# Freedom in the World

*Political Rights and Civil Liberties*
*1980*

# Freedom in the World

## Political Rights and Civil Liberties
## 1980

### RAYMOND D. GASTIL

*With a Study of World News Flow by*
Leonard R. Sussman

## FREEDOM HOUSE
### NEW YORK

Freedom House, 20 West 40th Street, New York, N.Y. 10018


**Library of Congress Cataloging in Publication Data**

Gastil, Raymond D.
    Freedom in the world.


   Includes bibliographical references and index.
       1. Civil rights.     I.    Sussman, Leonard R.,
joint author.    II.    Title.
JC571.G338      323.4      80–66430
ISBN 0–932088–02–3

Printed in the United States of America

# Contents

PART V. COUNTRY SUMMARIES

# Maps and Tables

## Tables

# Preface

The third edition of this yearbook, as its predecessors, ranges the world to assess the level of freedom in every country and territory. This edition goes on to examine other broad issues of liberty, as well as the overarching moral issues and human rights policy (Part IV).

As the two earlier volumes, this includes country studies (Part III): the struggle for democracy in Iran, and the elections in Zimbabwe Rhodesia. The latter assessments are the result of two extensive visits to the country (then Rhodesia) in April 1979 and February 1980. Against this backdrop one may view the developing political system in Salisbury. These election-monitoring missions provide more than an estimate of the quality of the elections. They describe the problems of initiating an electoral procedure in a country without a voting tradition or any effective representational history. The reactions of the electorate, whatever the ultimate success or failure of the Mugabe regime, encouraged those who believe a politically untutored population can readily learn to campaign, vote, and accept the decision of the polling place. Though these elections were conducted in a climate of fear and intimidation, the observers clearly noted the determination of the voters to regard elections as a serious business. This, itself, disputes the view that inexperienced voters are not ready to exercise their political rights.

This volume also focuses on the broad controversies that affect all countries (Part II). The problem of restructuring the flow of international news has been debated at global forums for a decade. Though it seemed in 1978 that a compromise declaration had been achieved at UNESCO, the controversies flared afresh this year in the MacBride Commission of UNESCO and underlay an April conference to transfer communications technology to developing countries. Late in 1980 these same controversies may reappear at the biennial general conference of UNESCO. Our analysis proposes some remedial steps for Western media managers, and the developed countries.

Part II also includes an important "index for trade union freedom"

ix

—the use of new criteria by which to judge the actions of governments in the field of trade unionism.

This edition provides once again in the Survey (Part I) and the Country Summaries (Part V) the information and assessments that provide a test of changing political and civil rights. These judgments are watched closely by governments themselves, as well as the mass news media, scholars, businessmen, and the general public.

Just as this edition assesses more than the year's levels of political and civil liberties, so the two previous yearbooks examined continuing, basic issues in the field. The 1978 volume included essays on the definitions and distinctions of freedom and democracy; diverse views of democracy; how democratic ideas became established; the relation of alternative political-economic systems to freedom; and self-determination, subnationalities, and freedom.

The 1979 edition featured a series of four essays by Sovietologists on supporting liberalization in the Soviet Union; as well as sections on freedom and equality; and national cultures and universal democracy.

*   *   *

We acknowledge, once again, the contribution made by the Advisory Panel for the Comparative Survey. The panel consists of:

Robert J. Alexander, Professor of Economics, Rutgers University; Richard W. Cottam, Professor of Political Science, University of Pittsburgh; Herbert J. Ellison, Professor of History, University of Washington; Seymour Martin Lipset, Senior Fellow, the Hoover Institution; Lucian Pye, Professor of Political Science, Massachusetts Institute of Technology; Leslie Rubin, lawyer, professor, and African specialist; Giovanni Sartori, the Albert Schweitzer Professor in the Humanities, Columbia University; Robert Scalapino and Paul Seabury, Professors of Political Science, University of California, Berkeley.

We are grateful for the financial support provided by the J. Howard Pew Freedom Trust, the John Dewey Foundation, the Earhart Foundation, and the Charles Stewart Mott Foundation. This support enabled Freedom House to maintain the Comparative Survey throughout the year, and produce this yearbook and other components of the Survey program. Since Freedom House neither solicits nor accepts funds from any government—nor has it done so in the forty years of its existence— private gifts and foundation grants are essential and deeply appreciated.

We also acknowledge the extensive editorial assistance of Jeannette Gastil and Patricia McCormack in producing this as the two previous yearbooks.—L.R.S.

# PART I

# The Survey in 1979

# The Comparative Survey of Freedom: Nature and Purposes

T he Comparative Survey of Freedom has been published at least annually since January 1973.[1] In spite of the obviously superficial knowledge of individual countries that they reflect, Survey ratings provide an objective reference point for those concerned with the state of freedom in the world.

An objective reference point for comparing levels of civil and political rights is desirable for several reasons. First, a recurrent American policy has been to go to the aid of other countries because their governments represented democratic systems similar to our own, or were struggling against forces hostile to democracy. But the policy can hardly be implemented if we cannot distinguish convincingly the more free from the less free states, particularly in the third world.[2] Secondly, opinion leaders in the developed democracies need a basis for a more balanced appraisal of the imperfections in freedom that they discover in their own societies. It is always important to protect democracies; like all systems they will continually fall away from their ideals. It is equally necessary to maintain perspective on these imperfections, to remember the difference between societies that have the means to discover, publicize, and often correct abuses of human rights and those that do not. Careless, fashionable pessimism about the level of freedom in imperfect free societies destroys the morale of their peoples; it encourages and nourishes the propaganda of those who truly hold their peoples in chains.

In the 1960's it was common for political analysts to avoid the issue of freedom by judging political systems primarily in economic and organizational terms. Such an analysis might see President Nixon as a poor manager of internal party affairs, or judge that Haile Selassie was overthrown because he failed to solve his nation's economic problems. Freedom in this analysis became an alternative means to administrative ends or the product of a certain stage of material and political progress. Such a view of freedom is a natural consequence of the materialistic, technocratic, "value-free" ethos of our time. The political analyst also

3

avoids the issue of freedom because its qualitative nature makes it hard to measure. It is easier to know if wheat production is higher this year than last, or if there are fewer beggars in the streets. However, those whose memories extend back as far as the thirties can never accept the claim that freedom inevitably accompanies economic or organizational progress, or that people who achieve material progress but are denied freedom necessarily prefer bread to liberty. Many questions go begging: How can we know what people think or want unless certain basic freedoms exist? Why is there so little evolution toward freedom in the Soviet Union, despite its advances in organization and technology? If freedom comes from material progress, why do so many Americans worry about the impact of further technological and organizational change upon freedom?

There is more to political organization than efficiency. By its simple existence the Freedom House Survey suggests that freedom is a goal that must be pursued separately from modernization. It inclines leaders of the new nations to notice that material results are not all that count. It suggests to citizens of developed democracies that the freedoms for which so many have struggled in the past will not inevitably triumph in the future. At the same time, a survey of freedom encourages people everywhere to reassess what they mean by freedom, its variations and its degrees, and to distinguish freedom more clearly from other desirable features in political systems.

Reassessment might also lead world leaders to a more acceptable understanding of modernization. Certainly the most dramatic revolution of recent years has been the revolt of the Iranian people against the Shah. Although led by conservative religious forces the revolt was inspired by years of political and social oppression.[3] The mistake of the Shah was not that he modernized the country too rapidly but that his efforts were unbalanced. Highly advanced technology in a few fields and the largest body of overseas students of any country in the world simply did not go with suppression of independent journalism, political imprisonment, the suppression of religious leaders, and dependence on the United States. Our leaders and the leaders of the third world should not forget that modernization in the image of the West and the establishment of free institutions cannot long be divorced.

In the Survey freedom is defined in terms of those *political rights* that allow people to participate freely and effectively in choosing their leaders or in voting directly on legislation, and those *civil liberties* that guarantee freedoms such as speech, privacy, and a fair trial. Of special importance for freedom in this sense are civil liberties making it possible to criticize the political, economic, and religious systems under which people live. This definition does not include the libertarian conception of liberty that denies majorities the power to regulate the nonpolitical public behavior of people in communities, nor does it include welfare interests, as in the rhetorical extensions "freedom from fear" or "freedom from want." In the Survey's definition independence may contribute to political freedom, but an independent state is not thereby "free." Whether the laws are codified or not, the freedoms of interest to the Survey must be guaranteed by a sense of law, by a regularized understanding of the forms and limits of government. Freedoms cannot be secure if they are continually threatened by the whims of personalities or even of majorities.

The rating a nation receives for political freedom is determined by factors such as the existence of two or more competing political parties or the independence of opposition candidates from government control. For a nation to achieve a high rating in the Survey, elections and legislatures have to demonstrate a significant opposition, and those elected have to be given real power. Civil freedoms include freedom of the press, the openness of public discussion, the existence of organizations separate from the government, an independent judiciary, and the absence of political imprisonment. Everything is in comparative terms. All nations fall short of perfection; on the other hand, perfect despotism would be hard to create or maintain. The sense of *degrees* of freedom that this approach produces is an important lesson in itself.

After placing countries on scales for political rights and civil liberties we divide all countries on this same basis into free, partly free, or not free categories. At the beginning of 1980 there were fifty-six independent nations in the world classified *not free,* fifty-one classified as *free,* and another fifty-four as *partly free.* In population terms this means that roughly forty-two percent of the world was considered not free, thirty-seven percent free, and the remaining twenty-one percent fell somewhere in between. To be sure, hundreds of millions classified as free were just marginally so, and almost as many classified as partly free could, with slight shifts of arbitrary category boundaries, have been considered not free.

The free states include those in Western Europe, the United Kingdom, and most overseas English-speaking nations, including the United States. The category also includes states such as Japan, Venezuela, India, and Fiji. Characteristic of all these states are a free press, an open political process, and a judiciary that often decides against the government. Among the partly free states are Mexico, Morocco, Senegal, and South Korea. Characteristic of such states are the maintenance of organized opposition groups and publicly expressed opposition. In these states there is repression of some important opposition groups;

here elections are a means of registering dissent rather than a way to seriously threaten the ruling group.

Among not free states are Uruguay, Zaire, Haiti, Tanzania, and most communist states. These are characterized by lack of significant public expression of opposition within either the electoral process or the legislature. Some criticism of policy implementation, of cultural tendencies, and of low-ranking officials may be allowed.

Critics have objected that the Survey's definition of freedom reflects nothing more than a generalization of the values of Western constitutional democracies. They see no reason why these values are necessarily of importance to the rest of the world, or why Americans should feel called upon to promote such standards for people in other countries.[4] The first reply to these objections is that the traditional world cultures that preceded Westernization play little role in any important political system today. For example, while cultural tones differ, the modern political systems of Japan and China are modeled on those of Western Europe and the Soviet Union respectively. One can understand more about the organization of Vietnam today by studying comparative communist administration than by studying a thousand years of pre-French Vietnamese history.

The second reply to the accusation of cultural ethnocentrism is that unless there are democratic freedoms, observers simply do not have any idea what a people wants. To outsiders populations often seem most satisfied when they are most hopelessly oppressed. Before Sihanouk was overthrown in Cambodia, we were assured by the media that, for all his faults, the Cambodian people loved him—he fit their style. After his downfall, reporters suddenly found no one in Phnom Penh with a good word for Sihanouk. The communists who conquered Cambodia ruled until January 1979 in a style neither media nor area experts prepared us for. Similarly, in India no one could imagine the strength of opposition to Mrs. Gandhi's oppressions in the mid-1970's before she put her rule to a vote. Most peoples accept tyrannies passively, either because tyrannies are all they have known, or they see no way of combining to overthrow tyrannies. When peoples learn of alternatives to tyranny, and see a chance of overthrowing it, they will grasp at the chance. Today the alternative they hope for is usually a version of Western democracy.

The Survey is often accused of being right-wing: certainly communist and one-party socialist regimes fare poorly. However, the Survey's only ideology is the importance of political and personal freedom. For this reason it should not be surprising that Chile was rated "free" under Allende, but "not free" under Pinochet (until this year when it was included marginally in the partly free group). The ratings of Chile illustrate the Survey's attempt to reflect the best information on current conditions, rather than reflecting what opposition groups report is "actually happening" in a country. It may be that Allende was trying to set up a left-wing dictatorship in 1973, but up to his ouster he had not succeeded, and the nation remained free. His successors set up a dictatorship. In the eyes of the military their actions may have been necessary; we note only that some military interventions under similar conditions elsewhere have been far less drastic, and have appeared to achieve all legitimate purposes.

The experience of the Survey suggests that it is difficult to maintain a high level of political rights alongside a low level of civil liberties; if the opposition cannot present its case, the right to vote is not very meaningful. On the other hand, people with strong civil liberties will soon clamor for more political rights. Increasing political rights is an obvious issue to raise, where it can be raised, by aspiring leaders that are currently out of power. If their demands are widely supported, incumbent leaders are forced either to increase political rights or to reduce civil liberties in order to cut off the discussion. Thus, ever since the peoples of the world became aware of the freedoms achieved in the West, developments toward or away from freedom have had an internal logic of their own. Once movement starts toward or away from freedom, it tends to continue inexorably through a process that might be described as the rectification of recurrent imbalances between civil and political freedoms. This is a primary reason communist regimes have been so fearful of even hesitant steps toward liberalization.

These last observations point up many issues related to the Survey that have not been carefully examined. Should independence itself be taken more seriously by the Survey? It may be said that the blacks in Tanzania "feel free" in a sense that blacks in South Africa cannot. This is very difficult to judge. One reason to doubt such a generalization is that most new states are made up of a variety of peoples, only some of which have access to rule. Secession may merely move the problem to a different plane. This was one of the paradoxes of the Ibo revolt in Nigeria, for within the rebel Ibo state of Biafra there were other smaller tribes that felt endangered in turn by the Ibos. This is nearly always the case. It is not at all clear that a Peruvian Indian or a Zairian pygmy feels happy to have a supposed norte-americano or European yoke replaced by the yoke of a native ethnic group. What we call a "people" from our distant vantage point frequently dissolves into many peoples when viewed up close.[5]

Similar questions arise when we try to define a "colony." The Soviet Union and China rule over a number of areas that are not populated by Russians or Chinese, and yet these areas are not normally con-

sidered colonies. If we consider Soviet Tadzhikistan a colony, would
not Northern Ireland also be a colony? In any event, in Northern
Ireland people have had a fair chance to vote on the issue of what
nation they belong in. In how many, even democratic, countries is this
the case?

Socialist critics believe we underrate the importance of economic
equality in the definition of freedom.[6] They think it ridiculous to call
India a free country in view of its great economic disparities, hunger,
and illiteracy. There is justice in the objection. Yet socioeconomic
equality cannot in itself be necessary for democracy: even the most
advanced democracies are oligarchies. Apparently competing party
organizations operate throughout India, people vote relatively freely,
and the results of their votes have a guiding power comparable to that
in richer, more egalitarian states.[7] Interest in freedom is not a reflec-
tion of prosperity. Indeed, a recent study of Turkey shows that the
poorest peasants are those most likely to vote; in India polls show
the poor are the most attached to democratic institutions.[8] Capitalist
critics of the Survey have perhaps an equally good case in arguing
that we should "take off points" for socialism or centralized planning.
Government control to the extent required by these systems reduces
civil liberties. Increasing the number of people directly dependent on
government inevitably restricts the population's ability to vote incumbents out of office.

More fundamentally, communism challenges our definitions of freedom both as they relate to internal and external policy. In communist
ideology, or Marxist "science," political power is always expressed in
favor of the interests of the dominant group in a society and against
the interests of everyone else. It follows that freedoms in any society
are meaningful only for the dominant and are nonexistent for others.
The difference between communist and noncommunist society becomes,
then, the difference in who is oppressed. Communists describe the
dominant group in noncommunist societies as those with control over
the means of production, and the dominant group in communist
(technically "socialist") societies as the workers and peasants. Since
workers and peasants make up a larger percentage of almost every
society than holders of productive property, it follows that there must
be more freedom in communist societies.[9]

The communist picture of reality is out of focus for two reasons. First,
while property is a significant form of power, and capitalists or large
landholders exert more than their share of power in noncommunist
states, property holders have only limited power in noncommunist
states. The increasing tax load borne by the wealthy in all noncommunist states is certainly an example of this limitation of control. It is

also a mistake to assume that adherence to principle and moral suasion cannot play a part in political life. The freedoms of the politically powerless, such as their rights to self-expression, choice of education, religious affiliation, or change of residence, are recognized most of the time in democracies today. The laws and principles of democracies, accepted in part as the basis for compromise among a number of conflicting groups fearful of one another's power, tend to be institutionalized in ways that redound to the benefit of all.

The first error of the communist analysis, then, comes from an underevaluation both of the significance for freedom of the conflicts within capitalist societies and of the importance of idealism. The second error of communist analysis comes from an overevaluation of communist idealism and a dogmatic identification of majority interests with communist party interests in communist societies, whether viewed hypothetically or empirically. There is no reason in communist ideology or human experience to imagine that a ruling group, especially when unchecked by regularly contested elections, will not twist the ruling ideology to its own interests rather than the interests of the people it serves. While revolutionary fervor may lead to moments of high idealism, communists in the long run cannot be expected to act unselfishly—and generally they do not. Communist ideologists have also allowed ideology to rule their social science by imagining that majorities of any people belong to an undifferentiated workers or peasants class that for more than the briefest moments has a unified set of interests and goals that can be expressed by an ideologically rigorous party platform. Even less is it likely that a party that does not provide itself with competitive and critical media is likely to know what the interests of the majority are. The communist theoretician's answer is that the party alone knows what the people essentially want, for they alone know what must be.[10] In ideological terms, communists believe that only when a people does what it must is it truly free.[11] A swimmer is free only if he knows how to swim.

But this turns the definition of freedom on its head; Marxist "science" has robbed it of the essential kernel of meaning with which the discussion began.[12] However we might disagree on the details, freedom must include the right to be wrong, express foolish opinions, vote for poor candidates.

It appears that communist analysis offers a useful reminder of the imperfections, necessary as well as remediable, in the freedoms of noncommunist societies. But it offers no sensible alternative. In an imperfect world it offers only a utopian mirage.

Whatever its faults, the Survey has become a monitoring facility by which people may become more responsibly concerned with the progress of freedom in their own and other countries. Since the Survey was initiated, several countries have lost freedom while others have gained it. Greece, Spain, and Portugal have given us hope, while Chile and the Philippines have been disappointments. The communist world has expanded in these years; freedom in the noncommunist world has also advanced. There is more freedom today in India, Sri Lanka, the Dominican Republic, Zimbabwe Rhodesia, Nigeria, and many other countries than there was a few years ago. And within the communist world, in Poland, China, and Hungary, freedom has also made gains.

Experience with the Survey suggests that people everywhere prefer freedom to tyranny in whatever form. But whether a country attains or sustains freedom depends on the willingness of elites to be satisfied with the limited power and compromise democracy requires. The Survey also suggests the degree to which the political trends of neighboring states, or of closely related states, are often copied. Elites will choose systems that are successful or fashionable and serve their interests.[13] Authoritarian military regimes look for legitimation, means of control, and international support to similar regimes, particularly in Latin America. Some elites find communism the best road to absolute power, as in Cuba or Kampuchea. In may developing countries the one-party socialist model, taken originally from communist countries, has become a popular official form (although the content given to socialism varies widely). This model is especially important for legitimating antidemocratic governments in Africa. During the period of the Survey Sierra Leone has moved away from freedom through imitation of Guinea; earlier Zambia had taken the same road, apparently in imitation of Tanzania. However, because of the inherent attractiveness of democracy to common people, the people with residual power in all societies, there repeatedly arise leaders in every society that look to the models of Western democratic institutions. In the 1970's we have seen such leaders arise in Thailand and India, Nigeria and Ghana, even South Korea and Taiwan. These are the people, often educated in the West, that we cannot afford to fail.

These observations suggest the importance of the ideological and informational warfare that ceaselessly goes on around us. It also suggests how the real world impinges on this struggle. If *one* free system fails competitively to perform as well as a nonfree, this failure hurts all free systems. If *one* relatively free society fails to maintain itself militarily this hurts all free societies.

Therefore, the first requirement for the victory of free societies is military and economic success. And today we find economic weaknesses in free societies; and we find military weaknesses, particularly because of the growing strategic strength of the USSR, its recently developed ability to project its power overseas, and the unwillingness of the United States after Vietnam to project its countervailing power.[14] The Soviet conquest of Afghanistan establishes as never before the expansionist tendency of the Soviet Union. Against losses on this scale, the modest gains for freedom we report have limited significance.

The second requirement for the success of freedom is ideological: democratic institutions must capture the imagination and allegiance of the educated elites of the world. This involves economic and military strength, but it also involves much more. It involves the identification of the liberal democracies with the idealistic longings of mankind, particularly in the area of human rights.

Pursuing military, economic, and idealistic strategies for protecting and expanding the arena of freedom in the world presents the publics and governments of free nations such as the United States or Japan with many dilemmas. The USSR is both a market for our goods and a danger to our existence. It punishes dissidents, and sometimes our protests seem only to make this punishment more severe. Revolutions in Iran and Nicaragua, partially with U.S. support, replaced pro-American autocrats in 1979. The resulting regimes have shown a tendency toward replacing one tyranny with another. We had to ask ourselves repeatedly: What should our policy be? Where should the pressure of public opinion be applied?

In the past the tendency of Western leaders and "responsible" publics has been to emphasize short-term material and military interests, and to resolutely stand up for freedom only when there is little conflict with these interests. This is commitment to freedom by exception. However, to win the ideological struggle and ultimately therefore the struggle for freedom everywhere we need to reverse these priorities and stand up for freedom regularly. With this priority we would ignore freedom only when this is demonstrably in our long- as well as short-run interest.

The strength of free institutions everywhere has been weakened when we as citizens or governments failed to criticize the Pinochet regime of Chile, General Somoza in Nicaragua, the Shah in Iran, the whites in South Africa, or when we ignored inhumanities in Indochina or Uganda, or the suppression of intellectual dissent by the cruel fabrications of Soviet courts. Consistency is justice, it builds, one case upon another, toward an international consensus that by its nature leaves totalitarianism out in the cold. Inconsistency makes all our actions, idealistic or Machiavellian, appear insincere, to be merely the manipulation of the pain of others for short-term advantage. For this reason a strategy for freedom must employ inconsistency most sparingly.

We have had many examples of the results of idealism by exception.

In the early sixties the king of Afghanistan attempted to establish a constitutional monarchy. In ten years the experiment had progressed, the press was freer, political activity was more open, the country had held its freest elections in history. Then Prince Daud staged a coup with the aid of the army and reestablished an authoritarian system. Neither official spokesman nor private citizens raised an alarm in the West. A government struggling to copy free institutions was swept under, and the Western public was told it was all just as well, Afghanistan had not really been a democracy anyhow.[15] In 1978 one of the parties nourished by that democratic experiment, driven underground, rose to take over the state and turn it into a fair copy of a totalitarian Soviet dictatorship. By 1980 the country appeared to be under direct Soviet rule.

In Greece the military suppressed democratic institutions for years, and too many Americans cheered them on. Yet the generals failed either to gain the support of their people or to achieve stability, and ended up precipitating the Turkish invasion of Cyprus. The Greeks managed in the aftermath to establish a democracy in spite of this legacy, but the ghost of America's role still haunts Grecian democracy.

In Ethiopia Western democracies supported a monarchical system that brooked no opposition, allowed little growth of free institutions, and maintained gross feudal inequities. When the revolution came, as we should have known it would, the free world was automatically the established enemy of the new order. The freest countries in the world were seen as the champions of oppression. The United States went along with the Portuguese dictatorship, viewed as the agent of stability. When the dictatorship collapsed, we almost lost Portugal to communism. We did lose all the African colonies—Angola, Mozambique, Guinea-Bissau, Cape Verde Islands, Sao Tome and Principe—to communist or quasi-communist systems. To the peoples of these colonies, who had no experience with democracy, and to whom the West was the oppressor, there seemed no other choice.

By early 1979 the Shah of Iran had gone into exile. His opposition had been in part a democratic, constitutionalist opposition, in part traditionalist and religious; the opposition of the Shah and the constitution, of king against mullah and bazaari is an old one in Iran. But in 1978-79 the opposition was also bitterly anti-American. It remembered the military and police support we had given the Shah and his legions, his spies, his military courts and regal pretensions over so many years. By the end of 1979 Iran appeared to be a barren ground for growth of a truly democratic society dedicated to Western liberties.

The point of these examples is that the policy of human rights by exception fails too often to maintain or achieve freedoms. It leads to failure in the struggle of systems materially, on the basis of who wins, and on the basis of "the system that rules next door." *And* this policy leads to failure in the worldwide ideological struggle because too often it suggests to the idealists who legitimize ideologies that the free world does not really care about extending its values to others, that the Western democracies are willing to let others suffer the inequities of tyranny as long as Westerners can enjoy the freedoms of their societies at home.

In many countries, including some developed democracies, political terror has become a part of political life. Of course, there will always be irrational, crazy, misguided persons for whom violence and idealism are an indigestible but addictive diet. Yet may it not be that the survival and growth of terrorist groups within Western societies is facilitated and sustained by the much larger penumbra of persons convinced that true respect for the freedoms of people, especially stateless peoples and people in the third world, is not to be found in the Western democracies?

In conclusion, experience shows that there are important strengths in the world of free nations. Peoples repeatedly choose freedom when given a choice by the elites that guide them. The progress of freedom is menaced, however, by certain dangers. There are the well-known military and economic problems. Equally important is the ideological problem of changing the balance of impressions of opinion-forming elites everywhere on the relative merits of liberal and authoritarian solutions to human problems, including the problem of individual freedom itself. Allegiance to Western democracies and their ideals must be shown to make a difference everywhere. The struggle for freedom will be won only when we turn away from supporting freedom by exception and adopt a personal and public policy of supporting freedom with consistency.

## NOTES

1. The first edition of the Survey was R. D. Gastil, "The New Criteria of Freedom," *Freedom at Issue,* no. 17 (January–February 1973). It has been published at least in every succeeding January–February edition of *Freedom at Issue.* The first Freedom House annual, *Freedom in the World* (New York and Boston: Freedom House and G. K. Hall), was published in 1978.

2. The other two reports used for making these distinctions are the Amnesty International Annual reports (latest: *Amnesty International Report 1979* [London: Amnesty International, 1979]) and the annual reports of the U.S. State Department to Congress on human rights (latest: "Country Reports on Human Rights Practices for 1979" [Washington: U.S. Government Printing Office 1980]). The purposes of these are complementary and supplementary to that of the Comparative Survey. Unlike the Survey both of these explicitly avoid com-

parative ratings. The topics of primary interest to Amnesty are political imprisonment, torture, and capital punishment. Table 6 (below) addresses Amnesty's special area of interest. Whenever it hears of an offense against its standards, Amnesty attempts by publicity to bring pressure. Therefore, where there is a great deal of information and its pressure seems likely to be productive Amnesty turns its spotlight. On the other hand, Department of State reports look at a broader group of factors than freedom, including efforts in areas such as employment or health services. With some notable exceptions State Department reports are forced by political considerations to avoid direct comparisons and to give as good a complexion to the human rights performances of other countries as possible. State Department reports would, for example, be most loath to bring up many self-determination questions. Profiting greatly from both of these sources, the Comparative Survey goes considerably further in attempting to judge relative condition or performance.

3. See Richard Cottam, "The Case of Iran," in Gastil, *Freedom in the World 1978,* pp. 88–108.

4. This issue was examined more theoretically in *Freedom in the World 1979,* pp. 75–82.

5. For an extended discussion of these issues see *Freedom in the World 1978,* pp. 180–215.

6. For more extended discussions of this issue see *Freedom in the World 1978,* pp. 163–179, and *Freedom in the World 1979,* pp. 63–74.

7. See Ram Joshi and Kirtidev Desai, "Toward a More Competitive Party System in India," *Asian Survey,* XVIII, no. 11 (November 1978), 1091–1116.

8. Ergun Özbudun, *Social Change and Political Participation in Turkey* (Princeton: Princeton University Press, 1976), pp. 56–161; and Samuel Huntington and Joan Nelson, *No Easy Choice* (Cambridge: Harvard University Press, 1976), pp. 82–83.

9. For this discussion compare Herbert Aptheker, *The Nature of Democracy and Freedom* (New York: International Publishers, 1967), especially pp. 60–74.

10. C. B. Macpherson, *The Real World of Democracy* (New York: Oxford University Press, 1966).

11. Aptheker, *The Nature of Democracy and Freedom,* pp. 71–73.

12. For our definition of freedom see *Freedom in the World 1978,* pp. 111–26.

13. This analysis·is developed in *Freedom in the World 1978,* pp. 147–62.

14. See International Institute for Strategic Studies, *The Military Balance 1979–80* (London, 1979), especially pp. 112–18.

15. For a discussion of this affair see *Freedom in the World 1978,* pp. 156–59.

# Survey Ratings and Tables
# for 1979

In spite of violence and oppression, 1979 was again a year of expanding freedom. Four of the worst governments of our time, those of Pol Pot in Kampuchea, Idi Amin in Uganda, Macias Nguema in Equatorial Guinea, and Bokassa in the Central African Empire (now "Republic"), were driven from power. Major advances in political and civil rights were made in Bangladesh, Bolivia, Ecuador, Ghana, Nigeria, and Thailand; among the declines that occurred in a few states the most notable was in Pakistan.

## THE TABULATED RATINGS

The accompanying Table 1 (Independent Nations) and Table 2 (Related Territories) rate each state or territory on seven-point scales for political and civil freedoms, and then provide an overall judgment of each as "free," "partly free," or "not free." In each scale, a rating of (1) is freest and (7) least free. Instead of using absolute standards, standards are comparative—that is, most observers would be likely to judge states rated (1) as freer than those rated (2), and so on. No state, of course, is absolutely free or unfree, but the degree of freedom does make a great deal of difference to the quality of life.[1]

In *political rights*, states rated (1) have a fully competitive electoral process and those elected clearly rule. Most West European democracies belong here. Relatively free states may receive a (2) because, although the electoral process works and the elected rule, there are factors which cause us to lower our rating of the effective equality of the process. These factors may include extreme economic inequality, illiteracy, or intimidating violence. They also include the weakening of effective competition that is implied by the absence of periodic shifts in rule from one group or party to another.

Below this level, political ratings of (3) through (5) represent successively less effective implementation of democratic processes. Mexico, for example, has periodic elections and limited opposition, but for many years its governments have been selected outside the public view by the

15

# Table 1
# Independent Nations:
# Comparative Measures of Freedom

| | Political Rights[1] | Civil Liberties[1] | Status of Freedom[2] | Outlook[3] |
|---|---|---|---|---|
| Afghanistan | 7 | 7 | NF | 0 |
| Albania | 7 | 7 | NF | 0 |
| Algeria | 6 | 6 | NF | + |
| Angola | 7 | 7 | NF | 0 |
| Argentina | 6 | 5 | NF | + |
| Australia | 1 | 1 | F | 0 |
| Austria | 1 | 1 | F | 0 |
| Bahamas | 1 | 2 | F | 0 |
| Bahrain | 5• | 4 | PF | 0 |
| Bangladesh | 3+ | 3+ | PF | 0 |
| Barbados | 1 | 1 | F | 0 |
| Belgium | 1 | 1 | F | 0 |
| Benin | 7 | 6• | NF | 0 |
| Bhutan | 5 | 5 | PF | 0 |
| Bolivia | 3+ | 3 | PF | + |
| Botswana | 2 | 2• | F | 0 |
| Brazil | 4 | 3+ | PF | + |
| Bulgaria | 7 | 7 | NF | 0 |
| Burma | 7 | 6 | NF | 0 |
| Burundi | 7 | 7 | NF | 0 |
| Cameroon | 6 | 6 | NF | 0 |
| Canada | 1 | 1 | F | 0 |
| Cape Verde Islands | 6 | 6 | NF | 0 |
| Central African Rep. | 7 | 6+ | NF | 0 |
| Chad | 6 | 6 | NF | 0 |
| Chile | 6 | 5 | PF+ | 0 |
| China (Mainland) | 6 | 6 | NF | 0 |
| China (Taiwan) | 5 | 5 | PF | 0 |
| Colombia | 2 | 3 | F | 0 |
| Comoro Islands | 4+ | 5• | PF | 0 |
| Congo | 7 | 7 | NF | 0 |
| Costa Rica | 1 | 1 | F | 0 |
| Cuba | 6 | 6 | NF | 0 |
| Cyprus | 3 | 3+ | PF | 0 |
| Czechoslovakia | 7 | 6 | NF | 0 |
| Denmark | 1 | 1 | F | 0 |
| Djibouti | 3 | 4 | PF | 0 |

**Notes to the Table**

1. The scales use the numbers 1-7, with 1 comparatively offering the highest level of political or civil rights and 7 the lowest. A plus or minus following a rating indicates an improvement or decline in 1979. A rating marked with a period (•) has been changed since the last Survey due to reevaluation by the author. This does not imply any change in the country.

2. A free state is designated by F, a partly free state by PF, and a not-free state by NF.

3. A positive outlook for freedom is indicated by a plus sign, a negative outlook, by a minus, and relative stability of ratings by a zero. The outlook for freedom is based on the problems the country is facing, the way the government and people are reacting to these problems, and the longer run political traditions of the society. A judgment of outlook may also reflect an imminent change, such as the expected adoption of a meaningful new constitution.

4. Official name of Cambodia.

5. Formerly the Gilbert Islands, territory of the United Kingdom.

6. Formerly territories of the United Kingdom.

16

|  | Political Rights[1] | Civil Liberties[1] | Status of Freedom[2] | Outlook[3] |
|---|---|---|---|---|
| Dominica | 2 | 2+ | F | 0 |
| Dominican Republic | 2 | 3•- | F | 0 |
| Ecuador | 2+ | 2+ | F+ | 0 |
| Egypt | 5 | 5 | PF | 0 |
| El Salvador | 5 | 4+ | PF | + |
| Equatorial Guinea | 7 | 6+ | NF | 0 |
| Ethiopia | 7 | 7 | NF | 0 |
| Fiji | 2 | 2 | F | 0 |
| Finland | 2 | 2 | F | 0 |
| France | 1 | 2 | F | 0 |
| Gabon | 6 | 6 | NF | 0 |
| Gambia | 2 | 2 | F | 0 |
| Germany (E) | 7 | 6 | NF | 0 |
| Germany (W) | 1 | 2 | F | 0 |
| Ghana | 4+ | 4 | PF | + |
| Greece | 2 | 2 | F | 0 |
| Grenada | 5- | 5- | PF- | - |
| Guatemala | 4• | 5• | PF | 0 |
| Guinea | 7 | 7 | NF | 0 |
| Guinea-Bissau | 6 | 6 | NF | 0 |
| Guyana | 4 | 4 | PF | - |
| Haiti | 6+ | 5+ | NF | 0 |
| Honduras | 6 | 3 | PF | + |
| Hungary | 6 | 5 | NF | 0 |
| Iceland | 1 | 1 | F | 0 |
| India | 2 | 2 | F | - |
| Indonesia | 5 | 5 | PF | 0 |
| Iran | 5 | 5 | PF | + |
| Iraq | 7 | 7- | NF | 0 |
| Ireland | 1 | 1 | F | 0 |
| Israel | 2 | 2 | F | 0 |
| Italy | 2 | 2 | F | 0 |
| Ivory Coast | 6 | 5 | PF | 0 |
| Jamaica | 2 | 3 | F | 0 |
| Japan | 2 | 1 | F | 0 |
| Jordan | 6 | 6 | NF | 0 |
| Kampuchea[4] | 7 | 7 | NF | 0 |
| Kenya | 5 | 4 | PF | 0 |
| Kiribati[5] | 2 | 2 | F | 0 |
| Korea (N) | 7 | 7 | NF | 0 |
| Korea (S) | 4 | 5 | PF | + |
| Kuwait | 6 | 4 | PF | + |
| Laos | 7 | 7 | NF | 0 |
| Lebanon | 4 | 4 | PF | 0 |
| Lesotho | 5 | 5 | PF | - |
| Liberia | 6 | 5 | PF | - |
| Libya | 6 | 6 | NF | 0 |
| Luxembourg | 1 | 1 | F | 0 |
| Madagascar | 6 | 6 | NF | 0 |
| Malawi | 6 | 7 | NF | 0 |
| Malaysia | 3 | 4 | PF | 0 |
| Maldives | 5 | 5 | PF | 0 |
| Mali | 7 | 6 | NF | 0 |
| Malta | 2 | 3- | F | - |

17

# Table 1—Continued

| | Political Rights[1] | Civil Liberties[1] | Status of Freedom[2] | Outlook[3] |
|---|---|---|---|---|
| Mauritania | 7● | 6 | NF | 0 |
| Mauritius | 2 | 4 | PF | 0 |
| Mexico | 3+ | 4 | PF | 0 |
| Mongolia | 7 | 7 | NF | 0 |
| Morocco | 4● | 4 | PF | 0 |
| Mozambique | 7 | 7 | NF | 0 |
| Nauru | 2 | 2 | F | 0 |
| Nepal | 5+ | 4+ | PF | + |
| Netherlands | 1 | 1 | F | 0 |
| New Zealand | 1 | 1 | F | 0 |
| Nicaragua | 5 | 5 | PF | + |
| Niger | 7 | 6 | NF | 0 |
| Nigeria | 2+ | 3 | F+ | 0 |
| Norway | 1 | 1 | F | 0 |
| Oman | 6 | 6 | NF | 0 |
| Pakistan | 6 | 5 | NF- | 0 |
| Panama | 5 | 5 | PF | 0 |
| Papua New Guinea | 2 | 2 | F | 0 |
| Paraguay | 5 | 5 | PF | 0 |
| Peru | 5 | 4 | PF | + |
| Philippines | 5 | 5 | PF | 0 |
| Poland | 6 | 5 | PF | - |
| Portugal | 2 | 2 | F | 0 |
| Qatar | 5 | 5 | PF | 0 |
| Rumania | 7 | 6 | NF | 0 |
| Rwanda | 6 | 6 | NF | 0 |
| St. Lucia[6] | 2 | 3 | F | 0 |
| St. Vincent[6] | 2 | 2 | F | 0 |
| Sao Tome and Principe | 6 | 6 | NF | 0 |
| Saudi Arabia | 6 | 6 | NF | 0 |
| Senegal | 4 | 4●- | PF | 0 |
| Seychelles | 6 | 6- | NF- | 0 |
| Sierra Leone | 5 | 5 | PF | 0 |
| Singapore | 5 | 5 | PF | 0 |
| Solomon Islands | 2 | 2 | F | 0 |
| Somalia | 7 | 7 | NF | 0 |
| South Africa | 5 | 6 | PF | + |
| Spain | 2 | 2 | F | 0 |
| Sri Lanka | 2 | 3 | F | 0 |
| Sudan | 5 | 5 | PF | 0 |
| Surinam | 2 | 2 | F | 0 |
| Swaziland | 5 | 5 | PF | 0 |
| Sweden | 1 | 1 | F | 0 |
| Switzerland | 1 | 1 | F | 0 |
| Syria | 5 | 6 | PF | 0 |
| Tanzania | 6 | 6 | NF | 0 |
| Thailand | 4+ | 4 | PF | 0 |
| Togo | 7 | 7●- | NF | 0 |
| Tonga | 5 | 3 | PF | 0 |
| Transkei | 5 | 6- | PF | 0 |
| Trinidad & Tobago | 2 | 2 | F | 0 |
| Tunisia | 6 | 5 | PF | 0 |

18

| | Political Rights[1] | Civil Liberties[1] | Status of Freedom[2] | Outlook[3] |
|---|---|---|---|---|
| Turkey | 2 | 3 | F | 0 |
| Tuvalu | 2 | 2 | F | 0 |
| Uganda | 6+ | 6+ | NF | + |
| USSR | 6 | 6 | NF | - |
| | | | | |
| United Arab Emirates | 5 | 5 | PF | 0 |
| United Kingdom | 1 | 1 | F | 0 |
| United States | 1 | 1 | F | 0 |
| Upper Volta | 2 | 3 | F | 0 |
| Uruguay | 6 | 6 | NF | 0 |
| | | | | |
| Venezuela | 1 | 2 | F | 0 |
| Vietnam | 7 | 7 | NF | 0 |
| Western Samoa | 4 | 2 | PF | 0 |
| Yemen (N) | 6 | 5 | NF | 0 |
| Yemen (S) | 6 | 7 | NF | 0 |
| | | | | |
| Yugoslavia | 6 | 5 | NF | 0 |
| Zaire | 6 | 6 | NF | 0 |
| Zambia | 5 | 5 | PF | 0 |
| Zimbabwe Rhodesia | 4+ | 4+ | PF | +/- |

leaders of factions within the one dominant Mexican party. Governments of states rated (5) sometimes have no effective voting processes at all, but strive for consensus among a variety of groups in society in a way weakly analogous to those of the democracies. States at (6) do not allow competitive electoral processes that would give the people a chance to voice their desire for a new ruling party or for a change in policy. The rulers of states at this level assume that one person or a small group has the right to decide what is best for the nation, and that no one should be allowed to challenge that right. Such rulers do respond, however, to popular desire in some areas, or respect (and therefore are constrained by) belief systems (for example, Islam) that are the property of the society as a whole. At (7) the political despots at the top appear by their actions to feel little constraint from either public opinion or popular tradition.

Turning to the scale for *civil liberties*, in countries rated (1) publications are not closed because of the expression of rational political opinion, especially when the intent of the expression is to affect the legitimate political process. No major media are simply conduits for government propaganda. The courts protect the individual; persons are not imprisoned for their opinions; private rights and desires in education, occupation, religion, residence, and so on, are generally respected; law-abiding persons do not fear for their lives because of their rational political activities. States at this level include most traditional democracies. There are, of course, flaws in the liberties of all of these states, and these flaws are significant when measured against the standards these states set themselves.

# Table 2
## Related Territories:
## Comparative Measures of Freedom

| | Political Rights[1] | Civil Liberties[1] | Status of Freedom[2] | Outlook[3] |
|---|---|---|---|---|
| **Australia** | | | | |
| Christmas Island (in Indian Ocean) | 4 | 2 | PF | 0 |
| Cocos Islands | 4 | 2 | PF | + |
| Norfolk Island | 4 | 2 | PF | + |
| **Chile** | | | | |
| Easter Island | 7 | 5●+ | NF | 0 |
| **Denmark** | | | | |
| Faroe Islands | 2 | 1 | F | 0 |
| Greenland | 2+ | 1 | F+ | 0 |
| **France** | | | | |
| French Guiana | 3 | 2 | PF | 0 |
| French Polynesia | 3 | 2 | PF | 0 |
| Guadeloupe | 3 | 2 | PF | 0 |
| Martinique | 3 | 2 | PF | 0 |
| Mayotte | 2 | 2 | F | 0 |
| Monaco[4] | 4 | 2 | PF | 0 |
| New Caledonia | 3●+ | 2●+ | F+ | 0 |
| Reunion | 3 | 2 | PF | 0 |
| Saint Pierre & Miquelon | 3 | 2 | PF | 0 |
| Wallis and Futuna | 4 | 3 | PF | 0 |
| **Israel** | | | | |
| Occupied Territories | 5 | 4 | PF | 0 |
| **Italy** | | | | |
| San Marino[4] | 2 | 2● | F | 0 |
| **Netherlands** | | | | |
| Neth. Antilles | 2 | 1 | F | 0 |
| **New Zealand** | | | | |
| Cook Islands | 3 | 2 | F | 0 |
| Niue | 2 | 2 | F | 0 |
| Tokelau Islands | 4 | 2 | PF | 0 |
| **Portugal** | | | | |
| Azores | 2 | 2 | F | 0 |
| Macao | 3 | 3 | PF | 0 |
| Madeira | 2 | 2 | F | 0 |
| **South Africa** | | | | |
| Bophuthatswana[5] | 6 | 6 | NF | 0 |
| South West Africa (*Namibia*) | 5 | 5 | PF | 0 |
| Venda[5] | 6 | 6 | NF | 0 |
| **Spain** | | | | |
| Canary Islands | 2 | 2 | F | 0 |
| Places of Sovereignty in North Africa | 2 | 2 | F | 0 |

**Notes to the Table**

1. 2., 3. See Notes, Table 1.

4. These states are not listed as independent because all have explicit legal forms of dependence on a particular country (or, in the case of Andorra, countries) in the spheres of foreign affairs, defense, etc.

5. The geography and history of these newly "independent" homelands cause us to consider them dependencies.

6. Formed out of the Trust Territory of the Pacific Islands, these territories are at various stages of evolution toward internal autonomy. "Micronesia" in the table this year refers to the much smaller Federated States of Micronesia.

| | Political Rights[1] | Civil Liberties[1] | Status of Freedom[2] | Outlook[3] |
|---|---|---|---|---|
| **Switzerland** | | | | |
| Liechtenstein[4] | 4 | 1 | PF | 0 |
| **United Kingdom** | | | | |
| Anguilla | 2 | 2 | F | 0 |
| Antigua and Barbuda | 2 | 2 | F | 0 |
| Belize | 1 | 2 | F | 0 |
| Bermuda | 2 | 1 | F | 0 |
| Brit. Virgin Islands | 3 | 2 | PF | 0 |
| Brunei[4] | 6 | 5 | NF | 0 |
| Cayman Islands | 2 | 2 | F | 0 |
| Channel Islands | 2 | 1 | F | 0 |
| Falkland Islands | 2 | 2 | F | 0 |
| Gibraltar | 1 | 2 | F | 0 |
| Hong Kong | 4• | 2 | PF | 0 |
| Isle of Man | 2 | 1 | F | 0 |
| Montserrat | 2•+ | 2 | F | 0 |
| St. Helena | 2 | 2 | F | 0 |
| St. Kitts and Nevis | 2 | 3 | F | 0 |
| Turks and Caicos | 3 | 2 | PF | 0 |
| **United States** | | | | |
| American Samoa | 2• | 2 | F• | 0 |
| Belau[6] | 4 | 2 | PF | + |
| Guam | 3 | 2 | PF | 0 |
| Marshall Islands[6] | 2 | 2 | F | 0 |
| Micronesia[6] | 3+ | 2 | PF | + |
| Northern Marianas[6] | 2 | 2 | F | 0 |
| Puerto Rico | 2 | 1 | F | 0 |
| Virgin Islands | 2•+ | 3• | F•+ | 0 |
| **France-Spain Condominium** | | | | |
| Andorra[4] | 4 | 3 | PF | 0 |
| **France-United Kingdom Condominium** | | | | |
| New Hebrides | 3 | 3 | PF | + |

Movement down from (2) to (7) represents a steady loss of the civil freedoms we have detailed. Compared to (1), the police and courts of states at (2) have more authoritarian traditions. In some cases they may simply have a less institutionalized or secure set of liberties, such as in Portugal or Greece. Those rated (3) or below may have political prisoners and generally varying forms of censorship. Too often their security services practice torture. States rated (6) almost always have political prisoners; usually the legitimate media are completely under government supervision; there is no right of assembly; and, often, travel, residence, and occupation are narrowly restricted. However, at (6) there still may be relative freedom in private conversation, especially in the home; illegal demonstrations do take place; underground literature is published; and so on. At (7) there is pervading fear, little independent expression takes place in private, almost no expressions of opposition emerge in the police-state environment, and execution is often swift and sure.

# Table 3  Ranking of Nations by Political Rights

| Most Free | | | | | | Least Free |
|---|---|---|---|---|---|---|
| 1 | 2 | 3 | 4 | 5 | 6 | 7 |
| Australia | Botswana | Bangladesh | Brazil | Bahrain | Algeria | Afghanistan |
| Austria | Colombia | Bolivia | Comoro Is. | Bhutan | Argentina | Albania |
| Bahamas | Dominica | Cyprus | Ghana | China (Taiwan) | Cameroon | Angola |
| Barbados | Dominican | Djibouti | Guatemala | Egypt | Cape Verde Is. | Benin |
| Belgium | Republic | Malaysia | Guyana | El Salvador | Chad | Bulgaria |
| Canada | Ecuador | Mexico | Korea (S) | Grenada | Chile | Burma |
| Costa Rica | Fiji | | Lebanon | Indonesia | China (Mainland) | Burundi |
| Denmark | Finland | | Morocco | Iran | Cuba | Central African |
| France | Gambia | | Senegal | Kenya | Gabon | Rep. |
| Germany (W) | Greece | | Thailand | Lesotho | Guinea-Bissau | Congo |
| Iceland | India | | Western Samoa | Maldives | Haiti | Czechoslovakia |
| Ireland | Israel | | Zimbabwe | Nepal | Honduras | Equatorial Guinea |
| Luxembourg | Italy | | Rhodesia | Nicaragua | Hungary | Ethiopia |
| Netherlands | Jamaica | | | Panama | Ivory Coast | Germany (E) |
| New Zealand | Japan | | | Paraguay | Jordan | Guinea |
| Norway | Kiribati | | | Peru | Kuwait | Iraq |
| Sweden | Malta | | | Philippines | Liberia | Kampuchea |
| Switzerland | Mauritius | | | Qatar | Libya | Korea (N) |
| United Kingdom | Nauru | | | Sierra Leone | Madagascar | Laos |
| United States | Nigeria | | | Singapore | Malawi | Mali |
| Venezuela | Papua New Guinea | | | South Africa | Oman | Mauritania |
| | Portugal | | | Sudan | Pakistan | Mongolia |
| | St. Lucia | | | Swaziland | Poland | Mozambique |
| | St. Vincent | | | Syria | Rwanda | Niger |
| | Solomon Is. | | | Tonga | Sao Tome | Rumania |
| | Spain | | | Transkei | & Principe | Somalia |
| | Sri Lanka | | | United Arab | Saudi Arabia | Togo |
| | Surinam | | | Emirates | Seychelles | Vietnam |
| | Trinidad & Tobago | | | Zambia | Tanzania | |
| | Turkey | | | | Tunisia | |
| | Tuvalu | | | | Uganda | |
| | Upper Volta | | | | USSR | |
| | | | | | Uruguay | |
| | | | | | Yemen (N) | |
| | | | | | Yemen (S) | |
| | | | | | Yugoslavia | |
| | | | | | Zaire | |

22

# Table 4   Ranking of Nations by Civil Liberties

| Most Free 1 | 2 | 3 | 4 | 5 | 6 | Least Free 7 |
|---|---|---|---|---|---|---|
| Australia | Bahamas | Bangladesh | Bahrain | Argentina | Algeria | Afghanistan |
| Austria | Botswana | Bolivia | Djibouti | Bhutan | Benin | Albania |
| Barbados | Dominica | Brazil | El Salvador | Chile | Burma | Angola |
| Belgium | Ecuador | Colombia | Ghana | China (Taiwan) | Cameroon | Bulgaria |
| Canada | Fiji | Cyprus | Guyana | Comoro Is. | Cape Verde Is. | Burundi |
| Costa Rica | Finland | Dominican Rep. | Kenya | Egypt | Central African Rep. | Congo |
| Denmark | France | Honduras | Kuwait | Grenada | Chad | Ethiopia |
| Iceland | Gambia | Jamaica | Lebanon | Guatemala | China (Mainland) | Guinea |
| Ireland | Germany (W) | Malta | Malaysia | Haiti | Cuba | Iraq |
| Japan | Greece | Nigeria | Mauritius | Hungary | Czechoslovakia | Kampuchea |
| Luxembourg | India | St. Lucia | Mexico | Indonesia | Equatorial Guinea | Korea (N) |
| Netherlands | Israel | Sri Lanka | Morocco | Iran | Gabon | Laos |
| New Zealand | Italy | Tonga | Nepal | Ivory Coast | Germany (E) | Malawi |
| Norway | Kiribati | Turkey | Peru | Korea (S) | Guinea-Bissau | Mongolia |
| Sweden | Nauru | Upper Volta | Senegal | Lesotho | Jordan | Mozambique |
| Switzerland | Papua New Guinea | | Thailand | Liberia | Libya | Somalia |
| United Kingdom | Portugal | | Zimbabwe | Maldives | Madagascar | Togo |
| United States | St. Vincent | | Rhodesia | Nicaragua | Mali | Vietnam |
| | Solomon Is. | | | Pakistan | Mauritania | Yemen (S) |
| | Spain | | | Panama | Niger | |
| | Surinam | | | Paraguay | Oman | |
| | Trinidad & Tobago | | | Philippines | Rumania | |
| | Tuvalu | | | Poland | Rwanda | |
| | Venezuela | | | Qatar | Sao Tome & Principe | |
| | Western Samoa | | | Sierra Leone | Saudi Arabia | |
| | | | | Singapore | Seychelles | |
| | | | | Sudan | South Africa | |
| | | | | Swaziland | Syria | |
| | | | | Tunisia | Tanzania | |
| | | | | United Arab Emirates | Transkei | |
| | | | | Yemen (N) | Uganda | |
| | | | | Yugoslavia | USSR | |
| | | | | Zambia | Uruguay | |
| | | | | | Zaire | |

23

A cumulative judgment of "free," "partly free," or "not free" is made on the basis of the foregoing seven-point ratings, and an understanding of how they were derived. Generally, states rated (1) and (2) will be "free"; those at (3), (4), and (5), "partly free"; and those at (6) and (7), "not free." When the ratings for political rights and civil liberties differ, the status of freedom must be decided by rough averaging. It must be remembered, however, that the ratings are not arithmetical units, but merely categories on arbitrary scales. There are, of course, marginal cases. A (6) and a (5) may lead either to a rating of "not free" or "partly free," depending on whether the (5) and (6) are a high (5) or low (5), a high (6) or low (6). In addition, political rights are given slightly more weight in marginal cases.

The tables also include an entry for "outlook." Since we are not in a position to adequately judge the futures of all the societies under review, this column reports many fewer trends than a more detailed study would discover. Primarily, we include cases where a forthcoming election appears likely to improve the freedoms of a country, or a downward trend is in prospect because a retrogressive process underway at the time of the Survey has not yet actually reached fruition. By the nature of the signals we use, more pluses are likely to appear under "outlook" than minuses.

The reporting period covered by the Survey (January 1 to December 31, 1979) of course does not correspond with the calendar of short-term events in the countries rated. For this reason the yearly Survey may mask or play down important events that occur during the year.

China and Iran may serve as examples. In mainland China the growth of the democratic movement led in December 1978 and January 1979 to the open presentation of ideas fundamentally questioning the country's control structure. These ideas were disseminated through wall posters, unauthorized but not always clandestine publications, and private discussion. Later the freedom of this discussion was restricted and the leaders of the movement arrested; by the end of 1979 China had fallen back to the levels of 1978, even though the period had included important experiments in freedom. The growth of freedom in Iran until August 1978 was followed by intermittent and ineffective repressions through the remainder of the year. Popular freedom to express opinion openly or to influence the political process reached its peak for most Iranians in January–February 1979. From this crest, the level of freedom again declined; Iran had little if any more freedom in late 1979 than late 1978, although what was controlled in the two periods was quite different.

## Significant Declines in Freedom

The main opposition party in *Grenada* overthrew the heavy-handed government of President Eric Gairy. The result has been a considerable decline in freedom, both because a coup is never a democratic process (although democratic elements in the process both here and in El Salvador caused us to rate both [5] for political rights) and because of the political imprisonment that followed the coup. Grenada's new rulers have followed these understandable actions by an indefinite postponement of elections and the closing of the chief opposition paper.

As an aside, Grenada presents a good example of the problem of the tilt of political analysis against right-wing regimes. Gairy had a poor human rights record, even for a country we only marginally rated as free last year. His gangs had reduced the rights of his opponents, especially in earlier years. However, his record was not nearly as bad as his reputation. For example, a moderate American political scientist's description of him in retrospect as a second-rank Idi Amin is ludicrous. The government Gairy headed was overthrown by a party that was represented in parliament for years, that operated in an environment with an opposition press, and was able to mobilize a large part of the population in its support. It appears that the leftists opposing Gairy were only interested in the fact *they* felt repressed, rather than in the injustice of repression itself. Paradoxically, they are now justifying Gairy's repressions by their greater ones. (This may also be the case in the leftist-leftist confrontation shaping up in Guyana. There is no fundamental validity to the cry for justice of those who would deny it to others. We would have little interest in such cries except that democracy may become the salient ultimate solution in the deadlock of non-democrats.)

In *Iraq* the Baath regime executed a number of the members of the government and of the communist party in a general suppression of the only legal counterweight to its absolutism. In *Pakistan* the military government executed the country's former president on the basis of questionable evidence, repeatedly imprisoned members of his party and family, silenced opposition media, introduced violent punishments, and called off promised but already emasculated elections. Numerous political arrests and harsher controls on both oral and printed discussion further reduced freedom in the *Seychelles*. Political arrests in *Transkei* suggested increasing tyranny.

*Malta* put increased pressure on journalists and other suspected opponents; it reduced the independence of labor.

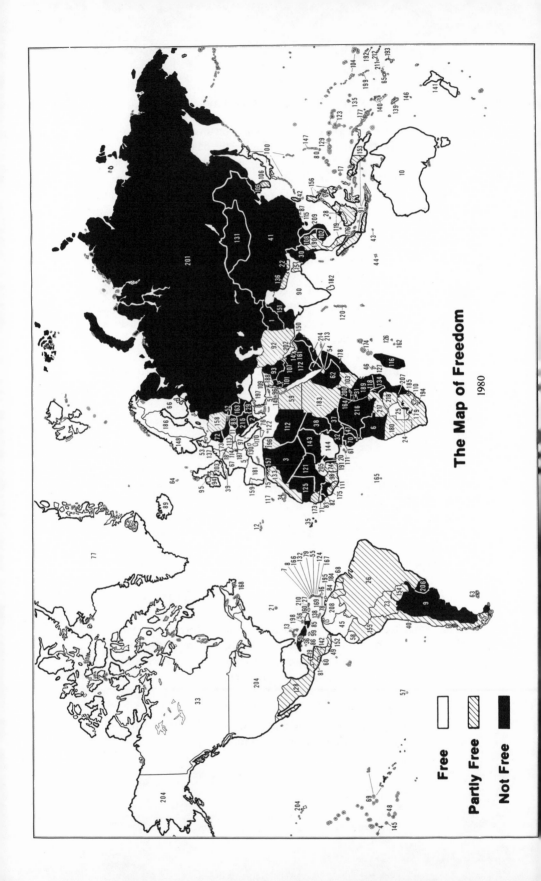

## The Map of Freedom

1980

- ☐ **Free**
- ▨ **Partly Free**
- ■ **Not Free**

# Free

## Nations

- 10 Australia
- 11 Austria
- 13 Bahamas
- 16 Barbados
- 18 Belgium
- 25 Botswana
- 33 Canada
- 45 Colombia
- 49 Costa Rica
- 53 Denmark
- 55 Dominica
- 56 Dominican Republic
- 58 Ecuador
- 65 Fiji
- 66 Finland
- 67 France
- 71 Gambia
- 73 Germany, West
- 76 Greece
- 89 Iceland
- 90 India
- 94 Ireland
- 96 Israel
- 97 Italy
- 99 Jamaica
- 100 Japan
- 104 Kiribati
- 114 Luxembourg
- 122 Malta
- 135 Nauru
- 137 Netherlands
- 141 New Zealand
- 144 Nigeria
- 148 Norway
- 153 Papua New Guinea
- 159 Portugal
- 167 St. Lucia
- 169 St. Vincent
- 177 Solomon Islands
- 181 Spain
- 182 Sri Lanka
- 184 Surinam
- 186 Sweden
- 187 Switzerland
- 195 Trinidad & Tobago
- 197 Turkey
- 199 Tuvalu
- 203 United Kingdom
- 204 United States
- 205 Upper Volta
- 208 Venezuela

## Related Territories

- 4 American Samoa
- 7 Anguilla (U.K.)
- 8 Antigua and Barbuda (U.K.)
- 12 Azores (Port.)
- 19 Belize (U.K.)
- 21 Bermuda (U.K.)
- 34 Canary Islands (Sp.)
- 36 Cayman Islands (U.K.)
- 39 Channel Islands (U.K.)
- 48 Cook Islands (N.Z.)
- 63 Falkland Islands (U.K.)
- 64 Faroe Islands (Den.)
- 75 Gibraltar (U.K.)
- 77 Greenland (Den.)
- 95 Isle of Man (U.K.)
- 117 Marshall Islands (U.S.)
- 123 Mayotte (Fr.)
- 127 Montserrat (U.K.)
- 132 Netherlands Antilles (Neth.)
- 138 New Caledonia (Fr.)
- 139 Niue (N.Z.)
- 145 Northern Marianas (U.S.)
- 147 Places of Sovereignty in North Africa (Sp.)
- 157 Puerto Rico (U.S.)
- 160 St. Helena (U.K.)
- 165 St. Kitts and Nevis (U.K.)
- 166 San Marino (It.)
- 170 San Marino (It.)
- 210 Virgin Islands (U.S.)

# Partly Free

## Nations

- 14 Bahrain
- 15 Bangladesh
- 22 Bhutan
- 23 Bolivia
- 26 Brazil
- 40 Chile
- 42 China, Taiwan
- 46 Comoro Islands
- 51 Cyprus
- 54 Djibouti
- 59 Egypt
- 60 El Salvador
- 74 Ghana
- 78 Grenada
- 81 Guatemala
- 84 Guyana
- 86 Honduras
- 91 Indonesia
- 92 Iran
- 98 Ivory Coast
- 103 Kenya
- 106 Korea, South
- 107 Kuwait
- 109 Lebanon
- 110 Lesotho
- 111 Liberia
- 119 Malaysia
- 120 Maldives
- 126 Mauritius
- 128 Mexico
- 133 Morocco
- 136 Nepal
- 142 Nicaragua
- 152 Panama
- 154 Paraguay
- 155 Peru
- 156 Philippines
- 158 Poland
- 161 Qatar
- 173 Senegal
- 175 Sierra Leone
- 176 Singapore
- 179 South Africa
- 183 Sudan
- 185 Swaziland
- 188 Syria
- 190 Thailand
- 193 Tonga
- 194 Transkei
- 196 Tunisia
- 202 United Arab Emirates
- 212 Western Samoa
- 217 Zambia
- 218 Zimbabwe Rhodesia

## Related Territories

- 5 Andorra (Fr.-Sp.)
- 17 Belau (U.S.)
- 27 British Virgin Islands (U.K.)
- 43 Christmas Island (Aus.)
- 44 Cocos Islands (Aus.)
- 68 French Guiana (Fr.)
- 69 French Polynesia (Fr.)
- 79 Guadeloupe (Fr.)
- 80 Guam (U.S.)
- 87 Hong Kong (U.K.)
- 113 Liechtenstein (Switz.)
- 115 Macao (Port.)
- 124 Martinique (Fr.)
- 129 Micronesia, Federated States of (U.S.)
- 130 Monaco (Fr.)
- 140 New Hebrides (Fr.-U.K.)
- 146 Norfolk Island (Aus.)
- 149 Occupied Territories (Isr.)
- 162 Reunion (Fr.)
- 168 Saint Pierre & Miquelon (Fr.)
- 180 South West Africa Namibia (S. Afr.)
- 192 Tokelau Islands (N.Z.)
- 198 Turks and Caicos Islands (U.K.)
- 211 Wallis and Futuna (Fr.)

# Not Free

## Nations

- 1 Afghanistan
- 2 Albania
- 3 Algeria
- 6 Angola
- 9 Argentina
- 20 Benin
- 29 Bulgaria
- 30 Burma
- 31 Burundi
- 32 Cameroon
- 35 Cape Verde Islands
- 37 Central African Republic
- 38 Chad
- 41 China, Mainland
- 47 Congo
- 50 Cuba
- 52 Czechoslovakia
- 61 Equatorial Guinea
- 62 Ethiopia
- 70 Gabon
- 72 Germany, East
- 82 Guinea
- 83 Guinea-Bissau
- 85 Haiti
- 88 Hungary
- 93 Iraq
- 101 Jordan
- 102 Kampuchea
- 105 Korea, North
- 108 Laos
- 112 Libya
- 116 Madagascar
- 118 Malawi
- 121 Mali
- 125 Mauritania
- 131 Mongolia
- 134 Mozambique
- 143 Niger
- 150 Oman
- 151 Pakistan
- 163 Rumania
- 164 Rwanda
- 171 Sao Tome and Principe
- 172 Saudi Arabia
- 174 Seychelles
- 178 Somalia
- 189 Tanzania
- 191 Togo
- 200 Uganda
- 201 USSR
- 206 Uruguay
- 209 Vietnam
- 213 Yemen, North
- 214 Yemen, South
- 215 Yugoslavia
- 216 Zaire

## Related Territories

- 24 Bophuthatswana (S. Afr.)
- 28 Brunei (U.K.)
- 57 Easter Island (Chile)
- 207 Venda (S. Afr.)

### SIGNIFICANT ADVANCES IN FREEDOM

*Bangladesh* continued its progress. A multiparty election resulted in the participation of opposition groups in parliament, although the president's power and that of his party remained supreme. The media were generally free, local centers of power were important, and university elections were won by third-force groups.

*Bolivia*'s democracy had a checkered advance. This year's election was fairer than that of 1978. Its ambiguous result led to the appointment of an interim president and a subsequent military coup when the government threatened court action against military figures. Compromise led to the reestablishment of civilian and parliamentary rule after this short-lived setback.

*Brazil* made further steps toward democracy with the release of most prisoners of conscience and the return of important political exiles. The media were reported to work in less fear, and union organization and strikes were conducted in a freer atmosphere. However, the government's new regulations for political parties were disquieting. Fear was greatly alleviated and expression somewhat freer in the *Central African Republic*. In *Chile* there were many conflicting signs. Yet disappearances and widespread arrests seemed to be in the past. Journalists showed more independence, peaceful antigovernment demonstrations occurred, the courts ordered the release of demonstrators, and the opposition won university elections. Restrictive labor laws have been enacted, but nongovernmental legal union activity and strikes continue. In the *Comoro Islands* parliamentary elections in late 1978 were seriously contested, and considerable local government was granted the constituent islands. In *Dominica* the parliamentary overturn of an entrenched leader seemed to accompany improvement in respect for legal safeguards.

Congressional and presidential elections in *Ecuador* returned the country by a fairly stormy passage to democracy. The new president represented new forces and partly for this reason was immediately locked in a struggle for power with his congress. Political prisoners were freed, and press and union freedom bolstered. In spite of continued violence, *El Salvador* moved toward freedom. The new junta contains important elements of the former political opposition, while the ousted government had become increasingly oppressive. Civil rights improved, political prisoners were released, and the media appeared freer. By the end of the year party formation was opened to all and elections were promised. Continued violence in early 1980 threatened this progress.

The democratic intentions of new rulers in *Equatorial Guinea* were unclear at last report, but at least the churches opened again and power initially was more equitably distributed. *Ghana* saw a return to democracy through presidential and parliamentary elections. The elections were competitive and fair, and yet they occurred alongside a military coup that led to a purge of the armed forces and the execution of a number of former leaders for corruption. The interveners then allowed the civilian government to take over, but their actions placed considerable doubt on the ability of civilians to go against military desires. In *Haitian* elections an opposition candidate was allowed to run and be elected. New political parties emerged, and the media courageously criticized the system. But violence and imprisonment were also used to limit the movement toward freedom.

*Mexico* held an election that saw the participation of new parties and the granting of television time to their spokesmen. Parliament became more competitive and meaningful. A number of political prisoners were released, but information on recent oppressions also increased. In *Nepal* demonstrations forced the government to agree on a referendum on the form of government. Campaigns began immediately, with considerable freedom exercised by those who want a return to a multiparty system. The parliament was given more power.

The most important victory for democracy was the return to civilian rule in *Nigeria* as the culmination of several years of progress. Five elections were held during the summer: Senate, House of Representatives, state legislatures, state governors, and presidential. Campaigns were meaningful, and the dispersion of votes ethnically and ideologically credible. It is true the military that gave the people this power can again lay claim to it, but compared to Ghana the Nigerian military recently has shown a much greater degree of commitment to noninterference.

In *Thailand* the political system moved decisively in a democratic direction through multiparty elections in which opposition elements showed themselves to be more popular than the government. However, a general remained in power through the power of an appointive senate in a manner reminiscent of the recent system of South Korea. Subsequently, parliament has shown considerable independence. The end of centrally directed lawlessness in *Uganda* is welcomed. Although installed by violence and foreign troops, new governmental institutions offered a measure of free popular participation. Anarchy and political imprisonment continued, but the churches regained their freedom, and the press and discussion were freer. Elections in *Zimbabwe Rhodesia* resulted in a black government. The elections were open to all parties and competitive. The police control of the countryside, the heavily controlled media, and the refusal of major insurgent parties to contest the elections under these conditions rendered them less than fully free.[2]

The temporary British government installed at the end of the year improved the civil liberties of many blacks considerably (and led to a second round of elections in 1980).

## FURTHER COMMENT ON CHANGES IN FREEDOM

The year saw the first direct participation of national electorates in electing a major international body, the European Parliament of the *European Communities*.[3] This not only extended direct popular control beyond the national level, but also helped to fix as a definition of community membership the democratic processes common to all members of the EC. The Parliament is not powerful, but the election is certainly a step forward. (If the Communities gain in unity, the Parliament will probably gain in strength; whether or not they gain in unity is probably an indifferent consideration from the standpoint of political rights.)

Three mini-states became independent during the year: *Kiribati* (formerly the Gilbert Islands in the Pacific), *St. Lucia*, and *St. Vincent and the Grenadines* (both in the Caribbean). All were formerly British colonies and all were essentially free both before and after independence.

The most important change among the "related territories," at least to those familiar with Mercator's projection, was the change of the Danish colony of *Greenland* from "partly free" to "free" status. A new home rule bill has been adopted that grants considerable internal autonomy for the first time. Greenland now has its own parliament and prime minister.

Review of evidence for *New Caledonia* indicates that it should now be regarded as among the "free" territories. Since 1977 it has taken over a large role in self-government, opposition and pro-independence parties have played a major role, and the political strengths and ethnic affiliations of those wishing to remain with France suggest that the territory is not retained against the wishes of its majority.

In South Africa *Venda* became the latest Bantustan to be granted independence. Because of its small size, location, and history, we are placing Venda along with Bophuthatswana as a "related territory" of South Africa rather than with Transkei, which we regard as independent.

During the year the *Canal Zone* was transferred from American to Panamanian control. Continuing devolution of the American Trust Territory of the Pacific Islands has created or is creating the new territories of *Belau*, the *Marshall Islands*, and the Federated States of *Micronesia*, in addition to the previously formed *Northern Marianas*. These territories have achieved or are rapidly achieving internal autonomy.

As mentioned above, this tragic year for the *Iranian* revolution began with an outpouring of free expression after years of repression. Two elections during the year, on the basic nature of the state and to elect representatives to a constituent assembly, were disappointing. The first referendum allowed no alternatives, campaigning against the new system was essentially impossible, and the secrecy of the ballot was hardly guaranteed. The second allowed choice, but some groups were not allowed to put up candidates. Since campaigning by secular groups was highly restricted, most of these groups boycotted the election. A third election approved the Constitution although some areas abstained. (The Presidential and Parliamentary elections in early 1980 led to an explosion of candidacies.) It was in civil liberties that the retreat from the hopes of January 1979 were most pronounced. Publications or organizations opposing the regime were closed down and their property confiscated; trials and executions continued without adequate guarantees and started to include some former opponents of the Shah who once again began to go into hiding. The autonomy of minority groups was violently oppressed. In conditions of near anarchy fear became a dominant theme in the lives of many.

Some readers will be surprised that after a year of revolution *Nicaragua*'s ratings should not change. However, politically there was a degree of freedom in the Somoza system, with a legal opposition, elections, and a partially free judiciary. This has been replaced by a government backed initially by popular enthusiasm and a number of political parties. But without elections, and without a previous electoral track record for those in power, a rating above (5) for political rights is not possible. In civil rights the media are about as free as they were under Somoza. Thousands of those connected with the Somoza government are still in jail, and have been joined by others arrested for new political reasons. The Bill of Rights continues in abeyance, leftists have been deported, and union organization restricted.

Oppressions in 1979 in East Germany, Czechoslovakia, the USSR and many other countries again did not show up as changes in the accompanying tables because comparatively these did not change prior ratings.

## Elections and Referenda

Evidence for political freedom is primarily found in the occurrence and nature of elections or referenda. Therefore, as a supplement to our ratings we have attempted in the accompanying Table 5 to summarize those national elections that occurred in independent countries in 1979. Indirect elections are included only in the more important cases. The reader should assume that the electoral process appeared comparatively open and competitive unless our remarks suggest other-

## Table 5
## National Elections and Referenda

| Nation and Date | Type of Election | Percentage Voting | Results and Remarks |
|---|---|---|---|
| **West European countries (European Parliament)** 6/7-10/79 | parliamentary | 61% | socialists largest single party but right stronger; first continent-wide party campaigning |
| **Algeria** 2/7/79 | presidential | 95% | single candidate receives 99% |
| **Austria** 11/5/78 | referendum | 64% | government's nuclear power plant rejected |
| 5/6/79 | parliamentary | 92% | socialists retain majority |
| **Bangladesh** 2/18/79 | parliamentary | 40% | government wins 2/3 of seats with 49% of vote; apparently fair and competitive |
| **Benin** 11/20/79 | parliamentary | 80% | no choice, 98% approve list |
| **Bolivia** 7/1/79 | general | NA | apparently fair; presidential decision reverts to parliament, parliamentary decision overturned by military; civilian caretaker government finally installed by parliament |
| **Botswana** 10/20/79 | general | over 50% | government wins 29 of 32 seats; opposition makes some gains in local elections |
| **Canada** 5/22/79 | parliamentary | NA | conservative opposition wins, although it polls fewer votes than liberals |

32

| Country / Date | Election type | % | Description |
|---|---|---|---|
| **Congo** 7/8/79 | general | 90% | constitutional referendum, parliamentary and local elections: apparently no choice or dissent |
| **Cuba** 4/8/79 | municipal | 97% | controlled nomination; some choice; municipal assemblies elect regional and national assemblies |
| **Denmark** 10/23/79 | parliamentary | 86% | government wins; centrist trend |
| **Ecuador** 4/29/79 | general | NA | competitive and free; some limits on nomination and party activity occurred in process |
| **Egypt** 4/19/79 | referendum | 90% | 99.9% approve government proposals—constitutional and Israeli treaty; opposition constrained |
| 6/7 and 6/14/79 | parliamentary | NA | government wins 80-90% of seats; several opposition parties excluded; discussion limited |
| **Finland** 3/18-19/79 | parliamentary | NA | social democrats lose but retain government in coalition |
| **Gabon** 12/30/79 | presidential | NA | only one candidate |
| **Germany (W)** 5/23/79 | presidential | NA | indirect, by Bundestag and Lauder delegates |
| **Ghana** 6/18 and 7/10/79 | general | under 50% | fair and competitive: under shadow of military power |
| **Haiti** 2/11/79 | parliamentary | NA | primarily one party, but independent, opponent of regime wins overwhelmingly in one case |
| **Iceland** 12/2/79 | parliamentary | NA | inconclusive; left declines |
| **Iran** 3/20-21/79 | referendum 90%(?) | 90%(?) | 99% or over for Islamic Republic; no real campaigning; not a secret ballot |
| 8/3/79 | constituent assembly | well under 50% | candidates selected by ruling party; most parties abstained; one or two independents, some competition; balloting less open |

# Table 5 — *Continued*

| Nation and Date | Type of Election | Percentage Voting | Results and Remarks |
|---|---|---|---|
| **Iran** (cont'd) 12/2-3/79 | referendum | NA | overwhelming support for new constitution; effective boycotts in some areas; not secret ballot; turnout may have been low |
| **Ireland** 7/5/79 | referendum | 28% | adoption and university representation issues |
| **Italy** 6/3-4/79 | parliamentary | 90% | communist decline, rise of new party |
| **Japan** 10/7/79 | parliamentary (lower house) | 68% | Liberals increase percentage but lose one seat; communists gain heavily in seats without increase in percentage of votes |
| **Kenya** 11/8/79 | parliamentary | 75% | hotly contested within one-party framework; relatives and friends of prohibited candidates did especially well as a popular protest; issues seldom debated |
| **Luxembourg** 6/10/79 | parliamentary | 86% | shift to right, new coalition |
| **Mali** 6/19/79 | general | NA | president receives 100%; single list 99.9% |
| **Mexico** 7/1/79 | parliamentary plus | 50% (of registered) | ruling party receives 68% of vote, 296 of 300 single member seats, but opposition groups receive 100 seats on proportional basis; more parties permitted than previously |
| **Nigeria** 7/7/79 | upper house | NA | five parties compete; national party leads in all, but no clear majority |
| 7/17/79 | lower house | NA | national party very weak in some southern states |
| 7/21/70 | state legislature | NA | |
| 7/28/79 | stage governors | NA | |
| 8/11/79 | presidential | NA | won by national party leader with plurality |

34

| Country / Date | Type | % | Notes |
|---|---|---|---|
| **Portugal** 12/2/79 | parliamentary | 88% | conservative victory; change in government |
| **St. Lucia** 7/2/79 | parliamentary | NA (high) | opposition wins |
| **St. Vincent** 12/5/79 | parliamentary | 62% | government wins; opposition increases strength in popular vote |
| **Seychelles** 6/23-26/79 | general | 50%(?) | one party; president uncontested; contests for most parliament seats |
| **Somalia** 8/29/79 | referendum | NA | 99% approve new one-party constitution |
| 12/30/79 | general | NA | no choice; 99.9% approve |
| **Spain** 3/1/79 | parliamentary | 67% | fair and competitive; little change in previous balance |
| 4/3/79 | municipal | under 60% | first in 48 years; elected also four provincial assemblies (many cities won by left) |
| 10/25/79 | regional referendums | 60% | Basques and Catalans overwhelmingly approve home rule statutes |
| **Sweden** 9/16/79 | parliamentary | 90% | little change; slight polarizing tendency; heavily defeated Centre party leads government coalition again |
| **Switzerland** 2/16-18/79 | referendum | 49% | oppose stricter controls on nuclear energy, bans on certain advertising and lowering voting age; approve footpath protection |
| 5/20/79 | referendum | 37% | approve controls on new nuclear plants, oppose value added tax (VAT) |
| 10/21/79 | general | 48% | little change, slight conservative shift |
| **Thailand** 4/22/79 | lower house | 25% | several parties, mostly conservative; Prime Minister's party receives few seats, but his appointive Senate ensures his reappointment |
| **Togo** 12/30/79 | general | NA | unopposed; president and parliament reelected on one-party basis; new constitution approved |

35

# Table 5 – *Continued*

| Nation and Date | Type of Election | Percentage Voting | Results and Remarks |
|---|---|---|---|
| **Tunisia** 11/4/79 | parliamentary | 81% | contested somewhat within one-party framework; opposition calls for abstention |
| **Turkey** 10/13/79 | parliamentary midterm | NA | shifts power to right-wing coalition |
| **USSR** 3/4/79 | parliamentary | 99.9% | no choice, although a handful voted against candidates (opposition group excluded from candidacy) |
| **United Kingdom** 3/1/79 | referendums | 64% Scotland 59% Wales | regional referendums on self-rule plan; Wales defeats, Scotland passes but participation too low to validate |
| 5/3/79 | parliamentary | 76% | conservative victory, regional parties decline |
| **Zimbabwe Rhodesia** 4/10/79 and 4/17-20/79 | parliamentary | 50% - 60% | open to all parties and competitive within limits; important segments of community boycotted process |

wise; extremely one-sided outcomes imply an unacceptable electoral process. Voter participation figures are often not comparable, even when available. Many states compel their citizens to vote, in others it is unclear whether participation is a percentage of those registered or of those of voting age.

## LEVELS OF POLITICAL TERROR

Contributing to the judgment of the level of civil liberties in a country is the degree to which its citizens are subject to political terror, either from government or from other groups within the society. Political terror, in turn, includes a variety of different aspects. Murder, torture, exile, passport restriction, denial of vocation, ubiquitous presence of police controls, threats against relatives—all contribute to the fear that is labeled political terror.

In the accompanying Table 6 five levels of political terror are distinguished.[4] The most general criterion is the extent to which the people live under a recognizable and reasonably humane rule of law. Countries on *Level A* live under a secure rule of law, people are not imprisoned for their views, and torture is rare or exceptional (though police and prison brutality may occur). Political murders are extremely rare. There is no detention without trial, and laws protect individual and group rights. On *Level B* there is a limited amount of imprisonment for non-violent political activity. However, few persons are affected, torture and beating are exceptional, and psychiatric institutions are not used to silence political opponents. Political murder is rare, or, if present, characteristic of small terrorist organizations. On *Level C* there is extensive political imprisonment, or a recent history of such imprisonment. Executions or other political murders and brutality may be common. Unlimited detention, with or without trial, for political views is accepted. Incarceration in mental hospitals and the involuntary use of strong drugs may supplement imprisonment. On *Level D* the practices of Level C are expanded to larger numbers. Murders, disappearances, and torture are a common part of life in some societies at this level. In others there is large-scale incarceration of ideological opponents in labor camps or reeducation centers. In still others the terror may stem primarily from the arbitrary and capricious manner in which opponents are punished. In spite of its generality, on this level terror affects primarily those who interest themselves in politics or ideas. On *Level E* the terrors of Level D have been extended to the whole population, and may result from religious, ethnic, or ideological fanaticism. The leaders of these societies place no limits on the means or thoroughness with which they pursue personal or ideological goals. The worst periods of Nazi Germany or Stalinist Russia characterize countries on Level E.

# Table 6
# Estimated Levels of Political Terror

| Level A | | Level B | | | |
|---|---|---|---|---|---|
| Australia | F | Algeria | NF | St. Lucia | F |
| Austria | F | Bahrain | PF | St. Vincent | F |
| Bahamas | F | Bangladesh | PF | Senegal | PF |
| Barbados | F | Benin | NF | Solomon Is. | F |
| Belgium | F | Bhutan | PF | Spain[6] | F |
| Botswana | F | Bolivia | PF | Sri Lanka | F |
| Canada | F | Brazil | PF | Sudan | PF |
| Costa Rica | F | Chile[2] | PF | Swaziland | PF |
| Denmark | F | Cyprus | PF | Thailand[1] | PF |
| Dominica[2] | F | Dominican | | Tonga | PF |
| Fiji | F | Republic | F | Trinidad & | |
| Finland | F | Ecuador[3] | F | Tobago | F |
| France[1] | F | Egypt | PF | United Arab | |
| Gambia | F | Gabon[5] | NF | Emirates | PF |
| Germany(W) | F | Guyana | PF | Upper Volta | F |
| Greece | F | Honduras | PF | Venezuela | F |
| Iceland | F | Hungary | NF | | |
| Ireland | F | India | F | | |
| Japan | F | Israel[4] | F | | |
| Luxembourg | F | Italy[6] | F | | |
| Nauru | F | Ivory Coast | PF | | |
| Netherlands | F | Jamaica | F | | |
| New Zealand | F | Jordan | NF | | |
| Norway | F | Kenya | PF | | |
| Papua New | | Kiribati | F | | |
| Guinea[1] | F | Kuwait | PF | | |
| Portugal[1] | F | Maldives | PF | | |
| Surinam[1] | F | Malta | F | | |
| Sweden | F | Mauritius | PF | | |
| Switzerland | F | Mexico | PF | | |
| Tuvalu[5] | F | Nepal | PF | | |
| United | | Nigeria | F | | |
| Kingdom[1] | F | Panama | PF | | |
| United | | Peru | PF | | |
| States | F | Poland | PF | | |
| Western Samoa[5] | PF | Qatar | PF | | |

This table measures the crimes against humanity of greatest interest to organizations such as Amnesty International. In doing so, it fills a gap in the explanation of how the Comparative Survey of Freedom relates to other human rights concerns and perceptions. Some critics have felt that there was a need to distinguish those countries that follow particularly evil practices from those that simply deny political and civil freedoms. Others have wondered how the Survey could continue to rate countries such as Lebanon, that have a high level of terror and violence, as highly as it does on the scales of political and civil freedoms.

This table establishes the point that in some cases fairly free institutions coexist with egregious violations of humanity. Comparison of the

## Level C

| | | | |
|---|---|---|---|
| Bulgaria | NF | Malaysia | PF |
| Burma | NF | Mali | NF |
| Burundi | NF | Mauritania[3] | NF |
| Cameroon | NF | Morocco | PF |
| Cape Verde Islands | NF | Nicaragua | PF |
| Central African Rep. | NF | Niger | NF |
| China (Mainland) | NF | Oman[3] | NF |
| China (Taiwan) | PF | Pakistan | PF |
| Colombia[6] | F | Paraguay | PF |
| Comoro Islands | PF | Philippines[6] | PF |
| Congo | NF | Rwanda[5] | NF |
| Cuba | NF | Rumania | NF |
| Czechoslovakia | NF | Sao Tome and Principe[5] | NF |
| Djibouti | PF | Saudi Arabia | NF |
| Equatorial Guinea[5] | NF | Seychelles | NF |
| Germany (E) | NF | Sierra Leone[3] | PF |
| Ghana | PF | Singapore | PF |
| Grenada | PF | Somalia | NF |
| Guinea[2] | NF | South Africa | PF |
| Guinea-Bissau | NF | Syria | PF |
| Haiti | NF | Tanzania[3] | NF |
| Indonesia[3] | PF | Togo | NF |
| Iran | PF | Transkei | PF |
| Korea (S) | PF | Tunisia | PF |
| Lesotho | PF | Turkey[6] | F |
| Liberia | PF | USSR | NF |
| Libya | NF | Yemen (N) | NF |
| Madagascar[5] | NF | Yugoslavia | NF |
| Malawi | NF | Zambia[6] | PF |

## Level D

| | |
|---|---|
| Albania | NF |
| Angola[6] | NF |
| Argentina[3] | NF |
| El Salvador[6] | PF |
| Guatemala | PF |
| Iraq | NF |
| Korea (N) | NF |
| Laos | NF |
| Lebanon[6] | PF |
| Mongolia[5] | NF |
| Mozambique | NF |
| Uganda[6] | NF |
| Uruguay | NF |
| Vietnam | NF |
| Yemen (S) | NF |
| Zaire[3] | NF |
| Zimbabwe Rhodesia[6] | PF |

## Level E

| | |
|---|---|
| Afghanistan[6] | NF |
| Chad[6] | NF |
| Ethiopia[3/6] | NF |
| Kampuchea[6] | NF |

**Notes to the Table**

1. Special situations, cases of terror in the recent past, or general political environment cast doubt on this rating.

2. Recent improvements have moved the country up to this level.

3. Recent improvements may have raised the country above this level.

4. Does not include occupied territories.

5. The situation was especially unclear.

6. This rating was due in large part to anti-government terrorism or civil war.

table with others will suggest that, while levels of freedom are obviously related to levels of terror, the correlation is not as high as might be imagined. It has been a surprising finding of the Survey that some societies—for example, several in Central America—exhibit a remarkable level of freedom in the face of widespread political violence, both governmental and nongovernmental. In part this is due to the unorganized, anarchic nature of violence in such countries, in part to the unwillingness of many of their citizens to be terrorized by others.

The categorization in the table of levels of political terror is obviously imprecise. It is based on very incomplete knowledge in some cases; it is confused by the attempt to integrate different types of terror in the

# Table 7  Political-

| POLITICAL ▸ | Multiparty | | Dominant-Party |
|---|---|---|---|
| | **Centralized** | **Decentralized** | |

**ECONOMIC**

**Capitalist — Inclusive**

| Centralized | | Decentralized | Dominant-Party |
|---|---|---|---|
| Bahamas F | Ireland F | Australia F | Korea (S)[1] PF |
| Barbados F | Italy[3] F | Belgium F[1] | Malaysia PF |
| Colombia[4] F | Japan F | Canada F | |
| Costa Rica F | Luxembourg F | Cyprus PF | |
| Dominica[4] F | Mauritius PF | Germany (W)[3] F | |
| Dominican | New Zealand[3] F | Lebanon PF | |
| Republic[4] F | Spain F | Switzerland F | |
| France[3] F | Surinam F | United States F | |
| Greece F | Trinidad & | | |
| Iceland F | Tobago F | | |

**Capitalist — Noninclusive**

| Centralized | Decentralized | Dominant-Party |
|---|---|---|
| Ecuador F | Botswana F | Haiti NF |
| Fiji[4] F | Papua New | Lesotho PF |
| Gambia[4] F | Guinea[1] F | Philippines PF |
| Guatemala PF | | Transkei[5] PF |
| Morocco PF | | |
| Thailand[1] PF | | |
| Upper Volta[3] F | | |

**Capitalist-Statist — Inclusive**

| Centralized | Decentralized | Dominant-Party |
|---|---|---|
| Ghana[1] PF | Brazil[1/3/4] PF | China (Taiwan) PF |
| Malta F | | Mexico PF |
| South Africa PF | | Singapore PF |
| Sri Lanka F | | |
| Turkey[4] F | | |
| Venezuela F | | |

**Capitalist-Statist — Noninclusive**

| Centralized | Decentralized | Dominant-Party |
|---|---|---|
| Bangladesh[1] PF | India F | Iran[2/4] PF |
| Bolivia PF | Nigeria[3/4] F | Indonesia[1/4] PF |
| Zimbabwe Rhodesia[4] PF | | Paraguay[1/3/4] PF |

**Capitalist-Socialist — Inclusive**

| Centralized | | Dominant-Party |
|---|---|---|
| Austria F | Netherlands F | Egypt[3/4] PF |
| Denmark F | Norway F | Grenada[2] PF |
| Finland F | Portugal F | Senegal[3/4] PF |
| Guyana PF | St. Lucia[3] F | Syria[1/4] PF |
| Israel F | St. Vincent[3] F | |
| Jamaica F | Sweden F | |
| | United Kingdom F | |

**Capitalist-Socialist — Noninclusive**

**Socialist — Inclusive**

**Socialist — Noninclusive**

## Notes

1. Military dominated.

2. Party relationships anomalous.

3. Close decision on capitalist-to-socialist dimension.

4. Close decision on inclusive/noninclusive dimension.

5. Over 50 percent of income from remittances of persons working in South Africa.

# Economic Systems

| One-Party | | | Nonparty | |
|---|---|---|---|---|
| **Socialist** | **Communist** | **Nationalist** | **Military** | **Nonmilitary** |
| | | Djibouti PF | Chile³ PF<br>El Salvador²/³ PF | Jordan³/⁴ NF |
| Sierra Leone PF | | Cameroon³ NF<br>Gabon NF<br>Ivory Coast⁴ PF<br>Kenya PF<br>Liberia² PF<br>Malawi NF | Chad NF<br>Honduras⁴ PF<br>Niger NF<br>Yemen (N)³ NF | Bhutan³ PF<br>Central Afr. Rep. NF<br>Comoro Islands PF<br>Maldives PF<br>Nepal³ PF<br>Solomon Islands² F<br>Swaziland PF<br>Tonga PF<br>Tuvalu F<br>Western Samoa PF |
| Libya¹/²/³ NF | | | Argentina NF<br>Panama³/⁴ PF | Bahrain PF<br>Kuwait PF<br>Nauru F<br>Qatar PF<br>Saudi Arabia NF<br>United Arab Ems. PF |
| | | Zaire¹ NF | Equatorial Guinea³ NF<br>Mauritania NF<br>Pakistan NF | Kiribati F<br>Oman NF |
| Seychelles³ NF<br>Tunisia⁴ PF | Poland³ PF<br>Yugoslavia³ NF | | Uruguay NF | Nicaragua²/⁴ PF |
| Burma¹ NF<br>Burundi¹/³ NF<br>Congo¹/³ NF<br>Somalia¹/³ NF<br>Zambia³ PF | | Madagascar¹/³ NF<br>Mali¹ NF<br>Rwanda¹/³ NF<br>Sudan¹ PF<br>Togo¹ NF<br>Uganda³ NF | Peru⁴ PF | |
| Algeria NF<br>Sao Tome and Principe³/⁴ NF | Albania NF<br>Bulgaria NF<br>China (Mainland) NF<br>Cuba NF<br>Czechoslovakia NF<br>Germany (E) NF<br>Hungary NF<br>Kampuchea NF<br>Korea (N) NF<br>Mongolia NF<br>Rumania NF<br>USSR NF<br>Vietnam NF | | | |
| Angola NF<br>Benin¹/³ NF<br>Cape Verde Is.³/⁴ NF<br>Guinea NF<br>Guinea-Bissau³ NF<br>Iraq¹/³/⁴ NF<br>Mozambique NF<br>Tanzania NF<br>Yemen (S) NF | Afghanistan NF<br>Laos NF | | Ethiopia³ NF | |

same scheme of judgment. As in the other tables, the degree of accuracy we strive for is to be never more than a category off for any country. For example, a B state should perhaps be placed on levels A or C, but we are quite sure it does not belong on Level D. The reader should also remember that while in most states the government is principally to blame for the level of terror, in some the government is simply too weak to control the terror.

## THE RELATION OF POLITICAL-ECONOMIC SYSTEMS TO FREEDOM

The accompanying table of political-economic systems (Table 7) fills two needs. It offers the reader additional information about the countries we have rated. For example, readers with libertarian views may wish to raise the relative ratings of capitalist countries, while those who place more value on redistributive systems may wish to raise the ratings of countries toward the socialist end of the spectrum. The table also makes possible an analysis of the relation between political and economic forms and the freedom ratings of the Survey. Examination of the table will show that freedom is directly related to the existence of multiparty systems: the further a country is from such systems, the less freedom it is likely to have. This could be considered a trivial result, since a publicly competitive political system is one of the criteria of freedom, and political parties are considered evidence for such competition. However, the result is not simply determined by our definitions: we searched for evidence of authentic public competition in countries without competitive parties, and seldom found the search rewarded. Both theoretical and empirical studies indicate the difficulty of effective public political opposition in one-party systems.[5]

The relation between economic systems and freedom is more complicated and, because of our lack of emphasis on economic systems in devising our ratings of freedom, is not predetermined by our methods. Historically, the table suggests that there are three types of societies competing for acceptance in the world. The first, or *traditional* type, is marginal and in retreat, but its adherents have borrowed political and economic bits and pieces from both of the other types. The second and third, the *Euro-American* and *Sino-Soviet* types, are strongest near their points of origin, but have spread by diffusion and active propagation all over the world. The Leninist-socialist style of political organization was exported along with the socialist concept of economic organization, just as constitutional democracy had been exported along with capitalist economic concepts. In this interpretation, the relation of economic systems to freedom found in the table may be an expression of historical chance rather than necessary relationship. Clearly, capitalism does not cause nations to be politically free, nor does socialism cause them to be politically unfree. Still, socialists must be concerned by the empirical relationship between the rating of "not free" and socialism that is found in tables such as this.

In the table, economies are roughly grouped in categories from "capitalist" to "socialist." Labeling economies as capitalist or socialist has a fairly clear significance in the developed world, but it may be doubted that it is very useful to label the mostly poor and largely agrarian societies of the third world in this manner. Raymond Aron, for example, casts doubt on the legitimacy of calling any third world, noncommunist society "socialist," regardless of what it may call itself.[6] However, third world states with dual economies, that is, with a modern sector and a preindustrial sector, have economic policies or goals that can be placed along the continuum from socialist to capitalist. A socialist third world state has usually nationalized all of the modern sector—except possibly some foreign investment—and claims central government jurisdiction over the land and its products, with only temporary assignment of land to individuals or cooperatives. The capitalist third world state has a capitalist modern sector and a traditionalist agricultural sector, combined in some cases with new agricultural projects either on family farm or agribusiness models. Third world economies that fall between capitalist and socialist do not have the high taxes of their industrialized equivalents, but they have major nationalized industries (for example, oil) in the modern sector, and their agricultural world may include emphasis on cooperatives or large-scale land reform, as well as more traditional forms.

States with *inclusive capitalist* forms are generally developed states that rely on the operation of the market and on private provision for industrial welfare. Taxes may be high, but they are not confiscatory, while government interference is generally limited to subsidy and regulation. States classified as *noninclusive capitalist*, such as Liberia or Thailand, have not over fifty percent of the population included in a capitalist modern economy, with the remainder of the population still living traditionally. In such states the traditional economy may be individual, communal, or feudal, but the direction of change as development proceeds is capitalistic.

Capitalist states grade over into capitalist-statist or capitalist-socialist nations. *Capitalist-statist* nations are those such as Brazil, Turkey, or Saudi Arabia, that have very large government productive enterprises, either because of an elitist development philosophy or major dependence on a key resource such as oil. Government interferes in the economy in a major way in such states, but not primarily because of egalitarian motives. *Capitalist-socialist* systems, such as those in Israel, the Netherlands, or Sweden, provide social services on a large scale through governmental or other nonprofit institutions, with the result that private control over property is sacrificed to egalitarian purposes. These nations still see capitalism as legitimate, but its legitimacy is accepted grudgingly by many in government. Governments of other states grouped here, such as Egypt or Poland, proclaim themselves to be socialist, but in fact allow rather large portions of the economy to remain in the private domain. Both variants have *noninclusive* versions, such as India or Madagascar.

*Socialist* economies, on the other hand, strive programmatically to place an entire national economy under direct or indirect government control. States such as the USSR or Cuba may allow some modest private productive property, but this is only by exception, and right to such property can be revoked at any time. The leaders of *noninclusive socialist* states have the same goals as the leaders of inclusive socialist states, but their relatively primitive economies or peoples have not yet been effectively included in the socialist system. Such states generally have a small socialized modern economy and a large preindustrial economy in which the organization of production and trade is still largely traditional. It should be understood that the characterizations in the table are impressionistic; the continuum between capitalist and socialist economies is necessarily cut arbitrarily into categories for this presentation.

Political systems range from democratic multiparty to absolutist one-party systems. Theoretically, the most democratic countries should be those with *decentralized multiparty* systems, for here important powers are held by the people at two or more levels of the political system, and dissent is legitimated and mobilized by opposition parties. More common are *centralized multiparty* systems, such as France or Japan, in which the central government organizes lower levels of government primarily for reasons of efficiency. *Dominant-party* systems allow the forms of democracy, but structure the political process so that opposition groups do not have a realistic chance of achieving power. Such limitations may be through vote fraud, imprisonment of opposition leaders, or other devices.

The now classical form of one-party rule is that in *one-party* states such as the USSR or Vietnam that proclaim themselves to be *communist*. The slightly larger group of *socialist one-party* states are ruled by elites that use Marxist-Leninist rhetoric, organize ruling parties very much along communist lines, but either do not have the disciplined organization of communist states or have explicitly rejected one or another aspect of communism. A final group of *nationalist one-party* states adopt the political form popularized by the communists (and the fascists in the last generation), but the leaders generally reject the revolutionary ideologies of socialist or communist states and fail to develop the totalitarian controls that characterize these states. There are several borderline states that might be switched between socialist and nationalist categories (for example, Libya). It should also be noted that "socialist" is used here to designate a political rather than economic system. A socialist "vanguard party" established along Marxist-Leninist lines will almost surely develop a socialist economy, but a state with a socialist economy need not be ruled by a vanguard party. It should be pointed out that the totalitarian-libertarian continuum is not directly reflected by this categorization.

Nonparty systems can be democratic, as in the small island of Nauru, but generally they are not. Such systems may be *nonmilitary nonparty* systems ranging from Tonga to Saudi Arabia. Much more important are the many *military nonparty* systems, such as that in Argentina.

## SOVIET AND COMMUNIST THREATS TO FREEDOM

The communist threat to freedom appears in three guises. First, Marxist-Leninist ideology is used in a wide variety of states to legitimize the undermining of the effectiveness of the so-called "bourgeois rights" to civil and political liberties. Secondly, the communist model is adopted by many new rulers and revolutionary groups struggling for power. At first this may be merely a way of attracting the money and arms communist nations provide those who use their slogans; later this early label may come to determine policy. Finally, the communist threat is expressed through the relative increase in the actual and perceived power of the Soviet bloc, a bloc whose leaders show remarkably little respect for freedom at home and abroad. It is the increase in the power of this bloc that holds the greatest long-term danger to freedom in the world, a danger that in the minds of many overshadows the short-term gains that the Survey reflects. Recent Soviet gains are not reflected in the Survey because they have occurred primarily in countries already with little or no freedom, such as Kampuchea and Afghanistan.

Whether a country is or is not in the Soviet bloc is of course open to much dispute. Two objective indicators can, however, be found in the last year. The Havana conference of Non-Aligned States in 1979 offers evidence for a pessimistic interpretation of Soviet success. Ninety-five countries were willing to attend as full members and several more as observers. Although many of the attendees objected to Cuba's allegiances, they nevertheless met in Havana and elected Castro president of the Non-Aligned Movement. This was in spite of the fact that Cuba and several other members of the Movement (notably Vietnam)

# Table 8
# The Roll Call

United Nations Resolution Demanding Soviet
Withdrawal from Afghanistan, January 14, 1980

### In Favor (104)

Albania
Argentina
Australia
Austria
Bahamas
Bahrain
Bangladesh
Barbados
Belgium
Bolivia
Botswana
Brazil
Britain
Burma
Cambodia
Cameroon
Canada
Chile
China
Colombia
Costa Rica
Denmark
Djibouti
Dominican
  Republic
Ecuador
Egypt
El Salvador
Fiji
France
Gabon
Gambia
Germany, West
Ghana
Greece
Guatemala

Guyana
Haiti
Honduras
Iceland
Indonesia
Iran
Iraq
Ireland
Israel
Italy
Ivory Coast
Jamaica
Japan
Jordan
Kenya
Kuwait
Lebanon
Lesotho
Liberia
Luxembourg
Malawi
Malaysia
Maldives
Malta
Mauritania
Mauritius
Mexico
Morocco
Nepal
Netherlands
New Zealand
Niger
Nigeria
Norway
Oman
Pakistan

Panama
Papua New
  Guinea
Paraguay
Peru
Philippines
Portugal
Qatar
Rwanda
St. Lucia
Samoa
Saudi Arabia
Senegal
Sierra Leone
Singapore
Somalia
Spain
Sri Lanka
Suriname
Swaziland
Sweden
Tanzania
Thailand
Togo
Trinidad and
  Tobago
Tunisia
Turkey
United Arab
  Emirates
United States
Upper Volta
Uruguay
Venezuela
Yugoslavia
Zaire

### Against (18)

Afghanistan
Angola
Bulgaria
Byelorussia
Cuba
Czechoslovakia

Ethiopia
Germany, East
Grenada
Hungary
Laos
Mongolia

Mozambique
Poland
Southern
  Yemen
Soviet Union
Ukraine
Vietnam

### Abstentions (18)

Algeria
Benin
Burundi
Congo
Cyprus
Equatorial
  Guinea

Finland
Guinea
Guinea-Bissau
India
Madagascar
Mali
Nicaragua

Sao Tome
  and Principe
Syria
Uganda
Yemen
Zambia

### Absent or Not Voting (12)

Bhutan
Cape Verde
Central African
  Republic

Chad
Comoros
Dominica
Libya

Rumania
Seychelles
Solomon Islands
South Africa
Sudan

were not in any sense non-aligned. The fact that Cuba failed in its attempt to define the Soviet Union as a special friend of the non-aligned world does not affect the significance of Castro's ability to treat the non-aligned movement, and thus most of the world, as a part of the Soviet camp. It was disappointing that opposition to Cuba at the conference was largely marshaled by countries such as Yugoslavia or China, themselves communist. We can only conclude that for the elites of most of the world, democratic and nondemocratic, the old concept that the left can do no wrong is alive and well.

However, under quite different circumstances the vote in the United Nations on January 14, 1980, calling for the immediate withdrawal of the USSR from Afghanistan provides a more optimistic and perhaps objective indication of the size of the Soviet bloc.[7] As the accompanying Table 8 indicates, the eighteen nations voting against the resolution can be thought to form the core of the Soviet bloc. Two of these are really parts of the USSR. Another, Grenada, is a worrisome addition, but its new leaders may have only a passing dependence on the bloc through reliance on Cuban military aid. A distinction should also be made between those bloc members under proven Soviet control—primarily those that border the USSR—and those that could perhaps break away from the bloc without incurring a massive Soviet intervention. These comments suggest that the "solid core" of the Soviet bloc is considerably less than eighteen states.

The nations shown not to be voting in Table 8 represent a variety of ideological viewpoints. Many, such as the Comoro Islands, were simply absent. Others such as Rumania no doubt chose to be absent. Such states, together with most of the eighteen abstaining states form a group of nations affected in one way or another by the shadow of Soviet power or support, but not yet forced into Moscow's empire. Finland is the now traditional example, but the number of such states in Africa is cause for concern. On the other hand, the willingness of states such as Jamaica and Malta to condemn the Soviet Union on this occasion indicate their continuing independence in spite of recent political signals.[8]

## Conclusion

This was a year of gains achieved in spite of the repressions that continued. Many peoples again showed their preference for liberty. But the centers of oppression, the imperial governments that would impose tyranny on all peoples, did not weaken. Through the success of Cuba in the third world and of Vietnam in Kampuchea, they advanced at the same time as the pricing policies of the Organization of Petroleum

Exporting Countries (OPEC) weakened the consumer-oriented democracies. Iran and Pakistan joined Libya in advancing Islam as a new ideological basis for oppression. Fortunately, these are not really powerful states, and Islam need not be politically interpreted in such a manner. The three leading states of this movement lack the uniformity of organization or ideology that characterizes Marxist-Leninist regimes.

We learned again this year how often world leaders are guilty of justifying the unjustifiable in the name of supposedly higher purposes. The horrors of Idi Amin in Uganda and Macias Nguema in Equatorial Guinea were abetted to the last by the Soviets and Libyans, those of Bokassa in the Central African Empire by the French, and of Pol Pot in Kampuchea by the Chinese. President Carter's human rights policy was seriously compromised when even the United States and its allies supported in the United Nations the right of self-determination of the Cambodian people represented by Pol Pot. We did not go this far in protesting the incursions that unseated Amin, but many of our African friends were more disturbed by Tanzania's interference in another country's affairs than pleased by the dictator's displacement.

Self-determination, the right of peoples to determine their own affairs, is a major component of political freedom. It is one that is often not sufficiently respected in national and international forums dedicated to the inviolability of borders. But to speak of self-determination in the absence of political processes allowing a people actually to determine who should rule them is often both sentimental and dangerous. By invading Uganda, Tanzania increased the probability of Ugandans determining their own affairs, and in Kampuchea the Vietnamese aided Cambodian self-determination even as they placed Cambodians under foreign tutelage. Self-determination goes far beyond politics: it includes the right to life, to talk with friends, to live with one's family. The humanism of our political categories must also include these rights.

Human rights are neither Eastern nor Western. It is a simple perversion of nationalism for President Duvalier to tell his Tontons Macoutes to ignore attempts from abroad to Westernize Haiti's political institutions, because models "dreamed up on the banks of the Potomac, the Thames and the Seine . . . retard our progress." [9]

In mainland China the dramatic declarations, trial, and conviction of the dissident Wei Jingsheng pointed up again the universality and undeniability of the desire for freedom. As Wei wrote to his fellow countrymen: "No leader can be given unconditional trust. He has our trust only so long as he puts into practice a policy which benefits the nation as a whole." This is the essential equality of the campfire or the village, which we express in modern life through political democracy. Wei was jailed essentially because he described this right to mistrust the claims of entrenched leaders as the "Fifth Modernization," the essential right of the "little man" for whom the Chinese Revolution was fought. As he stood in court he told his judges: "The prevailing current . . . is democracy . . . those who stand on the other side of democratic currents are counterrevolutionaries."[10]

## NOTES

1. For more discussion of methodology see R. D. Gastil, *Freedom in the World 1978*, especially pp. 7–30.

2. See Part III, "Report of the Freedom House Mission to Observe the Common Roll Election in Zimbabwe Rhodesia—April 1979," below pp. 000. It is also useful to compare the outcome as reported here with that forecast before the elections by a Zambian professor on the basis of a limited survey (Ronald T. Libby, "All-Party Elections in Zimbabwe: What Might Happen," *Africa Today* 26, no. 1 1979: 7–17). The results seem to indicate the fairness of the election, given the candidates that participated.

3. The journal *Government and Opposition* has devoted its Autumn 1979 issue (Vol. 14, no. 4) to the elections. See also *Keesing's Contemporary Archives,* pp. 29893–29900.

4. The reader may wish to compare this table with James Seymour's "Indices of Political Imprisonment," *Universal Human Rights* 1, no. 1 (January 1979): 99–103.

5. See William J. Foltz, "Political Opposition in Single-Party States of Tropical Africa" in R. A. Dahl, ed., *Regimes and Oppositions* (New Haven: Yale, 1973); also Giovanni Sartori, *Parties and Party Systems* (Cambridge: Cambridge University Press, 1976).

6. Raymond Aron, "My Defense of Our Decadent Europe," *Encounter* (September 1977), pp. 7–50, especially p. 33.

7. *New York Times,* January 15, 1980.

8. Discussion of self-determination, with tables of peoples denied these rights, will be found in *Freedom in the World 1978* and *1979.*

9. *Keesing's Contemporary Archives,* January 11, 1980, p. 30036.

10. *Far Eastern Economic Review,* November 2, 1979, pp. 22–24.

## PART II

# Special Concerns in Civil Liberties: International Communication and Union Organization

# Freedom of the Press: Problems in Restructuring the Flow of International News

## Leonard R. Sussman

The struggle between free and closed societies continues on many fronts, but perhaps none is more important than that on which the contesting parties struggle to advance their concepts of the proper forms and content of news flowing both within societies and between societies. Until recently we have assumed that the Western concept of freedom of the press was bound to be universally admired; indeed it has seemed to be enshrined in many international statements from the Universal Declaration on Human Rights to the Helsinki Accords. We assumed that tyrannical and authoritarian regimes would passively accept the concept whatever their actions in reality. However, in the past few years in international forums the concepts of an independent free press as it exists in Western countries and the private distribution of news internationally without control by the governments of either originating or receiving countries have been seriously challenged. The challenge has been complicated by the fact that it is made in the context of 1) the legitimate argument that there may be dangers to third world interests in the domination of international reportage by Western news services and 2) the legitimate request by weak third world states for technical and financial aid in developing their own communication capabilities. The skein of issues raised by these challenges must be seriously considered.

## I.  Recent History of International Attempts to Control or Restructure News Flows

### THE BIENNIAL CONFRONTATIONS

Nineteen eighty will be an important year for international communication. Since 1972 a new crisis has been expected at each biennial General Conference of the United Nations Educational, Scientific and Cultural Organization (UNESCO). Not only is 1980 a UNESCO biennial year, but the International Commission on the Study of Communication Problems is issuing its report, and the United States and other Western countries are expected to begin some significant transfers of communication technology to the developing countries.

In 1972 the Soviet bloc began introducing draft declarations that threatened to establish as a universal standard governmental control of the international news media. This standard would replace the free-flow-of-information model set in 1945. While Marxist ideology appeals only to a few developing countries, the Marxist-Leninist challenge to Western news-delivery systems has reinforced the desire of most third world countries for greater control over communications. Their aspirations have produced a mounting confrontation between the have-nots and the haves in international communication. Often, this takes the form of a clash between advocates of the "free flow" of information and those who seek a "balanced flow," with balance defined by governments.

Until the late 1960's, the desirability of a free flow of news was seldom challenged in international forums, although in practice most countries did not allow a free flow. Lack of challenge to news freedom encouraged news services that were not controlled by any government to roam the world for reportage. The rest of the world relied on the reports of free Western correspondents for their knowledge of world events. Necessarily news of the non-Western world was filtered through the tests of newsworthiness, general interest, and news style designed for a Western audience.

In pressing for a UNESCO document on the mass media, the Soviet Union originally appeared to have limited objectives. Soviet citizens and other Eastern Europeans were listening regularly to broadcasts from Radio Liberty and Radio Free Europe (since merged). Regarding such broadcasts as "intervention" in their internal affairs, the USSR hoped to persuade other nations to restrict the delivery of news and information across national borders. Most less developed countries (LDC's) had little desire to support this Soviet position, but year by year the Soviet pressure for *some* controls over nongovernmental international news media attracted many LDC representatives to the debate.

Failing in 1972 the Soviets tried again in 1974. The new Soviet text called for the "use" of the mass news media for specific (otherwise noble) objectives, such as strengthening peace or opposing racism. Western journalists did not immediately respond, and Western governments did little to alert the independent news media.

After a Latin American regional conference of UNESCO in Costa Rica, American journalists became aware in 1976 of the mounting campaign. Six months later, at the biennial in Nairobi, UNESCO itself faced a crisis of survival over the news media issue and the still-simmering denial of full regional committee status to Israel. The Israeli issue was soon resolved, but the information controversy has deepened and broadened. All forms of communication faced political challenge in far wider arenas: the United Nations General Assembly, the International Telecommunications Union (which allocates broadcast spectrum assignments, governing shortwave, radar and other signals, as well as outer-space agreements affecting military, economic, and geopolitical activities), and the UN Development Program, as well as UNESCO.

In 1976 the Soviet Union's draft declaration stipulated the "use" of the mass news media for certain purposes, and would make independent journalists subject to control by governments. The draft set forth "principles governing the use of the mass media in strengthening peace and international understanding and in combating war propaganda, racism and apartheid." The operative Article XII declared that "[s]tates are responsible for the activities in the international sphere of all mass media under their jurisdiction." Western governments, and the independent news media on their own, mounted a strong defense that won a two-year delay for rewriting the declaration. To save face for its supporters, a sixteen-person commission was created under the chairmanship of Sean MacBride, recipient of both the Lenin and Nobel Peace Prizes.

In addition to approving the creation of the MacBride Commission, the West, and particularly the United States, promised to make available to developing countries communications technology and training. With the assistance of black African countries the bargain was sealed: the mass media declaration was postponed for two years, the MacBride Commission would proceed, and technology transfers would begin.

UNESCO's 1978 biennial dealt with (1) a new declaration on the media, (2) an interim report of the MacBride Commission, (3) a separate examination of a New World Information Order (NWIO), and (4) programs in communications research and activities. Several mass media drafts had been written in the interim, but the version submitted in 1978 was almost as harsh as the 1976 draft. It still condoned manipulation of the press for ulterior purposes, and readily supported control and coercion. At the biennial, Western governments and independent journalists again negotiated extensively with groups of third world delegates. The West "sanitized" the declaration, eliminating all references to press controls. The Soviet representatives were largely unaware of the two-track negotiations conducted up to the evening before the final vote. While Soviet delegates were negotiating over their own press control draft, moderate third world and Western representatives were fashioning a different, control-free text.

By acclamation, on November 22 the delegates accepted a text that nowhere supported government interference in the free flow of news. This "Declaration on Fundamental Principles Concerning the Contribution of the Mass Media to Strengthening Peace and International Understanding, the Promotion of Human Rights and Countering Racialism, Apartheid and Incitement to War," clearly stated that interference in the free flow of information was a violation of a human right. It enjoined diversity of sources and means of information, as well as the journalist's freedom to report and fullest possible access to information. The text also supported "a new equilibrium and greater reciprocity," a balancing of news reports between the developed and developing countries, and among developing countries. This was an improvement over earlier drafts calling for a "balanced flow," the antithesis of a free flow. The declaration noted "the aspirations of the developing countries for the establishment of a new, more just and more effective world information and communication order," but did not call for a New World Information Order (NWIO), with its suggestion of a pre-ordained, fascist "order."

The 1978 UNESCO biennial approved a little-noted parallel declaration on the NWIO employing the compromise language of the media declaration. NWIO was not upper-cased, nor were the words of NWIO spelled out. Endorsement of "a new order" was explicitly avoided. Yet the NWIO concept remains the leading edge of the third world activists' challenge to Western communication media. Within hours after the UNESCO declarations were approved, the Special Political Committee of the UN General Assembly, with U.S. support, approved a consensus resolution linking the aspiration for a "new . . . order" to the maintenance of a "free flow and a wider and better balanced dissemination of information."

The 1978 UNESCO declaration provided a new trade-off. The softening of the text (just as the delay in approving a text in 1976) was accompanied by still firmer Western, particularly American, promises of technology and training assistance to third world communicators. Americans pledged specific technological and training assistance for third world communication systems. The United States promised some

$25,000,000 in satellite facilities and help in establishing six regional journalism and training centers in the third world. A consortium of thirty-two nongovernmental print and broadcast news services, editors and managers in the World Press Freedom Committee, would continue to provide equipment and training for third world communications. Thirty-six grants in sixteen countries were made through March 1980. Seminars and workshops were held in other countries in Africa, the Caribbean, and Central America. The International Press Institute (IPI) organized training seminars on editorial and technical subjects for journalists in Africa and Asia.

As the 1980 UNESCO biennial conference at Belgrade neared, the United States government delivered some of the promised communications assistance in 1979. It hosted a Washington conference to plan a major intergovernmental meeting in Paris the following spring. The American proposal for technology transfer would be funded through the United Nations Development Program, the International Telecommunications Union (ITU), and the World Bank. Third world activists rejected the American effort to attach these programs to several UN and international agencies. They favored UNESCO as the sole repository of information development.

But competition was developing within the UN. In December the General Assembly voted to examine the implications of a new information and communication order. The General Assembly's Third Committee created the UN Committee on Information with a membership of sixty-six states. While recognizing the central role played by UNESCO in informational matters, the new committee nevertheless was assigned a degree of primacy. It would expect progress reports from UNESCO's Director General on "the establishment of the new world information and communication order" following the conclusion of UNESCO's 1980 conference. The subject was added to the agenda for the next session of the General Assembly. The American delegate, Alfred P. Brainard, declared that there are "potential problems" in promoting the establishment of "new orders that require significant changes in international, and also national, structures such as are involved in both the call for a new international economic order and of a new world information and communication order."

The UN seems likely to develop its own programs and secretariat in 1980 to target further the performance of the mass news media on the world scene. Meanwhile, journalists and interested media-watchers around the world await the final text of the MacBride Commission's report. A prepublication reading of the report's conclusions reveals that while censorship and governmental controls are rejected, considerable support is given—between the lines in some cases, more openly in others—

for continued efforts to devise a code of ethics for journalists, which
ultimately implies the licensing of newspeople and the monitoring of
their output against a governmentally approved standard.

Technology transfer will also remain a primary third world expecta-
tion. If the American government's promises are not placed in the
pipeline by September 1980, ideological war could erupt anew at
Belgrade. Support by private sources such as the World Press Freedom
Committee, while generous in spirit, and helpful to many recipients,
cannot possibly match the needs. One wonders, though, whether some
LDC's could improve their communication capabilities by reordering
their own priorities. In 1977 some 117 third world countries spent
$96.9 billion on their defense budgets. Most notable, from 1973 to
1977, the developing countries bought $48.3 billion in arms from the
developed countries, East and West.[1]

## THE 1978 UNESCO DECLARATION ON THE MASS MEDIA

After this brief review of recent history we should consider in more
detail its most noteworthy products.

The declaration UNESCO adopted by acclamation in 1978 surprised
even its Western proponents. They had campaigned for six years to
kill any international declaration on the mass media. Merely negotiating
on the subject, they felt, would open the door to future intergovernmental controls of the press. Yet the clamor became so intense that
*some* document was deemed necessary. Given this assumption the
declaration was a Western victory.

While the 1978 text contained none of the restrictions on press
freedom in the earlier drafts, the declaration made two fundamental
assumptions that could plague the independent press. After reciting
obviously desirable objectives such as peace and human rights, the
declaration linked the assessment of the mass media to their performance
in contributing to the realization of these objectives. Thus, an intergovernmental agency, with the fully acclaimed approval of national
delegates, had "legislated" on transnational journalism, and assigned
to journalists responsibilities, however noble or vague.

The Soviets were among the most displeased delegates. At the last
moment, stipulations had been inserted that "freedom of opinion, expression and information" is an "integral part of human rights and
fundamental freedoms." Further, the public should have "access" to a
"diversity" of sources, and the journalist therefore must have "freedom
to report and the fullest possible access to information." Moreover,
to "promote human rights," the mass media are expected to report
the news of those "unable to make their voices heard within their own

territories." Thus, the declaration rejects the USSR's claim that journalistic activities in the Eastern bloc, and particularly coverage of Andrei Sakharov and the Soviet human rights activities, are an intrusion in the internal affairs of the Soviet Union.

The declaration noted the "inequalities in the flow of information to and from developing countries, and between those countries," and called for a "new equilibrium and reciprocity in the flow of information." It urged the transfer of resources to enable third world media "to gain strength and expand." UNESCO, not surprisingly, was enjoined to create "the conditions for a free flow and wider and more balanced dissemination of information" and "the protection" of journalists. These three elements—the transfer of resources to third world media, the institutionalization of free-flow campaigns at UNESCO, and efforts to assure the protection of journalists—set the stage for protracted, further controversies.

The declaration received a mixed reception. UNESCO's press release called the 2,000-word document "a triumph of the spirit of goodwill and international cooperation." The Associated Press described the consensus as "a personal victory for UNESCO Director-General Amadou Mahtar M'Bow," as well as a "significant diplomatic reversal in favor of the West and moderate developing nations." U.S. Ambassador John Reinhardt called it "a triumph that imposed no restraints on the role of the press." The Soviet spokesman asserted that his country's version (calling for press controls) "would have been preferable." An Austrian said the declaration was subject to different interpretations, "possibly not compatible with our basic freedoms." Said United Press International, "the real winner appears to be the third world." William Attwood, the only active newsman in the U.S. delegation, had gone to Paris with little hope that the press-control draft advocating the "duty of states to facilitate the application of the present declaration, and to ensure that the mass media coming directly under their jurisdiction act in conformity therewith" could be headed off. When in the event it was, Attwood wrote, "there were only two alternatives open to us: to vote against a Soviet-inspired declaration which would have passed overwhelmingly or to produce . . . a document that would be at worst innocuous and at best helpful to the free flow of information and the access of foreign correspondents to news sources. There simply was no other option."

American editors split sharply over the outcome. Of forty-two editorials that this writer examined, about half commented favorably in varying degrees. Six proclaimed flatly, "We won." Four regarded the declaration as falling short of a ringing endorsement of the free press, but far better than earlier drafts. The Chicago *Tribune* saw the declaration as "a significant step forward in a long struggle for universal freedom of expression." The *Tribune* is edited by Clayton Kirkpatrick who was the press member of the U.S. delegation to UNESCO when the Soviet draft was postponed in Nairobi in 1976. The *Christian Science Monitor* stated "[a] long festering threat to world press freedom was diverted in Paris."

Nearly half the editorials examined ranged from moderately to strongly negative. Three termed the declaration "meaningless," one observing, however, that it "did give UNESCO bureaucrats years of important-seeming work to do in fashionable watering holes." The Houston *Post* regarded the text as a dangerous precedent "for the organization's future involvement in these sensitive matters"—"a diplomatic foot in the door," the Phoenix *Gazette* called it. The New York *Times* found the declaration "a triumph of obfuscation." It said "the Americans who accepted it as the least offensive document they could write with 145 other nations were not speaking for the free press of the United States." The *Times* added, "there can be no free speech or 'balanced' news unless those who advocate racism and apartheid and, yes, war are also free to speak." The editorial said, "We do not negotiate codes of press behavior with our government and should not be negotiating them with any others."

William Attwood replied in the *Times* that there was "a rattlesnake of a declaration at large in the garden. The only chance of getting rid of it was by trying to replace it with a harmless garter snake." It was "academic" to argue that "we didn't need any snake." He was answered by Charles B. Seib, the Washington *Post*'s ombudsman: "The reptile we have accepted in our house may turn out to be not a harmless little garter snake but a baby rattler." He found objectionable the notion that the proper role of the press is "to help achieve certain goals rather than simply sustain the flow of information and ideas that will make the achievement of those goals possible."

The 1978 text ended the battle of the declarations. But it set the stage for new and more complex battles to control the content of news reporting. The chief Marxist analyst of news media issues, Kaarle Nordenstreng, president of the East-bloc's International Organization of Journalists, was dissatisfied with the 1978 declaration. It was, he said, "quite mild and vague." He said it emphasized "so-called 'help to poor countries' and 'action programs' " as a way of "preventing analyses and changes of a principal and structural nature." The declaration, he added, turned "attention away from the contents and performance of the media almost exclusively" and focused instead on "their more or less technical infrastructures." Nordenstreng observes that the UN General Assembly has passed "a much stronger declaration" that sets forth the "duty" of all states to "discourage advocacy of hatred and prejudice." Therefore, says the Finnish academic, "the mass media in large parts of the world have departed from the conduct of informational policies *as defined by international law*" (italics added). Consequently, he argues, "in view of international law the principle of freedom of information must be subordinated to such obligations as the promotion of peace and security and the prevention of propaganda for war and racism."[2]

## THE MACBRIDE COMMISSION REPORT: AN AGENDA
## FOR FUTURE CAMPAIGNS.

Establishing the MacBride Commission was a concession to the activists, particularly in the third world. The trade-off was not as clear as has been interpreted either in the third or first worlds. Since the MacBride Commission was seen as a forum in which they were outweighed about three to one, participation in its activities was seen by Western commissioners as an exercise in damage limitation. Some regarded the commission as a document-writing exercise. Since the final control was left to the next UNESCO General Conference to accept or reject the Commission's recommendations, it could always be hoped that another delaying formula could be found in 1980. Third world activists, however, assumed that for agreeing to a delay in adopting a document that would convert the free-flow doctrine into a balancing declaration, the third world had received a commission to spell out effective reforms in world news media systems. These reforms, the third world activists believed, would themselves reduce the "imbalance" in news volume that they felt favored Western interests.

In papers annexed to the Commission's final report, extensive efforts were made by Commissioners Masmoudi of Tunisia and Osolnik of Yugoslavia to define a New World Information Order (NWIO) and make explicit their demand for the transfer of communication power.

Masmoudi described communication as a "social goal and a cultural product, and not as a material commodity." Accordingly, "the right of those receiving information"—that is, the public—"should be regulated . . . as to ensure free and balanced flow of information." Hence, the document continues, each nation "should choose its information in accordance with its own realities and requirements." Governments thus should create their own national news agencies (as some 100 have done), and should share information through the existing nonaligned press agency pool. In respect of current news Masmoudi believes there must be: "regulation of the right to information by preventing abusive uses of the right of access to information; definition of appropriate criteria to govern truly objective news selections; regulation of the collection, processing and transmission of news and data across national frontiers . . ." A New World Information Order "must be considered as the essential corollary of the New International Economic Order."

The campaign to achieve *explicit, firm, internationally binding responsibilities* of states for the duties the mass media are commissioned to perform was conducted for two years within the MacBride Commission. One hundred documents were produced in addition to a five-part Final Report.[3] Of the sixteen members of the commission, no more than six could be expected to support unconditionally the traditional Western-style independence of journalists from governmental controls. The commission met in the presence of a secretariat mainly committed to advancing the position of third world activism. Sean MacBride repeatedly found himself at loggerheads with the secretariat over ideological as well as administrative matters. The secretariat maintained it was trying to prevent the chairman from committing member states to positions they had not formally approved. Repeatedly, drafts produced by the secretariat at the request of the Commission included ideas not approved by the commissioners. In some cases, ideas that had been rejected several times by commissioners emerged in later drafts. Turgid prose was regularly deleted, only to have it reappear in new versions. One such "final-draft" paragraph that had to be cut for the third time from the truly final draft stated:

> The increasing numbers of those possessing means of engaging in traditional, interpersonal or mediated communication is not an adequate sign of the expansion of social communication, or of its democratization . . . Over-information and the superabundance of the messages being transmitted are not tendencies to be fostered . . . We accordingly suggest that: 1) All countries adopt measures to enlarge the sources of mutual information needed by citizens in their everyday lives, as well as a guaranteed access thereto.

As this is written, the final report of the MacBride Commission has not been released. An advance copy of Part V, Communication Tomorrow, offers eighty-two conclusions and recommendations, and sets forth twelve other issues which the commissioners felt require further study.

The Commission's main conclusion is that because of the diversity of the countries and their communication systems—based on their "diverse patterns of social, economic and cultural life" and "their traditions, needs and possibilities"—"there is no place for the universal application of preconceived models."

"Communication"—the Commission states at the outset—"can be an instrument of power, a revolutionary weapon, a commercial product, or a means of education; it can serve the end either of liberation or of oppression, either of the growth of the individual personality or of drilling human beings into conformity." The Commission adds, "Each society will have to make its own choice in its own way."

Yet the Commission clearly assigns a responsibility to communication media: they must support the objectives of economic development.

The Commission strongly urges the elimination of imbalances and disparities in communication, its structures and information flows. But the Commission regards the right to seek, impart, and receive information as a fundamental human right, and a prerequisite for other rights. This right is an individual one, as well as a collective one, required by all communities and nations. The Commission supports UNESCO's insistence on the development of comprehensive national communication policies. This is a wedge through which governmental controls over the press for "just causes" can readily advance. In the United States, one can devise an elaborate communication policy for all the diverse agencies of the government that have domestic and international communications programs. Yet such a policy would not encompass the wide-ranging activities and impact of the independent American news and entertainment media. For them, the only "policy" the U.S. government needs is that stipulated in the First Amendment to the Constitution.

The MacBride report would provide a framework for the development of *a* new information and communications order. This is far less specific than speaking of *the* NWIO. Instead, the report regards the "order" as an "ongoing process of successive changes in the nature of relations between and within nations in the field of communication." The Commission calls for "crucial decisions" concerning communication development to promote "more understanding of diversity and plurality, . . . of peoples living in different conditions and acting in different ways."

The Commission supports the development of strong national news agencies, distribution of a series of small-format TV and radio systems, research for the production of cheap newsprint from widely available raw materials, reduction in tariffs for news transmission, integration of communication development with other forms of development, and strengthening cultural identity through national policies.

The Commission strongly attacks the privately owned mass media. Preference should be given to noncommercial forms when the media are expanded, the report states. The "negative effects" of market and commercial considerations on news flows should be reduced. The American commissioner, Elie Abel, responded:

> At no time has the commission seen evidence adduced in support of the notion that market and commercial considerations neces-

sarily exert a negative effect upon communication flows. On the contrary, the commission has praised elsewhere in this report courageous investigative journalism of the sort that can be sustained only by independent media whose survival depends upon their acceptance in the marketplace, rather than the favors of political leaders. The commission also is aware that market mechanisms play an increasingly important role today even in so-called planned economies . . .

Advertising is specifically condemned. "Effective legal measures" are advised "to limit the process of concentration and monopolization" in public or private ownership of the media. Concentration in free market societies is increasing but not always without ample editorial control retained in the local medium. The trend nevertheless, is worrisome. In most non-market countries the governments monopolize communication power. The Commission distinguishes between "owners and managers [of media] on the one hand and journalists on the other." The report calls for democratizing the management of the media so that journalists would have "a more active role in editorial policy and management."

In the final report the freedom and responsibility of the journalist are said to be indivisible. Freedom without a display of responsibility invites distortion, the report says. In the absence of freedom, it adds, there can be no exercise of responsibility. The Commission refrains, however, from recommending that a code of ethics be imposed on journalists. Sean MacBride repeatedly during the two-year period had spoken and written of a code to be tied to the protection of journalists. In return for their safety, journalists would accept a code of ethics. This code would be monitored, presumably by governments or an intergovernmental agency. Violators of the code could be penalized or their license to practice as journalists withdrawn. The Commission rejects licensing as well as the code, though it urges that new ways be developed for the public to assess media performance. The Commission rejects any special protection of journalists. It says that journalists will be fully protected only when everyone's human rights are protected and guaranteed. MacBride has written a document on protection of journalists to be appended to the final report. It is likely that questions of protection/licensing/code/responsibilities of the journalist will surface once again at the 1980 biennial of UNESCO in Belgrade.

Internal controversies within the Commission between the American and Russian representatives should also be noted. At an early Commission session in Stockholm in April 1978, Leonid Zamatin tangled with Elie Abel over the access of journalists to news sources. Zamatin, then the head of TASS, has since been elevated to information chief of the Central Committee of the Communist Party, Soviet Union. Abel, then dean of Columbia University's Graduate School of Journalism, was the only American on the Commission. Abel had said foreign journalists should be able to speak to citizens holding diverse viewpoints. Zamatin responded in anger, "Opposition ended in the Soviet Union in 1922!" Finally, they agreed on a formula: "all foreign correspondents requesting a visa must be authorized to do their job and assured access to the complete spectrum of opinion within the country." At the final session in November 1979, Zamatin's successor angrily rejected the commission's conclusion that balanced reporting necessarily involves "access to unofficial, as well as official sources of information, that is, access to the entire spectrum of opinion within any country." S. Losev, the new Soviet member, said this statement "doesn't correspond to the Helsinki Final Act." He would replace the paragraph and state that foreign correspondents must act "with due respect to the national sovereignty and the national identity of the host country." The Soviets often invoke Principle VI of the Final Act regarding intervention in internal affairs. Inherently, however, any topic treated in the Final Act constitutes a legitimate subject for review of the implementation of the act, and access of journalists is such a subject. Principle VI, therefore, does not prevent human-rights-minded observers from decrying the torture and inhumane treatment of citizens in another country.

## Institutionalization of News Media Analyses

From 1976 to 1980 there were scores of international and regional, professional and expert conferences and consultations on the flow of information and communication technology. There has also been a full-scale World Administrative Radio Conference (WARC) seeking to reassign the broadcast spectrums and adjudicate issues in outer space for the rest of this century. In all of these meetings (though less at the 1979 WARC than had been anticipated) the issues of national power and political status underlay discussions of the imbalance in the flow of information. The General Assembly of the UN has increasingly concerned itself with the question of a New World Information Order (NWIO). There are clear signs that the pressure on the Western nations to share the wealth through the New International Economic Order will be coupled with an institutionalized campaign to share information as a precursor to transferring more economic power to the developing countries.

The MacBride Commission has urged UNESCO to establish an International Center for the Study and Planning of Information and Communication. Its tasks would include promoting national communication systems in developing countries and improving the balance of international news flows; mobilizing and managing communication resources for these purposes; coordinating international aid programs in this field; and running training programs for journalists and other communication specialists. It is probable such an organization will be established.

Similar proposals were made at a regional media meeting in Asia, and at a conference run by the Soviet Union's national commission for UNESCO held at Tashkent, September 3-8, 1979. Although the Tashkent statement expressed Soviet support for "a new international information order," when third world activists proposed this at an early meeting of the MacBride Commission, Leonid Zamatin, the Soviet member, attacked the new "order" as unnecessary. The status quo, he said, was good enough because it defends national sovereignty. Zamatin did not want any international group—the UN or the Nonaligned—attempting to dictate to Soviet mass media. The Soviet's Tashkent approach moves closer to the third world's activist position, and ties information to economics as well as national power. "This new order," says the Tashkent statement, "understood as an integral part of the new international economic order, should be based on the generally recognized principle of international law, in particular as respect for national sovereignty and non-interference in internal affairs of other states." The meeting linked freedom of information to "responsibility," which, by inference, would be defined by national and international doctrines. The "free flow of information"—universally accepted since 1945—was described as a "grossly commercial concept serving the interests of transnational corporations," and should be replaced by a "concept ensuring the interest of all countries."

Thus, the broad ideological campaign to limit "free flow" by replacing it with a "balanced" or "more just" flow, continues. This campaign is sustained by the interaction between the third world activists and Marxist ideologues, on the one hand, and the UNESCO secretariat and UNESCO-recruited journalism research specialists (often drawn from the ranks of activists and Marxists), on the other hand. In addition to the one hundred research papers appended to the MacBride Commission's final report, another thirty studies were proceeding under UNESCO contract in the area of news flow in January 1980. Many of these may provide data on the movement of news to and from North America, Latin America, Asia, and Eastern and Western Europe. These are studies of "news dependence," the selection of news in Canada as a case study, the "balancing" of news through Tanjug (the Yugoslav agency that coordinates the Nonaligned News Pool), a comparison of third world news in the presses of the two Germanies, and some analyses of communication technology.

At a special UNESCO consultation in December 1979 in which the author participated, a new series of studies was proposed. The meeting recommended that UNESCO *inter alia* convene media experts to investigate the selection and processing of news and the meaning of truthful and responsible reporting; undertake case studies of international reporting; explore principles of journalistic ethics; convene seminars on the new information order to help journalists contribute to it; and encourage the establishment of professional organizations where they do not exist.

The effects of research and analysis on this scale cannot be fully predicted. It seems clear that journalists in countries having newspapers or radio and television independent of the respective governments will be increasingly required to defend their performance. Journalists who serve as government employees or loyalist supporters of their rulers—the system prevailing in two-thirds of the world—will be shielded from interference by international criticism or domestic response to international criticism or intergovernmental actions. "National sovereignty" will protect the government-controlled journalist; the independent journalist will fend for himself.

## II. *Basic Issues in the Debate*

There are four intertwined issues in the debate: the struggle between the concepts of free media and controlled media; improved media in the third world; the desire of third world countries for more power over the international flow of news; and the desire of these countries to emphasize development journalism. In spite of the rhetoric the first issue is the most important for most of the participants. Yet there are honest needs expressed by the other issues to which the developed world should respond.

### FREEDOM VERSUS DIRECTED JOURNALISM

Ever since Milton[4] argued that truth can emerge only by struggling with falsehood, governing elites have sought to tell their publics what is "true" and "false."

There are two basic journalistic systems in the world today:[5] government-controlled (mobilization) journalism paints the world, the nation, and the individual as the particular national elite would have them be; government-free journalism, when functioning according to its own standards, portrays the world and its parts as it is, or as a variety of elites would like it to be. (Mixed or loyalist systems refrain from serious criticisms of incumbents but are not required to actively promote particular views.) Neither system regards its opposite as compatible with it. The quality of the picture of the world drawn by the mobilization press has been described by the Soviet dissenter, Vladimir Bukovsky:

> A new holiday resort is being opened in Bulgaria; a typhoon hits Japan; workers in the Urals have surpassed their targets; thousands of workers on strike in France; a rich harvest is being gathered in the Ukraine; statistics about car accidents in the U.S. are monstrous; a new residential district is completed in Tashkent; student demonstrations are being broken up in Italy. Abroad, one long procession of natural disasters, catastrophes, demonstrations, strikes, police truncheons, slums, and a constant decline in the standard of living; while here, new holiday resorts, factories, harvests, boundless fields, beaming smiles, new homes, and the growth of prosperity. *There* the black forces of reaction and imperialism are grinding the faces of the workers and threatening us with war, *here* the bright forces of progress and socialism are building a radiant future and battling for a stable peace. And the forces of peace, socialism, and progress are bound to prevail. There is nothing else *at all*—nothing against.[6]

The defense of "national sovereignty," particularly in the UNESCO debates and the commission report, demonstrates the broad gap that separates the government-controlled from the government-free media. The most authoritative Marxist ideologues in the field of mass media research are Herbert Schiller, an American journalism professor at the University of California, San Diego, and the aforementioned Kaarle Nordenstreng, chairman of the Department of Journalism, University of Tampere, Finland. Schiller and Nordenstreng argue[7] that "the preservation of national sovereignty may be understood best as a step in the still larger struggle to break the domination of the world business system. In this ongoing effort, international communication has been an extremely effective and direct agent of the market system." The "overseers" of the system, say the authors, have insisted that communications are not only neutral but are beneficial to receiver societies and individuals everywhere. This, they add, is the rationale of those who imposed "the free flow of information doctrines on the world community, since the early 1940's." Despite this rationale, they add, the economic system and its media components "disregard human and social needs."

Ithiel de Sola Pool, of the Massachusetts Institute of Technology, Cambridge, responds:

> . . . people of the sincere left have been absorbed in classical doctrines of conservatism as a consequence of nationalism. Increasingly they find themselves pushed by the logic of their position to see themselves as

more opposed to liberalism than to traditional culture, to assert that the free flow of information is a goal that must be reconsidered, to conclude that preservation of traditional ways is more important than a rapid rise of GNP, and to justify the use of state power to control the communications that reach the people. Their ideological predecessors fought to liberate the print media from state control, but increasingly people who call themselves men of the left find themselves advocating state monopoly control of the newer media. Thus a strange alliance puts conservative military regimes or theocratic oligarchies at one with nominal progressives in defense of censorship. Needless to say, the things they want censored, what they want controlled, and by whom are quite different. But they unite in advocating restrictions on broadcasting and other instrumentalities of the free flow of information. . . . Indeed, it will often be the case that what is described as protection of the national culture is protection of the existing government . . .[8]

Although governments want to know more about everything, they do not want to hear criticism in public places, particularly if that criticism concerns a critical issue such as economic development. Circulation of unauthorized news of the failure of a crop or factory in a developing country can precipitate the hunt for an information leak not unlike the Watergate capers. In the third world, the national periphery—most of the country's population—is generally excluded by ignorance from publicly opposing policies of the ruling center, and the deficiencies of the society, which might be offset by some form of internal questioning, increase. Both government and people suffer from the absence of informed criticism or commonsense responses that might help improve conditions.

Third world countries are further hampered by deficient or gagged journalism. There are few experienced reporters and editors. The courageous journalists of colonial days often became a part of the new ruling establishment. They regarded journalism as a weapon in the struggle for independence. Once in power, these leaders effectively muzzled the press and radio lest a new opposition be strengthened by independent journalism. What journalism exists is weak and ineffectual, and the government's own information system suffers from not having to concern itself with authoritative responses from an alternative source.

This is the model of third world journalism that is understood widely in the West, and particularly among Western journalists. An interesting modification of that perception is provided by William A. Rugh.[9] He concludes that seven Arab countries (Egypt, Iraq, Syria, Sudan, Algeria, Libya, and South Yemen) have a *mobilization press*. The press is owned by agents of the regime and its purpose is to educate the public in government programs and policies. Though newspapers may display a contentious style and tone, they support and never criticize the basic

# Table 9
# News Media Control by Countries

| | Free[1] | Partly Free[1] | Generally Not Free[1] | Gov't News Agency[2] | Civil Liberties[3] |
|---|---|---|---|---|---|
| Afghanistan | | | PB | X | 7 |
| Albania | | | PB | X | 7 |
| Algeria | | | PB | X | 6 |
| Angola | | | PB | X | 7 |
| Argentina | | P | B | X | 5 |
| | | | | | |
| Australia | PB | | | X | 1 |
| Austria | PB | | | X | 1 |
| Bahamas | P | B | | | 2 |
| Bahrain | | | PB | X | 4 |
| Bangladesh | P | B | | X | 3 |
| | | | | | |
| Barbados | P | B | | X | 1 |
| Belgium | PB | | | X | 1 |
| Benin | | | PB | X | 6 |
| Bhutan | | | PB | | 5 |
| Bolivia | PB | | | X | 3 |
| | | | | | |
| Botswana | P | B | | | 2 |
| Brazil | P | B | | X | 3 |
| Bulgaria | | | PB | X | 7 |
| Burma | | | PB | X | 6 |
| Burundi | | | PB | X | 7 |
| | | | | | |
| Cameroon | | | PB | X | 6 |
| Canada | PB | | | | 1 |
| Cape Verde Islands | | | PB | | 6 |
| Central African Rep. | | | PB | | 6 |
| Chad | | | PB | X | 6 |
| | | | | | |
| Chile | | PB | | X | 5 |
| China (Mainland) | | | PB | X | 6 |
| China (Taiwan) | | PB | | | 5 |
| Colombia | PB | | | X | 3 |
| Congo | | | PB | X | 7 |
| | | | | | |
| Costa Rica | PB | | | | 1 |
| Cuba | | | PB | X | 6 |
| Cyprus | P | B | | X | 3 |
| Czechoslovakia | | | PB | X | 6 |
| Denmark | PB | | | X | 1 |
| Dominica | PB | | | | 2 |
| | | | | | |
| Dominican Rep. | P | B? | | | 3 |
| Ecuador | PB | | | X | 2 |

### Notes to the Table

1. P designates print media; B designates broadcast (radio and TV) media. Print media refers primarily to domestic newspapers and news magazines. Countries in which the media are too little developed or for which there is insufficient information to include in this table are: Comoro Islands, Djibouti, Kiribati, Rwanda, Solomon Islands, Tuvalu, and Western Samoa.

2. X designates the presence of a government news agency, with or without the availability of private news services also.

3. See Table 1 in Part 1.

| | Free[1] | Partly Free[1] | Generally Not Free[1] | Gov't News Agency[2] | Civil Liberties[3] |
|---|---|---|---|---|---|
| Egypt | | P | B | X | 5 |
| El Salvador | | PB | | | 4 |
| Equatorial Guinea | | | PB | | 6 |
| Ethiopia | | | PB | X | 7 |
| | | | | | |
| Fiji | PB | | | | 2 |
| Finland | P | B | | X | 2 |
| France | P | B | | X | 2 |
| Gabon | | | PB | X | 6 |
| Gambia | PB | | | | 2 |
| | | | | | |
| Germany (E) | | | PB | X | 6 |
| Germany (W) | PB | | | X | 2 |
| Ghana | | PB | | X | 4 |
| Greece | PB? | | | X | 2 |
| Grenada | | | PB | | 5 |
| | | | | | |
| Guatemala | | PB | | X | 5 |
| Guinea | | | PB | | 7 |
| Guinea-Bissau | | | PB | | 6 |
| Guyana | | PB | | X | 4 |
| Haiti | | PB | | | 5 |
| | | | | | |
| Honduras | PB | | | | 3 |
| Hungary | | | PB | X | 5 |
| Iceland | PB | | | | 1 |
| India | P | B | | X | 2 |
| Indonesia | | P | B | X | 5 |
| | | | | | |
| Iran | | PB | | X | 5 |
| Iraq | | | PB | X | 7 |
| Ireland | PB | | | | 1 |
| Israel | PB | | | | 2 |
| Italy | PB | | | X | 2 |
| | | | | | |
| Ivory Coast | | P | B | X | 5 |
| Jamaica | P | | B | | 3 |
| Japan | PB | | | X | 1 |
| Jordan | | | PB | X | 6 |
| Kampuchea | | | PB | X | 7 |
| | | | | | |
| Kenya | | P | B | X | 4 |
| Korea (N) | | | PB | X | 7 |
| Korea (S) | | PB | | X | 5 |
| Kuwait | | P | B | X | 4 |
| Laos | | | PB | X | 7 |
| | | | | | |
| Lebanon | | PB | | X | 4 |
| Lesotho | | PB | | | 5 |
| Liberia | | PB | | | 5 |
| Libya | | | PB | X | 6 |
| Luxembourg | PB | | | | 1 |
| | | | | | |
| Madagascar | | | PB | X | 6 |
| Malawi | | | PB | X | 7 |
| Malaysia | | P | B | X | 4 |
| Maldives | | P | B | | 5 |
| Mali | | | PB | X | 6 |
| | | | | | |
| Malta | | PB? | | X | 3 |
| Mauritania | | | PB | X | 6 |
| Mauritius | PB | | | | 4 |

71

# Table 9—Continued

| | Free¹ | Partly Free¹ | Generally Not Free¹ | Gov't News Agency² | Civil Liberties³ |
|---|---|---|---|---|---|
| Mexico | | PB | | X | 4 |
| Mongolia | | | PB | X | 7 |
| | | | | | |
| Morocco | | P | B? | X | 4 |
| Mozambique | | | PB | X | 7 |
| Nauru | PB | | | | 2 |
| Nepal | | P | B | X | 4 |
| Netherlands | PB | | | X | 1 |
| | | | | | |
| New Zealand | PB | | | X | 1 |
| Nicaragua | P | B | | | 5 |
| Niger | | | PB | | 6 |
| Nigeria | P | B | | X | 3 |
| Norway | PB | | | X | 1 |
| | | | | | |
| Oman | | | PB | | 6 |
| Pakistan | | | PB | X | 5 |
| Panama | | PB | | X | 5 |
| Papua New Guinea | PB | | | | 2 |
| Paraguay | | PB | | | 5 |
| | | | | | |
| Peru | | PB | | X | 4 |
| Philippines | | P | B | X | 5 |
| Poland | | | PB | X | 5 |
| Portugal | PB | | | X | 2 |
| Qatar | | | PB | X | 5 |
| | | | | | |
| Rumania | | | PB | X | 6 |
| St. Lucia | PB | | | | 3 |
| St. Vincent | P | B? | | | 2 |
| Sao Tome & Principe | | | PB | | 6 |
| Saudi Arabia | | | PB | X | 6 |
| | | | | | |
| Senegal | | PB | | X | 4 |
| Seychelles | | | PB | | 6 |
| Sierra Leone | | | PB | | 5 |
| Singapore | | | PB | | 5 |
| Somalia | | | PB | X | 7 |
| | | | | | |
| South Africa | | P | B | | 6 |
| Spain | PB | | | X | 2 |
| Sri Lanka | P?B? | | | X | 3 |
| Sudan | | | PB | X | 5 |
| Surinam | PB | | | | 2 |
| | | | | | |
| Swaziland | | | PB | | 5 |
| Sweden | PB | | | X | 1 |
| Switzerland | PB | | | X | 1 |
| Syria | | | PB | X | 6 |
| Tanzania | | | PB | X | 6 |
| | | | | | |
| Thailand | | P | B | | 4 |
| Togo | | | PB | X | 7 |
| Tonga | | | PB | | 3 |
| Transkei | | | PB | | 6 |
| Trinidad & Tobago | PB | | | | 2 |
| | | | | | |
| Tunisia | | P | B | X | 5 |
| Turkey | | P | B | X | 3 |

| | Free[1] | Partly Free[1] | Generally Not Free[1] | Gov't News Agency[2] | Civil Liberties[3] |
|---|---|---|---|---|---|
| Uganda | | | P?B? | X | 6 |
| USSR | | | PB | X | 6 |
| United Arab Emirates | | P | B | X | 5 |
| United Kingdom | PB | | | X | 1 |
| United States | PB | | | | 1 |
| Upper Volta | | PB | | X | 3 |
| Uruguay | | | PB | | 6 |
| Venezuela | PB | | | X | 2 |
| Vietnam | | | PB | X | 7 |
| Yemen (N) | | | PB | X | 5 |
| Yemen (S) | | | PB | X | 7 |
| Yugoslavia | | | PB | X | 5 |
| Zaire | | | PB | X | 6 |
| Zambia | | PB | | X | 5 |
| Zimbabwe Rhodesia | | P | B | | 4 |

## Table Summary

| | Countries (general rating) | | Print Media | | Broadcast Media | |
|---|---|---|---|---|---|---|
| | No. | % | No. | % | No. | % |
| Free | 51 | 31 | 52 | 33 | 37 | 24 |
| Partly free | 54 | 34 | 36 | 24 | 34 | 22 |
| Not free | 56 | 35 | 66 | 43 | 83 | 54 |
| | 161 | 100 | 154[1] | 100 | 154[1] | 100 |

This table suggests that governments in three-fourths of the world have a significant or dominant voice in determining what does or does not appear in the media. The definition of media control does not include regulation such as that practiced by the FCC; government control means control over newspaper or broadcast *content*. In some countries particular media (often broadcasting) may be government financed and indirectly government-managed like BBC, but still be regarded as largely free of government control of content.

In only one-fourth of the nations are both the print and broadcast media generally free; the press is free in one-third. Newspapers tend to be freer than radio or TV. The press is partly free in twenty-four percent, not free in forty-three percent; broadcasting is partly free in twenty-two percent, not free in fifty-four percent of the nations.

Nearly a half-century ago there were thirty-nine national news services in twenty-eight countries. Seventy percent of these were at least nominally independent of government (Robert Desmond, *The Press and World Affairs*, Appleton-Century, 1937). The number of government-operated news services has increased rapidly in the past five years in consequence of recommendations made by UNESCO. Sixty-eight percent of the nations have a government news agency: eighty-one percent of the not free, sixty-eight percent of the partly free, and fifty-seven percent of the free countries. Of nations with the lowest civil liberties rating (7), ninety-five percent operate government news agencies. National news agencies often use the world news services of the transnational Western media or TASS. They may then decide what world news may be distributed inside the country. Some national news agencies assign themselves the sole right to secure domestic news for distribution inside or outside the country.

foreign or domestic policies of the government. The papers may be critical of local services, such as shortage of power or sanitation assistance, but they do not hold national leaders responsible. However, the Egyptian papers have vitality, diversity, and professionalism not generally associated with an authoritarian state. The Egyptian press, particularly during the past three years, has been permitted increasing authority to select from official documents those to be reported each day as "news." The Egyption editors may choose not to publish the full text of President Sadat's speech. Egyptian newspapers also carry short stories or poetry which convey criticism through "symbolic fiction."

In six Arab countries (Jordan, Tunisia, Saudi Arabia, Bahrain, Qatar, and the United Arab Emirates), Rugh finds there is a *loyalist press*. Unlike the mobilization countries, this press is not widely used to generate popular support for particular forms of change, but it is expected to support the system at least passively. Papers are privately owned yet they consistently support the regime in power. They do not attack major government policies, although they may blame specific government officials for deficient local services. A loyalist editor can usually be persuaded by a call from a ministry to play up or down a particular story. The paper may be fined insignificantly for excessive criticism. Sensitive to the political environment, the editor does not need much official guidance.

Lebanon (before the civil war), Kuwait, and Morocco demonstrate the *diverse press*, in Rugh's terms. The newspapers in these countries are all privately owned, and their content, style, and political viewpoints vary. Some carry articles that do not support the regime in power. The diverse press, Rugh notes, "is therefore free, even if individual newspapers may be strong promoters of the regime, because some newspapers are somewhat independent of the regime and because the reader has more information and opinion to choose from." Despite the civil war, the Lebanese press in 1979 was still able to criticize the government, and disagreements were adjudicated in court.

Among the diverse press in third world countries outside the Arab region are newspapers that attack the regime despite strong counter pressures and even threats to nationalize the independent press. The *Daily Gleaner* in Jamaica is engaged in such a running battle with Prime Minister Michael Manley of Jamaica. In the freest developing countries such as Barbados and Costa Rica the press regularly criticizes both leaders and policies without government threats or reprisals.

The independence of the press in any country is ultimately linked to the nature of the nation's political system. A regime that permits the diffusion of political power is more likely to support an independent press than an elite that monopolizes political power.

The problem the free media face in international forums is that in both modern tyrannies and most traditional societies, independent criticism is not a part of the accepted social pattern. Not only in traditional African societies is the community—not the individual—the basis of life. There is no word in Russian for "privacy"—nor is there any privacy in the Soviet Union. All activity, as in the time of the Czar, is organized about the community, and every worker is subject to observation by a peer. Neighbors report on neighbors; children report on parents. It is expected, therefore, that the mass media will mobilize every aspect of the society and nation.

Newer societies elsewhere, whether or not they fully accept the complete Marxist-Leninist model, will probably adopt more socialist than capitalist techniques in constructing media as well as economic systems. And whether or not the number of totalitarian systems grows (they are slowly diminishing in number, as our Survey shows in Part I), 68 percent of the independent political systems are in the partly free or not free categories. Free journalists will have to operate for the foreseeable future in a world in which two-thirds of the countries accept grudgingly or not at all the government-free premises of American journalism.

In fewer than one-third of the countries will U.S. journalists find societies empowered by a civic culture that motivates a citizen to participate in the political process, join voluntary associations, make knowledgeable selections of reading and listening channels, or express citizen-views in countless other ways. In a civic culture, opinion leaders expect a significant number of journalists to be independent from government controls or pressures, the influence of corporate or commercial blandishments, or religious or partisan bias. They expect such journalists to instinctively search for the facts in the manner of professionals committed to excellence.

## THE AMERICAN CONCEPT OF JOURNALISM AND THE HAZARDS OF FREEDOM

The nature of American journalism must be considered in any analysis of the news flow around the world. U.S. world news managers who have sat in international conferences the past five years hear at every meeting the litany of complaints about the worldwide impact of American journalism. Yet American journalism has also brought a great volume of useful news and information. One difficulty lies in the fact that there is a single American journalism for both domestic and international audiences. There is need for distinctive news criteria and a separate writing style in providing specialized reports for developing countries.

News selection is the heart of journalism. American journalism strives for objectivity in the selection of events and personalities to report. Of course, bias in journalism cannot be entirely eliminated. Conscious as well as unconscious influences on correspondents and editors affect the way a reporter from a particular national or racial background perceives an event. Marxists believe economic considerations affect perception, and McLuhan points to the influence of the medium on the message. The writer's or publisher's political predisposition may influence the final product. News sources should always be considered in evaluating a news report.

Correspondents are more likely to be victims of warped perception than conscious bias. Herbert Gans concludes after extensive field study of four U.S. television and news magazine operations: "Successful pressure, leading to censorship or self-censorship, is rare."[10] Even "chilling effects," the vague sense that self-censorship may be expected, "are also few and far between," the sociologist found. Pressure is also minimal from news sources—the well known businessmen, politicians, or others of celebrity status. News is generally selected for its content rather than its sources.

Because the journalist's *perception* of an event may be influenced by cultural, technological, political, and other factors, there must be safeguards if the standard of objectivity is to be preserved. The ultimate safeguard is in diversity of coverage by any one newspaper or broadcaster, and the pluralism of having different kinds of media competing in the same society for attention (which for most outlets ultimately means commercial appeal). This diversity and pluralism are essential to the functioning of a democratic society. Choice of editor's viewpoints, news styles, story content, and selections of stories are as important as voter choice among political candidates and their policies. When the nation faces a tweedledee/tweedledum political election, the system suffers. If the major news media were consistently to carry the same stories from the same point of view, the country would sooner or later be in difficulty. Competitiveness within and among the media, including the important offbeat, alternative media, is a vital protection not only of the free flow but of a democratic society based on the need for diverse information. There is constant tension between the varied influences: government's aim to project information in a favorable light versus journalism's searching to know the full story; commerce's desire for positive publicity versus the consumer's need for protection; public interest in an individual's problems versus that person's right to privacy; and many other cross-influences. The more pressures on the journalist and the more diverse the pressures, the freer he will be to make his own choices.

News-power in the hands of authoritarian or totalitarian systems makes them omnipotent; news-power under the differentiated direction of competitive news services, newspaper publishers, book publishers, broadcasters, and television managers in the United States diffuses power. The "alternative" broadcasters of Pacifica Radio in New York and California daily attack the American political and economic systems. These stations can reach every radio receiver in the two most populous states, and beyond. If enough listeners were so moved by these radios they could initiate major changes in the local and national political and social systems. Alternate book publishers, magazines, and newspapers "keep honest" even the largest news services and publishers. After Watergate, even the semblance of a political or journalistic cover-up gains wide public attention. News-power in a free society then, does not reside solely in the hands of the dominant services.

This philosophy of journalism is liberating, but it is utterly unacceptable to governing elites in most countries, and to those in all but a handful of third world nations.

Our approach to news is admittedly imperfect. The New York *Times* eloquently noted in its 1979 Christmas editorial that the holiday "commemorates a colossal triumph of history over news." When Jesus was born, the *Times* recalled, "hardly anyone noticed that something stupendous had happened. Decades passed before the significance of the event was absorbed into human experience. The Bethlehem bureau really missed the story, and the editors of the day never even knew it." Now, despite the multinational news industry, "many prophets preach, but only some are heard." In any second coming, one may infer from the *Times'* preamble, even the best correspondents and fastest word processors may again miss the story; not by design, but by virtue of the small number of professional observers deployed over an increasingly complex world, stories of *process* or of intellectual *insight* can seldom be told in terms of events noticed on a given day, and so are not "news" in the all-too-generally-understood sense.

There are pragmatic disadvantages in the operation of free societies. The basic institution of journalism reveals the operational and intellectual difficulties of sustaining freedom of expression for large numbers of citizens. Communications technology now permits worldwide, virtually instantaneous transmission of a single voice or printed paragraph giving it vast power. Forty years ago John Dewey thought it would lead to greater superficiality in the content of messages.[11] The massiveness of the new audience, he said, created in a "large number of persons an appetite for the momentary 'thrills' caused by impacts that stimulate nerve endings but whose connections with cerebral functions are broken."

Third world critics charge that the Western media concentrate on natural disasters, coups, and oddities in the third world. They charge that Western media dominate the international information process. This, they say, is cultural imperialism or, at best, ethnocentric journalism. They tend to share Dewey's conclusions that the mass media provide "ready-made intellectual goods" akin to "ready-made foods, articles, and all kinds of gadgets." Marxist critics of the Western media go further. They say that ours is a market-based journalism—written and edited for an audience that is preconditioned to "buy" the kind of news or particular report; moreover, that Western news patterns parallel and support the interests of the multinational corporations and their allies, the Western governments. Dewey concluded that "we have to take into account the attitudes of human nature that have been created by the immense development in mechanical instrumentalities if we are to understand the present power of organized propaganda." (He, of course, was writing at a time of pervasive Nazi and Fascist propaganda, tempered only slightly by a halting countereffort by Britain and the United States. His argument was, nevertheless, sound.)

Fundamental changes are needed in the manner of perceiving and reporting news in the West. The answer, however, is not to be found in the proposals made so far by third world activists or their Soviet-bloc supporters. Salutary changes, we believe, should come from an understanding of ourselves, as Dewey advised:

> When habits are so ingrained as to be second nature [he said], they seem to have all of the inevitability that belongs to the movement of the fixed stars. The "principles" and standards which are stated in words and which circulate widely at a given time are usually only formulations of things which men do not so much believe in the intellectual sense of belief as live by unconsciously.

So it is with American (and Western) journalism. The three U.S. television networks, for example, broadcast nightly almost the same views of the world, from virtually the same point of view. There is no collusion. Far from it; there is competition—but against the same standards of experience and judgment of what Americans are supposed to *want* to know. There is little exercising of responsibility—social or journalistic—to present what Americans *ought* to know about the world (including, of course, the developing world).

How can such responsibility be generated and sustained? Third world activists have tried for five years to legislate "responsibility" among journalists. They propose a stringent code describing information which must, and other data which must never, be transmitted. This, of course, implies censorship. Even the thoroughly negotiated declaration on the mass news media approved unanimously at UNESCO, November 1978, carries the strong implication that governments somehow must oversee the "responsibility" of journalists acting under their flags.

Must there be the equivalent of Dewey's "moral factor" in a newly refined journalistic code of ethics? Would such a code convert reporters into evangelists, or editorialists into moralistic preachers? "Cooperation," said Dewey, "is as much a part of the democratic ideal as is personal initiative." Similarly, the educative function of providing broader and deeper contexts for today's developments (not merely newness as the primary definition of "news"); along with analyses of the human process (longer-term implications of issues and decisions taken today) should become operative functions of American journalism. Such writing appears in only a few publications, and not often enough. These are rare exceptions among the thousands of news outlets in America. That arithmetical factor alone determines the nature and quality of the two U.S. international news services—reinforcing that "appetite for the momentary 'thrills' " that Dewey mentioned in 1939.

Emphasis on the newsworthiness of cooperation rather than the present emphasis on adversarial activity is favored by moderate spokesmen in the third world. It is increasingly understood by a handful of astute U.S. news service managers, but by no means shared adequately with vast numbers of editorial gatekeepers throughout American journalism.

In essence, free journalism must continue to be concerned with the "problem of freedom rather than with solutions," as Dewey concluded. Indeed, to suggest an educative function for journalists is not to propose that they or we predetermine the *content* of reportage. Western newspeople must constantly defend the independence of the press against external and internal predispositions; but they must also distinguish real dangers from constructive criticism, even if it calls for major changes in orientation and journalistic procedures. Communication technologies and the temper of world events have changed dramatically these past fifty years; yet American journalists often imply there need be little fundamental change in their approach to the universe and its people.

This is the challenge facing the gatekeepers of the independent news media in all developed countries.

## THE CONTROL OF THE FLOW: REAL AND IMAGINARY ISSUES

In the Napoleonic period, the French dictator controlled all the news sources in Europe. His version of events affected banking and business transactions, as well as public understanding and morale in many countries. Napoleon's communicating center was finally broken by the audacity of the London Rothschilds who created their own news bureau. Their bureau beat everyone with word of Napoleon's defeat at Waterloo. The news that day earned a fortune for the Rothschilds.

News is money and power, as well as information of general public use. The conveyor of news, the communication center, exerts the power that comes with prior knowledge. The receiver of news, the communication periphery, suffers the weakness of learning late about economic, educational, and social progress, and even threats to political and military security. There is power and status at the center, less power or even impotence and lower status at the periphery.

Let us then examine the claims of the third world that it is dominated by news produced by and largely about the West, and that the domination by Western news centers seriously harm third world interests.

There have always been special reports written and edited by the world services for particular audiences in developing or developed countries abroad. The British and French services concentrated on fashioning such reports for audiences in Africa and Asia; the American services competed actively to provide Latin American editors with the coverage they wanted.

These efforts, however, have been insufficient to stave off attacks on the four Western news media: the Associated Press and United Press International in the United States; Reuters in the United Kingdom; and Agence France-Presse, France. Attacks are also made against Western, mainly American, news magazines, radio and television networks, commercial films, books, advertising, and ultimately all manner of computerized data flows. Entertainment as well as news reporting are now under blanket assault. Increasingly, the field of data processing as it relates to computerized news and, as well, to business data, will be targeted for new and quite different restrictions at international borders. Efforts to control the content of computerized transmissions across borders will come from Western countries as well as third world nations (this under the rubric of protecting privacy of nationals, yet permitting monitors to observe commercial secrets and news content). A full-blown controversy over data flows is just beyond the horizon.

The journalistic clock cannot be turned back any more than the people of La Gaude, a tiny medieval village in southern France, can be free of the odors of petrol blowing across the hills from traffic snarls in Nice. The French at first called this the Americanization of their beautiful village. "Every year (America) becomes less peculiar," Daniel Boorstin[12] reminds us. "The very same new forces that have given a special character of life in America now every year make the lives and fortunes of people everywhere more like the lives and fortunes of everywhere else." The new science and technological developments generate a "new convergence." The *problems* generated by Big Journalism are the same the world over. These are not the consequence of a will to dominate the world either on behalf of a political leadership or corporate multinationals. Yet the *effects* of Big Journalism are a matter of record. Moderate third world leaders properly read that record. New and still-arriving technology may only deepen and harden the domination of the news flow by a few Western gatekeepers.

Mass communication is a part of the process of the modernization of traditional societies, according to Majid Tehranian.[13] It "brings about the transition from *particularistic* to *universalist* values. Contact with the outside world and its contradictory values shakes up the traditional society," challenging its parochial views. The old hierarchial system of blood relations is slowly replaced by the competitive spirit. Ancient "notions of honor" are challenged by "notions of integrity" drawn from the individual's effort to assure both self-respect and self-advancement. The corporate structure of the traditional society is undermined by modernization and replaced by pluralistic structures and identities.

Choices emerge for schooling, housing, employment. The secular culture has few of the safety valves of the older religious cultures of traditional societies. "Instead," said Tehranian, there are "the burdens of freedom and choice." Perhaps feared most of all by the ruling elite is the loss of community. While the new communication technologies "seem to be useful vehicles for the propagation of a national culture, language and ideology," wrote Tehranian, "because of their weak links with traditional and nascent communications institutions, they produce a sense of alienation unparalleled in the historical experience of the Western countries." The Western publics developed alongside the growth of communication technology and voluntary associations; but not the publics of the societies undergoing rapid change today. The mass media can serve the emerging societies, Tehranian asserts, only if the media "enjoy relative autonomy from all pressure groups (including the most formidable of all—the government) while being accountable to all."

Above all, the burgeoning controversies over the domestic and international news media are struggles over political power and status within developing countries, among third world nations, and between them and the developed world. Just as the third world's striving for a New International Economic Order is as much about political power and status as economics, so the demand for a New World Information Order concerns political power and status as much as journalism and information. The debates in the United Nations and particularly UNESCO seldom emphasize the political objectives of the third world participants. The arguments, as in the economic sphere, stress national development, with the additional concern for protecting and enlarging indigenous cultures. These are, of course, legitimate interests of all nations. But an unreal quality pervades many of the debates, particularly in UNESCO, because the power element is attributed mainly to the superpowers and multinational corporations and is seldom regarded as an objective either of the Nonaligned Nations as a bloc or of the individual constituents. It should be acknowledged, however, that in considering any new "order"—economic or informational—a realignment of political power inevitably accompanies the change.

Journalists in the United States also tend to avoid seeing news in terms of power. The news purveyor enables corporations, generals, scholars, and the rest of society to function, and when he is changed or he alters his product he alters society. President Lyndon Johnson during the crucial Tet offensive in 1968 took some major steps on the basis of press reports, rejecting advice from his military or intelligence officers in Vietnam. Whether journalists have an ulterior objective in selecting one news report over another, their process of selection is critical. The term applied to the journalist making such choices, the *gatekeeper*, is apt. To control the gate is to affect power.

The struggle by third world countries for greater information power is directly related to their earlier and continuing demands for more economic power. The historic antecedents are clear. Western countries for more than a century colonized most of Africa, the Pacific islands, parts of Asia, and Latin America. The Russians and Chinese expanded over the territories of many Asian peoples in the last few centuries, and more recently the USSR has gone on to include Eastern Europe and Afghanistan within its sphere. But the Chinese and Russians are seldom mentioned in the third world information controversies. This is because in the third world the effective information power has been wielded mainly by France, the United Kingdom, and the United States. The metropolitan centers of these countries established the land lines for telephone and telegraph that went out to their respective colonies. The communications went, say, from London to Lagos in Nigeria, or from Paris to Lomé in Togo. It was impossible to phone or telegraph from Lagos to Lomé, a few hundred miles distant, without going through London and Paris and back to Africa. That added immensely to the cost and discouraged trade as well as cultural and other contacts between African neighbors. Many such communication anomalies persist across the continent of Africa, though radio and satellites have reduced this direct dependence of the periphery on the center.

The flow of information around the world overwhelmingly describes events and personalities in the developed countries where only one-third of the population lives. This undeniable fact is regarded by third world spokesmen as an imbalance. Some suggest the imbalance is structured to assure neocolonialist control of the communication-rich center over the poor periphery. The information-rich and -poor coincide roughly with the economically wealthy and impoverished. Yet there is *not* such a coincidence between the politically free and the economically rich. Sri Lanka and Upper Volta, among the poorest of nations, have a free press and free political systems; Argentina and Czechoslovakia, though industrialized, have neither free journalism nor political rights.

It is likely that even if third world editors controlled the four Western news agencies the flow of news from London, Washington, Moscow, Paris, Tokyo, and other high volume news centers would be little changed. These are the places where the action is; where financial, industrial, political, scientific, and educational advances are made that affect populations in all parts of the world. To be sure, the treatment would perhaps be altered by third world control of the major media. Many more stories would be written with third world audiences in mind. A drought in Ghana that affects cocoa production can be reported as the cause of increased world prices or as a blow to the economy of Ghana. A good journalistic account, no matter who is the editor or ultimate reader, should include a report of both major factors.

Detailed studies cast doubt on the third world charge that Western dominance has in itself had a detrimental effect on the cultures or development of poor countries. After its 1976 conference, UNESCO asked the International Association for Mass Communication Research (IAMCR) to study the national images presented in the media of different countries. Scholars in several nations agreed to undertake studies of press content during a period from April to June 1979.

Early results are available from the study of the news flow in Latin America. After examining newspapers from Argentina, Brazil, Mexico, and the United States, the study concluded that Latin American newspapers were similar to those in the United States and elsewhere. Traditional hard news such as foreign affairs, domestic politics, and economics received most space, but news of education, science, and culture "got more attention than one might have expected."[14] One finding ran directly counter to the common belief: "Disasters and accidents accounted for little foreign news coverage and even human interest stores—bizarre happenings, show business personalities, and the like—took up very little of the space devoted to foreign news. In fact, human interest material and accident and disaster news made up a higher proportion of Latin American coverage of North America than vice versa." As may have been expected, Western news agencies' service to Latin America included more news of that region than of any other area, slightly more than half the copy. The local use made of the news supplied by the world-news services showed that in two of three countries local editors underselected Latin American regional material. All three used more material about North America and Western Europe than the world-news services had supplied. The Latin Americans used little news from Asia, Africa, the Middle East, or Eastern Europe. In concluding, "the problems of third world journalism are really problems of journalism," the authors denationalize the problem significantly, and open the way to far more rational discussions of journalistic practice.

An Asian observer, Pran Chopra, described similar conclusions in 1977 at a UNESCO meeting on news agencies in Colombo. The problem in reporting across cultural boundaries is revealed not only internationally but domestically.[15] "The whole impetus behind the minority press in all countries," says Chopra, "is the belief of the minority that it does not get a fair deal from the majority press and it is only rarely if ever that the majority does not suspect the credentials of the minority press." In Asia, he says, "as anywhere else, a gate which frequently regulates the flow of news can be named 'What sells?' "—which news will interest most readers and also make the paper or broadcaster most attractive to advertisers. But, says Chopra, there is also "a gate which can be named 'Public Interest,' that is not mainly what *will* but also what *should* interest the public; that is, what is it in its interest to know, according ot the judgment of the journalist? In Asia, too, as much as in [Eastern] Europe, both these gates are suddenly replaced by another gate . . . This gate can be named 'State Policy,' meaning the current policy or what should be told when, by whom, to whom, by what means, and whether and how far it should conform to facts." For this and other reasons, Chopra states, some Asian governments control the news flow "in the name of development."

The criteria of news employed by Asian journalists stem from the interplay of Asian traditions and Western colonial influences. The indigenous patterns malformed the mass media as much as the influences of Western journalism, Chopra states. "The tendency to exaggerate, to oversimplify or otherwise distort is not a vice of Asian or Western journalism or an infection passed by the latter to the former as is sometimes alleged," says Chopra. "It has grown up as part of the malformation of the mass media as such." Such problems will persist, he adds, "even if Asian journalism becomes more Asian in content or the Western agencies working in Asia increase the Asian content in their services or the proportion of Asians on their staffs." Chopra concludes:

The majority of the influences upon the criteria applied by Asian journalists are indeed such that they inhibit the growth of interest in Asian affairs among the media in many Asian countries. The influence of the language in which some of the most prominent journalists and media conduct their professional business, and the status of this language in the community around them, the upbringing and education of many journalists, the historical linkages of many Asian countries with western Europe and America, the contemporary economic linkages, and the continuing effect of these upon the controlling interests in many Asian media, the meagreness of the traffic between many Asian countries, and the concentration of the media in the city and its effects upon the outlook of the media—all those factors have combined to make Asian media and media people turn away from each other and towards the more glittering even if more distant western horizons.

Reversing this trend, turning back from the "glittering horizons" by limiting world-news reception, or even demanding uncritical news coverage of local development, is unlikely to advance development, and certainly will not provide citizens with a realistic picture of the world.

Some third world journalists warn against governmental control of the news media. They maintain that a developing country is not strengthened by foreclosing debate of economic and political problems (just as some third world academics have shown that complete government control of agriculture and industry has generally not resulted in higher productivity in those sectors).

"Communications from abroad (including commercial ones) promote development, and even the development of the domestic media," says Ithiel de Sola Pool.[16] He denies that poor nations need to control the flow of communication either to prevent the submerging of their cultures or their media. Dismissing the argument that restrictions on free flow accelerate a country's development he notes that Taiwan, Korea, Brazil, and Mexico have not protected their media from competition, and their development has progressed rapidly. Burma, Vietnam, and Ethiopia have tightly controlled their media and their development is minimal.

Pool also rejects the assumption that the new technologies deepen the concentration of power. He maintains that computers, electronic communications, and related instruments "favor diversity," and do not have a "centralizing effect" on society. That technical fact, he adds, "will push society in the direction of the free flow of information." Governments may thus attack the new technology not because it concentrates power overseas but because it "threatens to throw everything wide open." The invention of printing broadened the reading public; the practice of censorship and the expurgatory index was the response of the Church and the Courts to their fear that the printed word might spread throughout the society.

The new technology permits highly individualized uses of information. Soon homes may have two-way videos on a switched network so that individuals can engage in two-way video conversations around the world. This technology makes every node an originating point as well as a receiver, Pool points out. But would regimes that regularly imprison their political or ideological opponents agree to such free flow of individual communication?

The technical communication network tends to ignore frontiers. As costs fall the restrictions become mainly political. Those who now demand of the world-news media a "right of reply" are not likely to accept the full implication of this demand: a worldwide open system of high speed communication directly into individual homes. The governments that reject such communication possibilities have been attacking for many years the American proposal for satellites that beam information across national borders. On the ground of defending "national sovereignty" they would block all communication not approved in advance. Yet neither the U.S. government nor American journalists should ignore either the facts of the culture shock faced by traditional societies emerging into the Information Age, or the arguments used by dominant elites to retain their dominance in the face of pervasive transnational news media.

## DEVELOPMENT JOURNALISM

Leaders of developing countries seek the magical formula that will lead to rapid development. Prior to their breaking away from the colonial center, many had regarded political independence as a guarantor of a better life. Independence, however, was soon found not to assure economic progress or even social stability. Literacy and the ability to communicate widely were soon seen to be necessary. But political independence did not guarantee the creation of a domestic communications system or access to adequate news and information about immediate or international consensus.

Nor did nationhood quickly integrate the often disparate ethnic, religious or tribal elements within the new borders. Lack of integration further deepened the problems of domestic communication. In many places there were critical issues of what language(s) to employ, or how to integrate cultural diversities. In many countries such problems have gone unresolved, though the ruling center has favored one cultural strain over another. Where differences of culture are extreme, limitation of conflict is managed mainly by use of state power.

The image of the nation in many less-developed countries remains underdeveloped. There is awareness of the tribal, regional, or ethnic commonality, but not the national. There is no civic culture. Leaders frequently rule without any sense that their people accept their rule as legitimate. (Elites in developed countries under authoritarian rule have the same uncertainty; they often arrange elections or referenda in which 99.9 percent of the voters are compelled to grant a pseudo-endorsement.) To become viable nations—not simply the headquarters of military or charismatic leaders—countries must become legitimate, accepted, unified societies.

Both capitalist or socialist third world governments believe themselves responsible for the economic well-being, education, and training of their people toward this goal. *Development* journalism is concentration by objective journalists on the *news*, the newness, of developments in education, agriculture, industry, communications, and applied science; developments that leaders hope will eventually produce economic success and a secure sense of national unity. The new technologies in agriculture and industry are intimately related to local employment opportunities and citizen skills, the system of education, the distribution of farm and consumer products, the nature and operation of the economy, and the blending of all projected changes with the traditional habits and culture of the society.

In development journalism the important problems of that society are reported as the underlying targets of the new technologies, systems, and improved education. The possibilities for improved health standards, increased consumer product distribution, greater economic security, and retaining family ties and traditional methods and beliefs become newsworthy when these developments affect large numbers of people.

The experience of other third world countries in recognizing similar problems and attempting solutions with demonstrated success or failure becomes locally relevant and newsworthy. The country-to-country exchange of news reports on development subjects should therefore benefit national development through the practice of interesting and relevant journalism.

Over the longer term, development journalism should explore the *process* by which change may come to a traditional society, keeping in focus (1) the long, grim past (during which problems went unnoticed, and being ignored, increased), (2) the comparatively brief recent period during which such problems have been recognized and for which solutions are still sought, and (3) the inevitably slow progress that even successful approaches can produce in the future. Such process stories could have the effect of putting development issues in perspective for both the third and first worlds, and explain to both why evolutionary change, while less bloody and less spectacular than revolutionary change, is both slower and more lasting.

The key word in the definition of development journalism is "objective." Development journalism should examine and report development news in balanced, authoritative fashion. The main thrust of an article on a new plant will be to assess the plant's effectiveness as an example of a technology or system for the generation of new products and new employment. The disappearance of a manager or the funds he departed with should not be the primary focus of the development-news report, although the disappearance may produce side effects that should be reported in perspective. At its best development news should not be regarded by the government as its tool to be used to advance economic progress. Such news will advance a nation's development, but the journalist should not be assigned responsibility for development nor be controlled by the government to guide his/her reporting. This kind of news should not be managed by government to advance or undermine political causes or their proponents. Nor should objective development journalists be denied access to development news, or their reports censored or otherwise restricted by representatives of the government.

To make development news either a tool or weapon of government is to transform this promising reportorial function into "developmental journalism" (a genre I have described extensively elsewhere).[17]

To what extent do the present news channels serve the purpose of development? Though the Western news flow carries little development information, nearly all developing countries purchase one or more transworld news services. They often reserve the content for the governing elites and censor the reports before relaying them to the average citizen. In some cases the Western news wire is retained because it is far less costly than maintaining an intelligence establishment abroad. The news services point out that they regularly ask clients how the service can be improved. There is competition between the AP and UPI, and among all four transnationals, to secure and serve clients in the third world as well as the West.

The four Western news services transmit about 300,000 words every day around the world. This is more than 80 percent of the international news flow. The decisions of which events and personalities to cover, and how to report them is made by a relatively few persons within those four services. While they function transnationally they are headquartered and owned in their Western capitals: Paris, London, and New York (with the American services providing the largest proportion of the reportage).

The four world services spend less than $300 million a year. They cannot cover 160 nations on that budget, particularly since it costs about $100,000 a year to maintain one American in a news bureau overseas. Hiring stringers locally, while less expensive, is not entirely satisfactory. The national, no matter how professional his attitude, may readily be pressured by his government. For example, Pakistan in 1979 jailed Salamat Ali, a native award-winning correspondent of the prestigious *Far Eastern Economic Review* published in Hong Kong. Outsiders may have similar problems. Indira Gandhi has demanded that only Indians report from India. During her "emergency," she expelled from the country those Western correspondents who, in her view, reported unfavorably. The world news services regularly face the dilemma in some third world countries of accepting government handouts, employing local stringers, or facing harassment and expulsion. If news services, because of financial strains, close or do not open bureaus in some small developing countries the services are charged with inadequate coverage. If the services send a correspondent occasionally to cover a little-reported group of countries in a developing region, such reportage is often said to be superficial and ill-informed. Such sporadic coverage, say third world critics, emphasizes disasters and spectacles. The daily problems of developing countries—sickness, hunger, illiteracy, and a lack of effective political structure—are not always treated in perspective. Perhaps most important, the development process that may be under way is ignored by the traveling journalist. He seeks hard news—today's corruption or tomorrow's coup—and is unlikely to report a long-term development prospect. Third world critics say they want Western journalism to deal sympathetically with entrenched problems and the projects designed to improve matters.

Development news will not always be regarded favorably by its subjects. An authoritarian elite is unlikely to welcome a foreign journalist who seriously examines the local agricultural or industrial scheme and finds it ineffective, poorly conceived, or its administrators corrupt. Doors may close as quickly on such development journalism as on the older forms of Western news reporting.

Efforts by Asian journalists to create a serious form of *development news* in the 1960's were scotched by the governments. "Under a process of imposed restructuring," according to Amitabha Chowdhury, director of the Press Foundation of Asia,[18] the governments feared the challenge of objective, professional journalists who were learning to examine the basic economic, scientific, and administrative factors in third world development economies. The regimes, moreover, found it more desirable to control the local press and restrict the transnational journalists. There is, says Chowdhury, a "startling reversal of direction that is visible all at the same time in all [Asian] countries." Such countries turned to

UNESCO and other forums to press their case for intergovernmental regulation of the news flow.

## III.   *American Responses to Legitimate Needs*

For the United States government the controversies over journalistic responsibility or a new world information order raise particularly difficult issues. Government policy can neither resolve nor even address the heart of the matter. Editorial, reportorial, publishing, and broadcasting prerogatives are clearly protected by the First Amendment. But in other areas the U.S. can respond: We pledged at Nairobi in 1976 and again at Paris in 1978 to provide concrete assistance to developing countries through supporting journalist training centers and a satellite program for the transmission of information to the third world. The United States hosted a planning conference in November 1979 and would be the major participant in a larger intergovernmental conference in April 1980. The purpose is to create a system of bilateral and multilateral transfers of communication technology for the developing countries.

Our pledges have led to some generally unpublicized but significant actions: 1) A cooperative satellite[19] program has begun in the Peruvian jungles. Through INTELSAT and low-cost earth stations, rural development of isolated villages and communities is being assisted. U.S. aid will make possible two-way telephone and conferencing services, radio broadcasting, telex, facsimile, and possibly slow-scan television. 2) Similar agreements are being considered in other parts of the world. A survey of the Caribbean area is being conducted by the University of the West Indies. AID will systematically share information from this and related programs with the international community. 3) The promised regional training centers have been delayed by UNESCO's reluctance to designate such centers. The U.S. International Communication Agency, however, expects to arrange to assist several such centers before the end of 1980.

Obviously, the USICA and AID can provide hardware. They cannot promise or deliver a "new order" in American journalistic *content*.

To continue to operate in most countries of the world, the American journalist will have to develop a new civic culture that matches global realities. There is taking place before our eyes the greatest acculturation ever before experienced, based on transmitting European and American ideas to the world. To be sure, much of this is the movement abroad of film, recordings, audio-visuals, books, broadcasting, and television. But the hundreds of thousands of words a day that speed around the world from the news services carrying news the people must have—that, too, is one form of idea-transferral.

Americans should acknowledge that they have great news-delivery systems. They will not and should not be dismantled, but they can be improved. While it may be hard to increase their volume of output, they can broaden the diversity of their content, if not each day then by providing over a period of weeks or months a cumulatively improved coverage of areas and countries now little noticed or reported.

American journalists should also acknowledge that some specialized procedures and news reporters are needed abroad. Fragile economic and political systems, for example, need far greater exploration and explication when corruption or obvious shortcomings are observed. There is a need for journalists who specialize in the development of third world societies. Roger Tatarian, former editor-in-chief of UPI, now a journalism professor at the University of California at Fresno, has proposed the creation of a first/third world agency that would specialize in development news. Tentatively called the North/South News Agency (NSNA), it would be managed, funded, and directed editorially, half by people from the developing countries and half from the developed nations. Several third world news agency chiefs met informally with AP, UPI, and Time Inc. representatives in 1979 under the auspices of the Murrow Center of the Fletcher School of Law and Diplomacy, Tufts University. The NSNA hit a snag when the Nonaligned Pool regarded it as competition (though the NSNA had invited the Pool to participate in creating the agency). The third world would be wise to support the NSNA and put the Western editors to the test. The most important barrier to the publication and broadcasting of third world news is not AP and UPI, but the judgment of end-users. Though their coverage is maintained at a financial loss, the news services devote twenty to thirty percent of their daily news budgets to third world news. In most newspapers in the United States little or none of this will appear in print, and very little will be heard or seen on the broadcast media.

The lack of American exposure to available news of the third world creates a problem for U.S. diplomacy as an information "order" becomes a factor in intergovernmental relations. It is also a problem for American citizens. It should not have been a shock for the President or his constituents when Soviet tanks rumbled across the Afghanistan border, nor should the failures of the Shah, or the successes of Moscow-supported liberation movements of southern Africa remain enigmas to the American people. Our major newspapers have expanded sports, living, shopping, entertainment, and science sections, but they have often reduced foreign coverage. Yet the real "living" section may ultimately prove to be those pages of foreign news that tell us what we need to know to live in a complex, increasingly dangerous world.

Some further guidelines are needed.

We need a new world communication system—not, as some UNESCO activists would have it, a New World Information Order. The distinction is important. A "communications system" refers to a network of technological and organizational arrangements, devices and agreements. An "information order," as defined thus far, implies prescriptions or controls over the *content* of communications. All manner of information can pass through a communication system. There should indeed be better arrangements for the flow of information among developing countries themselves and between them and the developed nations of the world. Enlarging and improving that flow of information will require enlarging and improving the global communications system. Some goals for improving that system are:

1. *General education—the starting point.* The earliest communication begins in the home and moves on to the schoolroom. The mass media of communication depend on early education to provide some tools of literacy and an ability to listen and speak. Not enough attention is given in our schools to generate an interest in the world and a context in which to view it. Each citizen needs to sort out important and useful information from the vast outpouring in this Information Age.

2. *Placing America in the world.* With a greater interest in the tools of communication should flow a heightened awareness of America's role in the world. This country, at gunpoint, has taken a crash course in the religion and politics of Iran, just as in the sixties we learned painfully about Indochina. With 100 other developing countries ripe for major changes often involving U.S. interests we must expand our citizens' understanding of other peoples and *their* interests. The schools alone cannot overcome our traditional American isolation. Generations whose formal education has ended must rely on mass communication. Americans are little different than virtually all other peoples: Africans seek little news of Asia, Asians care little about Latin America, and the latter show little interest in Asia or Africa. Americans, however, have easier access to effective communication systems and have a greater need to know about the rest of the world. The communication media should not leave generating interest to the schools, or assume that a tradition of information-isolation cannot be broken.

3. *Make positive use of the vast American communication systems.* By creating mass information- and data-transmitting technologies and communication systems, America has enabled far more news and information to reach far more people than ever before in history. We have also come to dominate the information flows around the world. Yet

Americans still are insufficiently interested and informed about the world and its needs. The major networks should be encouraged to produce more quality information programs and individual stations to present more than the minimal public-service time needed to maintain an FCC license. More space should be allotted for foreign news in newspapers and magazines. If the ideas and news of distant peoples were given greater attention, Americans would at least understand that our vast communication system should be better meshed with the fragile, primitive networks in the developing countries.

4. *Understand the nature of the attacks on the U.S. information services.* It is important for Americans to understand the challenges to the U.S. information systems—the two major transnational news services, television networks servicing clients abroad, news magazines with worldwide circulations, influential daily newspapers which also syndicate news and features, data-processing organizations, and radio/telegraph/satellite communication networks. Americans regard these as internally competitive: AP versus UPI, ITT versus RCA, IBM versus CDC. In the eyes of third world critics, these are all "American" and "Western." They are said to convey a single national orientation, a national bias. There is a growing homogeneity among the big information conveyors. Cultural imperialism, it is called abroad when U.S. ideas become pervasive. This is disadvantageous for America as well as for its critics. The reversal of homogeneity could improve the information flow for all. That requires policy decisions by the U.S. information system to encourage diversity at home and abroad, and welcome news and information about the developing world.

5. *A code of practice for the Information Age.* Professional journalists should explore the new potentials in communicating, and set down a voluntary, nongovernmental code of practice for the Information Age. This would take into account the time and physical limitations on the reader/listener/viewer, as well as his or her need-to-know as a citizen of the world. Governments have treatened to legislate a journalistic code. It behooves journalists to prepare or update their own. Schools of journalism should emphasize the values of such codes. In the past, voluntary codes have advised mainly on ethical and operational problems. To those concerns should now be added emphasis on improving the flow of information to and from the developing nations.

6. *Preferential tariffs and lower technology costs for the third world.* Telex, telephone, and other telecommunications costs tend to be more expensive for those least able to pay. Tariffs generally depend on the volume of traffic. Since far fewer words move to or from Lusaka than New York, the rate for comparable distances is higher to the former than the latter. High tariffs and technology costs should no longer divide the

poor two-thirds of the world from the richly communicating third. The PTTs of the developing countries (which themselves set high rates for international communications) should be compensated for lowering tariffs and encouraging a greater volume of information to pass their borders to both developing and developed nations. Every nation should be assisted in securing a modern satellite-receiving system, and shortwave linkages. These are now relatively inexpensive systems.

It is essential for the International Telecommunications Union and commercial carriers to arrange preferential tariffs as a relatively rapid and inexpensive way to spur communications among the developing countries. Bilateral efforts have begun to provide some heavy printing equipment for newspaper and magazine publishing in developing countries. The World Press Freedom Committee (WPFC) has made grants in third world countries to small papers, journalism schools, and media seminars, and offers retired U.S. specialists to train journalists abroad. UNESCO will hold a major conference in 1980 to coordinate international aid to third world journalists. There will still be the need for bilateral help, and especially for nongovernmental professional assistance from Americans.

7. *Low-cost communication instruments should be mass-produced.* There is a natural desire in developing countries to acquire the most advanced communications technology. In many situations this desire should be resisted. Far less expensive and less complex modes of communication should be expanded: the mimeograph, low-cost offset press, shortwave radio, public address systems, audiocassettes. Millions of persons in villages and small settlements in Africa, Asia, and Latin America could profit from such primary "mass" communication. Developed countries should produce such traditional instruments for distribution at little or no cost to developing countries.

8. *Support the North/South News Agency (NSNA).* This NSNA project discussed above deserves the support of American gatekeepers. The experiment is designed to meet persistent objections that present Western coverage of the third world ignores the long-range issues at the heart of the economic and social development of poor countries. The NSNA experiment would provide just such material, with interconnections to most other news agencies in the developing and developed world. To use NSNA dispatches, however, the four major world news services may have to waive exclusive rights to NSNA material, and also accept timeless copy focused on trends and processes rather than today's hard news.

9. *Stocking U.S. libraries abroad with computerized data.* There is a growing need in the developing countries for diverse economic, scientific, and general information. Radicals demand access to corporate and scientific research, whether or not protected by patent and copyright. While

this violates present international copyright conventions, there are broad areas of information in the public domain that could be shared through computer terminals in U.S. libraries abroad. Many kinds of basic scientific research could be provided, along with summaries of news and analysis going back many years. While the offering should not include current reportage in competition with independent news services, providing access to important news-background libraries would be a major contribution to journalists in developing countries.

10. *Sharing U.S. telecommunications facilities with third world journalists.* The United States has shared some of its satellite and shortwave facilities with other governments. The use of an American satellite for instructional purposes in India was a notable example. There should be more regularized offerings of other U.S. telecommunications systems for transmission from this country to home offices by third world journalists. There could be similar arrangements for using U.S. facilities between two points abroad.

# IV.  *Conclusion*

The struggle for a new world information order or system is primarily a struggle to enhance the power of particular leaders or states: the power of national leaders, not all in the third world, to control their citizens without competitive information permeating their societies; the power of ideological states such as the Soviet bloc and other ideological regimes to displace the marketing of news as well as the products of the free enterprise systems; and the power of relatively free, information-poor nations to sustain their own cultural and political orientations in the face of dominating information flows from a few Western news media. This last area of competition—the flow of diverse ideas—raises fundamental philosophical as well as journalistic issues. What should be the role of the news media in society, and how should journalists, while resisting governmental controls, nevertheless perform their mission under a code of social responsibility?

Confrontation between free-flow advocates and those who favor some form of controlled flow is inevitable. The free-flow advocates have (1) the tradition and practice of political freedom, and (2) vast communication infrastructures, technologies growing at ever-faster rates, and direct links to most centers of power in the world; third world activists generally have neither.

Western world-news services will continue to be challenged. They probably will continue to improve the quality of their third world coverage, but that will not prevent attacks from third world and Marxist activists. Western correspondents will occasionally suffer reprisals. Many third world and Marxist nationalists will continue to deprive their own peoples of the free flow of information, and, whenever they choose, hamper the flow of news across their borders.

That the controversy will persist suggests neither that American news media should not improve the quality and volume of the foreign news they deliver to the American people or to audiences abroad; nor that the U.S. government should continue to delay providing significant communication assistance to friendly developing countries.

The question of whether American journalism is either free or objective will continue to be challenged at home and abroad. That, too, is part of the democratic process. Up to the point of actual monopolization by one medium—a point by no means reached in any part of the American print or broadcast press—the diversity of information available in the United States and through it to readers and listeners abroad remains the best assurance that the flow will continue free. The diversity and competition of the market system also provide some counterpoint to the biases of many kinds that are bound to be reflected in reportage that is not dominated by a ministry of information. The most effective monopolists in the information field remain the *agitprops* of the Soviet Union, linked to vast information, disinformation, and intelligence services.

Even the most fragile developing countries, on balance, have more to gain from training journalists as responsible professionals and gradually freeing them to select information for publication than by narrowly restricting their freedom. In the free, developed nations there is a necessary tension between the people's right to know and the government's need to restrict access to some limited information for reasons of national security, commercial security, or personal privacy. The Freedom of Information Act, for example, gives the journalist and citizen unusual access to much information in government files. While this freedom increases the journalist's ability to know and to publish, it makes great demands on judgment, fairness, and sense of propriety.

American journalism should be as free to seek and transmit information as the First Amendment permits. In reporting from or serving third world countries, nevertheless, the American journalist will be wise to place current developments in broader and longer-range perspectives. As a link between civilizations and between peoples on different levels of development, and as a symbol of what it means to be free, the American journalist has a responsibility no one should underestimate.

## NOTES

1. United States Arms Control and Disarmament Agency. Personal communication.

2. *The Democratic Journalist,* December, 1979, pp. 1–3. Published by the International Organization of Journalists, Prague. More generally the material in section I of this paper is based on published and unpublished UNESCO and U.S. government documents, as well as personal communications.

3. The broad diversity of subjects and points of view reflected in these documents bears out the main theme in Leonard Sussman, "An Approach to the Study of Transnational News Media in a Pluralistic World," International Commission for the Study of Communication Problems (MacBride Commission), document no. 18. Written before the Commission began, this paper argued against a single standard or form of journalistic performance in a world of political pluralism.

4. "What wisdome can there be to choose, what continence to forbeare without the knowledge of evill?" *Areopagitica* (1644) (Reprint: New York: AMS Press, 1971), p. 20.

5. Leonard Sussman, *Mass News Media and the Third World Challenge* (Beverly Hills: Sage Publications, 1977); and Sussman, "Approach to the Study of Transnational News Media in a Pluralistic World."

6. Vladimir Bukovsky, "To Build a Castle: My Life as a Dissenter," *Quadrant,* September, 1979.

7. Kaarle Nordenstreng and Herbert Schiller, eds., *National Sovereignty and International Communications* (Norwood,, New Jersey: Abbex Publishing Co., 1979).

8. de Sola Pool, *in* Nordenstreng and Schiller, pp. 140–45.

9. William A. Rugh, *The Arab Press: News Media and Political Process in the Arab World* (Syracuse: Syracuse University Press, 1979).

10. Herbert G. Gans, *Deciding What's News: A Study of CBS Evening News, NBC Nightly News, Newsweek and Time* (New York: Random House, 1979), p. 252.

11. John Dewey, *Freedom and Culture* (1939) (1963 edition: Capricorn Books).

12. Daniel J. Boorstin, *The Republics of Technology* (New York: Harper and Row, 1978).

13. Majid Tehranian, "Modernization, Communication and Community Development," a paper delivered at the 1978 conference in Dubrovnik of the International Institute of Communications. Tehranian was director of the Iran Communications and Development Institute in 1978.

14. Robert L. Stevenson and Richard R. Coles, "News Flow Between the Americas: Are We Giving Our Own Hemisphere the Coverage it Deserves?", a paper delivered at the 35th annual meeting of the Inter-American Press Association, Toronto, 1979.

15. Pran Chopra, paper delivered at the UNESCO meeting on news agencies, Colombo, 1977.

16. Ithiel de Sola Pool, "The Communications Revolution in an Interdependent World," paper delivered at the 43rd annual meeting of the U.S. National Commission for UNESCO, Athens, Georgia, December 12, 1979.

17. Sussman, *Mass News Media and the Third World Challenge,* pp. 38–9; and *Index on Censorship,* January 1979, pp. 78–80.

18. Amitabha Chowdhury, "Report to the Annual Assembly of the International Press Institute," *IPI Report,* July 1976, pp. 1–2.

19. The U.S. National Aeronautics and Space Administration (NASA) in August 1975 launched a large SITE program using the ATS–6 satellite. This instructional satellite, parked in orbit 22,300 miles above the earth, enabled Indians to beam educational programs to 2,400 villages in six states. Another 2,500 villages were served by conventional TV transmitters.

# An Index for Trade Union Freedom

During the first three years of the Carter Administration the United States put great stress on the importance of human rights. Our government has spoken out on behalf of Soviet dissidents, reduced military aid to repressive Latin American regimes, and created a special human rights section in the State Department, headed by a new Assistant Secretary. In both government and the private sector, more attention has been paid to the subject, and more information on the status of human rights has been demanded. The subject has been publicized by reports on political prisoners from Amnesty International, and the annual reports by the State Department to Congress on human rights in the world. This new attention to human rights has often seemed to focus on the rights of the highly educated to freedom of speech and political action. Little specific attention has been devoted to those critical freedoms for the great majority of people, namely trade union rights, through which the workers and peasants can fill their basic economic needs for food, clothing, and shelter. To an unorganized worker receiving substandard wages, who cannot provide his or her family with proper food, the right to form a trade union to fight for higher wages is the most immediate human right of all. If we are to give a social content to our heightened concern for human rights, we must not limit our efforts to protecting freedom of expression for intellectuals and artists, but must also speak out for trade union rights, especially since the suppression of these rights is increasing alarmingly throughout much of the developing world.

To effectively attack this problem, we must first measure and analyze it. We must know how severe restrictions on trade unions are in a given country, how that situation compares with other countries, and whether

The presentation here of the general format for the Index is abstracted from the article "Criteria for an Index of Comparative Trade Union Freedom," published in *Conflict,* Volume 1, Number 4. We wish to thank the editors of *Conflict* for permission to reproduce this material here.

99

it is improving or worsening. If we are to use publicity to bring world opinion to bear on an offending government, we must show that especially grievous conditions exist for workers under its rule. If legislators and aid administrators are to use the reduction or expansion of U.S. foreign aid as a means of encouraging governments to respect trade union freedoms, they need measures to show trends in the toleration of unions as the aid-receiving nations react to these pressures. U.S. labor groups providing technical assistance to trade unions abroad must know where their efforts should be concentrated to produce results. For example, it is common for generally repressive, noncommunist dictatorships to allow local-level unions to function under freely elected leaders in particular industries or provinces. In such a case, it is with those unions that foreign assistance groups should work, both to use their presence to help protect these existing areas of worker freedom, and to try to expand them into other sectors still suffering from government repression.

This paper presents an index of comparative trade union freedom that will enable analysts to compare countries, and follow the rise and fall of worker rights in a given country. It then illustrates the use of the index by ranking five country situations in Latin America. This exercise suggests how widely the levels of worker freedom vary, even among countries with similar political systems.

## THE INDEX—GENERAL CONSIDERATIONS

It is impossible to construct a scientific, highly accurate index of trade union freedoms. However, the need remains for a format for ranking countries, even if that format can provide us with only a general idea of where some nations rank, and the rankings involve subjective judgments. Both cautions apply to the present index. If different experts, even of the same political outlook, were to rank the world's nations on this index, a number of countries would undoubtedly come out a bit higher or lower on one expert's list than on the other's. This is because the situation in each country at each time is unique—there is virtually no country situation that fits precisely into one of the categories in the index. The user of the index must put each situation in the category to which it comes closest. Although using the index will require subjective judgments, we believe the index presented here will be sufficiently reliable that variations in the judgments of different users will not be extreme. It should provide a satisfactory idea of how a nation compares with others in respect to workers' rights.

The index measures relations between workers and the state. It does not measure repression of workers by employers, such as the imposition of company unions, unless the state is involved in such repression. For example, one question asks whether national laws allow employers to dismiss workers for engaging in union activity. It does not ask whether employers engage in such practices, outside of or even in violation of the state's laws and policies.

However, where law and government practice differ, the index is generally concerned with the practice. Many nations have exemplary labor codes on paper, which appear to ensure full trade union rights, yet in practice unions are outlawed, strikes banned, and trade union leaders jailed and tortured. Some other nations still have on their books archaic laws that appear very restrictive of labor's rights, but these laws are not implemented, and the government's practice may be quite libertarian. In the Latin American case study (below) we have been guided by practice, not what is on paper, except where the index specifically states "in law" or "in law and practice."

## THE INDEX—PRINCIPAL CATEGORIES

The index ranks countries in five principal categories, giving both a numerical score and a percentile score for each, thus showing how each country ranks among all countries on each category. Then the five percentile scores are averaged into an overall score to determine the nation's general ranking. (See figure 1.)

The index is a comparative one. It does not establish absolute categories for degrees of freedom such as "free" or "party free," with a certain range on the numerical scores allocated to each category. We originally intended to devise absolute categories, but discovered that views on what "trade union freedom" requires vary too much to obtain any consensus on categories. For example, whether public employees should be allowed to organize and strike is a matter very much disputed at present even in democratic countries that pride themselves on offering freedom for workers. We therefore settled for a comparative index that simply ranks nations relative to each other, from the freest to the least free. All the experts on international labor interviewed recommended using this approach. In the example of public employees, a nation that allows them full trade union rights will rank higher than a nation that does not, but the latter will not be arbitrarily relegated to a certain category such as "partly free" because of its treatment of public employees.

The index ranks each country in terms of five categories of rights. The first three are the classic rights that everyone thinks of in regard to trade unionism: the right to organize, the right to bargain collectively, and the right to strike. The first two are also the rights on which the International Labor Organization (ILO) has adopted conventions:

# Figure 1
## An Index of Comparative Trade Union Freedom

| Right to Organize | | Right to Bargain Collectively | | Right to Strike. | | Right to Political Action | | Freedom from Specific Restrictions | | Overall Ranking | |
|---|---|---|---|---|---|---|---|---|---|---|---|
| Num. score | Percentile rank | Num. score | Percentile rank | Num. score | Percentile rank | Num. score | Percentile rank | Num. score | Percentile rank | Num. score | Percentile rank |
| | | | | | | | | | | | |

Number 87, on Freedom of Association and Protection of the Right to Organize, adopted in 1948, and Number 98, on the Right to Organize and Collective Bargaining, adopted in 1949. Both of these conventions have been ratified by over eighty countries.

As a fourth category, we have added the right to political action. If unions are to advance effectively the interests of their members, they must be able to act as powerful pressure groups on the national scene and play a role in determining who governs the nation.

In a developing nation, if a traditional elite owns most of the land and factories, controls the government, and receives a large part of the wealth, then unions that are allowed to bargain collectively, but are not allowed to engage in political action, can only bargain about the distribution of whatever crumbs the oligarchy leaves on the table. In a modern, industrialized country, it is the administration in power in the national government that decides on monetary and fiscal policies that affect levels of business activity, employment, and prices. That is, every worker has a stake, in terms of jobs, wages, and prices, in what group holds power nationally and to what extent it reflects the interests of labor or management. Enterprise-level collective bargaining by unions that cannot undertake political action would leave unions playing a game under rules made by others. Workers want a voice in making the rules of the game, and consequently the trade unionist views national politics as a legitimate union activity.

The first four categories involve fairly general concepts regarding union rights. Unfortunately, there are a multitude of detailed restrictions on trade unions that a government can impose, thereby greatly diminishing the value of general freedom to organize, bargain, strike, and take political action. As a corrective to the generalizations in the first four categories, we have included a fifth category entitled "Freedom from Specific Restrictions," which ranks nations on how free their unions are from forty common government violations of workers' rights. Taken together, the five categories provide a comprehensive picture of the state of trade union freedom in a given country.

*The right to organize.* The second page of the index (see figure 2) is devoted to the details of the right to organize free unions. The total of "yes" answers to the questions on this page constitutes the numerical score for the "Right to Organize" category on the first page.

This category does not measure the prevalence of trade unions but the prevalence of free unions, that is, ones in which the members can freely elect leaders of their own choice. There are many unions throughout the world, in nations ruled by totalitarian or military dictatorships, that will not show up on this scale. Our purpose is to measure how many unions exist that can defend workers' interests against the state. State

# Figure 2
# The Right to Organize Free Unions*

Are workers free in practice to organize AND to elect freely leaders of their own choice in:

Private sector, urban locals? ........................................ _____

Private sector, rural locals? ........................................ _____

Locals in autonomous state enterprises? ............................. _____

Locals in the public service? ........................................ _____

Province geographic federations? .................................... _____

National occupational sector federations? ........................... _____

National confederations? ............................................ _____


Are national unions free to affiliate, if they so desire, to the following kinds of international labor bodies of their choice?

International Trade Secretariats? .................................... _____

International regional confederations? ............................... _____

World-wide confederations? .......................................... _____

(For the numerical score, add the total number of "yes" answers:_____)


*On each question on this page, if workers have a considerable range of choice in leaders to elect or organizations with which to affiliate, but leaders or organizations of certain political colorations are eliminated from that range of choice, count a "½ yes" for that question.

---

labor fronts and "officialista" unions will not count toward "yes" answers on this page.

In this category, and throughout the index, separate answers are required for various union sectors, because of variations in union freedom among them. Urban workers may enjoy more freedom than rural workers, and usually private-sector workers have rights denied to those paid by the state. Throughout the index we have further subdivided the state's employees into two categories—those who work for "autonomous state enterprises" (state-owned factories, railroads, and so forth) and those who are in the public service proper (bureaucrats) and are thus engaged in the administration of the state.

A potential methodological difficulty exists in regard to nations with fully socialized economies. Even if they allowed free trade unions, they might get a low numerical score because, having no private sector, they would get fewer total "yes" answers. In the case of the Right to Organize category, this problem is not a real one, because no fully socialized state today allows any free unions at all, and such a state will get all "no" answers in any event.

Another problem arises on the Right to Organize page of the index in regard to countries that allow workers a reasonably wide range of political choice in electing leaders or selecting an international group with which to affiliate. In some countries adherents of all political parties except the Communists are allowed to compete in union elections, and the national level unions are free to affiliate with any international labor group except the Soviet-dominated World Federation of Trade Unions (WFTU). In some nations with military governments, the junta allows competition in union elections by all parties except the one ousted by the military in the coup that brought the junta to power.

In such cases of wide, but not unlimited range of choice, a "yes" answer would be too generous to a government, but a "no" answer would relegate it to the same low score as a dictatorship allowing no choice at all. Consequently, as the table footnote indicates a "½ yes" answer would be appropriate.

*The right to bargain collectively.* The third page of the index (see figure 3) measures who can bargain in a nation and what they can bargain about. A major problem arises from the great differences in national practice as to what matters are determined by national legislation and what are left to direct negotiations between unions and management. In some democratic countries with free labor movements, legislation is the major determinant of wages, hours, and welfare benefits. In other democratic nations, such as the United States, workers would consider it a great mistake to let legislators take over such a large portion of the decisions made through private-sector collective bargaining.

Since national preferences and customs vary so widely, the collective bargaining section of the index will *not* measure the division of decision making between bargaining and legislation. Our concern is the freedom of the unions versus the state. Therefore, the index asks on what topics unions in each sector can bargain for benefits going beyond whatever the national legislation does provide. If the legislative provisions constitute minima beyond which unions can bargain with employers for "more," then freedom to bargain collectively has not been abused. However, if the legislative provisions are maxima, with no bargaining for greater benefits allowed, then the right to bargain has been curtailed, and a "no" answer should be entered on the "bargaining" page of the index where such a situation prevails.

# Figure 3
# The Right to Bargain Collectively

| Issues which are allowed to be determined by collective bargaining: (beyond whatever minima are set by law) | Sectors | | | |
|---|---|---|---|---|
| | Urban Private | Rural Private | Autonomous State Enterpr. | The Public Service |
| Wages, unlimited* | | | | |
| Wages, within maxima set by government wage controls (if any) | | | | |
| Hours of work | | | | |
| Working conditions | | | | |
| Union security | | | | |
| Job security | | | | |
| Contract administration procedures | | | | |
| Health and welfare benefits | | | | |

(For the numerical score, total the "yes" answers)

(*If the answer to this question is "yes", then a "yes" answer should also be given to the next question.)

106

Though giving more points to nations without wage controls, the authors do not presume to judge whether such controls should be applied. The index merely measures the degree to which unions are free to bargain about wages, and ranks countries accordingly. If economic stabilization requires wage controls, there may be a good reason for restricting bargaining rights in this area.

*The right to strike.* This category of the index poses the most troublesome problems of all. First, despite the common usage of the phrase, the *right to strike* is not generally recognized in international covenants as are the rights to organize and bargain. The ILO has conventions (numbers 87 and 98) on the latter two rights, but not on the right to strike. No mention of the right to strike is found in the UN's Universal Declaration of Human Rights, the European Convention for Protection of Human Rights and Fundamental Freedoms, or the OAS American Declaration of the Rights and Duties of Man.[1]

Despite the silence of ILO conventions on the issue, the ILO's Committee of Experts and its Freedom of Association Committee have taken the position that a permanent ban on strikes in all sectors is "inconsistent with the principles of freedom of association," because the strike weapon is "a legitimate means whereby workers' organizations may defend their occupational interests."[2] Given this judgment by an organization that represents management, labor, and government sectors in virtually all nations, plus the emphasis put on the right to strike by trade unionists who view it as the workers' crucial "equalizer" to the influence and position of upper-income groups, we have included use of the strike as a right. Restrictions on this right will lower a country's overall ranking on the index.

Granted this decision, the problem arises as to how much a nation's ranking on the index should suffer if the right to strike is replaced by compulsory arbitration. This has been done in Australia and New Zealand, both fully democratic nations with labor movements generally considered free. Yet, they do not have legal resort to the strike, which has been replaced by arbitration procedures that are impartial and in which the parties concerned can participate at all stages.

Proponents of such participatory arbitration systems might contend that the right that workers possess is not to strike, but to a role of power and influence in the process of dispute settlement. This power might be exerted through the threat of a strike, or through a voice in setting arbitration procedures and selecting arbitrators. By such a definition, Australians might argue that their workers fully enjoy this right. The prevailing international consensus, as expressed through the ILO, does not accept this argument, but it is sufficiently presuasive that we have given democratic arbitration a fairly high ranking in the hierarchy of

# Figure 4 The Right to Strike

| Sector | Full freedom in law and practice when-ever negotiators are unable to agree (5 points) | Freedom in law and practice to strike after compliance with obligatory conciliation, me-diation and cool-ing-off period procedures* (4 points) | The practice of strik-ing is by far replaced by a compulsory arbitration system, with unions having a full voice in deciding proce-dures and choosing arbitrators (3 points) | Cumbersome legal procedures make "legal" strikes almost impossible, but many "illegal" strikes occur with-out government suppression of the strike or retal-iation against its leaders (2 points) | Few if any strikes allowed in practice; compulsory arbi-tration by the gov't; no union voice in deciding procedures or choosing arbi-trators (1 point) | Few if any strikes allowed in practice; no compulsory arbitration system (0 points) |
|---|---|---|---|---|---|---|
| Private, urban | | | | | | |
| Private, rural | | | | | | |
| Autonomous state enterprises | | | | | | |
| The Public Service | | | | | | |

*(If only certain industries or certain categories of strikes are affected by these procedures, give a score of 3½ points for that sector.)

(For the numerical score, add the total number of points)

situations presented on the "right to strike" page of the index. (See figure 4.)

*The right to political action.* The primary difficulty in considering figure 5 arises from the broad differences in national practice on types of political action engaged in by trade unions. In most of the world it is common for political movements of a social reformist nature to have two organization arms—a political party and a group of trade unions. Where this fused relationship prevails, the trade unions need not develop machinery for lobbying in the parliament, for the deputies from the movement the unions represent actually constitute a part of the parliament. An example of this pattern is the relationship between the DGB (union) and SPD (party) in West Germany. Where unions and parties remain separate, however, the lobbying function becomes very important, as in the United States, where both the AFL-CIO and most occupational federations maintain large staffs of lobbyists to deal with the Congress and the state legislatures. To German workers, freedom to lobby is not so important, because they have no need to exercise that right, while to U.S. workers the freedom to join with a political party into a single movement is of little concern because such a fusion is considered undesirable.

In the same way, variations in practice exist in regard to running union officers as candidates in national parliamentary elections, or to using the union movement to advocate a complete change in the system of ownership of the means of production. Some unions consider such actions vitally important, while others are totally disinterested in them.

To deal with such variations, the political-action page of the index does not measure the extent to which unions in each country engage in each type of political action. That is not the purpose of the index, which seeks instead to measure the degree of freedom allowed by the state. Therefore the index asks, "Are unions in practice free from prohibitions on exercising such of the following forms of political action as appear appropriate to the national circumstances?" If the unions appear free to engage in a certain type of political action, then the country should be given a "yes" answer for that item, even though its trade unions do not choose to undertake that type of activity.

*Freedom from specific restrictions.* This category is based on two ILO documents. One is a survey on "Freedom of Association and Collective Bargaining" made in 1973 by the Committee of Experts on the Application of Conventions and Recommendations.

The other is a digest published by the Freedom of Association Committee, which was created by the ILO's Governing Body in 1950. It is tripartite, composed of nine members drawn from the government,

# Figure 5 The Right to Political Action

| Sector: | Urban Private | Rural Private | Auton. State Enterpr. | The Public Service |
|---|---|---|---|---|
| Are unions in practice free from prohibitions on exercising such of the following forms of political action as appear appropriate to the national circumstances?: | | | | |
| Agitate for general social and economic reforms and changes in the system of ownership of the means of production? ...... | | | | |
| Assume a position in general opposition to the government in power and disseminate publicity critical of that government and its policies? ........ | | | | |
| Admit as candidates in freely contested union elections persons who favor joining the trade unions and a certain political party into a combined national political movement? | | | | |
| Lobby law-making bodies (parliaments, juntas) regarding labor's views on: | | | | |
| general economic, social, and political issues? ....... | | | | |
| wages, hours, working conditions, and trade union functions? ........ | | | | |
| Lobby executive-branch ministries regarding the details of implementing laws of decrees concerning: | | | | |
| general social, economic, and political policies? ...... | | | | |
| wages, hours, working conditions, and union functions? ........ | | | | |

Participate at the national level in mixed public/private commissions and boards which deal with such matters as minimum wages, economic development policy, etc?* .....

(The questions below pertain to countries in which contested elections determine who will hold political power at the national level. If no such electoral system exists, put a "no" for each sector on these four questions):

Formally endorse or condemn political parties or candidates campaigning for public office? ......................

Have their officials file as candidates for public office? ...

Coordinate participation of their members in the political campaign activities of parties or candidates favored by the unions? ..............................................

Coordinate contributions from their members to funds from which unions make donations to help finance campaigns of parties or candidates? ...............................
(In countries with public financing of campaigns, answer "not applicable" to this question, and count that as a "yes" answer in the total score)

*(Where such participation is by a national confederation to which unions in a given sector are affiliated, put a "yes" for that sector.)

111

employers', and workers' groups within the ILO Governing Body. The committee's task is to study complaints of violations of trade union rights and make recommendations to the Governing Body. In the past twenty-five years, this committee has dealt with over eight hundred cases and has codified into a digest the principles that these deliberations have produced.

The "specific restrictions" category in the index was developed by abstracting from the ILO materials a list of the forty most common specific government violations of trade union rights. Forty questions were then devised to ascertain whether unions were free from such restrictions. A nation's numerical score in this category is the total number of "yes" answers to these questions. (See figure 6.)

## APPLYING THE INDEX: A CASE STUDY OF LATIN AMERICA

Fortunately, great precision in the country rankings is not required by the uses for which the index is designed. Whether a country ranks 47th or 49th out of 110 nations is not important. Whether it ranks high, medium, or low is important, as is any considerable movement of a country up or down on the index over time. The ability of the index to indicate these general groupings and trends is suggested by a detailed consideration of workers' rights in some Latin American nations.

Before turning, however, to an analysis of labor freedom in Latin America, the reader should be able to place this analysis in the context of the rather dismal condition of workers' rights throughout the less developed world. Taking the world as a whole, the only areas in which workers enjoy a high degree of trade union freedom are Western Europe, North America, and the island nations of Japan, Australia, and New Zealand. In the communist countries we do not find a single free trade union in the entire arc from Eastern Europe to the USSR, North Korea, China, and Vietnam. Efforts to create free trade unions in Rumania and the USSR over the past two years have been snuffed out by arrests and deportations, just as demands for free unions were suppressed in Hungary in 1956, Czechoslovakia in 1968, and Poland in 1956, 1970, and 1976. In accordance with Marxist-Leninist theory, all labor organizations in those countries must be under the control and guidance of the ruling Communist Party.

In black Africa most labor movements are subject to widely varying degrees of government influence or control. Some of the movements with relatively greater autonomy are those in Senegal, Ghana, and Kenya. At the other end of the spectrum are the more tightly controlled unions in Ethiopia and Guinea. In Asia the pattern is similar—in addition to the fully controlled communist countries, labor in most of

# Figure 6
# Freedom from Specific Restrictions

1. Are the unions free from requirements that a government permit must be obtained before organizing of a union can be commenced?

2. Are the rural workers free from prohibitions on the entry of trade union officials into agricultural plantations for carrying on trade union activities?

3. Are the unions free from government-imposed requirements fixing the minimum number of members for a union, or the minimum percentage of workers in an enterprise who must join before a union can be formed, at such a high level that union organizing is seriously hindered?

4. Are unions free from legal requirements or de facto processes for registration of a union with, or granting of recognition or legal personality by, the government which allow arbitrary decisions at the discretion of executive-branch administrative officials on whether to accept such registration or grant such recognition?

5. Are the unions free from arbitrary power of executive-branch officials to certify a certain union as the exclusive bargaining agent for a given unit, without requirements that the officials apply objective criteria (such as unit elections to determine the most representative union)?

6. Are the unions free from legal requirements, dictating the form and content of union constitutions and by-laws, which violate the principles of freedom of association and which give the power of arbitrary approval or disapproval of such constitutions and by-laws to executive-branch authorities?

7. Are workers free from laws compelling them to join a certain union (usually that certified most representative) in order to keep their jobs?

8. Are the workers free from government prohibitions on workers of different races being members of the same union?

9. Are the unions free from the legal or de facto power of government executive-branch officials to "intervene" a union, imposing government-appointed leaders in place of the elected union leaders, or to dissolve a union, or to suspend its legal personality?

10. Are the unions free from limits imposed by the government in the name of "trade union unity" on the number of unions which can be organized at the enterprise, federation, or confederation levels?

11. Are the unions free from government requirements as to how many affiliated locals are needed for a federation to receive recognition by the state, or how many affiliated federations are needed for a confederation to receive state recognition?

12. Are the unions free from government-imposed compulsory affiliation to a certain national occupational federation or to a certain national confederation?

13. Are the unions free from government prohibitions on certain occupational sectors (for

113

# Figure 6—*Continued*

example, public servants or agricultural workers) joining together in federations with certain other occupational sectors?

14. Are the unions free from requirements that government permission must be obtained for labor unions to affiliate to international labor groupings?

15. Are union officials free from government restrictions on travel abroad to attend international labor meetings?

16. Are the unions free from government restrictions on visits to the country by representatives of international labor groups?

17. Are the unions free from government limits on the terms of office of elected union officials or on the right of such officials to be candidates for re-election?

18. Are the unions free from government requirements that elected union officials be employed in a certain occupation, or be employed by and/or work full-time at the enterprise, the workers of which the union represents?

19. Are the unions free from requirements that give the Ministry of Labor or other executive-branch administrative bodies the power to approve or disapprove union election results?

20. Are the unions free from government prohibition of those convicted of crimes being candidates for union office?

21. Are the unions free from legal or de facto government requirements that members and/or elected officials of unions must (or may not) belong to certain political parties or political movements?

22. Are the unions free from governmental legal or de facto authority to remove elected trade union officials from office by decision of state administrative authorities?

23. Are the unions free from the power of judicial authorities to dismiss elected union officials without having to apply precise criteria as to what acts warrant dismissal?

24. Are the unions free from legal or de facto requirements for government approval before a person can be a candidate for union office?

25. Are the unions free from laws or government regulations which allow employers to dismiss workers for engaging in normal trade union activity?

26. Are the unions free from requirements for government approval before union meetings can be held, and from any special requirements more onerous than those applied to applicants in general for parade and rally permits?

27. Are the unions free from requirements that a representative of the state be present during union meetings?

28. Are the unions free from requirements of prior government authorization to publish trade union publications, and from government censorship of those publications?

114

29. Are the unions free from arrest of trade union officials for engaging in trade union activity?

30. Are the unions free from searches of union offices by government officials lacking any judicially granted search warrants?

31. Are the unions free from requirements for government approval of trade union budgets and/or expenditures?

32. Are the unions free from dependence for their finances on a system under which the compulsory contributions of all workers are channeled through a state-controlled body?

33. Are the unions free from government bans on unions receiving financial or technical assistance from international labor groups?

34. Are federations of workers in a given occupational sector allowed to negotiate industry-wide on behalf of their various affiliated local unions?

35. Are collective agreements reached between workers and management free from requirements for prior approval by government authorities?

36. Are the unions free from limitations on the right to strike of workers of certain races?

37. Are the unions free from government prohibition on the calling of strikes by federations and confederations?

38. Are the unions free from government regulation as to how large a majority in favor of striking must be obtained in a strike vote before a union can declare a strike?

39. Are the unions free from government prohibition of strikes in essential services, which is not accompanied by adequate, impartial, and speedy conciliation and arbitration procedures in which the parties can take part at every stage?

40. Are the unions free from government prohibition of picketing during strikes?

(For the numerical score, add the total number of "yes" answers ) the area is subject to some degree of government influence. In some countries, such as Sri Lanka, labor is free.

In the Middle East and North Africa free unions are found in Turkey and Morocco; in Tunisia they are currently battling to remain autonomous. The brightest spot is Israel: unions are so powerful that Israel has sometimes been referred to as "a country with a union label." In most other Middle Eastern countries, labor is firmly under government control.

The general status of worker liberty in Latin America is not good, but on the whole the situation is certainly better than in communist countries, better than in the Arab nations, and certainly no worse than in Asia and black Africa.

Upon noting from the daily press that most Latin American nations are ruled by military regimes, the attentive newspaper reader would infer that trade unions must be in deep trouble in Central and South America. He would be correct in this conclusion, but what is not obvious from newspaper accounts is the wide variation in the degree to which trade union rights are respected in Latin America, not only between democracies and dictatorships, but even within these categories. To know that a Latin American country has a military government tells us little about the extent to which unions can be organized, contracts negotiated, and strikes called. Some military regimes have generally avoided oppressing labor, while others unleash campaigns of terror against labor leaders. The situation varies greatly from dictatorship to dictatorship, and often from time to time within each dictatorship. Among Latin America's democracies, some governments are much more liberal on trade union issues than others.

To illustrate the variety of situations, we have selected five cases. The governments in three of the cases were military regimes; the other two were civilian administrations. Our purpose is not to provide a comparison between the five countries at a particular time, but rather to compare certain kinds of situations, regardless of whether they all happened to coexist at the same moment. However, to keep the study topical, all five situations have been taken from one or another year of the late 1970's.

Basic information for the case study was obtained from published accounts of the status of workers' rights in Latin America in the mid-1970's.[3] To update this information, detailed interviews were conducted in 1978 and 1979 with persons working in or with the labor movements of the five countries concerned. Each interview lasted well over one hour, during which time the interviewee filled in each item on the work sheets of the index. Details about the various points were elicited by the interviewer. The persons interviewed were in many cases middle-level labor leaders from sectors of national labor movements associated with the political parties of the democratic left and affiliated to the Latin American labor organization ORIT. Others interviewed were European and North American labor specialists working in one of the five countries. All interviews were confidential. At least two persons were interviewed for each country; when their assessment of certain points differed, additional judgments were obtained from other knowledgeable sources. The authors feel the information on which the rankings in this article are based reflects fairly the views of democratic moderates concerned with labor in Latin America. (Rankings might vary somewhat from those obtained here if radical or conservative sources were to be interviewed).

The two cases of civilian rule chosen are Colombia in 1977–79 and the Dominican Republic under the administration of President Balaguer in 1977 and early 1978. In both cases, the governments in power were characterized by our sources as being conservative on social policy. In Colombia, the 1977–79 period began with President Alfonso Lopez Michelsen in office; presidential elections in June 1978 resulted in the accession to the presidency of Julio César Turbay Ayala in August. Both presidents represented the Liberal Party, which along with its only major competitor, the Conservative Party, is widely considered to reflect the interests of the higher-income groups in Colombia. Colombia has never developed a mass party of the democratic left, such as the Acción Democrática or the Aprista Party in the neighboring countries of Venezuela and Peru. Despite the conservative cast of Colombian politics, civil liberties and freedom for pluralistic institutions such as trade unions have been generally well observed.

The Dominican Republic does have a mass popular party, the PRD, which in 1977 was in opposition to the incumbent pro-business administration of President Joaquin Balaguer. (Later, in the May 1978 elections, the PRD came to power under President Antonio Guzman). Despite the dubious nature of the 1974 elections, from which the united opposition candidate withdrew because of fear of vote fraud, civil liberties appear to have been fairly well respected in the Dominican Republic under President Balaguer.[4]

The three cases of military regimes chosen for this sample are the situations in 1977 through early 1978 in Chile and Brazil, and 1976 through early 1977 in Ecuador. The policies of these governments toward labor varied widely. The Pinochet regime in Chile had almost totally repressed trade unions. Trade union elections, meetings, collective bargaining, and strikes all were banned. Many labor leaders had been jailed, beaten and exiled; and in the aftermath of the 1973 coup, some leftist leaders simply "disappeared." The Brazilian regime under General

Ernesto Geisel, continuing in the pattern set during President Vargas' *Estado Novo*, did not so much suppress trade unions as envelop them. Government stooges ("pelegos") were kept in leadership positions of many unions by various devices, and the government performed numerous functions (especially wage determination) that a large number of democratic theorists believe trade unions must do themselves if they are to be effective representatives of the workers' interests. (Beneath the surface of the apparently rigid system of control in Brazil, many local labor leaders not in the government camp were working to give their members effective representation. The pressures within Brazilian labor to break out of the *Estado Novo* mold produced the unprecedented wave of strikes in May 1978 and again in 1979. This case study ranks Brazilian labor's situation just prior to these events; interest is centered on the situation during the long period of military rule in Brazil from 1964 until the changes that began to appear in 1978).

The military government of Ecuador appears to have had a much better record from the time the triumvirate took power in January 1976 until it entered into a confrontation with labor beginning in May 1977. During this period the junta's rule was called a "dictablanda" (a mild dictatorship) rather than a "dictadura" (a harsh dictatorship), especially in comparison with the brutal repression in the "southern cone" countries of Argentina, Chile, and Uruguay. Trade unions in Ecuador in 1976 and early 1977 generally were able to organize, bargain freely, and sometimes strike, even under a military junta.[5]

*The right to organize.* In the cases of Colombia, the Dominican Republic, and Ecuador, our data indicate that workers were free to organize local unions and federations, *and* to elect freely leaders of their own choice, in the rural and urban private sectors, as well as in autonomous state enterprises. Only in Colombia, however, were even part of the public service workers allowed to organize trade unions. In Chile, Ecuador, and the Dominican Republic, only public employee "associations" were permitted. In Brazil, workers were free to organize only up to the level of national federations of unions in a given sector (communications, transport, etc.). No single national union confederation was allowed, and Brazilian unions were restricted in their choice of international labor groups with which they could affiliate.

Chile had the worst situation, because all trade union elections had been banned since the 1973 coup. The officers incumbent at the time of the coup simply continued, even if their terms of office had since run out. In rating Chile, we have given some credit for the existence of these unions with leaders who were at least elected freely at one time. In regard to affiliations with international groups, some Chilean unions remain affiliates of democratic Trade Secretariats and regional confederations, but affiliations to communist international labor bodies are banned.

When all the information on the right to organize is entered on the work sheets of the index, the resulting country scores are (out of 10):

| | |
|---|---|
| Colombia | 9.5 |
| Dominican Republic | 9 |
| Ecuador | 9 |
| Brazil | 5 |
| Chile | 4.5 |

The clearest distinction is not between the two civilian and the three military regimes, but between the regimes in Brazil and Chile on the one hand, and all the rest. (If Honduras [1977–78] were added to the sample, like Ecuador it would fall closer to the scores of the two civilian governments than to those of Brazil and Chile, even though Honduras also had a military regime).

*The right to bargain collectively.* None of the five sample countries granted public employees the right to bargain collectively; the differences between the countries lie in the private sector and some autonomous state enterprises. Colombia, the Dominican Republic, and Ecuador had unions in the private sector that usually could bargain freely on issues of wages, hours, working conditions, benefits, and trade union status. Autonomous state enterprise workers in all three cases were usually allowed to bargain over benefits and job security, but not over wages in Ecuador. In Brazil and Chile, collective bargaining was virtually unknown. Chile's score is equal to that of Brazil because we gave some weight to information that collective agreements signed before the 1973 coup remained in effect for those clauses which had not since been superseded by junta decrees. There was no indication that new contracts had been negotiated in Chile since the army seized power.

The total country scores on the right to bargain are (out of 32):

| | |
|---|---|
| Colombia | 24 |
| Dominican Republic | 24 |
| Ecuador | 16.5 |
| Brazil | 6 |
| Chile | 6 |

Again the dividing line between the two main groups of scores does not run between the civilian governments and the military regimes, but between the "dictaduras" on the one hand and the democracies and the "dictablandas" on the other.

*The right to strike.* The public employees' right to strike was so severely curtailed in all five sample countries that effectively it didn't

exist. In the private sector, only in Colombia and Ecuador was the right
to strike broadly respected. It was virtually unrestricted in practice in
Colombia, and limited in Ecuador only by unobjectionable requirements for compliance with mediation procedures before a strike could
be called legally. In the Dominican Republic strikes took place legally,
after a required period of conciliation, but once begun often were
terminated by labor courts, which then imposed obligatory arbitration
by the government. In both Brazil and Chile, few if any strikes were
allowed. Brazil required government arbitration of labor-management
disputes, whereas Chile gave the workers no recourse at all when their
demands were met by company intransigence.

When the details of the various national procedures concerning strikes
are compiled the country scores are (out of 20):

|                    |     |
| ------------------ | --- |
| Ecuador            | 11  |
| Colombia           | 10  |
| Dominican Republic | 4.5 |
| Brazil             | 4   |
| Chile              | 0   |

Although workers in the Dominican Republic could organize and bargain quite freely, they were severely restricted on the right to strike—
the right which would have given the workers real clout when negotiating. Our respondents attributed this to what they saw as the conservatism
and pro-business bias of the Dominican Republic's civilian government
under President Balaguer. The high score for Ecuador, which placed it
in the same range as democratic Colombia, shows that all is not
necessarily lost for the workers under a military regime. (The situation
for labor in Ecuador took a dramatic but temporary turn for the worse
after May of 1977.)

*The right to political action.* In many Latin American countries,
unions are much freer to undertake economic than political actions.
This is obviously the case in dictatorships, where the absence of elections
automatically deprives the trade unions of any opportunities to work
for candidates and parties of their choice in election campaigns. Under
the military government in Ecuador in 1976, for example, trade unions
were reasonably free to oppose the government publicly and to call
for social reforms, but there was little they could do in practice to change
the government without elections. Brazil and Chile were portrayed as
greatly restricting even non-electoral political activity by unions, but
as shown above, so was economic activity, such as collective bargaining.
The labor situation in those two countries was so bleak that no great
difference shows up in the rankings between economic and political
freedoms.

This difference did exist in practice under the civilian Balaguer government in the Dominican Republic, not because the government prohibited political action but because trade unions remained reluctant to test out how far they could actually go in politics. Under the decades of the Trujillo dictatorship, union political activity had been rigidly repressed. When Balaguer came into office, explicit restrictions were lifted, but an atmosphere of intimidation lingered on from the Trujillo days, reinforced by occasional assaults on labor leaders. The more politically oriented confederations, notably the Communist and Christian Democratic organizations, are said to have ventured farther into politics than did the other unions. The high ranking on political freedom for the Dominican Republic obscures the fact that little political activity was actually undertaken by labor during the Balaguer era.

In Colombia our data indicate that the freedoms of economic and political action went hand in hand. Trade unions were fully active, both in lobbying and partisan political activity, including work in election campaigns. Of the five sample countries, only in Colombia does it appear that the unions felt they could try to change the basic social power structure of the nation through political action. When this political information is listed on the index work sheets, the resulting scores are (out of 48):

| | |
|---|---|
| Colombia | 34 |
| Dominican Republic | 33 |
| Ecuador | 28 |
| Chile | 20 |
| Brazil | 17 |

*Freedom from specific restrictions.* The above general assessments of the status of the four main trade union rights are of interest to outside observers, but equally important to the trade union leaders in those countries is the daily freedom from, or subjection to, a large number of specific infringements of workers' rights. The country scores in regard to this category, as ranked on the index's list of 40 specific points, are (out of 40):

| | |
|---|---|
| Ecuador | 33.5 |
| Colombia | 30 |
| Dominican Republic | 27 |
| Brazil | 19 |
| Chile | 10.5 |

As expected, the regimes of Brazil and Chile, viewed as the most repressive, emerge as the most restrictive in specific application of their labor regulations. The Dominican Republic ranked in the middle.

Colombia and Ecuador appear the most permissive, with dictatorial Ecuador ranking surprisingly a bit higher than democratic Colombia in this category.

*Overall rankings.* Taking the scores in all five categories together, and giving each country five points for a first place, four for a second place, and so forth, the overall comparative rankings of the five countries are as follows (out of 25):

| | |
|---|---|
| Colombia | 23 |
| Ecuador | 20 |
| Dominican Republic | 19 |
| Brazil | 9 |
| Chile | 7 |

These overall rankings, like the more-detailed material presented above, show that there are notable differences in the degree of workers' freedom allowed, especially among the military regimes, but also between the two civilian governments.

*Conclusions for the case study and Latin America*:

The range in variation in union rights is so wide that a "dictablanda," like Ecuador in 1976, could be viewed as providing as free an environment for trade unionism as a civilian government such as the Dominican Republic.

Variations can be great between rights within a given nation. In the Dominican Republic, the data show that workers could organize and bargain freely, but strike only until arbitration was imposed, and engage in allowed political action only with considerable trepidation. In Chile, there also were variations—although the risk was certainly there, unions apparently spoke out on political issues to a surprising degree, while collective bargaining for new contracts remained totally banned.

The degree of freedom allowed to trade unions varies greatly over time in a given country, so new judgments must be made as the situation changes.

Though the spectrum of worker liberty in Latin America is a wide one, and there are a few bright spots such as Colombia and Venezuela, the situations range mainly through the dark end of the spectrum, reflecting the long night of military dictatorship in most of Central and South America.

There are no grounds for complacency about the existence of "dictablandas" in Latin America. The rulers always have the power to drop their tolerance of trade union activity overnight, as happened in Ecuador after May 1977. In the words of Martin Ward, Chairman of the International Affairs Committee of the AFL-CIO Executive Council: "Since arbitrary power, sooner or later, will always be abused, only the replacement of such power by popular rule can permanently end the threat of the torture chamber and the political dungeon."[6] Popular rule did return to Ecuador in 1979, and the trade unions greeted this event with expectations of greater security for workers' rights.

The wide variety of situations found and the abrupt changes in them make clear that worker freedom is not inescapably determined by socio-political conditions, nor is the existing situation likely to be permanent. There is a solid basis for hope that in Latin America we may soon see a shift of many countries from the dark to the bright end of the spectrum, bringing greater freedom for their workers.

## NOTES

1. Jenks, C. W., *The International Protection of Trade Union Freedom* (London: Stevens and Sons, 1957), pp. 21–22, 24–29, 357.

2. International Labour Conference, 1973, Report III, Part 4-B, *Freedom of Association and Collective Bargaining,* General Survey by the Committee of Experts on the Application of Conventions and Recommendations, p. 87; Also: International Labour Office, *Freedom of Association,* Digest of Decisions of the Freedom of Association Committee, 2d ed., (Geneva, 1976), pp. 122–123.

3. See especially the monograph *Trade Union Rights in Latin America,* Research Department, Inter-American Office, Postal, Telegraph and Telephone International, Washington, D.C., February, 1976. A more detailed version of this analysis was issued in Spanish by the PTTI in April, 1976, entitled *Las Condiciones de Trabajo en America Latina.* See also Rubén Rotondaro, "Trade Union Rights in Latin America," carried in the Spring, 1977 issue of *Comparative Labor Law.* For supplemental information, see *Libertad Sindical,* CTCA, Costa Rica, 1974.

4. Freedom House, in its January, 1978 survey, reflected this situation by giving the Dominican Republic a respectable "2" in its rankings on civil liberties, but only a mediocre "4" on political rights.

5. This article describes the situation in Ecuador prior to the general strike and the teachers' strike in May, 1977, and the massacre of 25 workers in October, 1977, which resulted in a political crisis, causing further serious violations of trade union rights. This situation points up how the iron hand can emerge very suddenly from the velvet glove of a "dictablanda."

6. Martin J. Ward, "Trade Unions, Human Rights, and Political Democracy," a paper presented at the Fifth Western Hemisphere Labor Economics Conference, Washington, D.C., November 13, 1979.

# PART III

# Country Studies:
# Iran and
# Zimbabwe Rhodesia

# The Struggle for Democracy in Iran

"The last few years have seen the modernizing authoritarian monarchy of Iran, a staunch and powerful ally of the United States in the Middle East, brought down by organized mob demonstration, only to be replaced by an obscurantist, populist, and repressive theocracy that is both unable and unwilling to operate either a modern economy or a democracy. A lesson to be drawn is that modernization and change cannot occur in backward countries without authoritarian systems to propel them. This being so, Americans need to avoid insisting on human rights in countries such as Iran. The result can only be slower growth and the eventual imposition of another regime equally or even more repressive than the one it replaced."

The foregoing is the lesson Euro-Americans have commonly drawn with the help of the media and its pundits. Yet I will argue that what has occurred is continuous with the history of struggle for democratic change in Iran, that this struggle is a meaningful part of Iranian history, and that there is in fact no moral or practical alternative to continuing its support. Democracy will only come to countries such as Iran after many false starts. Sooner or later responsible government will be achieved only through the hard experience of these attempts.

The lugubrious history of the Iranian Revolution of 1978–79 holds many lessons for all defenders of human freedom and humanity, if they can but read them. At the very least it provides an illustration of how historic struggles for freedom are determined in large part by the interaction of a wide variety of factors including current conditions, national histories, the movements of ideas, and the inevitable struggle between peoples desiring freedom and leaders desiring concentrated power. The final act of the struggle is, of course, determined by the way the actors play the earlier scenes. This drama is in turn subject to a set of laws that restrict the idiosyncracies of chance, laws that have been profitably studied by students of revolution.[1]

## THE COURSE OF REVOLUTION

The Iranian Revolution may be reviewed in terms of its initial context and successive stages.[2] In the mid-1970's the vast majority of Iranians acquiesced in the rule of the Shah. They enjoyed the benefits of good years without developing any deep commitment. More positive support came from those who had benefited most directly from his rule: the military, especially the officers, the "new" businessmen, the wealthier peasants who had benefited from land reform, the technocrats, most of the traditional elite, and the relatively highly paid skilled workers. But as pressure grew and appeals were made to the conflicting loyalties and the real grievances of these groups—corruption, income differentials, and irksome controls—their active support withered.

The protest movement that eventuated in Revolution had of course existed for years. Although its demands were various, almost all opposition groups agreed on the need to end repression, to return to constitutional monarchy, to spread the results of new income more evenly, and to change the long-standing pro-Western policy that included high military budgets and de facto support of Israel. The many branches of this opposition may be grouped most conveniently under 1) Shi'i clergy and their bazaari followers, strong within Iran (and Iraq), 2) middle class intellectuals and modernists, well represented everywhere in the Iranian community, and 3) radical leftists, especially common among students, some worker groups, and overseas Iranians. The first two strands of the opposition were able to openly continue their activities within Iran to a limited extent, while within Iran leftist groups, as well as some small fanatical religious groups, were necessarily almost entirely restricted to clandestine activity. The Freedom Front formed a bridge between clergy, students, and the older nationalist intelligentsia and was to provide the secular leaders of 1979 governments.

The first stage of the revolution, a period of reformist challenge, covered 1977 and the first half of 1978.[3] Leading intellectuals began to write openly on the mistakes of the government. In particular in June 1977 three leading members of the National Front wrote a widely distributed letter directly criticizing the Shah's rule and demanding wide-ranging reforms. (Two of the writers later served in the Bazargan government while the third was Shapour Bakhtiar.) The writers of such attacks were not imprisoned. Hundreds of lawyers and judges signed petitions demanding a return to the observance of the law.

Student demonstrations calling for the return of Ayatollah Khomeini in October and November 1977 led to clashes with security forces and several deaths. In January 1978 religious demonstrations in Qom led to more deaths; as a result all mosques in Teheran closed for a week.

The Qom deaths also led to nationwide mourning, as was traditional, forty days after the event. Riots in Tabriz on the occasion of this mourning led to more deaths; from now on forty-day intervals punctuated the events of the escalating movement.

During 1977 and early 1978 the government was making attempts at liberalization. Many prisoners were freed, torture declined, freedom of expression increased. But with more expression came more criticism, particularly from the intellectual parties. Parenthetically, perhaps for the first time the people learned of the severity of the repression as the prisoners emerged. By mid–1978 the Shah had abandoned the "one-party" he had organized only a few years before; everyone started to organize his own party, and multiparty elections were promised for 1979.

Liberalization stemmed from the Shah's desire to develop a "Spanish formula" that would allow his son at least to reign, from the persistent pressure of the United States under Carter's Human Rights program, and from the heightened willingness of students and intellectuals to speak out in this freer atmosphere.[4] But for whatever reason liberalizing moves only increased the pressure. In part this was because the organizing of the majority of Iranians that was at last occurring was the achievement of the clergy, while the liberalization that was occurring primarily served the interests or aspirations of students and intellectuals.

The second stage of the revolution (August–October 1978) represented an enhancement of the interplay of concession and demonstration. The Shah lifted most censorship, freedom of assembly was declared, the prime minister was replaced by one seemingly more religious, the Islamic calendar was restored, a cabinet position for women's affairs was eliminated. The arrests of merchants for economic crimes were halted. At last the real threat was understood and conciliation was directed at the alliance of the clergy and bazaar. And yet the riots got worse, the religious demonstrations bigger. Martial law was declared on "Black Friday." Hundreds were killed in Teheran and resulting mourning ceremonies drew immense crowds. The army was now being propagandized, infiltrated, and attacked; civilian armed groups grew, particularly the new groups organized by the clergy.

The "demands" of the opposition were becoming increasingly difficult to meet; the basic issue had become that of trust. Every liberalizing move was regarded publicly by the opposition as a deceitful trick. Meanwhile, free expression worked its will. Live broadcasts of parliamentary debates gave the public daily doses of denunciation of the system. (Although this legislature was to a degree "hand-picked" by the Shah, as things fell apart many members became strident supporters of the opposition.) Strikes led to substantial increases in wages, but the strikers turned to political demands. As Khomeini's intransigence and strength grew the other religious and secular leaders gradually fell in with his line, further reducing the possibility of compromise.

The third stage began in early November with bloody riots at Teheran University followed by extensive destruction in the capital. Military rule was proclaimed, but from this time on attacks and demonstrations were never effectively controlled. Military rule may have been indecisive in part because the Shah in his lingering fear of a military coup did not grant his commanders sufficient authority. The period was to be one of frustrated attempts to form a coalition that included opposition elements. Religious demonstrations became even larger, millions marched in Teheran and other cities demanding the replacement of the entire system and the creation of an Islamic Republic. Finally an important opposition intellectual leader, Shapour Bakhtiar, was persuaded to form a new government, on condition that the Shah leave. The Iran the Shah left Bakhtiar was one in which public administration had largely collapsed, a country the army felt no longer able to control. Parliament, the government, and the army existed in a state of enforced impotence from the Shah's departure on January 16 until the collapse on February 11, 1979. This regime offered all that had been wanted six months before, but the people could now be satisfied by nothing less than the destruction of the entire system and the elevation of the Ayatollah. With a few last battles the army surrendered the field and Khomeini and his committees took over Teheran. In the rest of the country resistance by isolated groups of soldiers soon faded. There had not been a civil war; deaths in the last few days were in the hundreds. Not a town or a large military unit mounted a sustained resistance.

The fifth stage of the revolution lasted from February 1979 through the end of the year. A government representing the more religious and less modernized of the intellectual party leaders, and appointed by Khomeini, came into existence alongside his more powerful Revolutionary Council with its network of local religious committees, religious courts, and Muslim militia. The Revolutionary Council retained the real power. The disarray of the prerevolutionary security forces, the de facto local power that emerged, and the success of some autonomist movements (especially in Kurdistan) made the sorting out and restructuring of power a slow and difficult process. Through a series of confrontations the secular government steadily lost power. The widely boycotted midsummer election of the Council of Experts (essentially a constituent assembly) led to rewriting a mixed, essentially liberal draft constitution into one dominated by the highest religious authorities. Foreign ministers were forced out for dealing with the West, opposition newspapers were closed or put under new supervision, separatist movements were violently attacked.

A comparison of the leading paper, *Ettela'at* over the last two years suggests that by fall 1979 the gains for press freedom achieved in 1978 and early 1979 had largely evaporated. Ayatollah Shari'atmadari was the main opposition voice still reported. However, in private there was certainly more open discussion of political questions than during the height of the Shah's rule.

The occupation of the U.S. Embassy in November and the subsequent hostage question led immediately to the downfall of the civilian government, and the resignations of Bazargan and Bani Sadr, prime minister and foreign minister respectively. Their resignations underlined the anarchical conditions even in Tehran. The government could not resist the occupying students because they had Khomeini's backing, but perhaps also because even support for Khomeini was unreliable. The referendum on the constitution that followed was perfunctory. Abstention was common, notably among Kurds, Baluchis, and Azerbaijanis.

In early 1980 a new breeze began to blow. The presidential campaign under the new constitution was not an open election, many candidates were denied equal access arbitrarily or ideologically; no one was allowed to oppose the system. Yet it was a secret ballot and voters could choose among a wide variety of candidates. Religious leaders were asked not to compete. Most voters chose Bani Sadr, only recently demoted as the result of the embassy occupation. The drawn-out parliamentary elections were poorly organized, but they offered a choice between individuals and groups from an even broader spectrum. A few "separatists" and far leftists were excluded, but not the regular communists. Of course, open criticism of the new system remained muted.

The Soviet invasion of Afghanistan, experience with the anarchy of the last months, reviving accusations of corruption, brutality, and inefficiency against the new order, and even the Ayatollah's illness might help the emerging elected government to establish a more democratic and responsible order. Yet when this went to press, several areas remained beyond central government control, parallel governments of mullahs and bureaucrats existed at every level of government along with parallel security forces, and semi-clandestine radical bands of left and right continued to exist alongside the disorganized security services.

## EXPLANATIONS OF THE REVOLUTION

Why did the Revolution occur and why did it succeed with such relative ease? The explanation of the theorists must lie in carefully describing the basic general weakness of the structure of control and why specifically there was a serious crisis at this time. In the first yearbook Cottam explained that a regime cannot continue to survive if it does not effectively and persuasively manipulate nationalist and religious symbols.[5] The weakness of the Shah's position was that he had failed to persuasively identify his regime with these symbols. He was regarded as a U.S. tool after his reestablishment of power with U.S. help, his continued identification with U.S. causes, and the purchase of American arms.[6] His father's activities, his own reforms, and particularly his covert support of Israel had blackened his record with the clergy. Therefore, his continued power was wholly dependent on steadily increasing the material rewards of the population and maintaining control over a repressive security force.[7]

Many theorists would generalize that after a long period of rising material standards and expectations, economic setbacks are likely to cause smoldering disaffection to burst into flame.[8] Largely because of oil revenues Iran had been dramatically improving its GNP/capita for several years. This improvement had to some extent reached the population as a whole through a combination of land reform and the influx of surplus rural labor into urban areas for new employment opportunities, particularly in construction. Yet in 1976–1978 the buildup had overreached itself; unemployment and inflation became more serious.[9] In addition, many educated Iranians had become displeased at the increasing dependence of the country on imported foodstuffs and very expensive advanced military technology, making necessary an influx of American technicians.

While the economic bonanza of oil revenues benefited all business, it tended to further shift the center of economic power from the traditional bazaar merchants and money lenders to modern capitalists with connections in court circles. The shift had also been a social shift in that the style of life and loyalties of the bazaari, even when wealthy, generally remained those of traditional Islam. The resentment of the bazaar was further deepened when the Shah courted popularity in 1974 by fighting inflation through sending 10,000 largely untrained inspectors into the bazaar with the power to punish merchants on the spot for profiteering and hoarding. They levied instant fines (or summary recommendations of stiff fines), closed shops, and deported merchants to remote areas. Thousands were imprisoned or deported without redress; 150,000 awaited trial when the inspectorate program was abandoned in mid–1978. The Shah had attempted to win popularity by attacking the class that had poured millions into Muslim welfare funds giving the clergy for the first time ample funds for political action or strikes.[10]

Three further weaknesses of the Shah's position should be mentioned. First, he persisted in supporting the largest overseas contingent of students of any country in the world.[11] These students were bound to resent the anachronisms of the regime and the difficulty of finding adequate opportunities outside of the bureaucracy on their return. For whatever reason, ideologically most overseas Iranian students lived in an unrelieved atmosphere of anti-Shah activism that the regime was unable to control. Secondly, the military forces were anything but homogeneous and self-confident. The Shah had carefully seen to the persistent separation of the services. He saw to the continual shifting of commands, preventing even communications among top officers that were not under his staff's control. It was a conscript army in which officers and men lived in different worlds.[12] Finally, the Iranian is a survivor, a person who characteristically hedges his bets, who sees little wrong in shifting his loyalties when it is in his interest. Dying to the last man out of loyalty to an individual has not been a characteristic of Iranian troops. (Dying for an idea, however, is in the Iranian tradition, but as we said above the Shah was never able to achieve popular identification with a significant idea.)[13]

These are the bare bones of causation. But here we are not so much interested in causation as in how the revolution and its aftermath fit in with Iranian tradition, how it expressed the democratic yearnings of this people. To do this let us first look at the religious aspect of the movement.

## THE RELIGIOUS INSTITUTION AND POPULAR HOPES

In 1979 Ayatollah Khomeini established, at least for a few months, an Islamic Republic, the dream of Islamic religious leaders since shortly after the time of Muhammed. In establishing the Islamic Republic Khomeini has been able to reject over a thousand years of Islamic history; indeed, he rejects Iranian history, for to him monarchy is not Islamic, or even reconcilable to Islam. Yet in the real world Iran has *always* been ruled by a monarch.[14]

We must understand Khomeini's dream to understand Iran, to understand the Islamic world, even to understand the longings that will sooner or later emerge of all peoples.

The Prophet Muhammed came from a middle class Meccan trading family.[15] When his revelation came to him he established a religious discipline that for a while allowed the more urbanized people of western Arabia to subdue and unite the more numerous and powerful tribes of Arabia with the cement of religious faith. After Muhammed, the first four "caliphs" (successors) were chosen through consensus by the community leaders of the faith, which increasingly meant that they were chosen by military leaders or important administrators. After the fourth caliph, Ali (the Prophet's son-in-law), military leaders and their male progeny came to rule Islamic countries. Therefore, in the eyes of the Islamic clergy, after Ali the de facto political leaders were no longer legitimate leaders, but usurpers to be suffered with varying degrees of acquiescence. This split between the ostensible power of God and man was particularly galling for Muslims because being highly legalistic and organizational in intent the Koran and Islamic tradition offer no legitimacy to a secular, political sphere separate from the religious. The depth of secular betrayal has been deepened for Shi'i divines because Shi'ism developed after Ali's death as a minority sect in Islam particularly concerned with the deprivation of the Muslim community of its legitimate leaders.[16] Its first martyrs to the tyranny of secular princes were the grandsons of the Prophet. The exaggerated suffering of Shi'i mourning celebrations have become its characteristic religious observance. Thus, although at times the Shi'i religious leaders attained power under the kings of Iran, the ostensible tradition has been one long record of usurpation. The identification of modern tyrants with the oppressors of the first martyrs has become an explicit part of commemoration of the ancient martyrdoms.

In Iran the tradition opposing Islamic legitimacy to secular monarchy has been sharpened in the last few centuries by historical events setting the country quite apart from the rest of the Islamic world. Safavid monarchs of Turkish descent established in the fifteenth to seventeenth centuries the borders of modern Iran and with or without force converted it to the "Twelver" sect of Shi'ism. At first they established their legitimacy by supporting a new class of theologians that were in part their creation, and by the unusual and heretical claim to be themselves divine incarnations. As the Safavids weakened and the special claims were forgotten, the doctrine that the *only* legitimate law was Islamic law as interpreted in each age by living mujtahids (religious authorities) came to be widely propounded.[17] The idea that the real ruler was the mujtahid and the king was only to be his minister, advanced in the seventeenth century, is closely paralleled by the relation established in the new Iranian Constitution between Khomeini and the prime minister. This doctrine was developed through centuries of weak Iranian monarchs and emerges today with renewed force in the views of Khomeini and his followers.

The heart of Islam has always remained the middle and lower middle-class bazaar where it began. The rulers of Islamic countries have almost universally come from upper-class or military backgrounds; frequently they have been tribal nobles of imperfect or very recent literacy. Such leaders needed the "technocrats" from the bazaar's religious schools, the limited legitimation they offered, and the money and trade of the bazaar, but the relationship was never an easy one, or one of mutual respect.

Socially, the extreme separation of the sexes and the prohibitions on liquor, drugs, and music were middle-class town conventions observed sporadically if at all in tribe or village. Particularly in Iran the consumption of alcohol was a common part of courtly life, further condemning this life in the eyes of the faithful.[18]

Looking at the history of Islamic countries Islam appears to have laid a foundation for tyranny and authoritarianism. But looked at from the vantage point of Islamic history and theology, Islam appears to have played a freeing and democratic role. The Iran Islam overwhelmed in the seventh century was rigidly divided into hereditary classes; even religious leadership was a hereditary privilege. Islam changed this world into one in which all believers were equal before the law, and poor peasants and tradesmen were able to rise to positions of importance. It was the contrast of this freeing effect of the Islamic faith and law with the hereditary and arbitrary principles of monarchical government and the uncontrolled imposition of secular taxes and arbitrary punishment that has been taught to countless generations of Iranian theology students.

It should be added that monarchical legitimacy has seldom had a secure basis even in secular terms. Since the Arab conquest, Iran's rulers have been foreigners for all but a few years; ruling groups were generally of Turkish tribal origin. The Pahlavi's were Iranian natives. On the other hand, they had no background in an old and honored family that could validate their pretensions in a society that still identifies leadership with lineage.

Traditionally the religious leader has acted as a go-between for the average person. He has been a mediator that the government had to listen to because of his direct access to the people of the bazaar and mosque. The chief spokesmen of the clergy in Shi'i Islam were the mujtahids (or ayatollahs), those who could directly interpret God's law in light of changing circumstances. Although without formal organization or hierarchical relations, such leaders were to be found in many towns, and cities would have several mujtahids. In each era, however, a few mujtahids would be widely recognized by most Shi'as in the Iranian area as preeminent.[19]

In modern times the mujtahids showed their power in the campaign mounted against the tobacco concession granted an English concern by the Shah in 1890–92.[20] For years Iranians had increasingly been upset by growing foreign influence; even before this concession was publicized religious leaders were speaking out against the government. The tobacco concession became the symbol of their discontent. Opposition was slowly mobilized, with religious leaders fomenting demonstrations in one city and then another. The exiling of two of the more important leaders only increased their influence, for now they, like the leading Shi'a mujtahid resident in Iraq, were beyond government control. Their movement could be orchestrated between distant cities and from Iraq because the invention of the telegraph provided a tool never before available (kept open paradoxically for the agitators by the English who built and controlled the lines). Finally the leading Shi'i divine declared from his Iraqi sanctuary that smoking was forbidden until the concession was cancelled. He was universally obeyed, and under the threat of a holy jihad, the government capitulated. For whatever reason the ulama failed to press for the more extensive changes in government they had been demanding, but they had established their power.

In the revolution of 1905–06 the alliance of mujtahids and the bazaar was again crucial for popular success. There soon developed a split within the clergy between liberals and conservatives fearful of any alternatives to holy law. Initially the liberal clergy were dominant and the king was forced to grant a Western-style constitution, to place his rule for the first time under limits. Iran thus became one of the first parliamentary states in the Middle East.[21] Although it was a period of chaos Iran retained constitutional forms and considerable civil liberty, at least in Teheran, until 1921.

In the 1920's Reza Khan, an army officer and the father of the recently deposed Shah, destroyed the Qajar monarchy. But when he crowned himself Reza Shah he effectively blocked the establishment of a truly independent and stable democracy that might have followed the elimination of the direct foreign intervention characteristic of the preceding period. The independence of ethnic minorities, tribes, and landlords was crushed. Reza Shah was openly contemptuous of the clergy, took education and the administration of the law away from them, drafted theology students into the army, prohibited important religious ceremonies, and introduced hated Western customs into social life.[22]

There was both a religious revival and a revival of democratic life under the relaxed early years of his son's reign after 1941. It seemed at last that the constitution of 1906 might be made to work. Then in 1951 the assassination of the prime minister by a radical religious group began the tumult of the Mossadegh years. Again one of the most important political actors was a religious leader, Ayatollah Kashani, a reactionary political leader as unwilling as the conservatives of 1905 (or Khomeini) to accept the idea that a secular constitution should have precedent over sacred law.[23] In 1951–1952 Kashani could bring larger numbers onto the streets than his competitors, yet by 1953 he had alienated so much of the bazaar and of his fellow clergy that the intellectual Mossadegh captured the nationalist leadership. Still without Kashani the parliamentarians could not command the crowds they needed in their crucial showdown with the military. In the end it was the crowds brought together by the conservative mullahs of Teheran that made possible the Shah's return.[24]

After 1954 the Shah ruled, but liberalization was again tried at the beginning of the 1960's. In 1963 reimposition of the Shah's one-man rule resulted in an outburst of religious rioting in the bazaar; the rioting soon developed into the most serious threat to the monarchy since 1953. The outbreak was led by the yet relatively unknown Ayatollah Khomeini; its suppression led to his expulsion, and contributed to his ultimate rise to national leadership.

Khomeini's success in bringing together the disparate elements opposed to the Shah in the late seventies can also be credited in part to the Shi'i doctrine of *taqiyye* that allows a pious Muslim to dissimulate his true beliefs.[25] Khomeini convinced his Western and liberal Iranian supporters that his goals were essentially limited. Shortly before his victory they could assert: "The Shi'ites are not interested in running the country, whatever the impression conveyed by the news media."[26] In spite of his earlier religious writings condemning the Constitution of 1906, Khomeini now appeared to say that he advocated restoring the Constitution of 1906,[27] and that the Shah's support for free elections would be the decisive change he desired. Neither could have been true statements of his intention.

It is significant that the first successful linking of modernist with traditional Islam in opposition to the Shah was engineered by the converted Armenian Malkam Khan and the chameleon Sayyed Jamal ad-Din al-Afghani.[28] Afghani posed as a Sunni religious reformer from Afghanistan, and as such became influential among both modernist and religious (anti-foreign) circles throughout the Islamic world. While propagandizing effectively in Iran, however, he revealed that he was really an Iranian Shi'a (and not from Afghanistan as his name deliberately suggested). His most effective work in Iran was in 1890 when from the sanctuary of a religious shrine he organized a secret society and taught his followers the technique of using appeals to religious traditions as a basis for attacks on the government. Thus while Khomeini has successfully disguised the rigidity of his medieval beliefs to achieve a traditional Islamic restructuring of society, Afghani disguised his essentially modernist goals to launch Iran into the constitutionalist era. In the Iranian context both clearly felt their ends more than justified their means.

In summary, the Islamic religious institution in Iran has traditionally played an important role in protecting the common people against arbitrary rule, both on a day-to-day basis and through mobilizing the people when opportunity arose to reclaim some of their always meager rights. Thus, what appears to the West as the black reaction of the mullahs appears as a populist expression of democratic hopes in the Iranian context.

A recent Iranian commentator has pointed out that Iranian religion and even the figure of Khomeini transcend Islam. Iranian Zoroastrianism and the Manichaeanism it produced depicted the world as an eternal struggle between good and evil, light and dark, Satan and God.[29] The ability of Ayatollah Khomeini to convincingly picture the world in these terms suggests that this unshaded view is still religiously dominant. It is also well to remember that "assassin" originally meant a fanatic disciple of the Isma'ili religious sect, sent forth from the sect's Iranian fortresses to purify the world of evil.

Iranian religiosity has many facets. The mystic, neo-Platonist, or Sufi tradition has been most important in art and literature; it was out of this tradition that much of Iranian poetry, Iranian art's most prized possession, was directly or indirectly evolved. Sufism always lived uneasily with the legalistic, worldly religion of the majority, and has been roundly condemned by many of the mujtahids or ayatollahs. The two strands of belief unite in their worship of God, but lead in different directions. In place of the rigidity and narrowness of traditional Islam, Sufism tends to be tolerant of all sects and religions, of wine and sex, of spiritual intoxication, and of a variety of heresies. Sufism has infected the thinking of Iranians at all social levels; it has inspired conservative Muslims, clergymen, and atheists. Unfortunately for democracy, its teaching leads to withdrawal, separation, and escape. Historically Sufi leaders have often played a leadership or mediator role similar to that of the mujtahids.[30]

Closely allied to the Sufi phenomenon is the religious creativity that has played such a large part in Iranian history. The proliferation of new sects that has characterized this history represents both the periodic tendency of individual Iranians to megalomania, to a belief that they are the appointed of God, or indeed God Himself,[31] and the tendency of popular dissatisfactions to be given religious form. Two examples are particularly important.

In a time of popular distress fifth century Iranians turned to a neo-Platonist, Zoroastrian priest for help. This Mazdak urged his starving followers to plunder the granaries of the wealthy, even of the king, and then convinced the king that religion demanded that the grain be divided. He taught that envy, anger, and hatred stemmed from desire and greed, and that these enemies of God could only be defeated by the division of wealth and the abolition of private property, including women. Property was divided so thoroughly that when a counterrevolution finally succeeded, special laws had to be enacted for the recovery of women and other property and the reestablishment of inheritance rights. The peasants managed to maintain some of their gains in spite of the counterrevolution. In the end Mazdak and his followers were slaughtered, yet revival of this sect was considered a threat to established Islamic monarchs hundred of years later.[32]

A characteristic belief in Islam (as in Zoroastrianism and other faiths) is in a saviour (Mahdi) who will return one day to mankind. Out of this tradition Baha'ism arose in nineteenth century Iran, a faith that later in international guise was to become a universal synthesizer of all religions. In Iran itself Baha'ism has been persecuted almost from the first, but it has at the same time gained adherents, particularly among surviving groups of the ancient Zoroastrian community. It appeals to some Iranians because of its modernism, its transitional nature, but to others perhaps because of the secrecy and air of mystery that surrounds it. Unfortunately, the traditional Islamic clergy has seen fit to portray the movement as traitorous to the nation and to regard its followers as heretics outside the law. That in the last few years they came to be identified with a monarch suspected of comparable crimes exposed them in 1979 to particular risk. (Although Baha'i properties have been attacked and confiscated, the extent of post-revolutionary individual oppression is unclear.)

It should also not be forgotten that Muslim intellectuals in Iran and throughout the Middle East have been much affected by the modernist ideas of Afghani and his many successors. Iranian mujtahids represent a wide range of ideological beliefs and degrees of submission to the literal word of the seventh century. The late Ayatollah Taleqani became a leader of the liberals during the revolutionary period, and his followers in the youth-dominated Mojahedin-e-Khalq continue to follow his line. Ayatollah Shari'atmadari has a nationwide, more conservative following, particularly strong in Azerbaijan. His careful pronouncements more adequately fuse faith with the desirability to separate religion and politics. Shaikh 'Ezz-ud-Din Husaini, the religious and political leader of the Kurds, expresses a similar moderate view.[33]

For most young educated Iranians the man who made Islam palatable was the modernist intellectual Ali Shari'ati (died 1977). Like Afghani, Parvaiz in Pakistan, and other modernists, Shari'ati strove to present Islam in a modern guise to a world familiar with Marx, Freud, and Darwin.[34] His rejection of the role of the mullahs and his emphasis on individual interpretation must, however, have caused his followers to seriously question Khomeini's Islamic order once this became dominant in 1979.

## THE FURTHER COMPLEXITY OF POPULAR INTERESTS

The hope of Iranian democracy may also be found amid a plethora of localistic and nationalistic appeals lying at right angles to the appeals of either the Shi'i clergy or leftwing modernizers. These come first from the tribes, which are generally not of Persian origin. Although most tribesmen are now settled peasants or townspeople, their leaders command a considerable following among the families and retainers of past chiefs. Tribal troops were the only effective forces in the country for most of its history, and the most effective military movements against the regime have been mounted by the tribes, most recently in 1963—when the clergy's struggle in Teheran was paralleled by a major tribal revolt in the South. However, in 1978–79 we have heard little of the power of tribal chieftains.

Attention has been focused instead on ethnic nationalism in recent years, particularly among the Kurds of the west, the Turkoman of the northeast, and the Arabs of the oil fields. Within living memory these peoples have had considerable independence, although not as national units. The Kurds have a long history of struggle against centralized government. In the nineteenth century Kurdish uprisings were often led by religious leaders or in terms of conservative Islamic symbols.[35] The more modern nationalism of this century is led by religious, leftist, and tribal notables. With millions in several states, the Kurds have a good claim to self-determination (and because of our shameful 1975 sellout of Barzani's movement in Iraq, the United States has an additional moral responsibility to support their claim.) The largest ethnic minority in Iran is the Azerbaijani. Yet since these Turkish-speaking people have played a decisive role in Iranian life for hundreds of years and have had a major role in modern Iranian nationalism, I find it unlikely they will see their interest in separation, unless separatism emerges as an expression of opposition to the ideological direction of a Teheran government.

The claims of Iran's ethnic minorities to self-determination have run up against Iranian nationalism—a belief by many Iranians of all ideologies in a unitary, powerful, and centralized state. Nevertheless, because the early stages of the Revolution granted territorial minorities greater control over their affairs, it served the purpose of advancing the self-determination of these Iranians—just as the general diffusion of power to local government enhanced the self-determination of all Iranians.

Shifting the angle of our focus a little further the Iranian nationalism that looks askance at minority movements, in turn, runs up against the Islamic universalism preached by the clergy. To the clergy the holy language of Iran is Arabic. Their training gives them natural affinity with Arabic causes, such as that of the Palestinians. It is true that Shi'ism is the dominant sect of Islam only in Iran, yet to the clergy this unfortunate fact is immaterial alongside the universal claims of Islam. To the clergy the first places of pilgrimage are Mecca and Medina, after this come the special Shi'i shrines of Najaf and Karbala in Iraq—on the third rung are the shrines of Qom and Mashhad in Iran.

Iran's bourgeois nationalists, even when anti-Shah, have for generations seen the Arab invasion as *the* great tragedy of Iranian history. To them Iran has a distinct culture from which Arab and Turkish elements should be excised. Indeed, credit for much of the calamitous medieval history of Iran is placed on Arabs and Turks, just as the disasters of this century are blamed on Russians, British, and Americans. This is the Iranian nationalism Shapour Bakhtiar echoed recently when he said, "Iran existed before Islam. I am Iranian and a human being before being Muslim."[36]

Many modern nationalists are still good Muslims; many more are not. Most modern Iranian literature has been blatantly anti-Islamic, contemptuous of the traditionalist clergy and their following.[37] It was humorous, but also sad, to watch modern Iranians mouth the slogans of Islam and put on the chador when Khomeini became the vehicle for overthrowing the Shah. For most educated Iranians Ayatollah Khomeini and strict observance of Islam are likely to be passing fads. Indeed, for this group, and most Iranians will become educated, the eventual downfall of Khomeini will be likely to destroy forever the romance of traditional religion.

Politically many members of the secular, modernist, educated class are left-wing; many more are essentially just striving to be part of the modern world as the media transmit it to them. It cannot be stressed too often that this modernized bourgeoisie forms a sizeable group both within and without Iran: it could not be otherwise with over 80,000 students overseas before the Revolution. When estimating the potential of this educated group in the political life of the country we should remember that India's relatively successful democracy is organized primarily by the three percent of the Indian population that speaks English.

Traditional Islam is not a religion of love, and Iranian history is a seldom-relieved story of cruelty. The Shah's willingness to accept torture as an aspect of governance is undeniable. Many of Ayatollah Khomeini's pronouncements suggest that he too would show little compassion. In a recent speech at a theological school he pointed out:

Islam grew with blood . . . For those who could be guided, the Koran

was their means of guidance; yet for those who could not be guided
and were plotters, the sword descended on their heads. Islam is a
religion of blood for heretics . . .[38]

Yet peoples evolve. Medieval Christianity was equally cruel. And liberalizing Iranians can equally quote the universalism of a poet such
as Sa'adi when he wrote: "The sons of Adam are parts of one another
created in the beginning from one seed. When one part is pained, the
other parts cannot remain unconcerned. No one should be called a man
who is not concerned with the troubles of others."[39] It is on the basis
of such sentiment that nationalist Iranians must build the sense of
humanity and respect for other opinions without which political and
civil rights can never be secured.

I have dwelt this long on the complexities of certain aspects of the
Iranian social and political scene in order to make the point that Iran
is not simply a backward country in which reactionary traditionalists
battle against progress, or exploiting capitalists struggle to maintain
privileges in the face of the demands of the poor.

The complexity of the argument has also been developed in order to
lay a more adequate groundwork for considering the sense it makes to
try to support political rights and civil liberties in Iran. The picture
developed above suggests that with the conflicting demands of the many
types of Iranians justice can only be provided by a pluralistic society.
Secondly, I have tried to show how the intermittent struggle of factions
in Iran, particularly the struggle of the clergy with the monarchy, has
represented one form of the eternal struggle of people to defend their
values as they see them against arbitrary power.

## DEMOCRACY ON THE FRONTIER

In the worldwide struggle for modern political and civil freedoms
Iran lies on the "democratic frontier." Constitutional democracy developed in Europe and North America and spread more or less successfully to the colonies of the Euro-American democracies.[40] The most
persistent attempts to spread democracy in areas without democratic
traditions have been made in Latin America. Many Americans are
inclined to smile at Latin American democracy. But democracy has in
fact provided hundreds of years of freedom to Latin Americans. And
at the beginning of 1980 Latin America had at least six operating democracies, in addition to several Caribbean democracies.

Democratic concepts also diffused from Western Europe and the
United Kingdom to Eastern and Southern Europe and the Middle East.
Democracy has had a rocky, but not entirely unsuccessful, course in

Central and Eastern Europe. Its achievements have fundamentally been blighted by outside interference. To the south the Mediterranean states have repeatedly gained and then lost democratic liberties since they were first attained in the nineteenth century. Today, democracy functions along the whole southern flank, in Portugal, Spain, Italy, and Greece. Although beset with problems, Turkey and Israel are democracies, while ethnically divided Cyprus and Lebanon try to preserve as much liberty as they can.

The ideas of the modern world, including political and civil liberties, had hardly penetrated Iran in 1850. Then, through Turkey and Russia, through the media of traveling Englishmen and Iranians returning from Europe, constitutionalist concepts came flowing in. The most important example for Iran was Turkey (the Ottoman Empire) which, more exposed to Europe, took on European ways of life more quickly than Iran. After World War I the reforms of Ataturk were copied by Reza Khan, to be copied in turn by King Amanullah in Afghanistan. Unfortunately this was the age of Mussolini, and Mussolini served as an example to Ataturk that was copied in turn by the new Persian king. Russian experience was also crucial in this awakening. It was not by chance that Iran's constitutionalist revolt of 1905–06 corresponded with events in Russia—and with the Japanese defeat of the Russian monarch.

When Iranian intellectuals looked for the ideas on which their new society should be founded, they learned from the English who both repressed and supported their democratization; from France, the intellectual mentor of the older generation of Iranians; and from the smaller European countries, such as Belgium from which much of the 1906 Constitution was borrowed.

Since World War II the struggle for democracy in the Iranian region has been intense. Turkey has largely succeeded in achieving a working system, thanks to the growth of party organization and a tough military willing to intervene but not to rule. Democracy in Greece emerged from the struggle with communism that followed the war, only to be submerged by the colonels in the 1960's. With tyranny now overcome democracy in Greece seems to have even better prospects than in Turkey.

Post-World War II glimmers of democratic rule in Iraq were completely crushed by a succession of leftist military regimes. Experiments with limited democratic forms developed in Afghanistan in the early fifties; and a semi-democratic system in 1963–73 was crushed by military force, later to be replaced by a weakly based, Soviet supported communist intellectual tyranny. In spite of repeated tries Pakistan has never quite made it to a fully democratic society. There have been some years with a fair degree of freedom: its relatively strong press and educated class, even much of the military is democratic by inclination and aspiration if not action. Unfortunately, Pakistan's inability to achieve legitimacy as a nation, even in the eyes of its own people, has made democratic development extraordinarily difficult. Further east, India and Sri Lanka have had remarkable success in preserving democratic forms in societies economically much poorer than Iran's.

It is on this democratic frontier that the Iranians have struggled for popular freedom since World War II. In the first years much was achieved. But the challenge to the Shah by Mossadegh and the repression following his defeat led to a gradual wearing away of the democratic freedoms of the country. It seems apparent that for many years, even as late as 1963, the Shah agreed with the educated classes that Iran should be a democratic state, because that is what "modern" states were. But the Shah also wanted unchallenged rule, and the two desires proved in the end to be incompatible.

Essentially an anarchical people, Iranians have been, and are likely to remain, poor at organizing political parties. The communist, Tudeh, party achieved considerable organization by 1953 but was destroyed. Even then its strength among the peasants and working class was never extensive. The Shah was notably unable to organize an effective party in his own support, either in a one- or two-party state. The Ayatollah's Islamic Republican Party appears to be an ad hoc group formed for present purposes; it is likely to collapse as new problems and leaders arise.

Yet aside from the extreme left and that part of the clergy that denies the legitimacy of both legislation and liberal tolerance, the bulk of Iranian opinion wants a competitive democracy, and a predictable legal structure with a considerable scope for civil liberties. Their inability to institutionalize a viable democratic process does not negate this recurrent desire.

Iran will remain for generations a difficult land in which to institutionalize democracy. Yet I suggest Iranians will repeatedly try, that they will be unsatisfied with anything else, and that in fact no other system will be found more "suited" to them. For all the propaganda and all the glorification and all the reforms, when the Shah fell only a handful stood by him. Whether they were peasants or university graduates, teachers or army officers, Iranians simply had not liked living with the fear and arbitrariness of tyranny. If the Revolution establishes a new tyranny, these people will soon feel cheated and strive again for freedom. In this struggle American actions cannot be decisive, but certainly we have a responsibility not to turn our back and once again opt for the false security of tyranny in the wishful belief that this is what the Iranian people really want.

## THE DEMOCRATIC VERSUS MARXIST ANALYSIS OF IRAN

The Marxist interpretation of history is commonly applied by Iranian intellectuals and Western students of Iran to its modern history.[41] According to this analysis Iran's rulers since the late nineteenth century have allied themselves with international capitalism in order to maintain power and exploit the economy. The nationalist bourgeoisie, consisting of bazaar merchants, some landlords, religious leaders, and professionals, emerged as a challenge to this alliance in the 1890's, and intermittently since then. The social and economic base of the nationalist bourgeoisie has steadily grown, particularly in the period since World War II. In spite of its growth, this group has been defeated repeatedly. The repressive apparatus has simply been too strong, the nationalist leadership has been coopted, and their challenge was diffused by fear among this class that by pushing too hard for reforms they would risk the loss of their position to the workers and peasants challenging them from beneath.

In this analysis the true saviours are, of course, eventually to be the workers and peasants, groups that have not yet played a decisive role on the Iranian stage. Peasants have been inactive politically, except when struggling for local nationalisms, or after migrating to towns to enter the urban work force. Workers have shown some determination when organized, but national organizations have never been created, and the government has been able to destroy or fractionate most developments of a true workers movement. In addition, the competing obscurantist religious leaders allied to the nationalist bourgeoisie have evidently been more successful than labor leaders in organizing the bulk of the working class—a class still predominantly engaged in small, craft-like businesses. Although these leaders express the working man's anger at the exploitation and tyranny of the international capitalist system imposed upon him, traditionalist religious leaders do not envisage the fundamental revision in the social system that would fundamentally improve the position of workers or peasants.

The Marxist interpretation is, then, that the struggle will go on in Iran until a truly socialist system is attained that organizes the economy for the benefit of the many instead of the few. Although this analysis raises important issues, it is subject to serious criticisms.

The first criticism is that the identification of the international politics of more or less capitalist states as "international capitalism" is misleading. Much of the interference of foreign powers in Iran has been primarily an expression of their ability to relatively easily advance their national interests at Iran's expense. Capitalism had little to do with the desire of England to block Russian expansion or secure its naval oil supplies before World War I, or the desire of the allies to occupy Iran to secure communications to the USSR in World War II. Iranian capitalists in the modern sense hardly existed in Iran prior to World War II and, in so far as they did, were not particularly supportive of the government. As in past centuries, the Shah and his retainers used the possession of power to rule, where rule involved the exploitation of both the Iranian people and of any foreign individuals or governments that wanted to play a part in Iran.

Since World War II economic development and modernization, including the breaking of the power of feudal landlords and the conversion of some property into agribusiness and modern corporations. developed a capitalist class supportive of the monarch alongside the still powerful bazaar merchants loyal primarily to the religious establishment. However, the support of the monarchy by this capitalist class was quite unimportant. From the 1930's the modern economy had been largely in the hands of the government, increasingly so as oil came to dominate all activities. The new capitalists exploited, or operated in, the system as far as they could, but their money and loyalty were hardly necessary. The Shah controlled the money, and his army and his political tools were decisive.

International capitalists also operated in Iran since World War II. But again their relations were primarily with the Iranian or American governments; it was national interests as defined by these governments that were served, rather than corporate economic interests. Until the late 1960's the United States primarily wanted to help the development and security of Iran because it was a poor country and because it was a front-line country in our containment strategy. From then on we increasingly sold arms to Iran because we saw it as a country with common security interests and because arms sales became a way to redress the balance-of-payments drain occasioned by the rise in oil prices. Pressure for these sales came at least as much from the Shah and those around him as from the United States. American companies played their part primarily by supporting the process once it began rolling. The irrelevance of capitalism was true for other countries in the Iranian trade, where often the suppliers were government-owned companies.

Only if we see the world as a giant theatre in which countries labeled "international capitalists" struggle against those labeled "socialist," is it meaningful to see recent Iranian history as the story of domination by international capital. Unfortunately for the theorists these would remain nonpredictive labels; the Soviets and Chinese proved as quick to ally with the Shah when it served their interests as did the capitalists.[42]

The theory of international capitalism also fails to explain recent Iranian history because it ignores the critical weakness of Iranian counteraction to outside pressure. This weakness makes the history of this century seem more the story of Iranian inaction than of the oppression of others. The overthrow of Mossadegh is said to be the result of foreign interference. Yet where were the foreign troops or even threats? Iranians overthrew Mossadegh, no matter how much they may have been urged on by a handful of Americans. The causes must be found either in Iranian anarchy and nihilism or in widespread opposition within the Iranian population to what they saw as the direction of Mossadegh.

The critical problem with Marxist analysis is that it fails to respect the true complexity and continual changeability of human beings in real countries with real traditions. Whether workers or merchants or students, Iranians are not and hopefully never will be a "mass." They represent many classes, occupations, religious groups, nationalities, and inclinations. The fact that workers and peasants have not yet seen their true interests as defined by Marxism is explained both by their incomplete mobilization and the fact their interests are simply much broader and often of a different quality than the Marxists would have them be.

The future Marxist-Leninists paint for Iran would be the future desired by the vanguard party that knows right from wrong opinion. It would mete out justice as the party sees justice, not necessarily as the majority sees justice. Specifically it would destroy the traditional power of religion. Perhaps its leaders would walk carefully, but just as likely they would follow the lead of the Albanians who have banned religion in a formerly religious country, or the Somalis who executed mullahs for opposing women's rights, or the Cambodians of Pol Pot. In either case the response of a Marxist-Leninist government to religious values in Iran would be just as destructive of the values of many Iranians as the Ayatollah's attempt to put Iranians into the straight-jacket of medieval religiosity.

Inevitably, too, a socialist Iran on this model would develop the new bureaucratic class that has bedeviled every communist state, exploiting now in the name of the workers as other exploiters employed other symbols. In these states the promise of political and civil freedoms, even if initially made, would soon be forgotten, its dismissal legitimated by the logic of the vanguard concept, the experience of other Marxist states, and the natural egoism of any ruling class. This is the future of Iranian "socialism" as a political model. Economically all societies today are to a degree socialist, Iran to a high degree. The balance between government cooperatives, or private enterprise in a future Iran should be decided pragmatically, as needs change, and as the people learn of the advantages and disadvantages of each form for particular applications.

The future that holds out the greatest promise for ending exploitation and injustice in Iran is one that has the modest goal of working steadily toward their elimination within the untidy confines of democratic process. A free press, jails without political prisoners, and periodic competitive elections will insure that the interests of the peoples of the Iranian mosaic, and their continually changing interests, will be approximated in the decisions of Iranian governments. This future will at the very least deny to any group the fundamental injustice of allowing ideological elites excessive power over others in the name of whatever cause. It will be a hard future for Iranians to achieve, but Iran offers no easy road to justice.

## CONCLUSION: LESSONS FOR AMERICAN POLICY

American policy toward Iran has been based on a variety of interests. At first in the Schuster mission of the earlier part of the century, America's technical aid came to fulfill the U.S. commitment to poorer countries. As a neutral power America sought to help Iran resist the threat of the Russian and British Empires. In the 1940's we appeared along with the United Kingdom as direct interventionists. Yet since our intervention caused the ending of Reza Shah's tyranny, we played a positive role in furthering the freedom of Iranians. After the war our ability to force the Soviets to withdraw from Iran was welcomed by most Iranians. Although this meant the ending of the Azerbaijan and Kurdish states established by the Soviets, only in Kurdistan is there likely to be the feeling that the United States supported oppression in this way.

The late forties were years of technical aid, with the United States developing new plans for large-scale foreign assistance. These were also relatively good years for political and civil liberties. With the struggle of Mossadegh in the early fifties Iran fell into the cold war pattern in which the United States felt it had to prevent communist success at all cost. At the beginning Americans feared Mossadegh falling under communist control or being replaced by communists. Religious leaders evidently feared the same thing; most of them deserted Mossadegh and allowed the army to return the Shah to power.

It must be remembered that the Shah at this time was not the dictator of years later. He had served as a constitutional monarch, and at the time could claim indeed that Mossadegh was the usurper of the constitution. In helping to organize the forces that made possible his return, the Americans involved did not think of our support as a choice between democracy represented by Mossadegh and dictatorship represented by the Shah. Those involved could argue that preventing a communist takeover was in the long run the best guarantee of democracy in Iran. The people in the streets made it appear to some Americans to be the "popular cause."[43]

The very limited nature of our actual involvement in the events of 1953 should be contrasted with the physical interventions of U.S. troops in Vietnam or the Dominican Republic, or of communist forces more recently in Ethiopia, Angola, Cambodia, Laos and most dramatically Czechoslovakia and Afghanistan. The record suggests that the USSR was in fact more actively intervening than we were in the events of 1953 and subsequently. The Soviets supported and continue to support an organized political party; a quality of political involvement not available to the United States. The recent Iranian charges of U.S. rule through its puppets is sheer fantasy. At most ours was a blocking action intended to prevent the subverting of Iranian sovereignty by the Soviet Union. To this goal the international and other advantages obtained by Americans have always been secondary. The interpretation by Iranians that we practically took over in 1953 is unfortunate but one with which Americans, at least, need not be burdened.[44]

After 1953 the continued adherence of most democratic groups to Mossadegh's cause and the reliance of the regime on the army made relaxation of the Shah's authoritarianism very difficult. Still, in the remainder of the fifties Iranian society was relatively open. Although there were executions of political opponents, it is well to remember that after a lengthy and well-recorded trial Mossadegh himself was not harmed.

The United States in this period played several roles. On the one hand, we aided the Shah in the development of his secret police and military forces. On the other hand, we promoted education and agricultural development, and urged the Shah toward relinquishing his estates and promoting more general land reform.

The Kennedy administration urged a return to more democratic institutions in the early 1960's and with the prime ministership of Ali Amini and a return to political parties the Shah tried again. This time the opposition, joined with the religious leadership, threatened both the Shah's control and the modernizations that both he and the United States had used partially to legitimize that control.

Iran now slipped deeper into authoritarianism. The relation of the United States to the Shah became closer even though as oil revenues increased we phased out our financial aid. It is important to note that U.S.-Iranian trade or investment was to this point relatively insignificant.

It was certainly not the cause of our association. The cause was rather that the Shah was a reliable ally in an area of probable Soviet expansionism, a friend of Israel in a generally hostile area, and a useful balance to Arab oil. We also saw the Shah's development policy as making possible a new center of power and development. The generally accepted belief was, we must remember, that democracy and well-being only follow social and economic development. Again it should be remembered that we *wanted* a strong Iran and thought the Shah was the way to get it; this is quite the opposite of imperialism.

In the last decade the rapid increase in Iranian wealth led to American investments, arms sales, and trade opportunities that could sustain the charge of exploitation, although the strength of this charge will vary widely with personal ideology. But again the old relationship was continued, with the power of the Shah growing with wealth and time and as an American-Iranian lobby came to be established within American bureaucracies. The Shah was granted unique power to veto government studies of Iran and American contacts with Iranians. Internally his opposition was silent or in exile, exhausted except for a few radical students and the smoldering priests.

President Carter came into power talking of human rights, reinvigorating opposition to tyranny everywhere in the world, and in private admonishing tyrants that their oppressions could no longer be tolerated. Soon the government of Iran collapsed disastrously from either an American or Iranian point of view.

The policy errors that led to this result were of two kinds: those that laid the anti-American foundation for the Iranian Revolution, and those that made the Revolution take the direction it did.

Turning to the first error, anti-Americanism grew out of our special relation to the deposed Shah. We developed this relation because we wanted to obtain allies and to prevent communist control of Iran. But in obtaining these goals we paid too high a price both in Iranian and world terms. Let us consider what we could have lost if we had not closely associated ourselves with the Shah. The main negative probabilities would have been a socialist autocracy with occasional communist overtones as in Iraq, a noncommunist but occasionally anti-American monarchy, a military regime on the order of present-day Pakistan, or a Soviet supported quasi-communist regime such as now struggles in Afghanistan. For more positive evolutions we might look to present-day Turkey, Bangladesh, or Nigeria. In most of these alternatives the future of the country would be with democrats whether ruling or in exile, and the experience for the world would redound to America's credit.

With the choices we made the memory left behind in much of the world and for most Iranians is an ugly one, however undeserved this might be, and the future holds little promise. Iran certainly will not contribute to America's defense in the future, but then it never did. Its oil production and pricing will not be as we desire, but then the Shah had become a leader in raising oil prices. We have lost a lucrative if dangerous market for our arms.

Since World War II we have needed to gamble more often on democracy. Mossadegh was not a communist and many of the people around him were not. Could we not have aided them in their struggle as we aided the Shah? Secondly, in friendly countries we must insist on maintaining contact with all significant groups, both in and out of power. The development of pro-American factions or connections and of confining most of our contacts and support to these is in the long run neither in their interest nor ours. We must strive to understand the interests of even those who seem most foreign to us, and try to respond as far as possible to their concerns. Third, we must not fall for the thesis propounded by every autocrat around the world that there are peoples not ready for democracy, that "nation building," "political development," "economic growth," or "economic democracy" must be achieved first. Tyranny promotes tyranny. Often it can be overcome only from the outside and we should stand ready to provide that help.

A more sophisticated but for that reason more dangerous anti-democratic thesis is the doctrine of cultural impenetrability, according to which the United States should not attempt to impose its democratic ideal on the world because 1) this is ethnocentric and 2) impossible.[45] Of course, no country will or should become "like us," but the world's people are struggling for more power, they *will* have new systems, and we have every reason to think that certain positive aspects of our systems should and can be exported. The West Germans and Japanese hardly looked like good candidates to make democratic processes work forty years ago: today they are freer in some respects than many older democracies. India is culturally far removed from Iowa, yet Indian democracy has shown remarkable staying power against great obstacles. In the great struggle of ideologies that occupies three-fourths of the world it would be both immoral and foolish to stand aside.

But more important we must never allow our short-run national and ideological interests to allow us to countenance inhumanity. Political executions are not necessary for rule anywhere outside of situations of open warfare. Still less necessary is torture. I do not know how much the United States (or Israel) was actually involved in the cruelties of the Iranian secret police, SAVAK, or even the extent of these. But the evidence is persuasive that SAVAK did imprison, torture, and kill its opponents, and apparently the American government continued to support SAVAK in spite of this knowledge. The fact Iran (and many other countries) has had a cruel history of such atrocities or that "we could not stop them if we wanted to" does not lessen the shame for the United States, or more pragmatically erase Iranian memories of our association with these activities. The ability of the Carter administration to lessen such practices shows what could have been done long before.

Iran had more students in the United States than any other country, and yet the Revolution the students supported was bitterly anti-American. We must pay more attention to the foreign students. Apparently many students learned little of American democracy and developed little attachment to our ideals. At the same time American colleges became organizing centers for radically anti-American revolutionists. Allowing SAVAK agents on U.S. campuses was part of this problem, but simple inattention to this positive potential of foreign students for foreign relations was another.

Turning to our inability to affect the revolutionary process as it developed, the main lesson is that devising a strategy for change toward freedom must accompany pious demands for greater attention to human rights. If the Shah actually wanted to follow the Spanish example after 1976, seminars on the Spanish experience, talks with Spanish politicians, and so forth, might have been arranged. In 1978 the Shah should have been encouraged to hold a real election, the religious advisors promised by the constitution should have been brought in before the flood of priestly power began its buildup, and an earlier abdication should have been considered. Clearly actions rather than promises were needed, and they needed to precede the events that rendered them insufficient.

On the other hand, more consistency and intelligence in crowd control was needed. The methods of the United Kingdom in Northern Ireland against the unarmed were needed alongside enforced prohibitions on arms. Released prisoners might have been kept from the press for an interim period.

Obviously, these suggestions are easy to make in retrospect. Just as obviously they are not as useful as the longer-term policy suggestions. Yet the main point is that it is in periods of rapid liberalization that both governments and oppositions need maximum U.S. help, help not to preserve or prevent or react, but to change. I doubt if we were prepared to offer such help to either the Shah or his opponents. The two classes of errors are of course interconnected: we could not successfully offer help in a transition to freedom because we had not developed the quality or quantity of relationships with Iranians that would have made such help acceptable.

## NOTES

1. Crane Brinton, *the Anatomy of Revolution* (New York: Random House, 1965); and James Davies, "Political Stability and Instability: Some Manifestations and Causes," *Journal of Conflict Resolution* 1969, 13, pp. 1–17.

2. Based on an expansion of the stages defined by Sepehr Zabih, *Iran's Revolutionary Upheaval* (San Francisco: Alchemy Press, 1979), pp. 46–71. See also Richard Cottam, "Revolutionary Iran," *Current History,* January 1980 (78, 453) pp. 12–17ff; and Fereydoun Hoveyda, *The Fall of the Shah* (London: Weidenfeld and Nicolson, 1977). The basic record may also be found in *Keesing's Contemporary Archives,* pp. 28939–40 (April 21, 1978), pp. 29383–89 (January 5, 1979), and pp. 29733–46 (July 27, 1979). Personally, I followed these events in *Iran Express,* a largely Persian language weekly published in Washington and quoting widely from Persian sources.

3. On this period see especially Robert Graham, *The Illusion of Power* (New York: St. Martin's Press, 1979), p. 206ff.

4. The importance of U.S. policy in these events was emphasized in Richard Cottam, "The Case for Iran," in R. D. Gastil, *Freedom in the World 1978* (New York and Boston: Freedom House and G. K. Hall, 1978), pp. 88–108. The Iranian Committee for the Defence of Liberty and Human Rights formed in December 1977 was in large part a response to Carter's policy. See also Helmut Richards, "Carter's Human Rights Policy and the Pahlavi Dictatorship," in A. R. Nobari, *Iran Erupts* (Stanford: Inter-American Documentation Group, December 1978), pp. 90–116.

5. Richard Cottam, "The Case of Iran."

6. This is the view of the Shah's opposition, and is widely held by educated Iranians. The Shah and his father were, of course, far more than simply tools of foreign powers. Even the Marxist Fred Halliday (*Iran: Dictatorship and Development* [Harmondsworth, England: Penguin Books, 1979], pp. 38–102) points out that Iranians overestimate the Shah's dependence on foreign support. The tendency to shift blame for lack of democracy onto successive foreign governments is a critical and debilitating tendency most Iranians share.

7. For general interpretations of what led up to the Revolution see Cottam, "The Case of Iran," Halliday, *Iran: Dictatorship and Development,* and Zabih, *Iran's Revolutionary Upheaval.*

8. James Davies, "Political Stability and Instability"; also Mansour Olsen, Jr., "Rapid Growth as a Destabilizing Factor," *Journal of Economic History* 1963, 23(4): 529–558.

9. See Abul Kasim Mansur (pseud.), "The Crisis in Iran," *Armed Forces Journal,* January 1979, pp. 26–33(29).

10. In addition to Zabih, *Iran's Revolutionary Upheaval,* pp. 27–38, see Amir Taheri, "The Bazaar," *Iran Express,* December 23, 1978, and G. Thaiss, "Religious Symbolism and Social Change," in Nikki Keddie, ed., *Scholars, Saints and Sufis* (Berkeley and Los Angeles: University of California Press), pp. 349–366. There may also be something in Hoveyda's belief that the Shah's policy in the 1960's made real gains but that he lost touch and relapsed into megalomania in the 1970's. (Hoveyda, *The Fall of the Shah,* pp. 50–52, 81–116).

11. Halliday, *Iran,* pp. 218–219.

12. In addition to the foregoing references see James A. Bill, *The Politics of Iran: Groups, Classes, and Modernization* (Columbus: Merrill, 1972), and James

A. Bill, "The Patterns of Elite Politics in Iran," in G. Lenczowski, ed., *Political Elites in the Middle East* (Washington, D.C.: American Enterprise Institute, 1975), pp. 17–41; and Marvin Zonis, *The Political Elite of Iran* (Princeton: Princeton University Press, 1971).

13. On Iranian national character see R. D. Gastil, "Middle Class Impediments to Iranian Modernization," *Public Opinion Quarterly XXII* Fall 1958): 325–329, and more fully the Ph.D. dissertation (unpublished), "Iranian General Belief Modes as Found in Middle Class Shiraz," Harvard, May, 1958.

14. On the views of Khomeini see the series Hokūmat-e-Eslāmī, November 1978–February 1979 in *Iran Express,* written originally as *Velāyat-e-Faqih* (The Rule of the Islamic Theologian). In this series Numbers Four and Six are especially important, for they point out the necessity to have no ruler but the holy law; that no government is today (pre-1978) ruled by this law; that neither majorities in democracies nor kings in monarchies have the right to make laws; that monarchies are illegal in Islam; and that the only acceptable rulers are those with knowledge of the holy law. Sepehr Zabih also defines the Islamic Republic in similar terms (*Iran's Revolutionary Upheaval,* pp. 95–99). The historical background to Khomeini's thinking is offered by N. Keddie and Hamid Algar in Nikki Keddie, ed., *Scholars, Saints, and Sufis* (Berkeley and Los Angeles: University of California Press, 1972).

15. See H. A. R. Gibb, *Mohammedanism* (London: Oxford University Press, 1949); Tor Andrae, *Mohammed, the Man and His Faith* (New York: Harper and Bros., 1960 [1936]); and Muhammad 'Ali, *The Religion of Islam* (Lahore: Ahmadiyya Anjuman, 1950).

16. On Shi'ism see Dwight Donaldson, *The Shi'ite Religion* (London: Luzac & Company, 1933). On oppression, martyrdom, and ritual see also N. Keddie and G. Thaiss in *Scholars, Saints, and Sufis,* pp. 211–232, 349–366.

17. See Nikki Keddie, "The Roots of the Ulama's Power in Modern Iran," in N. Keddie, ed., *Scholars, Saints, and Sufis,* pp. 211–230.

18. For a comprehensive picture of Iranian life under Islam see Edward G. Browne, *Literary History of Persia* (Cambridge: Cambridge University Press, 1902–1925 [1951–1959]).

19. An excellent summary of the religious structure as found today is Amir Taheri, "Return of the Mosque," *Iran Express,* October 28, 1978, p. 11. See also the modern histories by Cottam and Upton referenced below.

20. On the tobacco concession see Nikki Keddi, *Religion and Rebellion in Iran: The Tobacco Protest of 1891–92* (London: Frank Cass, 1966). More general references including this event and the subsequent period are Richard Cottam, *Nationalism in Iran* (Pittsburgh: University of Pittsburgh Press, 1964), and Joseph Upton, *The History of Modern Iran: An Interpretation* (Cambridge: Harvard Center for Middle Eastern Studies, 1960).

21. In addition to the foregoing references, see Edward G. Browne, *The Persian Revolution of 1905–09* (Cambridge: Cambridge University Press, 1910); Edward G. Browne, *The Press and Poetry of Modern Persia* (Cambridge, 1914); and Ahmad Foroughy, "Repression in Iran," in A. R. Nobari, *Iran Erupts,* pp. 51–68.

22. On the Reza Khan period see also L. P. Elwell-Sutton, *Modern Iran* (London, 1941); and Amin Banani, *The Modernization of Iran* (Stanford: Stanford University Press, 1961).

23. The discussion of the post-war years is based largely on Cottam, *Nationalism in Iran.*

24. Cottam, *Nationalism in Iran,* especially pp. 150–57. Ayatollah Kashani was not regarded as a leading ayatollah theologically, but was seen by most Iranians as primarily a politician. The views of the ayatollahs span a considerable spectrum; appearances of unanimity should always be viewed skeptically.

25. See, for example, Ameer Ali, *The Spirit of Islam* (London: Christophers, 1922 [1952]), pp. 335–6.

26. William Dorman and Ehsan Omeed, "Reporting Iran the Shah's Way," *Columbia Journalism Review,* January/February 1979, pp. 27–33.

27. Nobari, *Iran Erupts,* pp. 15, 23. Compare the references in Note 12.

28. See Nikki Keddie, *Religion and Rebellion in Iran,* pp. 15–29 (and reference note 19), 141–144.

29. See William Pfaff, "Reflections," *New Yorker,* December 10, 1979, pp. 208–214.

30. See Keddie, ed., *Scholars, Saints, and Sufis.*

31. See Edward G. Browne, *A Year Among the Persians* (London, 1893); and Gastil, "General Belief Modes . . ." The claim of the Baghdad Sufi Halladj "I am God" was echoed by many Isma'ili leaders and of course the Safavid monarchs mentioned above.

32. A. Christensen, *L'Iran sous les Sassanides* (Copenhagen: Munksgaard, 1944); E. Browne, *A Literary History of Persia,* Volume 1 (Cambridge: Cambridge University Press, 1951); and A. Firdowsi, *The Shahnameh* (Teheran: Amir Kabir, 1931), pp. 714–717. See also Reuben Levy's translation, *The Epic of the Kings* (Chicago: University of Chicago Press, 1967), pp. 317–323; Franz Altheim, *Utopie und Wirtschaft* (Frankfurt am Main: Klostermann, 1957); Eldridge Colby, "Religion and Politics in Early Persia," *Open Court* 36 (1922): 401–413; and Paul Luttinger, "Mazdak," *Open Court* 35 (1921): 664–686.

33. See interview in *Iran Express,* December 22, 1979, p. 15.

34. Ali Shari'ati, *On the Sociology of Islam,* (translated by H. Algar) (Berkeley: Mizan Press, 1979). See also the interpretation of his importance in Cottam, "Revolutionary Iran."

35. See R. D. Gastil, "In Defense of Islam: Some Kurdish Revolts of the Nineteenth Century," unpublished paper, 1956; Frederick Barth, *Principles of Social Organization in Southern Kurdistan* (Oslo, 1953): and C. J. Rich, *Narrative of a Residence in Koordistan* (London, 1836).

36. *New York Times,* August 1, 1979. The whole history of Iranian monarchy since Islam is similarly rejected by Foroughy in A. R. Nobari, *Iran Erupts.*

· 37. See for example the writings of Sadegh Hedayat, Iran's best known modern writer.

38. *Iran Voice,* September 10, 1979.

39. Sa'adi, *Golestan,* Part I.

40. On the importance of diffusion of democratic ideas see R. D. Gastil, *Freedom in the World 1978,* pp. 147–162.

41. For an exceptionally reasonable presentation see Fred Halliday, *Iran: Dictatorship and Development.* For a more typical but paranoid version of the capitalist/imperialist exploitation argument see A. H. Banisadr and Paul Vielle, "Iran and the Multinationals," in A. R. Nobari, ed., *Iran Erupts,* pp. 24–34. According to these authors Iran's rulers have deliberately destroyed the country's

agriculture and developed trade with communist countries at the behest of international capitalism.

42. Halliday, *Iran,* pp. 258–266.

43. See Kermit Roosevelt, *Countercoup: The Struggle for the Control of Iran* (New York: McGraw-Hill, 1979).

44. See Cottam, *Nationalism in Iran,* pp. 221–236; also Roosevelt, *ibid.* See also Sepehr Zabih, *The Communist Movement in Iran* (Berkeley: University of California Press, 1966).

45. See Edward Stillman and William Pfaff, *Power and Impotence* (New York: Harper and Row, 1967), and most recently Pfaff's "Reflections," *New Yorker,* December 10, 1979, pp. 208–214.

# Elections in
# Zimbabwe Rhodesia

## PREFACE

F reedom House sent a nine-member delegation to observe the common roll election in April 1979. While, given the context, we judged the election to be not fully democratic, we thought it was a step toward democracy, and so it proved to be. Our recommendations following this report were that the United States welcome the progress that had been made and urge further steps toward full democracy as the U.S. government moved by slow stages toward recognition.[1] We were clear that democracy must eventually involve all of the major political forces, and the reestablishment of full civil liberties in a post-war settlement.

Events, however, moved more rapidly than we had imagined on both the political and military fronts. The success of Bishop Muzorewa's government, finally established in June, depended in large part on peace and the increase in a sense of security in both the white and black populations. This did not occur. At the same time the new government of Zimbabwe Rhodesia was offered in the early fall not the recognition they had hoped for from the new Conservative government of the United Kingdom but a chance to participate in negotiations for an all-party settlement and new elections. The government of Zimbabwe Rhodesia had no choice but to participate and get the best deal it could. The resulting Lancaster House Agreements led to the elections we observed in February 1980.

The April 1979 Freedom House Mission was chaired by Roscoe Drummond, syndicated Washington columnist, and Bayard Rustin, president of the A. Philip Randolph Institute. Both are Freedom House trustees. The Mission also included Leonard Sussman and Raymond Gastil of Freedom House, Robert Henderson, of the Center for Strategic and International Studies of Georgetown University, Allard Lowenstein, former Congressman and U.S. Ambassador to the U.N. Commission on Human Rights, Howard Penniman, of Georgetown University and the American Enterprise Institute, Leon Weaver of Michigan State University, and Maurice Woodard of Howard University.

Because of the larger number of observers and journalists attending the 1980 elections, the observer group for the second election had to be

157

limited to four persons: Raymond Gastil, Howard Penniman, Bayard Rustin, and Leonard Sussman. However, the final report for the 1980 election was written in consultation with the other members of the original mission. Allard Lowenstein was killed in New York shortly before this consultation. In 1979 Lowenstein contributed to the formulation of Congressional Legislation that formed the basis of subsequent U.S. policy.

We would also like to thank Professors Marshall Murphree and Hasu Patel of the University of Rhodesia for their advice while in the field.

We have included below the major sections of the Freedom House reports on the April and February elections. The report on the April election (Section I, below) is more extensive because we felt it necessary initially to develop at greater length the background and context of the election and our methods of investigation. The second, shorter report of the February election (Section II, below) begins with the Interim Report the group produced in the field several days before the results were announced but after the first day of voting. This was included in the final report because it was necessary to separate our thoughts on the process at that point from any influence the dramatic election results might have had on our evaluation. The Interim Report is followed by our later analysis of the voting and the results, as well as recommendations for the future.

# I. The Common Roll Election—April 1979

## INTRODUCTION

Rhodesia (now Zimbabwe Rhodesia) represents one of the last vestiges of white colonialism in Africa. Originally colonized at the end of the nineteenth century by South African and British settlers, its small white population was more than doubled through immigration after World War II. The white settlers formed their own legislature but the British government maintained the right of intervention in local affairs in matters dealing with the treatment of the African population. In 1953, the colony was incorporated with the British protectorates of Northern Rhodesia and Nyasaland under a scheme to promote regional economic growth within a multiracial federation. Agitation against this federation by the African populations in the protectorates that feared they would have difficulty in achieving independence led to the federation's dissolution in 1963.

Negotiations for the independence of the colony of Rhodesia had broken down by 1964 over the issues of African representation in the parliament and eventual majority rule. The white minority government of Ian Smith eventually rejected the authority of the British government, which led in 1965 to the Unilateral Declaration of Independence. Diplomatic isolation and international economic sanctions were imposed in 1966, after efforts by the UN to negotiate a settlement failed. Until recently the white Rhodesian government adamantly continued to resist pressures for political change including majority rule.

The white ability to conquer and rule the country with a population that seldom exceeded five percent of the total resulted from superior white organization and technology. With this advantage white Rhodesians had by the 1960's managed to direct the construction of a relatively modern society by African standards, but also a society with great disparities of wealth and opportunity between black and white. Most of the best agricultural land, with the best soil and highest rainfall, was given over to white development; the majority of the black population either had to subsist in generally more marginal land or work as dependents for white farms or businesses. White education, homes, and wages were far superior; whites had created a pleasant world, but one of special privileges. At the same time Christian missions and the government had come by the 1960's to provide Rhodesian blacks with education, health care, agricultural technology, and transportation that otherwise would have been absent. And through setting aside definite areas for blacks the complete destruction of black tribal organization and land claims had at least been avoided. A small black electorate had been developed, and parliament did have a small black representation.

Black consciousness and the modern political activity it engenders began in the 1950's. By the early 1960's several political organizations had been formed, only to be quickly banned and their leaders detained. This experience led many blacks to turn to guerrilla or terrorist activity. They received outside support, but poor organization, internecine strife, the continued self-confidence of the Rhodesian whites, and South African aid kept insurgent activities from achieving notable success for many years.

In the mid-1970's the Portuguese Revolution and the subsequent formation of radical Marxist states in Angola and Mozambique increased greatly both the capabilities and prospects of the insurgents. The attitude of South Africa changed, and under United States pressure it added its voice to those supporting fundamental change in the country. The country had weathered UN, OAU, American, and British sanctions and diplomatic isolation, but now the impact of the sanctions, combined with economic dislocations stemming from continued warfare, caused the economy to falter.

Under these pressures the Salisbury government seriously began to seek an alternative political structure. Prime Minister Ian Smith announced in September 1976 that his government would agree in principle to the concept of one man/one vote in Zimbabwe Rhodesia and a transfer of political power to the overwhelming black majority. After attempts to achieve this result through an all-parties conference failed, negotiations on the terms of a settlement were undertaken with Bishop Abel Muzorewa, the leader of the United African National Council (UANC), the Rev. Ndabaningi Sithole, leader of the internal wing of the Zimbabwe African National Union (ZANU), and Senator Chief Jeremiah Chirau, a leader of Zimbabwe United People's Organization (ZUPO).

These internal leaders signed an agreement on March 3, 1978, that resulted in the establishment of an Executive Council with a rotating chairmanship. This Transitional Government would guide the country through an interim period that would produce a new constitution and organize elections for a new parliament (originally scheduled for December 31, 1978). The elections were delayed by the mass of administrative detail that faced the civil service. A referendum on the new constitution was held in early 1979 in which only the white population was permitted to vote. This vote affirmed the transition to majority rule. The elections for the parliament authorized by the new constitution were finally held on April 17–21, 1979.

## THE GOALS AND ACTIVITIES OF THE OBSERVER MISSION

The international isolation of Zimbabwe Rhodesia has been based on the continuance of white minority rule in the face of the hostility of the surrounding black states and the insurgent forces they support. The elections represent an effort by the government of Zimbabwe Rhodesia to break out of this isolation by satisfying, at least in part, the desire of the outside world for black majority rule. Both the American and British governments had explicitly made transfer of power to the blacks a precondition of recognition and the lifting of sanctions. As the elections drew near, many commentators, public and private, suggested that it was conceivable that this election might signify transfer of power to the black majority, and that the only way to find out whether a transfer of power was occurring was to send observers that would critically evaluate the election's significance in the establishment of black majority rule. Some also felt that the presence of observers might improve the quality of the election. Others hoped that the success of a moderate government, based on a compromise of black and white interests, could conceivably serve as a model of peaceful, democratic evolution for Namibia and South Africa.

It was in the spirit of these concerns that Freedom House sent a nine-man observer group to Zimbabwe Rhodesia. It should also be mentioned that one immediate cause of the Mission was the breakdown of the effort in the U.S. Congress to send an official observation team in the light of the legal tie it had erected between continuation of sanctions and lack of majority rule. When this effort failed, many felt that private observers would be necessary and desirable if U.S. policy were not to remain uninformed. For analogous reasons and because of the announced decision of the Zimbabwe Rhodesian government to welcome observers, many observer teams were dispatched to the scene of the elections in mid-April, from Europe, the United States, Australia, and South Africa.

The primary assignments of the Freedom House Mission were:

To determine whether the electoral process was designed to produce a free and meaningful election.

To discover whether the mechanics of the electoral process were carried out efficiently and were substantially free of irregularities.

To measure to what degree the difficult conditions under which the voting took place—the continuing civil war directed from outside the country, the status of civil liberties inside the country, the high visibility of necessary security forces, and the extent of martial law—kept the voting from reflecting the political desires of the electorate and thereby diminished the full value of the election.

*The questions addressed by the mission.*

1. Who were deemed eligible to vote, and was the process of determining eligibility carefully executed?

2. Was the right to vote genuinely open to all eligible voters, and the opportunity to vote readily accessible?

3. Were all political parties that wished to contest for seats in the parliament free to nominate slates of candidates and to campaign?

4. Did the press and media give reasonably balanced coverage of the contesting parties and candidates?

5. Did the Transitional Government do its part to explain and publicize the voting process to the black people most of whom were previously unfamiliar with the national election process?

6. Did the Transitional Government resort to methods that would have pressured people to go to the polls in a way that could distort the vote, and did private employers either in the urban or farming areas do so?

7. Were the leaders of the two political parties in the "Patriotic

Front" outside the country able to use their forces to intimidate any substantial number of voters from casting their ballots?

8. Was any significant pressure brought to bear on the voters—other than through legitimate campaigning—to influence them to cast their ballots for particular candidates?

9. Was martial law, which was in effect to protect against the activities of identifiable terrorists, unfairly used to deter the people who wanted to campaign openly against the elections?

10. Were there any substantial irregularities at the polling places?

11. Were the ballots safely impounded before counting them? Was there evidence that the impounded ballots were tampered with?

*The investigative activities of the mission.* The nine members of the observer team spent a considerable part of four of five days of balloting visiting a widely separated and diverse range of voting booths in every part of the country, scrutinizing the procedures, and examining the care with which they were being carried out. For security reasons most of the trips were made with the advance knowledge of government officials, but on one day members of the Mission were able to travel to balloting sites of their own choosing.

Members of the Mission investigated the presence of officials of the parties at the impounding and the counting of the ballots, examined the impounding of the ballot boxes, and witnessed their re-opening to begin counting.

Members of the group interviewed—often with non-government translators—considerable numbers of voters in different election districts to find out whether they felt coerced to vote or not to vote, about why they voted, about what they thought of the elections, how they decided which candidates to vote for, how they thought the elections would change their lives and whether an end to the fighting would soon come about. The Mission sought to assess the visible presence of armed security forces in the vicinity of the voting booths.

In our effort to get the widest cross section of thinking about the political climate in which the election was taking place and its impact on the result, members of the Mission discussed the election with political leaders of the participating parties and with identifiable representatives of the opposition in the "Patriotic Front," including some detained in prison. Useful conversations were held with informed correspondents, academics, and others with experience in Zimbabwe Rhodesia, and experiences were exchanged with other international observers.

Three members of the group (Henderson, Weaver, and Woodard) stayed in Zimbabwe Rhodesia through the counting, tabulation, and announcements of the results of the common roll election. The integrity of the process was investigated by several methods. Henderson and

Weaver witnessed the opening of a ballot box that had been sealed on Saturday in Dr. Weaver's presence. There were spot checks on counting locations in Salisbury and in surrounding rural communities. Observers from other teams were present in other parts of the country on the first morning of the counting. There were also officials from the various political parties present at counting stations throughout the country.

No serious irregularities surrounding the counting or tabulation of the poll were reported by the members of the Freedom House team, other international observer teams, or from the various party officials. A series of party officials present during the counting were interviewed and no reports of widespread irregularities were mentioned.

All participating party leaders had publicly expressed confidence in the election process after the conclusion of polling. However, when the results were announced Rev. Sithole alleged that massive fraud had occurred in the electoral process. To learn the substance of these allegations, members of the Executive Committee of ZANU (internal) and parliamentary candidates from the districts in which irregularities were reported were interviewed. The information given to us was not substantive enough to challenge the information we had already received on the electoral process. Infractions cited were isolated and minor in terms of their overall impact on the vote. Our informants had very little to assert about the counting and tabulation of the final vote. The Freedom House Mission had already documented cases of intimidation and coercion. It was felt that cases of inter-party conflict instigated by respective auxiliaries balanced themselves out in the total poll.

## THE CONTEXT OF THE COMMON ROLL ELECTION

The common roll election must be understood against the background of the continual conflict and shifting of allegiances that have characterized the recent history of Zimbabwe Rhodesia. It was in this context that the Rhodesian government and three of the major personalities in the black community had finally agreed on an internal settlement that would transfer some major aspects of power and responsibility to the black population. Those participating in the agreement felt that the settlement offered a viable compromise that would serve the interests of all races. On this basis the constitution negotiated by Ian Smith and the black leaders was approved in a referendum by the white community.

The new constitution provides for the election of a parliament, an indirectly elected upper house with 20 of 30 positions to be filled by blacks, and a directly elected lower house in which 72 out of 100 members are elected on the common roll, and thus will almost surely be black. The Prime Minister is to be the person commanding a majority in the lower house. The constitution inhibits major changes for at least ten years in the command of the security forces, judiciary, and civil services. These constraints are included, along with the constitutional guarantee of civil liberties, among the "entrenched clauses" that require the approval of 78 members of the lower house. After ten years the question of whether whites will continue to have the specially guaranteed group of 28 positions in the lower house will be reviewed.

After the constitution was approved the common roll election of the 72 black members of the lower house was organized on a party basis. Political parties were to propose slates of candidates for the eight electoral districts. Seats were allocated to these districts on the basis of population; election of candidates within each district was to be determined proportionately on the basis of the division of votes in each district. Four parties submitted slates for all districts and one party for one district. The best known parties were those already established by the three black leaders who had signed the internal settlement. The major party leaders had established popular followings, particularly in certain districts, and at least two had played a significant role in the national struggle for black rule.

Two major black leaders and their followers, however, remained outside of the country and opposed to the internal settlement. (The ethnic and political relations of groups in the nationalist struggle are examined at greater length below, pp. 172–177.) Although asked to return to take part in the settlement and to offer slates in the election, the external leaders refused on the grounds that the constitution was unfairly biased in favor of the white minority and that the holding of free elections while the administration and security forces remained essentially under white control was impossible.

The external leaders decided to continue their attempt to wrest control of Zimbabwe Rhodesia from the white minority through insurgency and a diplomatic offensive that has crippled Zimbabwe Rhodesia's way of life, economy, and to an extent military capability through the maintenance of sanctions and nonrecognition. Their opposition to the election was expressed more directly through an announced intention to campaign against the election and to disrupt it violently.

The consequent division among black nationalist groups meant that the common roll election had to be carried on in the face of a considerable insurgency, an insurgency that was likely to become more intense as the election neared. This meant that providing security to those involved in each stage of the election process would force the process to take place under the continuous surveillance of pervasive security forces.

The security situation in the weeks preceding the election led to a major mobilization, especially among the white population. Although statistics are unreliable there are no doubt several thousand insurgents living in the country, mostly operating in small units in the Tribal Trust Lands. Several more thousand insurgents in bases outside the borders could be sent into the country at any time. The insurgents do not attempt to control territory, but rather try through terrorist attacks to establish their existence, separate the people from the government, and cause its administrative and economic collapse. They may also be laying a basis through recruitment and training for major military action at a future date.

As a result of the security situation many people in the Tribal Trust Lands have lost the economic bases of their lives and been gathered, forcibly or willingly, into Protected Villages where they live directly under the protection of a variety of security forces, including local militias. Elsewhere in the tribal lands Protected Villages are absent, but there is a heavy presence of security forces throughout the more heavily populated areas. Finally, there are rural areas, generally of low population density, where security forces are present only during police or military operations. Around major cities, on the other hand, and in many of the better European farming areas military and police presence is relatively less conspicuous. During the course of the election campaign and polling these variations in the presence of military or police force did of course continue, although the security effort was more intense everywhere. Necessarily within the country this effort had a more than usual defensive role because security forces had to protect a larger than usual number of fixed targets for at least a temporary period.

The security requirement was all the greater because for most of the ninety-six percent of the potential voters who were black this was the first modern voting process in which they had participated. It was difficult to reach potential voters in rural areas with the election message, and the fact that most voters were functionally illiterate increased the difficulty. For a meaningful election political parties had to rapidly develop a completely new organization in many areas in order to carry their message to the people under conditions of considerable danger.

The election context was also affected by the level of civil liberties, in particular those guaranteeing freedom of expression. The modern media, including publications directed to the black population, are almost exclusively under the control of the white population. Assembly and publication in opposition to the internal settlement occurred, but were very limited. Many members of the opposition have been detained; and this is under conditions of martial law in most of the country. The major black paper favorable to the external parties was forced to cease publication in fall 1978, and there was no opposition paper generally available in the campaign period. The censored white media are encouraged to present an almost uniformly favorable picture of the internal settlement, the election process, and the country's security and judicial services. The reasons for much of this control, grounded in history and the present security situation, are understandable, but this situation nevertheless affected the election.

Another important aspect of the election context was the wide gap between the white and black races, reflected until recently in legally enforced discriminatory treatment. Established patterns of dependence on white leaders, employers, or officials cannot help but have been reflected in the behavior of many potential black voters. The independence of these voters could not have been as great as that of a population familiar with life in a society founded upon legal equality. Transition to full personal independence is never instantaneous.

## ISSUES OF PRIMARY SIGNIFICANCE IN THE EVALUATION OF THE ELECTION

The common roll election took place on April 17–21. Over 1,800,000 votes were cast, of which three and one-half percent were spoiled ballots. Since estimates of the number of potential voters varied, this represents from fifty to sixty-four percent of the potential voters in the country. Counting took place on April 23 and 24. The final results showed Bishop Muzorewa's UANC winning a total of fifty-one seats, with two other parties dividing the remainder. But the significance of this outcome can only be determined after an evaluation of the many controversial issues surrounding the election that have cast doubt on the result.

The purpose of the election in the minds of both white and black Zimbabwe Rhodesians was to make possible the establishment of black majority rule. Since the constitution under which those to be elected would attempt to exert black rule was approved this spring by white voters only (although important black leaders had taken part in its formulation), and since both constitution and election were opposed by external political leaders well known in the country, a large, uncoerced turnout at the polls would be considered by most observers to represent tacit acceptance of the internal settlement's version of majority rule. Indeed, it was for this reason that the external parties violently opposed voting itself (or voting acceptable ballots) rather than particular parties on the ballot, and why in spite of its own political preferences the government's efforts in the campaign were directed almost entirely toward achieving a maximum poll rather than the success of any particular party.

It is also the character of "black majority rule" that the details of the selection of particular black candidates seem less important than the fact that a largely black electorate has come together to elect a black leader or black-dominated parliament. The interest of observers must be primarily in the willingness of the voter to accept the mechanism of this election to reach this goal rather than the particular party choices made.

If we ask, then, whether "all political and population groups were permitted to participate freely" (the language of the Case-Javits Amendment) in this election, then we must approach the question somewhat differently from the way we would approach most elections. On the one hand, there is no evidence that significant parties or individuals were arbitrarily excluded from the process. Although in the campaigning and election there were reports of unfair pressures being exerted in favor of dominant parties in certain areas, especially by local militias (security forces originally organized by political parties), and there was no doubt a great deal of pressure in areas loyal to particular figures, these pressures do not appear to have been so widespread or comparatively so unusual as to generally invalidate the election as an expression of popular preference. It should be noted that most parties chose to concentrate the bulk of their efforts in areas of known strength and prior organization.

On the other hand, since the primary issue in the election was the election itself, the extent of full participation by those parties opposed to the election must also be considered. Judging this issue appropriately is not easy. Since violent opposition cannot be a part of the democratic process, the fact that such opposition was suppressed as far as possible by security forces cannot be criticized. However, channels of nonviolent communication of opposition positions were also extremely limited in the country, with the exception of areas of accepted opposition such as the university in Salisbury. Uncoerced, purposive nonvoting or spoiling of ballots in these areas or in areas of traditional support for external leaders was accepted in the election process, but it was extremely difficult to communicate the message of these opposition political groups to the great bulk of the population and thus for their message to have a marked effect on the results. In this sense the full freedom of the election was restricted.

In most elections it is felt that encouragement of the population to participate fully in the election process serves to enhance the degree of majority control over the result. From this point of view the government did an exemplary job with limited resources. They encouraged participation wherever possible and educated the populace in the forms of the election and the available candidates. They encouraged and protected both campaigning and voting.

However, again the issues were different. The very government effort to get out the vote was a campaign for the most important issue—the election and the constitution it represented. This does not diminish the achievement, but its significance becomes ambiguous. The important question becomes the extent to which the government went beyond an educational and security effort by exerting significant pressure on voters to participate. There were cases in which pressures were applied, particularly by white farmers or other employers who gave time and transportation to the polling stations to employees perhaps so used to following orders and so relatively unsophisticated as to be unable to resist. There were also reports of party activity coercing both voting and choice of candidates. However, our judgment on the basis of many contacts with the process throughout the country is that the government generally did not bring out the vote by compelling the population to participate. In many localities people did not vote in large numbers, and local government officials seemed simply to accept that fact. We saw little evidence that people in Protected Villages or otherwise under close government protection were coerced into participation. Thus, while the pervasive presence of security forces helped constrict opposition to the election, these forces did not appear to be used for its positive promotion.

In evaluating the degree to which there was an element of compulsion in the effort to get people to the polls, it must also be remembered that an undetermined number of people were physically prevented or deterred by fear from voting or campaigning, particularly in remote areas. Insurgents often made it clear that voters would suffer immediate or delayed retribution; in some areas it was too dangerous even to provide polling facilities at a reasonable distance from the potential voters. Land mines were planted near polls, and a number of people were killed while in transit to or from polling stations. While these efforts were not as great as had been anticipated, it is likely that without this form of coercion the total poll would have been several percentage points higher.

The argument might also be made that with a population unfamiliar with both national politics or modern elections the degree of participation of the more urbanized and politicized portion of the populace should be especially important in judging the degree to which the results of the election represented meaningful expression of willingness to accept this constitution's version of majority rule. By this measure, the higher and by our impression more understanding participation in urban areas was evidence that the election was significant to an important portion of the electorate.

The common roll election did not seem to us to be open to important criticism on the basis of the organization of the voting process itself. Because of the security situation (in which the population might see a registration roll as a potential "hit list" for terrorists or insurgents), and the impracticality of administration of both registration and election in the few months available, the election was carried out without registration. A chemical identification system used elsewhere in many previous elections was employed to prevent multiple voting, and each polling booth had a local person to check the identities and qualifications of voters. Most rejected voters were underage. It appeared as though some ineligible individuals could and did vote, but it also appeared to us that the percentage of such voters was insignificant. There could, of course, be unobserved stuffing of ballot boxes for or against candidates, or to enhance totals. But we found no reason to believe this occurred. It is significant that sweeping criticisms of the process by one candidate after the results were announced did not focus on the mechanics of the election itself.

On these bases, we believe the fact that over fifty percent of the potential voting population of Zimbabwe Rhodesia participated in this election provides evidence that the majority of the population support generally and freely the government that will emerge from this election.

While not a part of the election process itself, the constitution that the election served must be judged to transfer a significant share of governing power in Zimbabwe Rhodesia to the black majority before the election can be judged a significant step toward majority rule. The constitution grants to the white voters for at least ten years 28 out of 100 seats, although they constitute only three or four percent of the population. Arithmetically, such inequalities have been accepted by many states considered to be democracies. The U.S. Senate itself falls short of the one-man/one-vote standard; like the Senate's representational formula that of Zimbabwe Rhodesia was made necessary by political compromise. However, in this case the inequality seems particularly significant because it represents an unequal allocation of parliamentary power to the very group that also possesses overwhelming economic power. Its significance is enhanced by additional constitutional provisions that serve to maintain white administrative control (because of seniority and entrance requirements) in the judiciary, civil service, and the military and police command for at least ten years.

While we attempt in this report to make no definitive judgment on the constitution, our examination of the situation leads us to believe that the powers granted to blacks through control of a two-thirds or greater majority of both houses of parliament and the bulk of ministerial positions, as well as through the general elimination of racially discriminatory laws that has already occurred, represents a major transfer of power. Administratively, the transfer is incomplete, yet a more sudden transfer of administrative power to relatively inexperienced or untrained individuals might endanger as well as enhance majority rule. Furthermore, we believe that the degree of power granted to the black population by this constitution can be used by black parliamentary leaders to advance the attainment of full equality more rapidly than the constitution appears to suggest in those areas where these leaders feel that it is in the country's interest. Given these judgments, the argument that attainment of majority rule is impossible under this constitution appears to be based on an insufficient appreciation of political realities.

## CONCLUSIONS

On the basis of the foregoing considerations our conclusions were:

1. The level and threat of guerrilla activity in many areas required a high degree of visibility and activity of the security forces if the elections were to be held. The extension of martial law to much of the country had a coercive as well as a reassuring effect. Under these conditions, carrying out a fully free election was difficult. Given these factors, and the previous unfamiliarity of much of the population with the national election process, the effort of the Zimbabwe Rhodesian government to involve the people in the election appears to have been creditable.

2. All major groups that desired to compete for parliamentary seats in the election were free to nominate slates and campaign.

3. The technical arrangements for the election were adequate for the achievement of a democratic expression of majority preference.

4. There was a high turnout under the circumstances. Because of varying population estimates and methods of calculation, the percentage participating cannot be precisely determined but estimates place it between fifty and sixty-four percent.

5. The campaigns of the contending parties gave a significant percentage of voters a sense of meaningful choice. A much larger proportion of voters saw the election as a chance to vote for peace or black rule in Zimbabwe Rhodesia, or to express communal affiliation.

6. There were direct and indirect pressures on people to vote. There were efforts by guerrilla or terrorist forces to prevent potential voters from going to the polls. The extent or degree of these pressures cannot be precisely established but a large proportion of voters apparently felt free to vote or abstain from voting.

7. There were pressures to vote for a particular party. In some areas majorities for certain candidates may have been illegally inflated for local favorites by overlooking the participation of ineligible voters. It is our judgment these activities did not affect the final returns sufficiently to discredit the general results of the election. Before the results were announced leaders of most participating parties announced that they

were satisfied with the elections. Although the results were subsequently disputed, they conformed reasonably well with pre-election estimates of relative party strengths, estimates that had remained fairly stable for some time.

8. The Mission could not precisely estimate the extent to which the use of police power to suppress most campaigning or media expression opposed to the election affected the ability of insurgents and their supporters to persuade people to reject the election by abstention or spoiling ballots. To the extent it did, the full value of the election as an expression of all potential viewpoints was diminished.

9. Under the new constitution of Zimbabwe Rhodesia this election will give the black majority control of parliament and a major role in government. Whites will continue to exercise power disproportionate to their numbers.

10. In spite of the several ways in which this election is open to reasoned objection, it is the Mission's judgment that the election represented a significant advance toward multiracial majority rule in Zimbabwe Rhodesia. The country had never had so inclusive and free an election. Elections in most developing countries are less free. In a world in which peaceful change does not and cannot occur all at once, this election was a useful and encouraging step toward the establishment of a free society in Zimbabwe Rhodesia.

# Annex 1

## THE RESULTS OF THE COMMON ROLL ELECTION

Some 1,869,077 persons or 64.45 percent of the government's estimated 2.9 million eligible voters voted in Zimbabwe Rhodesia's first inclusive, national elections. If one accepts the highest estimate of eligible voters, 3.5 million, the level of turnout was 53.34 percent.

Some 66,319 voters or 3.35 percent cast spoiled ballots, that is unmarked, mismarked, or shredded ballots. The provinces with the highest rate of spoiled ballots were Matabeleland South with 9.7 percent, Matabeleland North with 6.25 percent, and Victoria with 5.15 percent. The lowest level of spoiled ballots was in Mashonaland East with only 2 percent. These figures generally reflect the level of guerrilla activity on the one hand, and inversely, the levels of education and income on the other hand—the higher the level of guerrilla activity and the lower the levels of income and education, the higher the percentage of spoiled ballots. The lowest level of 2 percent spoiled ballots came in the province that included the capital city of Salisbury which is also the home of the national university, and the center with the highest average income.

The UANC headed by Bishop Muzorewa led all parties with a total vote of 1,212,635, which gave the party 51 of the 72 black seats in Parliament. ZANU, under the Reverend Sithole, followed with a vote of 262,928, and 12 seats. The UNFP led by Chief Ndiweni with a vote of 194,546, and 9 seats was the only other party to win seats.

The support for a party reflected to a degree the tribal affiliations of the party leaders. Bishop Muzorewa who is a member of the Shona-speaking Manyika tribe did best in the three Mashonalands where he captured all seats, in Midlands where he won seven of eleven, and in Manicaland where he took six of ten seats. His superior organization and financing were sufficient to win his party at least one seat in every province.

Rev. Sithole, whose mother was of a Matabele tribe and whose father was a Ndau tribesman, won seats in every province where one or another of these tribes was represented. Ndiweni won his nine seats in the two Matabelelands, Victoria, and Midlands reflecting his tribal background and probably his appeal for a federal state to protect minority tribes.

The level of turnout and of spoiled ballots reflected predictable patterns of conflict and of education and income. The vote for candidates reflected at least to some extent the tribal affiliations of party leaders plus the excellent organization and financing of Bishop Muzorewa's UANC. Each of these patterns appears to support the reasonableness and validity of the election results.

## Annex 2

### POLITICAL, ETHNIC, AND GEOGRAPHIC ASPECTS OF THE NATIONALIST STRUGGLE IN ZIMBABWE RHODESIA

This report's discussion of the electoral context and recent history raise several questions about the nationalist movement: Why have the insurgents, who have fought for fifteen years in the name of over ninety-five percent of the population, achieved so little control of the population that they were unable to disrupt a nationwide election? Why has the insurgent movement repeatedly been wracked by dissension, even bloody warfare? Why did certain popular leaders disassociate themselves from the insurgency and participate in the election? The answer to this latter question will provide insight into whether those who took part in the election can simply be defined as white collaborators vis-à-vis the more dedicated nationalist and insurgent leaders who opposed it.

Nationalist opposition in the early 1960's was organized by Joshua Nkomo and his ZAPU organization. In 1963 the movement split into

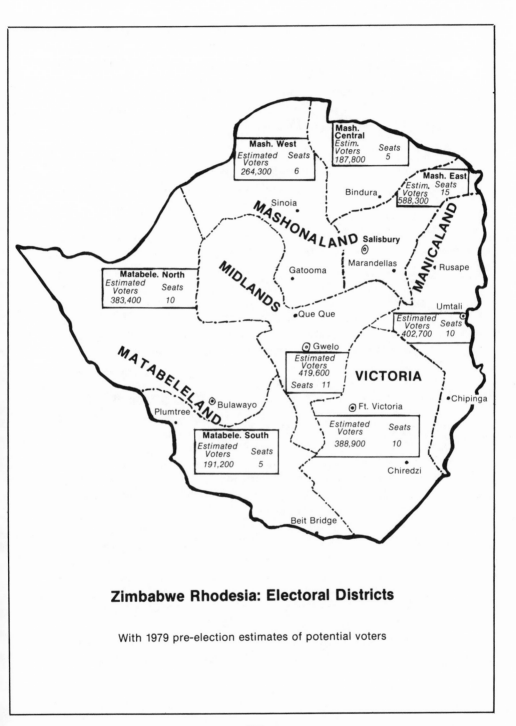

**Mash. West**
Estimated Voters 264,300
Seats 6

**Mash. Central**
Estim. Voters 187,800
Seats 5

**Mash. East**
Estim. Voters 588,300
Seats 15

MASHONALAND

Sinoia

Bindura

Salisbury

Gatooma

Marandellas

Rusape

MIDLANDS

MANICALAND

**Matabele. North**
Estimated Voters 383,400
Seats 10

Que Que

Umtali

Estimated Voters 402,700
Seats 10

Gwelo

Estimated Voters 419,600
Seats 11

**VICTORIA**

MATABELELAND

Bulawayo

Plumtree

Ft. Victoria

Chipinga

**Matabele. South**
Estimated Voters 191,200
Seats 5

Estimated Voters 388,900
Seats 10

Chiredzi

Beit Bridge

# Zimbabwe Rhodesia: Electoral Districts

With 1979 pre-election estimates of potential voters

ZAPU and ZANU over the question of Nkomo's arbitrary rule and alleged unwillingness to face jail. Although at first all tribal factions were included in both parties, the split has increasingly been between an Ndebele recruited ZAPU of Nkomo and a Shona recruited ZANU of Sithole and Mugabe. This split was further sharpened after the formation of FROLIZI out of ZAPU in 1970, one of several attempts to create a middle ground. Within ZANU there increasingly broke out a struggle between the backers of Sithole and Mugabe which culminated in an ostensibly complete split between the two leaders. A revolt within the ZANU forces in Zambia in 1974 was viciously suppressed and led indirectly to the murder of a civilian leader of ZANU. Zambia's intervention in this struggle led to the virtual exclusion of ZANU from Zambia which henceforth operated primarily from Mozambique.

Another attempt at unity, this time with emphasis on achieving an internal settlement, was the ANC (African National Council), formed by leaders from both ZANU and ZAPU (and as so often by individuals in detention or prison). To mobilize internal opinion against the proposed Anglo-Rhodesian settlement in 1972 this group chose as its leader a popular individual who had remained aloof from party politics—Bishop Muzorewa. He accepted the job and was completely successful.

At first the ANC and its work was favorably received by all nationalist groups. But as it began and continued talks with the Smith regime it came under increasing criticism, in particular by Sithole and Mugabe (together at this time in a Salisbury prison). ZAPU and Nkomo were more friendly. Yet in December of 1974 all groups agreed on paper to unite under the ANC as a unifying force.

Returning to the country the new leaders found popular opinion had swung away from Nkomo to the ANC and particularly to the ZANU (Sithole) faction. Therefore, after Sithole's subsequent arrest only Nkomo continued talks with Smith. Meanwhile in Zambia ZANU's offices were turned over to the new ANC. Soon Muzorewa was in exile and considered head of the external wing of the ANC. Out again, Sithole worked beside him as commander of both ZANU and ZANLA (see below). Nkomo had in effect split off to become head of the internal wing of ANC, as well as remaining head of ZAPU. In 1976 Nkomo continued talks with the Smith regime while a new front organization incorporated ZANLA insurgents under the ANC with the Bishop as their official commander.

But the insurgent organization was little affected by these changes. Soon Sithole had taken ZANU out of the ANC, and in turn the insurgent commanders by rejecting Sithole came entirely under Mugabe's direction. Unable to continue the external operation Bishop Muzorewa returned to Rhodesia to link up with Nkomo; but popular support for his ANC (later UANC) appeared so strong that he felt he could do without Nkomo. The latter immediately set out for the frontline states to organize the Patriotic Front with Mugabe.

The fact that most top leaders had been jailed or detained repeatedly and for long periods led to the parties forming both internal and external wings, and, inevitably, to occasional hostility between these wings. In addition, insurgent forces have often been out of political control. These forces also go by different names than the parties they are attached to. As a result we find ZANU (internal) and ZANU (external). ZAPU is largely external; internally it has been called the PCC or ANC (Nkomo). ZIPRA refers to the armed forces of ZAPU, and ZANLA to the armed forces of ZANU (external or Mugabe). Both are included on paper and for the benefit of the leaders of the frontline states in the Patriotic Front, the military forces of which are labeled ZIPA. However, the Front and its forces are merely umbrellas uniting for certain purposes forces that either stay apart from one another or actually engage in armed warfare in the field.

Thus, as events moved toward the internal settlement and the eventual elections, the main divisions of the nationalists were among ZAPU, ZANU (internal), ZANU (external), and the UANC. The other main figures in the election represented conservatives supporting Shona chiefs —Chirau—and conservatives and Nkomo supporters of Ndebele or other minority afflliation—Ndiweni.

This political history has meant that an unknown number of insurgents may be in their hearts loyal to internal political leaders such as Muzorewa, Sithole, or their lieutenants. It also means that the relative lack of success makes many insurgents and their families look earnestly for peace. It has also reflected the relatively nonideological nature of much of the leadership. But there are also other ethnic and geographical considerations that should be mentioned.

Aside from the white, and even smaller Asian and coloured, communities, the black population of Zimbabwe Rhodesia is grouped into Ndebele related tribes (19 percent), Shona related tribes (77 percent), and other, usually more primitive tribes (4 percent). The Ndebele are recent arrivals, having entered and conquered the country in the middle of the nineteenth century. The Shona are in turn divided into a number of important subgroups: Korekore, Zezuru, Manyika, Karanga and Ndau. Very proud of their noble traditions as nomadic warriors and cattle herders the Ndebele are relatively poorly represented in urban areas, even in their southwestern region. Largely farmers, the Shona dominate most of the country, including its urban centers. For many Zimbabwe Rhodesians, new ways of life and tribal intermarriage have greatly reduced the importance of tribal affiliations; this is especially true of the many blacks from neighboring countries who work in the cities and on industrialized farms. Yet for the overwhelming number of Zimbabwe Rhodesians times of stress bring out the saliency of tribal affiliations.

Geographically the heartland of the country is a high plateau with good rainfall and soil. Here are the main cities and the white farms. This is surrounded by a "middle veld" of poorer soil and lower rainfall and a "low veld" with even poorer conditions. The latter two areas contain most of the Tribal Trust Lands, still to some extent under the tribal control of chiefs; the low veld generally has very low populations and is given over in many areas to wildlife parks. The humid and unhealthy Zambezi valley forms the northern border. Only along the mountainous eastern border does relatively dense population and good agricultural land extend to the country's border.

The insurgency in Zimbabwe Rhodesia has had to deal with the fact that in most areas insurgents must cross large expanses of difficult, largely unpopulated or unwatered terrain to reach the main populated areas of the country. Insurgents are also confounded by the fact that the dependence of insurgents on certain tribal groups restricts areas of effective operation. The ZAPU movement of Joshua Nkomo receiving Zambian backing consists largely of Ndebele recruits, yet for geographical reasons and in order to remain a national movement its units must cross large areas occupied by different peoples, peoples which in a war characterized largely by terrorist killings of blacks are not likely to become friendlier. ZAPU must use Tongas to help its penetration across the Zambezi in the northwest, while in the north its units attempt to operate among tribal Shona. Its greatest success apparently comes from the longer route of sending units through Botswana, from which they can directly enter the tribal areas of the Ndebele people in the southwest.

Since a larger portion of the country is Shona, and the center of the Shona-based external ZANU (ZANLA) forces operate from Mozambique in the east, their geographical-ethnic problems should be less intense. However, as problems developed within ZANU they were increasingly exacerbated by secondary tribal divisions within Shona, so that by 1975 all external leaders of ZANU were said to belong to the Karanga tribe.[2] In addition, with the split between ZAPU and ZANU becoming increasingly open, ZANLA forces are reported to have opened a southern "offensive" to cut off ZAPU forces. But here ZANLA forces must operate in and subsist among the Venda people, a people hostile to the Shona and historically allied to the Ndebele. Partly as a result of this poor matching of insurgents and people, most insurgent activities have remained based on infiltrators rather than on groups organized within the country, and isolated actions have continued to have more a terrorist than military character. Thus, in spite of considerable support from neighboring countries, from the Soviet Union and its allies, and (at least formerly) China, the insurgency remains in its beginning stages.

## BIBLIOGRAPHY

*African Research Bulletin* (monthly press review on African affairs; particularly strong on Zimbabwe Rhodesia).

Blake, Robert. *A History of Rhodesia*. New York: Knopf, 1978.

Bowman, Larry W. *Politics in Rhodesia: White Power in an African State*. Cambridge: Harvard University Press, 1973.

Cary, Robert, and Diana Mitchell. *African Nationalist Leaders in Rhodesia Who's Who*. Bulawayo: Books of Rhodesia, 1977.

Davidson, Basil. *Let Freedom Come: Africa in Modern History*. Boston: Little Brown, 1978.

Legum, Colin. *African Contemporary Record*, Volume 9. New York: Holmes and Meier, 1977.

Murphree, M. W., B. J. Dorsey, G. Cheater, and B. D. Mothobi. *Education Race and Employment in Rhodesia*. Salisbury: Artca Publications, 1975.

Nelson, Harold D., *et al*. *Area Handbook for Southern Rhodesia*. American University Foreign Area Studies, Washington, D.C., 1975.

O'Meara, Patrick. *Rhodesia: Racial Conflict or Coexistence?* Ithaca: Cornell University Press, 1975.

Raeburn, Michael. *We Are Everywhere: Narratives from Rhodesian Guerrillas*. New York: Random House, 1979.

Sithole, Masipula. *Zimbabwe: Struggles Within the Struggle*. Salisbury: Rujeko Publishers, 1979.

In addition to the above we examined a number of documents directly relevant to the elections. Many of these were materials provided by the Zimbabwe Rhodesian government, local newspapers, and local groups opposed to the election. They also included:

Moose, Richard. "Rhodesia," Testimony by Assistant Secretary of State for African Affairs, Richard M. Moose, before the Senate Foreign Relations Committee, March 7, 1979.

Palley, Claire. "Memorandum on the Rhodesian Election Campaign, on whether Elections were Fair and Free and whether Principles Required for Rhodesian Independence have been Satisfied." April 19, 1979.

Wilkinson, Anthony R. "The Impact of the War in Zimbabwe: Some Critical Indicators." Statement presented to the Solarz Subcommittee, 1979.

"Zimbabwe." A Position Paper Prepared by the Catholic Commission for Justice and Peace on the Elections, April, 1979.

(After this report appeared we should add at least:

Meredith, Martin. *The Past is Another Country: Rhodesia 1890-1979*. London: Andre Deutsch, 1979.)

## II.  *The Common Roll Election—February 1980*

### INTERIM REPORT OF THE FREEDOM HOUSE OBSERVATION GROUP MARCH 1, 1980

Since Rhodesia became a British colony nearly a century ago, the white settlers have maintained an economic and political system that severely limited the rights of Africans. Colonialism, in Rhodesia as elsewhere, rested upon a social base of racism. The white minority effectively managed the agricultural, mining, and industrial development of the country. Africans, while suffering social humiliation, shared only marginally in this material development and not at all in the effective political system.

In the early 1960's African nationalists demanded independence and racial equality. The white minority sought independence from Great Britain to avoid fundamental changes in the racial structure of the society. Inevitably, demands for ending racial discrimination and national independence became intertwined.

Britain did not respond effectively to black demands for equality and independence, and white Rhodesians similarly failed to respond adequately to African pleas for greater political responsibilities. Protracted insurgency and international pressures finally forced the white government to reach the internal settlement with important segments of the black community in 1978. Under the subsequent Salisbury Agreement elections in April 1979 produced the first black prime minister, though whites retained significant power. Racial laws were abolished and more equitable social interaction between the races began.

Less than six months after the internal black nationalists were installed in office, the conference at Lancaster House resulted in new elections and a renewed promise of national sovereignty under majority rule.

The rulers of the new state would inevitably be black. But neither black nor white majority or minority rule assures the creation or preservation of a democratic society.

In this context the Freedom House observation group considered its task to be the evaluation of the extent to which the 1980 election:

1) represented progress in the transfer of power to the majority of the Zimbabwean people,
2) is a sincere, adequate attempt by the British and Rhodesian administrations to support this transfer,
3) is likely to represent an outcome provisionally acceptable as an expression of the will of the people, and
4) provides an adequate basis for the continuation and perfection of democratic rule.

Without the availability of the final election results or information on

any major defects that may come to light, we offer these preliminary
conclusions.

*A comparison of elections with democratic criteria.* A democratic system requires elections that do not exclude major sections of the adult
population from either active participation in the campaign or voting
processes. Voting must be secret and the counting of ballots must be
fair. Electoral campaigns must allow for the competitive presentation of
policies and programs by organized parties in a reasonably free atmosphere. All parties must have access to the communications media, and
ideally the media should represent a variety of viewpoints. Finally, the
constitutional system must provide elected representatives with the power
to rule the country. In general, voters should be represented in the
parliament in proportion to their numbers, except in so far as constitutional agreements making possible the continuation or establishment of
the nation give special but not unreasonable weight to the interests of
particular ethnic, religious, or sectional groups. The creation and continuance of the democratic system requires commitment to the processes
and principles of the system.

In these terms we judged the common roll election held in April 1979
to be a "relatively free expression of the will of the people of Zimbabwe
Rhodesia and to constitute a necessary step toward unfettered majority
rule." We believe that subsequent events have confirmed this judgment.
Nevertheless, we noted then a number of objections to the April elections. Two major political groups did not participate because they did
not accept 1) the constitution produced by the internal settlement, and
therefore 2) the legitimacy of the election.

Although there was an authentic contest among participating parties,
the primary electoral struggle was between the externally based parties
that opposed voting and the government that promoted it. In this context enforced participation in the poll and enforced abstention were
widely reported. There were no media generally available to the parties
that urged abstention, meetings and demonstrations opposing the elections were generally prevented, and many of those urging abstention were
in detention. Some observers also argued that the constitution provided
by the internal settlement gave unreasonable weight to the white ethnic
interest.

Judged against the background of the last election, the present election
represents on the surface a further step toward the perfection of democratic rule. In this election parties representing all major interests are
competing, there are publications representing the major political viewpoints (although most have had limited distribution), and the messages
of the competing parties have been broadcast on radio and television.
Although limited by time, resources, or fear, to some extent all parties

have been able to hold legal meetings and engage in other forms of campaigning in all provinces in which they competed. Unfortunately intimidation in this election remains at a high level, yet the fact that voter participation is not the central question in the 1980 election should have made direct coercion of voter behavior less effective. The constitutional framework within which the government elected this February will operate, if properly enforced, is more favorable to majority rule than that provided for in the internal settlement.

*Intimidation.* On the most general level, the open or implicit threat by the formerly externally based parties that they would renew the insurgency should they not win represented an important indirect form of intimidation. Threats by white or black African states of nonrecognition or intervention in the event of particular electoral outcomes represented an external form of intimidation.

The intimidation most in people's minds is the direct threat to individuals or families that they would lose their jobs, be beaten, or killed if they showed any sign of considering a party other than the intimidator's, if they campaigned for such a party, or voted for such a party. Although it is impossible to judge the effectiveness of these threats, in many areas of the country such threats, or the anticipation of such threats, effectively blocked the free presentation of the positions of competing parties. This particularly affected the chances of the weaker parties, but all parties had difficulties in one or more areas. Adherents of the three major parties have been those primarily accused of intimidation, but for a variety of reasons, the formerly externally based parties appear to have been most able to maintain areas in which the messages of other parties could not be effectively presented. As a result of the campaign the bulk of the population nonetheless was conscious of the messages of two or more competing parties.

The majority, perhaps because of the secrecy campaign and the experience of the April election, apparently believed that their votes would be secret. This reduced the effect of intimidators on electoral choices. In the last election the fact of voting could hardly remain unknown, and both sides could apply direct and effective pressure on the public act of going to the polls. Intimidators in this election, however, generally had to rely on more indirect means of influencing voters, for all parties desired a high turnout. Still, the climate of fear permeating much of the country significantly reduced the freedom with which the voter cast his or her ballot. The people have suffered so long from violence, and in many areas are so used to seeing opposing political parties as dangerous and violent groups, that the degree to which fear has played a role in voter choice in this election cannot be determined.

*The administrative and security effort.* The pervasive history of violence and the still incomplete acceptance and development of democratic institutions required far greater resources and more time than was available to the Governor to fully achieve his objectives. The system was simply unable to provide the average person the atmosphere a fully free democracy requires.

The cooperative attempt by the British government, the interim administration, and the security services to hold a "free and fair" election is creditable. The mechanics of last April's election were generally acceptable; with experience, the additional guarantees of the British presence, and the changes introduced, the mechanism this time appears to be even more reliable. It has been alleged that there has been an insufficiency of polling stations; we judge that lack of adequate stations has not greatly affected the result.

It is widely alleged that the security forces, and particularly the auxiliaries, have been allowed a free rein while the forces of the formerly external parties have been kept in camps, and that this as well as bias in reporting campaign violence, represents an attempt by the combined administration of the country to use the government machinery to defeat the formerly external parties, and particularly ZANU (PF). We believe that a nationwide, active security effort was essential and that given his resources the Governor used the services most likely to secure a fair result. Obviously, many of those in charge of the country personally oppose transfer of power to former insurgents, but most officials appeared to operate within a legal framework. Given its recent participation in government, one party exercised to some extent the incumbent advantage common to any election. Our interviews, however, indicate that the identification of the administration and security services with this party harmed its campaign more than aided it.*

Governor Soames and the Rhodesian bureaucracy should be credited with the substantial campaign to get out the vote and persuade the voter his ballot was secret. This campaign would be incomprehensible if the government and the Governor were attempting to use the security forces to intimidate voters to vote for a particular party. The campaign for secrecy strengthens the government's claim that the bulk of voter intimidation was not by the security forces, and that the formerly externally based forces maintained a politically effective presence outside the assembly points.

*Conclusions on the election.* The Governor and the Rhodesian bureaucracy have made a sincere attempt to involve all major sections of

---

*Afternote. Correspondingly, Governor Soames' biased ascription of intimidation to ZANU(PF) redounded to the benefit of ZANU(PF).

the Zimbabwean population in determining their affairs. However, given
the criteria expressed in this report, and if we define *free* as referring to
the degree to which the government provides for open competition and
guarantees the electoral process, and *fair* as referring to the ability of
the parties equitably to compete among one another; then the election
was essentially free but not entirely fair. Although political leaders
were not given a fully fair chance to achieve electoral success, the
electoral result will approximately represent the distribution of current
political force within Zimbabwe's black population. In this sense the
election process may be judged a further step toward majority rule.

*The election and the future of democracy in Zimbabwe.* As societies
strive to establish democratic systems, they frequently find that some
parties use democratic means to attain power without commiting themselves to maintain free institutions. Unfortunately, the commitment of
major parties to maintaining the openness and pluralism attained in the
last year of struggle in Zimbabwe has not been established. This problem
is compounded by the fact that some participants in the election will
have reason to believe that the outcome was determined by the distribution of partisan military or insurgent force.

Whatever the outcome, we hope the people of Zimbabwe remain
vigilant in the defense of those democratic institutions they already have
acquired. They must maintain their rights to think and choose freely,
and to change their minds and their leaders after experience with the
choices they have made.

Democracy requires compromise, and only compromise will bring an
end to violence and allow for the reconstruction that Zimbabwe's
people, particularly its poorest people, need. Democracy also implies
readiness to accept defeat, and to join with a will to resolve the problems
that face the community as a whole. To assure the freedom and peace
of Zimbabwe we hope those in the government emerging from this
election will temper partisanship and ideology, and strive to unify the
country and institutionalize its freedoms. Ultimately those who achieve
power must be prepared once again to face the free choice of the
electorate.

Africa has been plagued by apartheid, racism, tribalism, economic
exploitation, authoritarianism, and vicious dictatorships of both right
and left. In many countries civil liberties are denied and foreign armies
support continued oppression.

Protestation, economic measures, resolutions by the UN or OAU
have not been able significantly to alter or eradicate these conditions.

A free, democratic Zimbabwe can be a lesson not only for Africa but
for any place in the world where racism and exploitation exist. Such a
state could be the challenge that the world and the other peoples of

southern Africa need to begin the process of evaluation of their institutions that perhaps only a living example can give. In particular, South Africans would have before them the example of a society where black Africans have the major political power but where all citizens are treated with respect and equality in a free society.

Against this background Zimbabwe could offer a clear demonstration that a multiracial, economically viable state can be created that places democracy and individual freedom above all else, including black rule. For without democracy first, black governments can exploit both black and white.

## SUPPLEMENTARY ANALYSIS OF THE ELECTION

In terms of the Lancaster House Agreements the lower house was to consist of 100 members, 20 to be elected by the 103,000 registered white, coloured, and Asian voters and the other 80 by the black voters.

The white election on February 14 saw only six of twenty constituencies contested. In the event, the Rhodesian Front (of Ian Smith) won all twenty seats. In spite of the rapidly growing pragmatic acceptance of black rule and the even more meaningful end of segregation by the non-black community, the result seemed to indicate a tightening of a negative sense of racial identity in the face of a frightening and imminent black election.[3]

The black poll occurred on February 27, 28, and 29. 2,700,000 votes were cast, comparing favorably with the 1,870,000 votes in the previous election. Since 100,000 of the 1979 voters were non-black, nearly one million additional black votes were cast this February. As in 1979 the actual percentage of potential voters participating cannot be determined since the eligible population was only vaguely estimated. If 59 percent of the eligible black population voted in April 1979, about 84 percent voted in 1980.

Voting took place in eight electoral districts or provinces in both elections. In several provinces increases were modest—in Mashonaland West there was an actual drop in the estimated participation of potential voters. However, in three provinces where voting had been light last time increases were well over 100 percent. Most extreme was Victoria Province with an increase of 160 percent; the two Matabelelands were not far behind.

While the size of the poll was viewed as a sign of success for the civil service and the British Election Commissioner, it suggested in some cases an inability to prevent the formerly externally based parties from forcing people to vote on a scale we had not anticipated in our interim report. The Election Commissioner reported:

The massive turnout in these areas (Victoria Province, part of Manica-land and part of the Midlands) on the first day was largely achieved by aggressive "herding" of voters by party supporters, who escorted voters to the polls, patrolling up and down or insinuating themselves into the queues to ensure support for their party by sounds and gestures backed by threats. Many voters were frightened into voting by threats of death and the aged, infirm and pregnant were denied the opportunity to abstain. Many voters by-passed nearer polling stations in obedience to party instructions, to swamp other polling stations more distant where no doubt their party discipline and control was more rigid. Some voters were so anxious to demonstrate their obedience that they declared orally or by display of their ballot papers (eg. to be visible at a window in the polling station) that they had voted as instructed. Voting in these areas took place in an atmosphere of fear and under evident compulsion.

Elsewhere the Election Commissioner points to the possible serious-ness of "intimidation exerted on queues of voters by young party sup-porters joining the queue for the purpose of proselytizing—or worse." It also appears that party workers watching the lines moving in and out of the polls may have exerted in the highly charged and dangerous atmosphere a kind of polling intimidation far more widespread than the Election Commissioner had direct evidence for. One must also assume that "herding" of a less obvious kind may have occurred in many more areas than those officially detected.

The election results were as follows:

| Party | Percent of Valid Votes | Seats |
|-------|------------------------|-------|
| Zanu (PF) (Mugabe) | 62.99% | 57 |
| PF (Nkomo) | 24.11% | 20 |
| UANC (Muzorewa) | 8.28% | 3 |
| ZANU (Sithole) | 2.01% | 0 |
| Other Parties | 2.61% | 0 |
|  | 100.00% | 80 |

The result may be compared with the last election in which Mugabe and Nkomo did not compete. That time Muzorewa received 51 of 72 black seats, Sithole 12, and Ndiweni (in part a stand-in for Nkomo) 9. It may also be compared with estimates made before the election of party strengths. On the basis of a survey of knowledgeable Rhodesians in Lusaka in May 1978 a professor at the University of Zambia estimated (on a corrected basis) that in an inclusive election at that time Mugabe would receive 21 seats, Nkomo 30, Muzorewa 22, and Sithole 9.[5] This estimate would, of course, reflect the pro-Nkomo tendency of Lusaka observers. In its December 12, 1979, edition *Africa Confidential* esti-mated the outcome of the proposed election would be: Mugabe 23,

Nkomo 20, Muzorewa 23, Sithole 9, others 5. Shortly before the election itself many people were estimating Mugabe in the low 30's, with fewer seats for Nkomo and the minor candidates than in the *Africa Confidential* estimates. In its February 19 special edition on Rhodesia the *London Times* assumed no candidate would win a majority, as did apparently the pro-Mugabe weekly *Moto* as late as February 23.

Explaining the size of Mugabe's triumph is a chancy exercise at best. Clearly Muzorewa's victory in April hurt the Bishop greatly. He had promised peace and black government, with an evolutionary movement toward equality. The electorate expected peace and change. Bishop Muzorewa ruled effectively for not more than four months, and there was no peace and not enough visible change, certainly not for the electorate. We heard many say that they voted for Muzorewa last time but would vote for Mugabe (or Nkomo) this time for this reason. Many voters saw the government still in white hands, yet paradoxically they blamed the black government for still killing black guerrillas in the bush (and in Mozambique and Zambia where, in an attempt to force peace, attacks intensified in 1979). As we pointed out in the interim report the more the security forces seemed to support the UANC, the more the people identified the Bishop's party with the white enemy. In a youth and male dominated society identification of the Bishop with women may also have hurt, as did identification of Sithole, Nkomo, and Chikerema with the old in other parts of the country.

We remarked in the interim report on the several kinds of intimidation, most of which favored ZANU (PF) or the Patriotic Front. This apparently carried over into the voting process itself; shortly after our interim report was completed we learned this influence extended more into the urban areas than we had imagined.

It should also be remarked that the dividing line in election results between Mugabe and Nkomo support appeared to follow almost exactly the line of division between Shona speaking groups (Mugabe) and Ndebele and related groups (Nkomo). Rigidity of tribal determination seemed to have been more important than recent guerrilla force domination. For example, in Matabeleland South, an area of significant ZANLA (Mugabe) guerrilla success in the last few years and of ZIPRA (Nkomo) retreat, Mugabe only received 6.8 percent to Nkomo's 86.4 percent of the vote. This suggests that the effect of intimidation on voter behavior was accomplished through long-term political-military controls rather than the simple area presence of outside military units. This conforms with our previously expressed opinion that auxiliary intimidation (for the Bishop) would appear to have had little positive effect.

Decisive in the size of the Mugabe-Nkomo victory also appeared to be the growing realization in the last days of the campaign that Mugabe-Nkomo would win. For people afraid of their physical future if they ended up on the losing side, a fear often expressed, this realization probably led many to leave their previous inclinations and join the expected winners, thereby inflating the size of the margins. Effectively preventing campaigners of other parties from entering some areas further added to the strength of this effect. In some areas little more than government workers, soldiers, and outsiders must have voted against the sweep by the formerly externally based parties.

With these conflicting pieces of evidence and argument we cannot conclude, as the press generally seems to, that Mugabe and Nkomo would have gotten over fifty seats together without intimidation (enough to form a government), or that they would not have. Clearly they had considerable non-coerced support, but its dimensions cannot be estimated.

## FINAL REMARKS

Zimbabwe is now launched into fully recognized "majority rule government." Our experience in two elections suggests the extreme care with which the authenticity of elections of this kind must be viewed by outsiders in the context of violence. Superficial interviews hardly suffice as a means to understand the problem, no matter how necessary they may be. Comparison of April with February results also demonstrates the tendency, noted worldwide, for voters to ignore boycotts and vote for the candidates they are offered (as in April 1979). This should make outside observers skeptical of the legitimizing value of any election in which a narrow range of candidates is offered (as in one-party states).

Our observation of election observers led us to the conclusion that good observation results not so much from the time spent in the field or the number of observers as it does from the extent and nature of institutional limitations under which the observers work. We felt that many observing groups, particularly the official delegations, were so tied to the political interests of their governments that an independent verdict was impossible. In situations of this kind private observation groups should be more helpful; unfortunately many private groups seemed to have come with their minds made up—in some cases reversing their judgment of the election when the election results started to appear. All observation groups make bureaucracies and governments more careful, and in this sense all groups were desirable.

There are two interpretations of the meaning of the election results for Zimbabwe. According to the first, Mugabe and Nkomo merely used the rhetoric of Marxism-Leninism and the finances, supplies, and training of the communist world as a means to black power. Once in power they will adjust to the realities of Zimbabwe and establish a mixed socialist society comparable perhaps to that of socialist Egypt. More than in Egypt, it is assumed the present balance of forces will preserve civil liberties and opportunities that will allow later free and fair elections on the model of neighboring Botswana. Early post-election statements by Mugabe and his formation of a coalition government would seem to support this projection.

The alternative interpretation of the new Zimbabwe is that the present government is in the process of consolidating power in a delicate situation in which the preponderance of military force remains under white commanders. Once the reins of power are taken firmly by ZANU (PF), a rapid radicalization will occur that conforms with the hard-line party manifestos released as late as January. The society will then be regimented and disciplined along the lines of other one-party African states, for instance Mozambique, with tight administrative control and party discipline. Following the logic of this projection, the resulting closed and centralized system will not allow another free election with civil liberties and authentic choice. It is assumed that even should Prime Minister Mugabe not wish such a radicalization, many of his younger supporters and guerrilla leaders will force him in this direction.

The first interpretation conforms with our hopes in the interim report that Zimbabwe might become a model that would assist South Africa in the transitions it will soon face. This interpretation is closer to what our investigations would lead us to suppose the average Mugabe voter wants and expects, and is certainly what the voters for the other parties would desire. The second interpretation of Mugabe's success would not lead us to expect benefits from the election for either the Zimbabwean people or the peoples of southern Africa.

Although desirable American foreign policy directions in regard to Zimbabwe are not greatly clarified by the inconclusiveness of this analysis, it is clear that we should act in a way that increases the likelihood that events will unfold as suggested in the first interpretation. The political parties of both Nkomo and Mugabe contain a variety of factions along a continuum from moderate to radical. This strengthens the hope that a policy differentiating between support for a democratic and a totalitarian future might be productive.

The transition period the new government faces will be critical for the eventual shape of the political system and traditions of political culture that emerge. Prime Minister Mugabe has an opportunity to rise above narrow racial, tribal, factional, or ideological interests in the organization of the new Zimbabwe. Certainly he must go beyond narrow interests if Zimbabwe is to become a prosperous counterexample to the other nations under Marxist domination in southern Africa. Black power *and* a better life is what the Patriotic Front fought for.

The symmetry of pressures that brought the internal authorities and the external parties to the negotiating table at Lancaster House has been considerably altered by the election result. However, since the losers may still possess the power to support or obstruct the future development of the state, continuing recognition and employment of the full variety of political and military groups would be the ideal solution to the problems of transition. The new political leadership will be responsible for the decisions that are made, but in many ways they will be dependent on the people who were there before them—managers and technicians, military and police officers, defeated parties, and coalition partners. This distribution of power must be taken into account in the interim period. How this period is handled will have a decisive effect on Western governments or private institutions hoping to assist in the country's development.

The aid envisaged in the economic assistance package recommended for fiscal year eighty-one is a useful means of initiating a positive relationship between the United States and Zimbabwe following the establishment of diplomatic relations. Refugee resettlement assistance and health and educational aid reflect interest in the special problems of transition. It should be clear from the start of relations, however, that significant increments of American economic assistance, and political and moral support are contingent on the maintenance of those democratic institutions that brought the Mugabe government to power.

We counsel decision makers of democracies to follow again the careful approach we proposed after the April election: a democracy should not undertake quickly any major new initiatives in regard to Zimbabwe; it should welcome the progress that has been made toward a more inclusive polity, but predicate its continued support on the preservation and expansion of political and civil liberties. In so far as these rights are denied or the justification of their denial becomes government policy, a democracy should refrain from further government-to-government aid. Just as a democrat cannot support rule by a narrow white elite, he cannot justify supporting the rule of a narrow communist elite—no matter how much it claims to be acting in the interests of the people.[6]

## NOTES

1. "An Approach to a New American Policy on Zimbabwe Rhodesia." Testimony before the Subcommittees on Africa and International Organizations of the Foreign Affairs Committee of the House of Representatives, by Clifford P. Case, Bayard Rustin, and Leonard Sussman, May 16, 1979.

2. *See* Masipula Sithole, *Zimbabwe: Struggles Within the Struggle* (Salisbury: Rujeko Publishers, 1979), p. 69.

3. *See* M. W. Murphree, "Voting for White Seats in the February 1980 Elections: A Research Note" (Unpublished, 1980).

4. *See* "Common Roll Election 1980: Interim Report by Sir John Boynton, MC, British Election Commissioner." Salisbury, March 3, 1980.

5. Ronald T. Libby, "All-Party Elections in Zimbabwe: What Might Happen," *Africa Today*, 26, no. 1, 1979, pp. 7-17.

6. *See* note (1) above.

# PART IV

# Human Rights Policy and Moral Values

# The Need for a New International Basis for Human Rights Actions

The past year provided an extensive menu of situations in which the American government had an opportunity and responsibility to place American influence on the side of freedom. Unfortunately, it often failed to take these opportunities. Its failures derived from insufficient commitment to promoting freedom, poorly understood responsibilities, and a lack of effective means for the expression of American values. If we do not learn how to operate in defense of our values soon, we shall no longer be able to legitimate or defend them.

1979 saw four of the world's most tyrannical or violent regimes brought to violent ends—in Cambodia, the Central African Republic, Uganda, and Equatorial Guinea. Three of these had directly attacked their entire populations and killed hundreds of thousands arbitrarily and capriciously. Law no longer had meaning, traditional values were trampled upon, and no one dared to raise his voice. The actions of these governments approximated and in some cases surpassed those in Germany and Eastern Europe in the worst years of Nazi brutality—although their focus was not as explicitly on a particular group. The destruction of these regimes should have led to rejoicing in Washington. Yet by and large the American government stood mute. In the case of Uganda we were inclined to be more disapproving than approving because the convention of not crossing national boundaries had been broken to effect change; in the UN we voted for the Pol Pot regime's legitimacy; Equatorial Guinea was largely ignored by the United States both before and after the removal of its tyrant.

American reluctance is partly understandable. In Cambodia, Uganda, and the Central African Republic change of government required essentially foreign invasions. We have come a long way since World War II in affirming the sanctity of borders on a worldwide basis. In all four cases American leaders could reasonably fear that the successor governments would end up little better than their predecessors. In the two principal cases many Americans had little ideological sympathy with

193

the aggressors. Indeed, Vietnam was by its aggression completing its conquest of Indochina: indirectly it was expanding the realm of Soviet communism, the expansion that poses the most explicit international threat to the democracies. By heralding Vietnam's destruction of Pol Pot we would also be offending the Chinese communists, our allies of convenience in the big-power standoff.

But if we are to stand for our values in the world, this stand must include supporting effective action, however uncomfortable its source, against regimes that treat their peoples like animals. Since the international community failed to act, others acted, and in spite of their further sins or the unfortunate *machtpolitik* repercussions, we should have applauded these actions. Ideally we should have participated in the overthrow of such tyrannies. Properly accomplished, such participation would have helped our image, advanced our ideals, and made for a better prognosis for the countries themselves.

In Iran and Palestine 1978-79 saw the United States taking positive steps to defend the rights of the oppressed, yet the steps were incomplete and to the rest of the world our role seemed at best ambiguous. Through the Camp David agreement we made possible the reestablishment of the rights of Egyptians and Palestinians in the Sinai and Gaza. But in the West Bank there was a continued and even progressive erosion of the rights of Palestinians. Our feeble complaints to Israel led to a one step backward two steps forward movement by the Israelis. Pro-Arab opinion was building in the United States that combined with political realities would forever reverse this policy, but movement was very slow. The fact that Palestinian, Syrian, and Israeli interventions in Lebanon continued to make impossible the Lebanese reorganization of their polity in spite of a UN presence offered another opportunity for decisive U.S. action, but it did not come.

The Iranian situation changed between mid-1978 and mid-1979 from one in which we were simultaneously trying to liberalize and maintain in power the Shah's regime to one in which we were critical but supportive of the populist but tyrannical Islamic regime that replaced it. There was a natural ideological clientele of American policy in Iran—moderate, democratic, liberal rights-oriented groups with Western educated leaders. We had failed to support this clientele adequately under the Shah—although the Carter administration took important steps in this direction—and we have failed to support it adequately under the Islamic suppression. As the Soviets saw the left wing crushed under the weight of the mullahs, their propagandists came thundering to the assistance of the left; we continued to hesitate in the name of good intergovernmental relations.

Late in the year the U.S. government made the tactical error of allowing the Shah in for medical treatment. An explosion of hatred and the taking of hostages inevitably followed. Our position continued to deteriorate, and with it that of freedom for the Iranians. Perhaps it was morally defensible to take in the Shah but this morality surely clashed with other U.S. human rights and foreign policy interests.

In neighboring Afghanistan 1979 saw a Soviet-backed regime imprison thousands, bomb villages, torture peasants, and repress intellectuals and religious leaders. We wrung our hands while the Soviets ferried in government troops and Soviet officers led army units against the oppressed. We took a negative official attitude to events in Afghanistan; still for fear of offending the Soviets and because of our poor relations with both Pakistan and Iran, we did not propose concerted action that might support the many groups that struggled against oppression. At the end of the year the Soviets simply occupied the country, shot its ruler, and put in a thoroughly subservient puppet. *Then* we made Afghanistan an international issue, but it was the Soviet troops not the oppression that moved us.

Our African policy has been a web of contradictions. In spite of the long-admitted justice of the Eritrean revolt, backed by a people with little historical relation to Addis Adaba, and the brutally murderous policy of the present rulers of the country, we failed to lift a hand to support any of the rebel factions. The flagrant intervention of the Soviets and Cubans could not move us, nor could the popularity of the Eritrean cause with many Arab countries, countries with which our government could use improved relations.

Our inaction in Eritrea and Uganda was defended on the basis of our commitment to leave Africa to the Africans, to follow the lead of the OAU, to search for African friends no matter what their politics or human rights record. The nadir of this policy was perhaps reached in 1979 when President Carter received with honor President Touré of Guinea. Touré's barbarous leftwing government had been noted for the execution, torture, and imprisonment of its enemies. Apparently Touré's movement away from the USSR and quite recent conversion to moderation were enough for our support. It used to be said the United States would support any leader as long as he was anti-communist; now it apparently is enough if he is anti-Soviet; this policy is no more charming, nor is it likely to be more rewarding than mindless anti-communism.

After the fall of Amin the only African country against which we exercised sanctions during 1979 was Zimbabwe Rhodesia. It is true that in the midst of war it held political prisoners and practiced censorship. It is true a small white minority had the most power and lived at a much higher standard than the black majority. But in 1978-79 the society was changing rapidly. Elections were held under a compromise constitution in April in which the elected were mostly black and in which there was real political competition.[1] The state of civil liberties and wartime conditions made the election only a partial step toward freedom. Yet by mid-1979 Zimbabwe Rhodesia was a freer country than many on the African continent and was moving toward a further expansion of its freedom. This was in stark contrast to the situations in neighboring Mozambique or Angola. While flawed the April elections were certainly freer than those in one-party Zambia or Tanzania. Yet the imperatives of African black racism, according to which any black government is "freer" than any with even lingering white influence, would have us condemn Zimbabwe's rulers while praising their neighbors. For Machiavellian reasons, dictated by both internal and external politics the United States followed the lead of this racism and refused to end our embargo on trade or open diplomatic relations. Only the ability of the British Conservatives to work out a compromise between Salisbury and the guerrillas and temporarily regain control of the country allowed us finally to abandon our biased policy. Whatever the final outcome, the awkward human rights issues of 1979 cannot be denied.

In Central America U.S. policy again trailed behind events. There were communists in the rebel movements of Guatemala, Nicaragua, and El Salvador, but by vacillating for this reason in our support of decisive improvements in human rights, we have appeared determined to create self-fulfilling prophecies that change will mean communist rule. In Nicaragua we pressed for improvement in human rights with Somoza. At times he responded by reducing the severity of his regime—which in any event was not very repressive by third world standards. But our subsequent praise of these limited improvements placed us paradoxically on the side of repression as the violence on both sides escalated. This was analogous to the dilemma faced in Iran; when the Shah liberalized in response to our pressure, our resulting praise of the improvements made us appear to legitimize the repression that remained. In both cases the failure of our human rights public relations was largely due to the long record of American association with the old regime, a relation President Carter's human rights team could not erase with the limited moves within its control. But even where a historical background of this kind does not poison our efforts, our need to praise small improvements in human rights often conflicts with our ultimate goal of creating a democratic world. States rejecting American models and allegiances are less likely to build that world.

These examples of indecision, inaction, or ineffective action resulted partly from the incomplete acceptance of human rights objectives within American bureaucratic and political communities, the unavoidable need to consider trade-offs between a variety of national interests, and the passivity produced by the expensive Vietnam failure. But our ineffectiveness also stemmed from the absence of an effective international organizational forum through which the United States might express and defend its values.

Three kinds of cases should be distinguished. In the first it seems probable that international opinion will have an effect upon the internal situation. The liberals of Iran believed that they had found such a point when in 1892 they addressed a plea for help to the Western embassies in Teheran. It read, in part:

> We, sons of Iran, call for the intervention of the Western Powers at this critical moment. Such an intervention must of course be collective and pacific. The nations of Europe must constitute themselves umpires between the Persian people and government. An armed intervention would, on the contrary, be of no avail to anyone, least of all to Persia, already torn by internal feuds. You have no need to take any official step; your influence alone with our oppressor would be sufficient.[2]

For the violations of human rights today in Brazil and El Salvador, or a few years ago in India or Iran, this type of intervention could be decisive. In several of the situations listed above for 1979 it could have been of some value, but in many cases such international "jawboning" will not be effective. UN resolutions could not bring the American hostages home; UN resolutions were likewise unable to affect the Soviet occupation of Afghanistan.

Solving cases of this kind require either the dispatch of effective intervention forces by international agreement, or international support of opposition elements through the provision of arms and advice. The former is needed in Lebanon; the latter would be more effective in Afghanistan.

Common to all three of the strategies, if they are to be effective, is an international consensus supporting the action. Ideally this would be a universal, UN consensus. But its very universality has pulled the teeth from the UN and pointed its actions toward a limited number of less than critical situations. As demonstrated repeatedly on the borders of Israel and in Cyprus, even when agreement is reached UN forces do not fight and generally are not expected to.

Regional organizations such as the Organization of African Unity (OAU) or the Organization of American States (OAS) have proved equally ineffective and for essentially the same reasons. National boundaries and existing governments are sacrosanct, except in special ideological situations in which criteria tangential to human rights are used to define pariah states. (However, because of the special U.S.

relationship in the case of Nicaragua, reliance on the OAS was an important option.)

As proposed in *Freedom at Issue* a few years ago effective multilateral, international action must be organized through a more limited grouping.[3] The "Council of Free Nations" proposed there would be able to decide in conformity with the democratic values of its members on collective actions. These would not always be actions reflecting U.S. interests, but active consensus on American goals would be far more likely than through the mechanism of a UN under the control of a majority of anti-democratic or less than democratic states.

Such a Council of Free Nations might emerge from case by case American reliance on like-minded states for consensual intervention over a period of years. Relatively small international forces from such groupings might be able to police the borders of southern Lebanon and eventually the West Bank. They might have been able to eject Amin at an appropriate point, or to occupy Phnom Penh. Such actions would offer direct benefit to local populations and help establish the principle that the democratic international community will not put up with governmental behavior below a certain standard, irrespective of the competing principle that national borders shall be inviolable. Where we could not take these actions with the aid of an international grouping, such a grouping might at least support those who were able to act.

In other cases, such as Afghanistan, the international grouping might provide arms and integration to rebel movements. In still others, such as the Indonesian suppressions of West Irian or East Timor the grouping might bring the kind of pressure to bear that the Iranian liberals of 1892 requested: they might bring moral pressure or act as an umpire. This would require on-the-spot investigation and subsequent recommendations. A democratic regional power would in some interventions play the major role, while in others all parties would prefer that pressure come from further away.

By following this approach human rights concerns could be effectively extended to the world as they have been extended to the margins of western and southern Europe by the Council of Europe. The approach would diffuse criticisms at home, internationally, and in the host countries that always stem from unilateral U.S. action, and would increase the effectiveness of outside action.

It will be said that Korea and Vietnam proved our inability to effectively get other states to cooperate with us on international action. But our actions in these cases were of a decisiveness and scale unlikely in the future; in the future the United States may not act at all without international cooperation. Korea and Vietnam were also cold war actions;

however defensible, they are of a different order than the concerted actions in defense of human rights that the free nations must agree upon if they are to build a human and just future.

## NOTES

1. For extended analyses by Freedom House, see Part III, above.

2. Nikki Keddie, *Religion and Rebellion in Iran: The Tobacco Protest of 1891-92* (London 1966), p. 154.

3. R. D. Gastil, "Affirming America's Ideals in Foreign Policy," *Freedom at Issue*, 38 (November/December 1976), pp. 12-15.

# Moral Value and Freedom

Those who strive to extend political rights and civil liberties are open to the criticism that they are contributing to the nihilistic devaluation of modern life. Eventually, unlimited freedom must destroy itself, for the inevitable result of nihilism is the destruction of freedom.

One of the earliest criticisms of the Comparative Survey pointed out the degree to which the Survey seemed to ignore alternative goals such as order, piety, and justice.[1] In particular the critic pointed to the inability of a democratic system to operate if everyone acted without constraint in pursuit of his own private goals.

In spite of communist history and the libertarian milieu in which it continues to thrive in noncommunist states, communist regimes have often been remarkably puritanical. In their propaganda they emphasize the negative relationship of Western freedoms with nihilistic decadence. Authoritarian noncommunist regimes often justify their repressions by picturing themselves as the defenders of traditional values and standards against dissolute innovation. Most recently Iran's Ayatollah Khomeini preaches the identification of the liberal freedoms with prostitution, alcoholism, and pornography. As the Ayatollah says to his critics: "You do not believe in any limits to freedom. You deem license to be freedom."[2]

For an American to identify political freedom with license appears to be historically mistaken, although in recent years the First Amendment has certainly been used, though apparently misused, to support libertarian interests. Our Revolution was seen by the overwhelming majority of its participants as a way to preserve liberties they believed London was steadily taking away from them. These liberties of popular consent and rational criticism offered no license. More problematical were the liberties of individuals or at least communal conscience: these were to become the basis of libertarian thinking, but to their authors meant primarily choice among a variety of roads to God.[3]

Clearly freedom can be expanded, and in the West sometimes has been, until it eliminates even those barriers that make its preservation possible.

To escape capture by this paradox we reiterate that in promoting freedom we affirm 1) that freedom is only one among several values necessary for a healthy society, 2) that freedom and liberty do not necessarily imply libertarianism, 3) that political and civil freedoms must be balanced by other concerns, and 4) freedom, like any other basic value, becomes meaningful to the extent that it places limits or restrictions on other values.

It may help to understand this position if we place social freedom[4] within a more encompassing framework for humanistic evaluation.[5] The values that have traditionally interested thinkers may be classified as hedonistic, distributional, transcendent, and reverential. Hedonistic values are those commonly of most concern to utilitarians and materialists. Food, shelter, sex, and entertainment are core values of this class. Distributional values are those expressed by the concept of justice. We want people to have the material values they require, but we also want the division of these values among persons to accord with an acceptable concept of justice. For some thinkers justice implies that all people receive the same material benefits, for others justice means that all should receive a just reward for effort, or that there be an equal chance in the lottery of life. Negatively, justice implies that those who injure others or harm the social order should receive a reasonable or to some degree compensating punishment.

The spiritual values of transcendence and reverence are equally important. Transcendence includes all those human activities that rise above the limits of untrained biological nature, whether the accomplishment be in athletics, science, art, or some other field. Since concern for morality is itself a learned mastering or refocusing of the egoistic and narrowly altruistic (for example, parental) concerns of biological humanity, transcendence is the most basic of moral concerns. Reverence means the capacity of human beings to place some matters beyond calculation out of respect for the values they honor. It means a willingness to accept limits positively, to constrain the full possibilities of action for reasons not reducible to material, distributional, or transcendent analysis. Murder, for example, may restore balance in human relations or bring justice; Nietzsche would see some murders as a form of self-assertion or of transcendence of triviality. But most people recoil from murder because of the reverence for human life implied in the simple "Thou shalt not kill." Reverence comes in many other forms, such as the feeling food should be blessed before it is consumed, or in the preservationist's concern to preserve wildlife or traditional ways of life from destruction.

Freedom in this framework can be seen from two vantage points. First, the value of freedom is comparable to the distributional concern with equality. As we pointed out in the 1979 yearbook,[6] freedom as understood in America is not as much an alternative value to equality as it is identical to it. Freedom to us means that in certain essential respects all people are to be treated equally and to have an equal right to participate in the affairs of the community. In so far as this equality is not practically reflected in equal power, Americans have generally accepted a limited inequality as required by the needs of society and differences in the histories of particular individuals. Against these needs freedom and equality must be considered together.

Freedom and equality are also supported in certain respects by the existence of a reverential concern for the basic value of each human being. In particular, the advocate of freedom believes that no group of people or government has a right to kill, imprison, or torture other human beings for their nonviolent beliefs. For whatever reason, human beings cannot be treated as objects for the greater good of mankind or placed in mental institutions for ideological mistakes.

Libertarianism means that all individuals or groups should have a right to act as they please, irrespective of the desires of the society as a whole, in so far as the individual actions do not directly take the same rights away from others. However, the fact is that a minority of individuals too often can disrupt the achievement of a majority's values. In our view the libertarian would grant such minorities unequal and unfair political and civil rights.

To illustrate this defect of libertarianism let us consider the desire of a majority to restrict temptations such as those of sex, drink, or gambling that they believe are essentially damaging to themselves and others when submitted to. Members of this majority may be fully aware that individually they are attracted to the activities they wish to prohibit, and indeed consider this fact an important reason to remove the temptations. Libertarians believe there should be no prohibitions. Of course, if people with this belief are in a majority, no prohibition can be maintained. But if they are not in the majority, the majority should not feel that it is destroying the birthright of a free people to introduce prohibitions.

For this reason we argue that it is access to the decision-making power of the free society that is critical to freedom rather than the degree to which that society applies rigid or relaxed constraints on the public behavior of its citizens.

Freedom is also constrained by the fact that social life demands that we must emotionally accept a variety of role-dependent moralities as our individual lives develop. Social roles may be seen as either descriptive averages of what people do in particular positions in life; or prescriptive, ideal descriptions of what people should do in these positions. Most prescriptive roles are to a considerable degree biologically and culturally defined for us. Yet their acceptance is not automatic. Each individual must necessarily through a transcendence of his ego adopt appropriate roles as his own if he is to make a maximum contribution to the happiness and well-being of those around him. A child sacrifices something in cleaving to the role of a child, just as a parent sacrifices in doggedly playing his or her role, or as political leaders or other public figures do in their roles. While there are exceptions, escape from such role expectations almost always harms those about us, *and* harms the generation to follow by corrupting or tarnishing the models that they would wish to copy.

This moral requirement of roles might be called by some philosophers the freedom to do what one must. But it is better seen as a limit on freedom that society and each of us places on individuals so that other social goals, whether material or spiritual, may be obtained.

This view of social freedom as a constrained and limited, albeit basic value, is consistent with the concept of freedom as a value that by itself is insufficient. Historically the free societies of history—such as peasant Iceland or Switzerland—were not centers for creation of great art, science, or religious faith, nor were they outstanding in the creation of a material surplus of general benefit for mankind. It does not deny the contribution of these societies or the nobility of their free peoples to point to their incompleteness.

Mankind would not only be diminished if freedom became the only value of a society, but such a society could not exist. Obviously, all human life depends on the values of material benefit and pleasure. While we have argued that these can be satisfied at many levels, and that given traditional material standards human beings will be at least as interested in non-material as material goals,[7] nevertheless providing the minimum material expectations of each generation is clearly a basic value for social stability and human satisfaction.

The necessity for societies to develop or maintain spiritual values other than freedom is suggested by the persistent drive for human beings to make sense of the world and their place in it—to understand. No one is likely to believe he is on earth simply to be free. There has to be a freedom for something. Without this, there is a deep hollow in the soul that makes life hard to bear.

It is this hollowness that destroyed the Weimar Republic, that makes possible the persistent fanaticism of the young, mirrored so well in the communist Vietnamese cadres that, however misguided, *were* more willing to sacrifice themselves for their cause than the noncommunists they faced. While the search for ideals may lead one generation to riot and lead the next to passive withdrawal and materialism, the search never ends. Underneath, a society erodes that does not provide a framework or frameworks within which at least partial answers may be found.

To understand the need for spiritual meaning, we must not overintellectualize. Meaning for most, perhaps all people, lies more in the realm of action than ideas. Meaning is found when life is so understood that it is worthwhile renouncing some of life's possibilities to affirm it. For God one may renounce marriage and family, pay the tithe, contribute labor free of charge to the church; for communism one may risk his life, reject trivial relationships, immerse himself in study; for Krishna one may shave his head and dance in the streets. Intuitively, there is meaning in what we do if there is sacrifice, renunciation, or what may be called reverence or limits. For a mother, a child is meaningful to the degree it has placed limits on her life, and thereby fulfilled it.

For many, of course, there must be a transcendental value that carries beyond this, that places the sacrifice of parent or soldier in an intellectual framework. Indeed, serious scientists devote their lives to perfecting, block by block, an edifice of meaning that transcends what the generation before could know. But sacrifice seems the more fundamental answer. The failure of our society to maintain a legitimating scheme for sacrifice, one that fits its ever higher level of sophistication, is one of its most critical weaknesses.

In a society that cannot tie its deepest values to freedom, freedom is itself endangered. The danger from without comes from the inbalance between societies that by allowing the expression of all beliefs and behaviors and by requiring no sacrifice cast doubt on all belief and behavior *and* those societies that by restricting access to alternatives and daily requiring sacrifice are able to maintain beliefs and spiritual habits of sacrifice. The danger from within comes from the search of unbounded lives for bounds, bounds that may ultimately be found in narrow belief systems and organizations that reject freedoms and develop sufficient power to overwhelm liberal but dissolute majorities.

The free society paradoxically faces the ever present danger of succumbing to the dangers inherent in its defining value. All values, like all verities, are fruitful within limits, but carried to extremes negate themselves.

To meet this challenge the free society has several strategies. First it must emphasize the essential rather than the more questionable extensions of freedom. Such essentials include limited majority rule, free rational expression and organization, pluralism, and privacy. The free society must allow majorities to maintain the material and spiritual values they cherish, including those limitations on public lifestyles and modes of nonrational expression they feel appropriate. Secondly, the free society must cherish the multitude of minority belief systems, organizations, and traditions it contains, allowing the supporters of each to maintain its strengths and characteristics, at least in so far as the action of minorities do not seriously interfere with the rights of other groups or legitimate majority concerns. Finally, the free society must emphasize the spiritual values inherent in, or attached to, the concepts of political and civil freedom, particularly the respect for human individuality and value they represent. This emphasis will not make freedom a basic spiritual value, however, unless there goes with it the clear message that we must at times sacrifice other values for freedom. Nothing worth having is without this cost. This may mean the sacrifice implied in military preparedness or even war, but it also means the sacrifice of American material interests inherent in a diligent, long-term pursuit of an international human rights policy. We must be taught, administration after administration, that we cannot maintain the value of our freedoms without sacrificing some of our material benefits for the freedoms of others.

## NOTES

1. Theodore A. Sumberg, "Social Disorganization as a Threat to Freedom," *Freedom at Issue* 28 (November/December 1974), pp. 12-14.

2. *Iran Voice* 1, 15 (September 10, 1979). Publication of the Embassy of the Islamic Republic of Iran.

3. *See* Oscar and Mary Handlin, *The Dimensions of Liberty* (Cambridge: Harvard University Press, 1961); Glenn T. Miller, *Religious Liberty in America: History and Prospects* (Philadelphia: Westminster Press, 1976).

4. *See* R. D. Gastil, *Freedom in the World 1978* (Boston and New York: G. K. Hall and Freedom House, 1978), pp. 111ff, for definitions of social freedom.

5. For a fuller discussion of this approach see R. D. Gastil, *Social Humanities* (San Francisco: Jossey-Bass, 1977), pp. 96-131.

6. R. D. Gastil, *Freedom in the World 1979* (Boston and New York: G. K. Hall and Freedom House, 1979), pp. 63-73.

7. *See* R. D. Gastil, "Pluralist Democracy and the Third World," *Worldview*, October, 1978, pp. 37-42.

# PART V

# Country Summaries

# Introduction

The following country descriptions summarize the evidence that lies behind our ratings for each country. They first bring together for each country most of the tabular material of Part I. Then, political rights are considered in terms of the extent to which a country is ruled by a government elected by the majority at the national level, the division of power among levels of government, and the possible denial of self-determination to major subnationalities, if any. While decentralization and the denial of group rights are deemphasized in our rating system, these questions should not be ignored. The summaries also contain consideration of civil liberties, especially as these include freedom of the media and other forms of political expression, freedom from political imprisonment, torture, and other forms of government reprisal, and freedom from interference in nonpublic group or personal life. Equality of access to politically relevant expression is also considered. In some cases the summaries will touch on the relative degree of freedom from oppression outside of the government arena, for example, through slavery, labor bosses, capitalist exploitation, or private terrorism; this area of analysis is little developed at present.

At the beginning of each summary statement the country is characterized by the forms of its economy and policy. The meanings of the terms used in this classification may be found in Part I, "The Relation of Political-Economic Systems to Freedom," and its accompanying Table 7. The classification is highly simplified, but it serves our concern with the developmental forms and biases that affect political controls. The terms employed in Part I and Table 7 differ from those used in the following summaries only in that the capitalist-socialist term in the former discussion is divided into two classes in the summaries. *Mixed capitalist* systems, such as those in Israel, the Netherlands, or Sweden, provide social services on a large scale through governmental or other nonprofit institutions with the result that private control over property is sacrificed to egalitarian purposes. These nations still see capitalism as legitimate, but its legitimacy is accepted grudgingly by many in government. *Mixed socialist* states such as Iraq or Poland proclaim themselves to be socialist but in fact allow rather large portions of the economy to remain in the private domain. As in Table 7 the terms *inclusive* and *noninclusive* are used to distinguish between societies in which the economic activities of most people are organized in accordance with the dominant system and those dual societies in which they remain largely outside. The system should be assumed to be inclusive unless otherwise indicated.

Each state is categorized according to the political positions of the national or ethnic groups it contains. Since the modern political form is the "nation-state," it is not surprising that many states have a *relatively homogeneous population.* The overwhelming majority in these states belong to roughly the same ethnic group; people from this group naturally form the dominant group in the state. In relatively homogeneous states there is no large subnationality (this is, with more than one million people or twenty percent of the population) residing in a defined territory within the country: Austria, Costa Rica, Somalia, and West Germany are good examples. States in this category may be ethnically diverse (for example, Cuba or Colombia), but there are no sharp ethnic lines between major groups. These states should be distinguished from *ethnically complex states,* such as Guyana or Singapore, that have several ethnic groups, but no major group that has its historic homeland in a particular part of the country. Complex states may have large minorities that have suffered social, political, or economic discrimination in the recent past, but today governments in such states treat all peoples as equals as a matter of policy. In this regard complex states are distinguishable from *ethnic states with major nonterritorial subnationalities,* for the governments of such states have a deliberate policy of giving preference to the dominant ethnic group at the expense of other major groups. Examples are Burundi or China (Taiwan).

Another large category of states is labeled *ethnic states with (a) major territorial` subnationalities(y).* As in the homogeneous states there is a definite ruling people (or *Staatsvolk*) residing on its historic national territory within the state. But the state also incorporates other territories with other historic peoples that are now either without a state, or the state dominated by their people lies beyond the new border. As explained in *Freedom in the World 1978* (pp. 180–218), to be considered a subnationality a territorial minority must have enough cohesion and publicity that their right to nationhood is acknowledged in some quarters. Events have forged a quasi-unity among groups only recently quite distinct—as among rebels in the Southern Sudan. Typical countries in this category are Burma and the USSR; more marginally states such as Peru or Laos are also included. *Ethnic states with major potential territorial subnationalities* fall into a closely related category. In such states—for example, Ecuador or Bolivia—many individuals in the ethnic group have merged, with little overt hostility, with the dominant ethnic strain. The assimilation process has gone on for centuries. Yet in these countries the new consciousness that accompanies the diffusion of nationalistic ideas through education may reverse the process of assimilation in the future, especially where the potential subnationality has preserved a more or less definable territorial base.

There are a few truly *multinational states* in which ethnic groups with territorial bases coexist in one state without a clearly definable ruling people or *Staatsvolk*. In such states the several "nations" each have autonomous political rights, although these do not in law generally include the right to secession. India and Nigeria are examples. One *trinational* and a few *binational* states complete the categories of those states in which several nations coexist.

The distinction between truly multinational states and ethnic states with territorial subnationalities may be made by comparing two major states that lie close to the margin between the categories—the ethnic Russian USSR and multinational India. In the USSR, Russian is in every was the dominant language. By contrast, in India Hindi speakers have not achieved dominance. English remains a unifying lingua franca, the languages of the several states have not been forced to change their script to accord with Hindi forms, and Hindi itself is not the distinctive language of a "ruling people"—it is a nationalized version of the popular language of a portion of the population of northern India. (The pre-British ruling class used a closely related language with Arabic, Persian, and Turkish infusions; it was generally written in Persian-Arabic script.) Unlike Russians in the non-Russian Soviet Republics, Hindi speakers from northern India do not have a special standing in their own eyes or those of other Indians. Calcutta, Bombay, and Madras are non-Hindi speaking cities, and their pride in their identities and culture is an important aspect of Indian culture. By contrast, many Soviet Republics are dominated by Russian speakers, a situation developing even in Kiev, the largest non-Russian city.

Finally, *transethnic heterogeneous states*, primarily in Africa, are those in which independence found a large number of ethnically distinct peoples grouped more or less artifically within one political framework. The usual solution was for those taking over the reins of government to adopt the colonial approach of formally treating all local peoples as equal, but with the new objective of integrating all equally into a new national framework (and new national identity) as and when this would be possible. Rulers of states such as Senegal or Zaire often come from relatively small tribes, and it is in their interest to deemphasize tribalism. In some cases the tribes are so scattered and localistic that there is no short-term likelihood of secession resulting from tribalism. However, in other cases portions of the country have histories of separate nationhood making the transethnic solution hard to implement. In a few countries recent events have placed certain ethnic groups in opposition to one another or to ruling circles in such a way that the transethnic state remains only the *formal* principle of rule, replaced in practice by an ethnic hierarchy, as in Congo or Liberia (until 1980).

The descriptive paragraphs for political and civil rights are largely self-explanatory. Subnationalities are generally discussed under a subheading for political rights, although the subject has obvious civil liberties aspects. Discussion of the existence or nonexistence of political parties may be arbitrarily placed in one or the other section. These paragraphs only touch on a few relevant issues, especially in the civil liberties discussion. An issue may be omitted for lack of information, because it does not seem important for the country addressed, or because a particular condition can be inferred from the general statement of a pattern. It should be noted that we have tried to incorporate the distinction between a broad definition of political prisoners (including those detained for violent political crimes) and a narrow definition that includes those arrested only for nonviolent actions—often labeled "prisoners of conscience." At the end of each country summary we have included an overall comparative statement that places the country's ratings in relation to those of others. Countries chosen for comparison are often neighboring or similar ones, but juxtaposing very different countries is also necessary for tying together the system.

The following summaries take little account of the oppressions that occur within the social units of a society, such as family and religious groups, or that reflect variations in the nonpolitical aspects of culture. In particular, the reader will note few references in the following summaries to the relative freedom of women. This may be a serious gap in the Survey, but with limited resources we felt that it was better to omit this range of issues than to only tangentially include it. We suspect that including the freedom of women would not affect the ratings a great deal. Democracies today have almost universally opened political and civic participation to women on at least a formal basis of equality, while most nondemocratic societies that deny these equal rights to women also deny effective participation to most men. In such societies granting equal rights may have limited meaning. It is little gain for political and most civil rights when women are granted equal participation in a totalitarian society.

# AFGHANISTAN

**Economy:** noninclusive socialist    **Political Rights:** 7
**Polity:** Communist one-party       **Civil Liberties:** 7
**Population:** 18,000,000*            **Status of Freedom:** not free

An ethnic state with major territorial subnationalities

**Political Rights.** Afghanistan is now ruled by a communist party under the tutelage and direct control of the Soviet Union. It has no electoral or traditional legitimization. Soviet forces control the major cities but their control is contested by a variety of resistance movements throughout the country.

*Subnationalities.* The largest minority is the Tadzhik (thirty percent), the dominant people of the cities and the western part of the country. Essentially lowland Persians, their language remains the lingua franca of the country, although it has been government policy to require equal use of the language of the Pathan majority, especially in the bureaucracy. The Persian speaking Hazaras constitute five to ten percent of the population. Another ten percent belong to the Uzbek and other Turkish groups in the north.

**Civil Liberties.** The press is government owned and under rigid censorship. Antigovernment organization or expression is forbidden. Conversation is guarded and travel is restricted. There are thousands of political prisoners; torture and brutality are common; thousands of executions occurred in 1979 in addition to war deaths and massacres. The objectives of the state are totalitarian; their achievement has been limited by the continuing struggle for control.

**Comparatively:** Afghanistan is as free as Vietnam, less free than Iran.

# ALBANIA

**Economy:** socialist                **Political Rights:** 7
**Polity:** communist one-party       **Civil Liberties:** 7
**Population:** 2,600,000             **Status of Freedom:** not free

A relatively homogeneous population

**Political Rights.** Albania has been a communist dictatorship under essentially one-man rule since 1944. While there are a number of elected bodies, including an assembly, the parallel government of the communist party (three percent of the people) is decisive at all levels;

---

*Population estimates for all countries are generally derived from the 1979 World Population Data Sheet of the Population Reference Bureau, Washington, D.C.

elections offer only one list of candidates. Candidates are officially designated by the Democratic Front, to which all Albanians are supposed to belong. In the 1970's several extensive purges within the party have apparently been designed to maintain the power of the top leaders.

**Civil Liberties.** Press, radio, and television are completely under government or party control, and communication with the outside world is minimal. Media are characterized by incessant propaganda, and open expression of opinion in private conversation is rare. Political imprisonment is common; torture is frequently reported. All religious institutions were abolished in 1967; religion is outlawed; priests are regularly imprisoned. Apparently there are no private organizations independent of government or party. Economic disparities are comparatively small: all people must work one month of each year in factories or on farms, and there are no private cars. Private economic choice is minimal.

**Comparatively:** Albania is as free as Kampuchea, less free than Yugoslavia.

# ALGERIA

**Economy:** socialist
**Polity:** socialist one-party
**Population:** 19,000,000

**Political Rights:** 6
**Civil Liberties:** 6
**Status of Freedom:** not free

An ethnic state with a potential subnationality

**Political Rights.** Algeria has combined military dictatorship with one-party socialist rule. Elections at both local and national levels are managed by the party; they allow little opposition to the system, although individual representatives and specific policies may be criticized. Recent elections resulted in ninety-nine percent favorable votes. However, the pragmatic, puritanical, military rulers are probably supported by a fairly broad consensus. *Subnationalities*: about twenty percent of the people are Berbers: revolt in their areas in the Kabylia (1963–64) suggests continuing desire to run their own affairs.

**Civil Liberties.** The media are governmental means for active indoctrination; no opposition voice is allowed, and foreign publications are closely watched. Private conversation appears relatively open. Although not fully independent, the regular judiciary has established a rule of law in some areas. Several important prisoners were released during 1979, but other prisoners of conscience are still held. No appeal from the decisions of the special Revolutionary Courts for crimes against the state is allowed; there have been reports of torture. Land reform has transformed former French plantations into collectives. Although government goals are clearly socialist, many small farms and businesses remain. Travel is generally free. Eighty percent of the people are illiterate; many are still very poor, but extremes of wealth have been reduced. Islam's continued strength provides a counterweight to governmental absolutism. There is religious freedom.

**Comparatively:** Algeria is as free as Tanzania, freer than Iraq, less free than Morocco.

# ANGOLA

**Economy:** noninclusive socialist  
**Polity:** socialist one-party  
**Population:** . 6,900,000

**Political Rights:** 7  
**Civil Liberties:** 7  
**Status of Freedom:** not free

A transethnic heterogeneous state with major subnationalities

**Political Rights.** Angola is ruled by a communist-style socialist party in which military commanders may wield considerable power. The ruling party has relied heavily on Soviet equipment and Cuban troops to win the recent civil war and to stay in power. In 1977 a serious revolt within the top level of the ruling party decimated its leadership. *Subnationalities*: The party is not tribalist, but is opposed by groups relying on particular tribes or regions—especially in Cabinda, the northeast, and the south central areas. The UNITA movement among the Ovimbundu people actively controls much of the south and east of the country.

**Civil Liberties.** There is no constitution; the nation remains in a state of war, with power arbitrarily exercised, particularly in the countryside. The media in controlled areas are government owned and do not deviate from its line. Political imprisonment and execution is common; repression of religious activity is reported. Private medical care has been abolished, as has much private property—especially in the modern sectors. Strikes are prohibited and unions tightly controlled. Agricultural production is held down by peasant opposition to socialization.

**Comparatively:** Angola is as free as Vietnam, less free than Zambia.

# ARGENTINA

**Economy:** capitalist-statist  
**Polity:** military nonparty  
**Population:** 26,700,000

**Political Rights:** 6  
**Civil Liberties:** 5  
**Status of Freedom:** not free

A relatively homogeneous population

**Political Rights.** Ruled today by a military junta, Argentina oscillates between democracy and authoritarianism. The military's last intervention probably had initial popular support because of the high level of both right- and left-wing terrorism, and the corrupt and ineffective regime it replaced. The continued use of violence by the regime and its supporters to silence opposition has eroded this support. The regions are now under direct junta control. The government has only limited control over its security forces.

**Civil Liberties.** Private newspapers and both private and government broadcasting stations operate; to a limited degree they report unfavorable events and criticize the government. Yet both self-censorship and newspaper closings are common. Censorship of media and private expression also occurs informally through the threat of terrorist attacks from radical leftist or rightist groups (with the latter apparently supported by, or associated with, elements of the military and police). The universities are closely controlled. While courts retain some independence, arbitrary arrest, torture, and execution have been common. Recently this has been mostly by semiofficial rightist terrorists. The church and trade unions continue to play a strong opposition role, although there is frequent pressure on the unions. For non-Catholics religious freedom is curtailed.

**Comparatively:** Argentina is as free as Yugoslavia, freer than Uruguay, less free than Chile.

# AUSTRALIA

**Economy:** capitalist
**Polity:** decentralized multiparty
**Population:** 14,400,000

**Political Rights:** 1
**Civil Liberties:** 1
**Status of Freedom:** free

A relatively homogeneous population with small aboriginal groups

**Political Rights.** Australia is a federal parliamentary democracy with strong powers retained by its component states. With equal representation from each state, the Senate provides a counterbalance to the nationally representative House of Representatives. There have been recent changes in government, with the Labour Party gaining control in 1972 only to lose it again in 1975. The British appointed Governor General retains some power in constitutional deadlocks. Trade unions (separately and through the Labour Party) and foreign investors have great economic weight. The states have separate parliaments and premiers, but appointed governors. The relative power of rural peoples and aborigines has recently been strengthened, particularly through the establishment of the new Northern Territory.

Civil Liberties. All the newspapers and most radio and television stations are privately owned. The Australian Broadcasting Commission operates government radio and television stations on a basis similar to BBC. Although Australia lacks many formal guarantees of civil liberties, the degree of protection of these liberties in the common law is similar to that in Britain and Canada. Freedom of choice in education, travel, occupation, property, and private association are perhaps as complete as anywhere in the world. Relatively low taxes enhance this freedom.

Comparatively: Australia is as free as the United Kingdom, freer than Italy.

## AUSTRIA

Economy: mixed capitalist          Political Rights: 1
Polity: (centralized) multiparty   Civil Liberties: 1
Population: 7,500,000              Status of Freedom: free

A relatively homogeneous population

Political Rights. Austria's parliamentary system has a directly elected lower house and an upper (and less powerful) house elected by the provincial assemblies. The president is directly elected, but the chancellor (representing the majority party in parliament) is the center of political power. The two major parties have alternated control since the 1950's but the government often seeks broad consensus. The referendum is used on rare occasions. Provincial legislatures and governors are elective. *Subnationalities*: Fifty thousand Slovenes in the southern part of the country have rights to their own schools.

Civil Liberties. The press in Austria is free and varied, while radio and television are under a state-owned corporation that by law is supposed to be free of political control. Its geographical position and neutral status by treaty places its media and government in a position analogous to Finland, but the Soviets have put less pressure on Austria to conform to Soviet wishes than on Finland. The rule of law is secure, and there are no political prisoners. Banks and heavy industry are largely nationalized.

Comparatively: Austria is as free as Belgium, freer than Greece.

## BAHAMAS

Economy: capitalist               Political Rights: 1
Polity: centralized multiparty    Civil Liberties: 2
Population: 225,000               Status of Freedom: free

A relatively homogeneous population

**Political Rights.** The Bahamas have a parliamentary system with a largely ceremonial British Governor General. The ruling party has a large majority, but there is an opposition in parliament. Most islands are administered by centrally appointed commissioners. There is an independence movement in Abaco Island, one of the more important islands in the group.

**Civil Liberties.** There are independent newspapers, but through restricting income and preventing hiring or keeping desired employees, the government has exerted pressure on the opposition press. Radio is government owned and is not completely free of government control. In other respects Bahamas' freedoms seem reasonably secure.

**Comparatively:** Bahamas is as free as Venezuela, freer than St. Lucia, less free than Barbados.

# BAHRAIN

**Economy:** capitalist-statist
**Polity:** traditional nonparty
**Population:** 300,000

**Political Rights:** 5
**Civil Liberties:** 4
**Status of Freedom:** partly free

The citizenry is relatively homogeneous

**Political Rights.** Bahrain is a traditional shaikhdom with a modernized administration. Direct access to the ruler is encouraged. At present the legislature is dissolved, but powerful merchant and religious families place a check on royal power. There are local councils. *Subnationalities*: The primary ethnic problem has been the struggle between the Iranians who once ruled and the Arabs who now rule; in part this is reflected in the opposition of the ruling Sunni and majority Shi'ite Muslim sects.

**Civil Liberties.** The government and private press seldom criticizes government policy. Radio and television are government owned. Although freedom of expression and assembly are cautiously expressed, a climate of fear does not exist. The legal and educational systems are a mixture of traditional Islamic and British. Short-term arrest is used to discourage dissent, but there are few long-term political prisoners. In security cases involving violence fair and quick trials are delayed and torture occurs. Rights to travel, property, and religious choice are secured. There is a record of disturbances by workers groups, although union organization is restricted. Many free social services are provided. Citizenship is very hard to obtain; there is antipathy to foreign workers (but unlike neighboring shaikhdoms most people in the country are citizens).

**Comparatively:** Bahrain is as free as Kenya, freer than Saudi Arabia, less free than Turkey.

# BANGLADESH

**Economy:** noninclusive capitalist-statist

**Political Rights:** 3

**Civil Liberties:** 3

**Polity:** centralized multiparty

**Status of Freedom:** partly free

**Population:** 87,000,000

A relatively homogeneous population with Hindu and Bihari minorities

**Political Rights.** Bangladesh is ruled by a president and parliament. Recent parliamentary and presidential elections have shown a satisfactory degree of competition. The shadow of the violent military rule of the recent past still hangs over election processes and parliamentary independence. *Subnationalities*: Fighting with minor tribal groups along the border continues; the Bihari minority suffers discrimination.

**Civil Liberties.** The press is private, government, and party. The papers are not censored but there are still some controls. Radio and television are government controlled, but are not actively used for mobilization. The existence of a broad spectrum of political parties allows for the organization of dissent. There have been numerous arrests and executions following coup attempts during recent years, and torture is reported. It appeared that by the end of 1979 there were few prisoners of conscience. The courts can decide against the government. In spite of considerable communal antipathy, religious freedom exists. Travel is generally unrestricted. Although they do not have the right to strike, labor unions are active and strikes occur. Corruption remains a major problem.

**Comparatively:** Bangladesh is as free as Bolivia, freer than Burma, less free than India.

# BARBADOS

**Economy:** capitalist

**Political Rights:** 1

**Polity:** centralized multiparty

**Civil Liberties:** 1

**Population:** 250,000

**Status of Freedom:** free

A relatively homogeneous population

**Political Rights.** Barbados is governed by a parliamentary system, with a ceremonial British Governor General. Power alternates between the two major parties. Local governments are also elected.

**Civil Liberties.** Newspapers are private and free of government control. There are both private and government radio stations, but the government-controlled radio station also controls the only television station on the BBC model. There is an independent judiciary, and general freedom from arbitrary government action. Travel, residence, and religion are free. Although both major parties rely on the support of labor, private property is fully accepted.

**Comparatively:** Barbados is as free as the United Kingdom, freer than Jamaica.


# BELGIUM

Economy: capitalist                           Political Rights: 1
Polity: decentralized multiparty              Civil Liberties: 1
Population: 9,800,000                         Status of Freedom: free

A binational state

**Political Rights.** Belgium is a constitutional monarchy with a bi-cameral parliament. Elections lead to coalition governments, generally of the center. Linguistic divisions have produced considerable instability. *Subnationalities*: The rise of nationalism among the two major peoples—Flemish and Walloon—has led to increasing transfer of control over cultural affairs to the communal groups. However, provincial governors are appointed by the national government.

**Civil Liberties.** Newspapers are free and uncensored. Radio and television are government owned, but the director of each station is solely responsible for programming. The full spectrum of private rights is respected, but voting is compulsory.

**Comparatively:** Belgium is as free as Switzerland, freer than France.


# BENIN

Economy: noninclusive socialist               Political Rights: 7
Polity: socialist one-party                   Civil Liberties: 6
Population: 3,500,000                          Status of Freedom: not free

A transethnic heterogeneous state

**Political Rights.** Benin is a military dictatorship buttressed by a one-party organization. Regional and tribal loyalties may be stronger than national. A parliament was elected in 1979 on a single list. Local assemblies are closely controlled.

**Civil Liberties.** All media are rigidly censored; most are owned by the government. Opposition is not tolerated; criticism of the government often leads to a few days of reeducation in military camps. There are few if any long-term political prisoners, but the rule of law is very weak.

Private schools have been closed, Jehovah's Witnesses are banned, independent labor unions forbidden. Potential dissidents are not allowed to leave the country. Economically, the government's interventions have been in cash crops and internal trade, and industries have been nationalized; control over the largely subsistence and small entrepreneur economy remains incomplete.

**Comparatively:** Benin is as free as Burma, freer than Togo, less free than Senegal.

# B H U T A N

**Economy:** preindustrial
**Polity:** traditional nonparty
**Population:** 1,300,000

**Political Rights:** 5
**Civil Liberties:** 5
**Status of Freedom:** partly free

An ethnic state with a significant subnationality

**Political Rights.** Bhutan is a hereditary monarchy in which the king rules with the aid of a council and the indirectly elected National Assembly. There are no legal political parties and the Assembly does little more than approve government actions. Villages are traditionally ruled by their own headmen, but districts are directly ruled from the center. The Buddhist hierarchy is still very important in the affairs of the country. In foreign policy Bhutan's dependence upon India has been partially renounced; it is still dependent for defense. *Subnationalities*: The main political party operates outside the country, agitating in favor of the Nepalese minority (about 250,000) and a more open system.

**Civil Liberties.** The media are government owned and operated. There are few if any prisoners of conscience. The legal structure exhibits a mixture of traditional and British forms. There is religious freedom and freedom to travel. Traditional agriculture, crafts, and trade dominate the economy.

**Comparatively:** Bhutan is as free as Maldives, freer than Burma, less free than India.

# B O L I V I A

**Economy:** noninclusive capitalist-
              statist
**Polity:** centralized multiparty
**Population:** 5,000,000

**Political Rights:** 3
**Civil Liberties:** 3
**Status of Freedom:** partly free

An ethnic state with major potential subnationalities

**Political Rights.** Bolivia is a multiparty democracy with frequent military interference. In 1979 military attempts to overturn elections were ultimately resisted after compromises. Provincial and local government is controlled from the center, but there are strong labor, peasant, and religious organizations in many areas that exert quasi-governmental power. *Subnationalities*: Over sixty percent of the people are Indians speaking Aymara or Quechua; these languages have been given official status alongside Spanish. The Indian peoples remain, however, more potential than active nationalities.

**Civil Liberties.** The press and most radio and television stations are private. Although the government sometimes interferes, there is general freedom of the press. An organized private group fights human rights violations. Freedom is also restricted by the climate of violence, both governmental and nongovernmental. Normal legal protections have often been denied during frequent states of siege, but it is possible to win against the government in the courts. At the end of 1979 there were no known prisoners of conscience, nor travel restrictions. Peasant and union organizations are powerful. The people are overwhelmingly post-land reform, subsistence agriculturists. The major mines are nationalized; the workers have a generous social welfare program, given the country's poverty.

**Comparatively:** Bolivia is as free as Cyprus, freer than Paraguay, less free than Colombia.

# BOTSWANA

**Economy:** noninclusive capitalist    **Political Rights:** 2
**Polity:** decentralized multiparty    **Civil Liberties:** 2
**Population,** 750,000                  **Status of Freedom:** free

A relatively homogeneous population

**Political Rights.** The republican system of Botswana combines traditional and modern principles. The assembly is elected for a fixed term and appoints the president who rules. There is also an advisory House of Chiefs. Nine districts, led either by chiefs or elected leaders, have independent power of taxation, as well as traditional power over land and agriculture. Elections continue to be won overwhelmingly by the ruling party as they were even before independence, yet there are opposition members in parliament and local governments. There is economic and political pressure from both black African and white neighbors. *Subnationalities*: The country is divided among several major tribes belonging to the Batswana people, as well as minor peoples on the margins. The latter include a few hundred comparatively wealthy white farmers.

**Civil Liberties.** The radio and most newspapers are government owned; however, there is no censorship, and South African media present an available alternative. Rights of assembly, religion, and travel are respected; prisoners of conscience are not held. Judicially, civil liberties appear to be guaranteed, although on the local scale the individual tribesman may have considerably less freedom.

**Comparatively:** Botswana is as free as Gambia, freer than Zambia, less free than Barbados.

# B R A Z I L

**Economy:** capitalist-statist
**Polity:** decentralized multiparty
        (military dominated)
**Population:** 119,000,000

**Political Rights:** 4
**Civil Liberties:** 3
**Status of Freedom:** partly free

A complex but relatively homogeneous population with many small, territorial subnationalities

**Political Rights.** Brazil has been governed by a president, essentially elected by the military, and a popularly elected but weak assembly. Legislative elections in 1978 gave a majority to the opposition, although the opposition did not gain legislative majorities. Party organization is controlled, but party activity is increasingly competitive; only the communist party remains banned. Illiterates do not have the vote. There are independently organized elected governments at both state and local levels, though the army has sometimes interfered at these levels. *Subnationalities*: The many small Indian groups of the interior are under both private and public pressure. Some still fight back in the face of loss of land, lives, and culture.

**Civil Liberties.** The media are private, except for a few broadcasting stations. The powerful press is now free of overt censorship. Radio and television practice limited self-censorship. The atmosphere of terror has largely dissipated; there are few if any prisoners of conscience. Political exiles returned in 1979. Private violence against criminals and suspected communists may continue outside the law. Opposition voices are regularly heard—including parliamentarians, journalists, and officials of the church. Union organization is powerful and strikes are widespread, though not allowed in all industries. There is considerable large-scale government industry, but rights to property, religious freedom, travel, and education of one's choice are generally respected.

**Comparatively:** Brazil is as free as Mexico, freer than Uruguay, less free than Jamaica.

# BULGARIA

**Economy:** socialist
**Polity:** communist one-party
**Population:** 8,900,000

**Political Rights:** 7
**Civil Liberties:** 7
**Status of Freedom:** not free

A relatively homogeneous population

**Political Rights.** Bulgaria is governed by its communist party, although the facade of a parallel government and two-party system is maintained. The same man has essentially ruled over the system since 1954; elections at both national and local levels have little meaning. Both economically and politically the country is subservient to the Soviet Union. *Subnationalities*: The Muslim Turkish minority of about one million is persecuted in several ways.

**Civil Liberties.** All media are controlled by the government or its party branches. Citizens have few if any rights against the state. There are hundreds or thousands of prisoners of conscience, many living under severe conditions. Brutality and torture are common. The detained may also be banished to villages, denied their occupations, or confined in psychiatric hospitals. Believers are subject to discrimination, particularly Muslims. The most common political crimes are illegally trying to leave the country, criticism of the government, and illegal contacts with foreigners.

**Comparatively:** Bulgaria is as free as Mongolia, less free than Hungary.

# BURMA

**Economy:** noninclusive mixed
socialist
**Polity:** socialist one-party
**Population:** 32,200,000

**Political Rights:** 7
**Civil Liberties:** 6
**Status of Freedom:** not free

An ethnic state with major territorial subnationalities

**Political Rights.** Burma is a one-party socialist, military dictatorship. The government's dependence on the army makes its strengths and weaknesses more those of a military dictatorship than those of a communist regime. Elections are held at both national and local levels; the only candidates likely to win are those nominated by the single party. *Subnationalities*: The government represents essentially the Burmese people that live in the heartland of the country. The Burmese are surrounded by millions of non-Burmese living in continuing disaffection or active revolt. Among the minorities in the periphery are the Karens, Shan, Kachins, Mon, and Chin.

**Civil Liberties.** All media are government owned, with alternative opinions expressed obliquely if at all; both domestic and foreign publications are censored. Organized dissent is forbidden; in part, this policy is explained by the almost continuous warfare the government has had to wage since independence against both rebellious subnationalities and two separate communist armies. This state of war has been augmented since the 1960's by the attempts of civilian politicians to regain power by armed force or antigovernment demonstration, as well as recent plots within the army itself. There are hundreds or thousands of political prisoners. The regular court structure has been replaced by "people's courts." Religion is free; union activity is not; both internal and external travel are very difficult. Although the eventual goal of the government is complete socialization and there are to be steady moves toward agricultural collectivization, an official announcement in 1977 temporarily reserved significant portions of the economy for private enterprise.

**Comparatively:** Burma is as free as Rumania, freer than Kampuchea, less free than Thailand.

# BURUNDI

**Economy:** noninclusive mixed
**Polity:** socialist one-party
     (military dominated)
**Population:** 4,000,000

**Political Rights:** 7
**Civil Liberties:** 7
**Status of Freedom:** not free

An ethnic state with a majority, nonterritorial subnationality

**Political Rights.** Burundi is ruled by a Supreme Revolutionary Council led by a military officer, with the assistance of the single party. There is now no elected assembly. *Subnationalities*: The rulers continue to be all from the Tutsi ethnic group (fifteen percent) that has traditionally ruled; their dominance was reinforced by a massacre of Hutus (eighty-five percent) after an attempted revolt in the early 1970's.

**Civil Liberties.** The media are now all government controlled and closely censored. Lack of freedom of political speech or assembly is accompanied by political imprisonment and reports of brutality. Under current conditions there is little guarantee of individual rights, particularly for the Hutu majority. In recent years Hutu have been excluded from the army, secondary schools, and the civil service. There are no independent unions. Traditional group and individual rights no doubt persist on the village level: Burundi is not a highly structured modern society. Travel is relatively unrestricted. Education is controlled, missionary activity closely regulated. Although officially socialist, private or traditional economic forms predominate.

**Comparatively:** Burundi is as free as Somalia, less free than Kenya.

# CAMBODIA
## (See Kampuchea)

# CAMEROON

**Economy:** noninclusive capitalist
**Polity:** nationalist one-party
**Population:** 8,300,000

**Political Rights:** 6
**Civil Liberties:** 6
**Status of Freedom:** not free

A transethnic heterogeneous state with a major subnationality

**Political Rights.** Cameroon is a one-party state ruled by the same person since independence in 1960. The government has steadily centralized power. Referendums and other elections have little meaning; voters are given no alternatives and provide ninety-nine percent majorities. Provincial governors are appointed by the central government. An attempt has been made to incorporate all elements in a government of broad consensus. *Subnationalities*: The most significant opposition has come from those opposing centralization, particularly movements supported by the country's largest ethnic group, the Bamileke (twenty-six percent). Other ethnic groups are quite small.

**Civil Liberties.** The media are closely controlled and self-censorship common; works of critical authors are prohibited. Freedom of speech, assembly, and union organization are limited, while freedom of occupation, education, and property are respected. Prisoners of conscience are detained without trial and may be ill-treated. Allegations have been made of torture and village massacres. Internal travel and religious choice are relatively free; foreign travel may be difficult. Labor and business organizations are controlled. The government has supported land reform; although still relatively short on capital, private enterprise is encouraged wherever possible.

**Comparatively:** Cameroon is as free as Gabon, freer than Niger, less free than Ghana.

# CANADA

**Economy:** capitalist
**Polity:** decentralized multiparty
**Population:** 23,700,000

**Political Rights:** 1
**Civil Liberties:** 1
**Status of Freedom:** free

A binational state

**Political Rights.** Canada is a parliamentary democracy with alternation of rule between leading parties. The provinces have their own democratic institutions with a higher degree of autonomy than the American states. *Subnationalities*: In an attempt to prevent the breakup of Canada, the government has moved toward granting French linguistic equality; French has become the official language in Quebec. In addition, Quebec has been allowed to opt out of some national programs and maintains its own representatives abroad.

**Civil Liberties.** The media are free, although there is a government-related radio and television network. The full range of civil liberties is generally respected. In Quebec rights to choose education and language for many purposes have been infringed. There has been evidence of the invasion of privacy by Canadian security forces in recent years, much as in the United States. Many judicial and legal structures have been borrowed from the United Kingdom or the United States, with consequent advantages and disadvantages.

**Comparatively:** Canada is as free as the United States of America, freer than Italy.

# CAPE VERDE ISLANDS

**Economy:** noninclusive socialist  **Political Rights:** 6
**Polity:** socialist one-party      **Civil Liberties:** 6
**Population:** 330,000              **Status of Freedom:** not free

A relatively homogeneous state

**Political Rights.** The party ruling the Cape Verde Islands also rules Guinea-Bissau. Established and originally led by Cape Verdeans, the party achieved its major preindependence success on the mainland. Its secretary-general is president of the Cape Verde Islands. The single party is small and tightly organized.

**Civil Liberties.** Neither private nor government media may criticize the government. Prisoners of conscience are frequently detained, often without trial; rights to organized opposition, assembly, or political expression are not respected. For its region Cape Verde's seventy-five percent literacy is very high. The Island's plantation agriculture has been largely nationalized, but endemic unemployment continues to lead to emigration. Religion is relatively free, although under political pressure; labor unions are government controlled.

**Comparatively:** Cape Verde Islands is as free as Tanzania, freer than Ethiopia, less free than Ivory Coast.

# CENTRAL AFRICAN REPUBLIC

**Economy:** noninclusive capitalist  
**Polity:** nonmilitary nonparty  
**Population:** 2,400,000  

**Political Rights:** 7  
**Civil Liberties:** 6  
**Status of Freedom:** not free  

A transethnic heterogeneous state

**Political Rights.** The Central African Republic is a dictatorship without representative institutions. Prefects are appointed by the central government in the French style. Heavily dependent on French economic and military aid, the recent change of government was due to a direct French military intervention.

**Civil Liberties.** All media are government controlled; there are political prisoners. Religious freedom is generally respected, as are other personal and economic freedoms.

**Comparatively:** Central African Republic is as free as Congo, freer than Togo, less free than Kenya.


# CHAD

**Economy:** noninclusive capitalist  
**Polity:** military decentralized  
**Population:** 4,300,000  

**Political Rights:** 6  
**Civil Liberties:** 6  
**Status of Freedom:** not free  

A collection of semi-autonomous ethnic groups

**Political Rights.** Chad is governed by a national union government representing a variety of ethnic and military factions. Anarchy remains a threat; most of the country is under de facto factional control. (Violent factional struggle characterized early 1980.) *Subnationalities*: Ethnic struggle pits the southern Negroes (principally the Christian and animist Sara tribe) against a variety of northern Muslim groups (principally nomadic Arabs). No group is now clearly dominant.

**Civil Liberties.** The media are controlled by the government, although journalists show some independence. In conditions of mixed anarchy, and varying degrees of local and national control rights have little meaning. Many have been killed or imprisoned without due process. Anarchy gives certain freedoms to local groups. Not an ideological state, traditional law is still influential.

**Comparatively:** Chad is apparently as free as Saudi Arabia, freer than Central African Republic, less free than Sudan.

# CHILE

**Economy:** capitalist
**Polity:** military nonparty
**Population:** 11,000,000

**Political Rights:** 6
**Civil Liberties:** 5
**Status of Freedom:** partly free

A relatively homogeneous population

**Political Rights.** Chile is a military dictatorship. A 1978 plebiscite confirming government policy allowed an opposition vote of twenty percent. All power is concentrated at the center; there are no elective positions. An appointive Council of State is supposed to represent most sectors of society.

**Civil Liberties.** All media have both public and private outlets; newspapers are primarily private. The media, although censored and often threatened with closure, express a considerable range of opinion, occasionally including direct criticism of government policy. Students, church leaders, and former political leaders regularly express dissent. While one can win against the government, the courts are under government pressure. After years of terror, disappearances and other extralegal repressions appear to have ceased. There remain prisoners of conscience and occasional torture. Unions are restricted but have some rights, including a limited right to strike. Rights to private property have been greatly strengthened both in the country and city, with government control of the economy now being limited to copper and petroleum.

**Comparatively:** Chile is as free as Poland, freer than Czechoslovakia, less free than Peru.

# CHINA (Mainland)

**Economy:** socialist
**Polity:** communist one-party
**Population:** 950,000,000

**Political Rights:** 6
**Civil Liberties:** 6
**Status of Freedom:** not free

An ethnic state with peripheral subnationalities

**Political Rights.** China is a one-party communist state under the collective leadership of the Politburo. A National Peoples Congress is indirectly elected within party guidelines, but does not function as a competitive parliament. National policy struggles are obscured by secrecy; choices are sharply limited. Recently there have been some more open local elections. *Subnationalities*: There are several subordinated peripheral peoples such as the Tibetans, Uighurs, or Mongols. These are granted a very limited degree of separate cultural life. Amounting to not more than five percent of the population, non-Chinese ethnic groups have tended to be diluted and obscured by Chinese settlement or Sinification.

**Civil Liberties.** The mass media remain closely controlled, the limited underground and wall poster literature of 1978–79 has largely been suppressed. Non-political cultural freedom has, however, greatly expanded. The new constitution places an emphasis on legal procedures that has been lacking until recently. Although this may herald movement toward "socialist legality" on the Soviet model, court cases often appear to be decided in political terms. There are unknown thousands of political prisoners, including those in labor-reform camps; the government has forced millions to live indefinitely in undesirable areas. Although now less common, political executions are still reported. Millions of Chinese have been systematically discriminated against because of "bad class background," but such discrimination has recently been curtailed.

Compared to other communist states popular opinions and pressures play a considerable role. Recurrent poster campaigns, demonstrations, and evidence of private conversation show that pervasive factionalism has allowed elements of freedom and consensus into the system; repression in 1979, including imprisonment, equally shows the government's determination to keep such campaigning from becoming a threat to the system or its current leaders. Rights to travel and emigration are limited, as are other economic and religious freedoms.

**Comparatively:** China (Mainland) is as free as Algeria, freer than Mongolia, and less free than China (Taiwan).

# C H I N A   (Taiwan)

**Economy:** capitalist-statist
**Polity:** centralized dominant-
            party
**Population:** 17,300,000

**Political Rights:** 5
**Civil Liberties:** 5
**Status of Freedom:** partly free

A quasi-ethnic state with a majority nonterritorial subnationality

**Political Rights.** Taiwan is ruled by a single party organized according to a communist model (although anticommunist ideologically). There is a parliament to which representatives from Taiwan are elected in fairly free elections; a few members oppose the regime but no effective opposition party is tolerated. Most parliamentarians continue to be persons elected in 1947 as representatives of districts in China where elections could not be held subsequently. The indirect presidential election is *pro forma*, but the election of a Taiwanese as vice president in 1978 was significant. Important local and regional positions are elective, including those in the provincial assembly which are held by Taiwanese.

*Subnationalities*: The people are eighty-six percent native Taiwanese (speaking two Chinese dialects), and an opposition movement to transfer control from the mainland immigrants to the Taiwanese has been repressed. Since nearly all Taiwanese are also Chinese, it is difficult to know the extent to which non-Taiwanese oppression is felt.

**Civil Liberties.** The media include government or party organs, but are mostly in private hands. Newspapers and magazines are subject to censorship or suspension, and practice self-censorship. Nineteen seventy-nine saw a number of new publications and new suppressions; in late 1979 a major confrontation led to the closing of publications and the imprisonment of major leaders of the opposition. Television remained one-sided. Rights to assembly are limited. There are several hundred political prisoners, but there has been only one recent political execution and reports of torture are now rare. Union activity is restricted; strikes are forbidden. Private rights to property, education, and religion are generally respected; there is no right to travel to the mainland.

**Comparatively:** China (Taiwan) is as free as Singapore, freer than Poland, less free than Malaysia.

## COLOMBIA

Economy: capitalist               Political Rights: 2
Polity: centralized multiparty     Civil Liberties: 3
Population: 26,000,000             Status of Freedom: free

A relatively homogeneous population with scattered minorities

**Political Rights.** Colombia is a constitutional democracy. The president is directly elected, as are both houses of the legislature. Although campaigns are accompanied by both violence and apathy, there is little reason to believe they are fraudulent. Members of the two principal parties are included in the government and the list of departmental governors. Both of the leading parties have well-defined factions. There is one major third party; among the minor parties several are involved in revolutionary activity. The provinces are directly administered by the national government. The military is alleged to be only partly under government control.

**Civil Liberties.** The press is private, with some papers under party control, and quite free. Radio and television include both government and private stations. All media have been limited in their freedom to report subversive activity. Personal rights are generally respected; courts are relatively strong and independent. Riots and guerrilla activity have led to periodic states of siege in which these rights are limited. Assemblies are often banned for fear of riots. In these conditions the security

forces have infringed violently personal rights, especially those of peasants or Amerindians in rural areas. Although many persons are rounded
up in antiguerrilla or antiterrorist campaigns, people are not given prison
sentences simply for their nonviolent expression of political opinion.
Torture occurs. The government encourages private enterprise where
possible; union activity and strikes for economic goals are legal.

**Comparatively:** Colombia is as free as Turkey, freer than Panama,
less free than Venezuela.

# COMORO ISLANDS

**Economy:** noninclusive capitalist
**Polity:** decentralized nonparty
**Population:** 400,000

**Political Rights:** 4
**Civil Liberties:** 5
**Status of Freedom:** partly free

A relatively homogeneous population

**Political Rights.** The Comoran government came to power by armed
attack in 1978. Subsequently, the voters approved a new constitution
and president. The majority probably support the new system—the
previous ruler had become very oppressive and the new president had
been prime minister in the recent past. There were contested parliamentary elections in late 1978. The new constitution grants each island
an elected governor and council. (The island of Mayotte is formally a
part of the Comoros, but it has chosen to be a French dependency.)

**Civil Liberties.** Radio is government owned; there is no press. Some
outside publications and meetings have been banned. There are political
prisoners resulting from the recent coup, and pressure is reported
against opposition groups. There is a new emphasis on Islamic customs.
The poor population depends almost entirely on subsistence agriculture
and emigration.

**Comparatively:** Comoro Islands appears to be as free as Kenya,
freer than Seychelles, less free than Mauritius.

# CONGO

**Economy:** noninclusive mixed
**Polity:** socialist one-party
    (military dominated)
**Population:** 1,500,000

**Political Rights:** 7
**Civil Liberties:** 7
**Status of Freedom:** not free

A formally transethnic heterogeneous state

**Political Rights.** Congo is a military dictatorship with lethal factional
infighting. One-party elections allow no opposition. *Subnationalities*:
Historically the country was established out of a maze of ethnic groups,

without the domination of some by others. However, the army that now rules is said to come from tribes with not more than fifteen percent of the population.

**Civil Liberties.** The news media are heavily censored. Executions and imprisonment of political opponents are common; trials exhibit little interest in justice. Only one union is allowed; it is not allowed to strike. Religious groups are limited. At the local and small entrepreneur level private property is generally respected; many larger industries have been nationalized.

**Comparatively:** Congo is as free as Iraq, less free than Cameroon.

# COSTA RICA

**Economy:** capitalist
**Polity:** centralized multiparty
**Population:** 2,200,000

**Political Rights:** 1
**Civil Liberties:** 1
**Status of Freedom:** free

A relatively homogeneous population

**Political Rights.** A parliamentary democracy, Costa Rica has a directly elected president and several important parties. No parties are prohibited. This structure is supplemented by an independent tribunal for the overseeing of elections. Elections are fair; in 1978 they brought the opposition to power. Provinces are under the direction of the central government.

**Civil Liberties.** The media are notably free, private, and varied; they serve a society ninety percent literate. The courts are fair, and private rights, such as those to movement, occupation, education, religion, and union organization are respected.

**Comparatively:** Costa Rica is as free as Ireland, freer than Colombia.

# CUBA

**Economy:** socialist
**Polity:** communist one-party
**Population:** 9,900,000

**Political Rights:** 6
**Civil Liberties:** 6
**Status of Freedom:** not free

A complex but relatively homogeneous population

**Political Rights.** Cuba is a one-party communist state on the Soviet model. Real power lies, however, more in the person of Fidel Castro and in the Russian leaders upon whom he depends than is the case in other noncontiguous states adopting this model. Popular election at the municipal level has recently been introduced. Provincial and national assemblies are elected by municipalities but can be recalled by popular vote. The whole system is largely a show: Political opponents are excluded from nomination by law, many others are simply disqualified by party fiat; no debate is allowed on major issues; once elected the assemblies do not oppose party decisions.

**Civil Liberties.** The media are state controlled and publish only as the state directs. Thousands of political prisoners have been released recently, mostly into exile. Torture has been reported only in the past, but hundreds who have refused to recant continue to be held in difficult conditions, and new arrests are frequent. There are hundreds of thousands of others who are formally discriminated against as opponents of the system. There appears to be some freedom to criticize informally. Freedom to choose work, education, or residence is greatly restricted; most people are forcibly prevented from leaving; new laws force people to work harder. The practice of religion is discouraged by the government.

**Comparatively:** Cuba is as free as Tanzania, freer than Czechoslovakia, less free than Mexico.

# CYPRUS

**Economy:** capitalist
**Polity:** decentralized multiparty
**Population:** 650,000

**Political Rights:** 3
**Civil Liberties:** 3
**Status of Freedom:** partly free

A binational state (no central government)

**Political Rights.** At present Cyprus is one state only in theory. Both the Greek and the Turkish sectors are parliamentary democracies, although the Turkish sector is in effect a protectorate of Turkey. Elections have seemed reasonably fair in both sectors, but in the violent atmosphere pressure has been applied to all nonconforming groups or individuals. Greek Cypriots in the North are denied voting rights. *Nationalities*: Greeks and Turks now live almost exclusively in their own sectors. Eighty percent of the population is Greek, sixty percent of the land is in the Greek sector.

**Civil Liberties.** The newspapers are free and varied in both sectors, with the constraints mentioned above. Radio and television are under the respective governments or semigovernmental bodies. The usual rights of free peoples are respected in each sector, including occupation, labor organization, and religion. Because of communal strife and invasion, property has often been taken from members of one group by force (or abandoned from fear of force) and given to the other. Under these conditions rights to choose one's sector of residence or to travel between sectors are greatly restricted.

**Comparatively:** Cyprus is as free as Bolivia, freer than Lebanon, less free than Turkey.

# CZECHOSLOVAKIA

**Economy:** socialist  
**Polity:** communist one-party  
**Population:** 15,200,000  
A binational state

**Political Rights:** 7  
**Civil Liberties:** 6  
**Status of Freedom:** not free

**Political Rights.** Czechoslovakia is a Soviet-style, one-party communist state, reinforced by the presence of Soviet troops. Elections are noncompetitive and there is essentially no legislative debate. *Subnationalities*: The division of the state into separate Czech and Slovak socialist republics has only slight meaning since the Czechoslovak Communist Party continues to run the country (under the guidance of the Soviet Communist Party). Although less numerous and poorer than the Czech people, the Slovaks are probably granted their rightful share of power within this framework.

**Civil Liberties.** Media are government or party owned and rigidly censored. However, some private and literary expression occurs that is relatively free. Freedom of assembly, organization, and even association are denied. Rights to travel, occupation, and private property are restricted. Heavy pressures are placed on religious activities, especially through holding ministerial incomes at a very low level and curtailing religious education. There are a number of prisoners of conscience; exclusion of individuals from their chosen occupation is a more common sanction. The beating of political suspects is common. Successful defense in political cases is possible, but lawyers may be arrested for overzealous defense. Travel to the West and emigration are restricted. Independent trade unions and strikes are forbidden.

**Comparatively:** Czechoslovakia is as free as Rumania, freer than Bulgaria, less free than Poland.

# DENMARK

**Economy:** mixed capitalist  
**Polity:** centralized multiparty  
**Population:** 5,100,000  
A relatively homogeneous population

**Political Rights:** 1  
**Civil Liberties:** 1  
**Status of Freedom:** free

**Political Rights.** Denmark is a constitutional monarchy with a unicameral parliament. Elections are fair. Since a wide variety of parties achieve success, resulting governments are based on coalitions. Districts have governors appointed from the center and elected councils; local officials are under local control.

**Civil Liberties.** The press is free (and more conservative politically than the electorate). Radio and television are government owned but relatively free. All other rights are guaranteed, although the very high tax level constitutes more than usual constraint on private property in a capitalist state. Religion is free but state supported.

**Comparatively:** Denmark is as free as Norway, freer than Finland.

# DJIBOUTI

Economy: capitalist
Polity: centralized one-party
Population: 115,000

Political Rights: 3
Civil Liberties: 4
Status of Freedom: partly free

Independence led initially to a Somali majority ruling over a territorial Afar minority

**Political Rights.** Djibouti is a parliamentary democracy under French protection. In the elections of 1977, only one list of parliamentary candidates was presented, a list dominated by the majority Somali people. Resulting governments have included representatives of all former political parties and ethnic groups and appear to be broadly representative.

**Civil Liberties.** Law is based on French codes and modified overseas French practice. The media are mostly government owned and apparently apolitical. There is no direct censorship. In an atmosphere of violence there are political imprisonments and torture. Labor has the right to strike in a free market economy.

**Comparatively:** Djibouti appears to be as free as Malaysia, freer than Somalia, less free than Israel.

# DOMINICA

Economy: capitalist
Polity: centralized multiparty
Population: 75,000

Political Rights: 2
Civil Liberties: 2
Status of Freedom: free

A relatively homogeneous population with a minority enclave

**Political Rights.** Dominica is a parliamentary democracy with competing political parties. Change of government through shifts of parliamentary allegiances in 1979 appeared to enhance the legitimacy of the system. The rights of the native Caribs are said not to be fully respected.

**Civil Liberties.** Press is private and the radio public. The press is generally free and critical, and radio presents alternative views. Rights of assembly and organization are guaranteed. There is a rule of law with no remaining cases of political imprisonment. A special law on the Rastaferians is discriminatory. Otherwise, personal freedoms of travel, residence, union rights of workers, and property rights are secured.

**Comparatively:** Dominica is as free as Nauru, freer than Guyana, less free than Barbados.

# DOMINICAN REPUBLIC

**Economy:** capitalist
**Polity:** centralized multiparty
**Population:** 5,300,000

**Political Rights:** 2
**Civil Liberties:** 3
**Status of Freedom:** free

A complex but relatively homogeneous population

**Political Rights.** The Dominican Republic is a presidential democracy on the American model. Fairly contested elections in 1978 were won by the opposition. The ensuing regime has greatly reduced military influence. Provinces are under national control, municipalities under local.

**Civil Liberties.** The media are privately owned and free; pressure on broadcasting is alleged. Public expression is generally free; the spokesmen of a wide range of parties openly express their opinions. The communist party was recently legalized, but far left groups still find holding public meetings difficult. In the recent past guerrilla activity has led to government violence in which rights have not been respected. Although the government has shown itself quick to detain persons suspected of plotting against it, there are few, if any, prisoners of conscience. Labor unions operate under constraint.

**Comparatively:** Dominican Republic is as free as Colombia, freer than Guatemala, less free than Barbados.

# ECUADOR

**Economy:** noninclusive capitalist
**Polity:** centralized multiparty
**Population:** 8,000,000

**Political Rights:** 2
**Civil Liberties:** 2
**Status of Freedom:** free

An ethnic state with a potential subnationality

**Political Rights.** Ecuador is governed by an elected president and parliament. Elections in 1978–79 establishing the system were essentially free and widely contested. There were, however, some restrictions on party activity and nominations. *Subnationalities*: Perhaps forty percent of the population is Indian and many of these speak Quechua. However, this population does not at present form a conscious subnationality in a distinctive homeland.

**Civil Liberties.** Newspapers are under private or party control and quite outspoken; censorship has ceased since the return to civilian government. Radio and television are mostly under private control. There are no prisoners of conscience. The court system is not strongly independent, and imprisonment for belief may recur. Unions are powerful and independent. Personal freedoms to travel, residence, education, and religion are secured. Although there are state firms, particularly in major industries, Ecuador is essentially a capitalist and traditionalist state.

**Comparatively:** Ecuador is as free as Portugal, freer than Peru, less free than Costa Rica.

# EGYPT

**Economy:** mixed socialist
**Polity:** centralized dominant-
              party
**Population:** 40,600,000

**Political Rights:** 5
**Civil Liberties:** 5
**Status of Freedom:** partly free

A relatively homogeneous population with a communal religious minority

**Political Rights.** Egypt is a controlled democracy. Within limits political parties may organize: communist and religious extremist parties are forbidden. Referendums have received unlikely ninety-eight and ninety-nine percent approval. The ruling party won ninety percent of parliamentary seats in the 1979 election, but other parties achieved representation. *Subnationalities*: Several million Coptic Christians live a distinct communal life.

**Civil Liberties.** The Egyptian press is mostly government owned. Radio and television are under government control. All media are governmental means for active indoctrination, but opposition journals are allowed to appear sporadically; a fairly broad range of literary publications has recently developed. There is limited freedom of assembly. Severe riot laws have led to large-scale imprisonment, but the independence of the courts has been strengthened recently. Many prisoners of conscience have been arrested in the last few years; but few are held for long periods. Women's rights have improved. In both agriculture and industry considerable diversity and choice exists, although within a loose socialist framework. Unions have developed some independence of the government. Travel and other private rights are generally free.

**Comparatively:** Egypt is as free as Panama, freer than Saudi Arabia, less free than Mexico.

# EL SALVADOR

**Economy:** capitalist (transitional)
**Polity:** military nonparty
**Population:** 4,500,000

**Political Rights:** 5
**Civil Liberties:** 4
**Status of Freedom**: partly free

A relatively homogeneous population

**Political Rights.** At the end of 1979 El Salvador was ruled by a revolutionary military junta with the backing of major political parties. In much of the country a bloody struggle continued between rightist and leftist organizations.

**Civil Liberties.** Newspapers and radio are largely in private hands. The media are under strong pressures from all sides. There have been major opposition papers throughout the recent turmoil, and by year's end the full spectrum of opinion was available in the media. The rule of law is weak; assassination common. Guerrilla war reduces the security of all. The judiciary has shown considerable independence both before and after the 1979 coup. Freedom to organize and assemble was widely exercised throughout the year in spite of attempts at control. Human rights organizations have been very active. Although still a heavily agricultural country, rural people are to a large extent involved in the wage and market economy.

**Comparatively:** El Salvador appeared to be as free as Guatemala, freer than Haiti, less free than Mexico.

# EQUATORIAL GUINEA

**Economy:** noninclusive capitalist-
statist
**Polity:** military nonparty
**Population:** 300,000

**Political Rights:** 7
**Civil Liberties:** 6
**Status of Freedom:** not free

An ethnic state with a territorial minority

**Political Rights.** Equatorial Guinea is a military dictatorship. The coup that replaced the former dictator was popular, but the population as a whole played and plays little part. The minority Bubi people do, however, have a fairer share in power than in 1978.

**Civil Liberties.** All media are government owned. The atmosphere of terror no longer exists and there are said to be few if any political prisoners. Religious freedom was reestablished in 1979. The country is to a considerable extent dependent on plantation agriculture.

**Comparatively:** Equatorial Guinea appears to be as free as Central African Republic, freer than Congo, less free than Tanzania.

# ETHIOPIA

**Economy:** noninclusive socialist    **Political Rights:** 7
**Polity:** military nonparty    **Civil Liberties:** 7
**Population:** 31,000,000    **Status of Freedom:** not free

An ethnic state with major territorial subnationalities

**Political Rights.** Ethiopia is ruled by a military committee that has successively slaughtered the leaders of the *ancien régime* and many of its own leaders. A spectrum of mass organizations has been established on the model of a one-party socialist state. Popular control in the villages may be significant.

*Subnationalities.* The heartland of Ethiopia is occupied by the traditionally dominant Amhara and acculturated portions of the diffuse Galla people. In the late nineteenth century Ethiopian rulers united what had been warring fragments of a former empire in this heartland, and proceeded to incorporate some entirely new areas. At this time the Somali of the south came under Ethiopian rule; Eritrea was incorporated as the result of a UN decision in 1952. Today Ethiopia is crosscut by linguistic and religious divisions: most important is separatism due to historic allegiances to ancient provinces (especially Tigre), to different experiences (Eritrea), and to the population of a foreign nation (Somalia).

**Civil Liberties.** Individual rights as we know them are unprotected under conditions of despotism and anarchy. Political imprisonment, forced confession, execution, and torture are common—by the government, its supporters, and no doubt, some of its opponents. Many thousands have been killed aside from those dying in civil war. Education is totally controlled. What independence there was under the Ethiopian monarchy (of churches, the media, and unions) has been largely lost, but lack of centralized control has led to some pluralistic freedom in expression and increased local control, benefits supported in some degree by the land reform that the revolution has accomplished. Choice of residence and workplace is often made by the government. The words and actions of the regime indicate little respect for private rights in property or worker rights to independent organization.

**Comparatively:** Ethiopia is as free as Kampuchea, less free than Sudan.

# F I J I

**Economy:** noninclusive capitalist    **Political Rights:** 2
**Polity:** centralized multiparty       **Civil Liberties:** 2
**Population:** 600,000                   **Status of Freedom**: free

A binational state

**Political Rights.** Fiji has a complex political structure designed to protect the interests of both the original Fiji people and the Indian people, who now form a slight majority. The Lower House is directly elected on the basis of both communal and national rolls. The Upper House is indirectly elected by a variety of electors (including the council of chiefs, the prime minister, and the opposition leader). Local government is organized both by the central government and by a Fijian administration headed by the council of chiefs. In 1977 the opposition won its first election, but was unable to hold together a majority that could rule. This inability led to its decisive defeat in a subsequent election later in the year.

**Civil Liberties.** The press is free and private; government radio is under a separate and independent commission. The full protection of the rule of law is supplemented by an ombudsman to investigate complaints against the government. Right to property is limited by special rights of inalienability that are granted to the Fijians and cover most of the country. Strong unions have full rights. Religion, travel, and other personal rights are secured. The nation may be about evenly divided between a subsistence economy, based on agriculture and fishing, and a modern market economy.

**Comparatively:** Fiji is as free as Gambia, freer than Tonga, less free than New Zealand.

# F I N L A N D

**Economy:** mixed capitalist             **Political Rights:** 2
**Polity:** centralized multiparty        **Civil Liberties:** 2
**Population:** 4,800,000                  **Status of Freedom**: free

An ethnic state with a small territorial subnationality

**Political Rights.** Finland has a parliamentary system with a strong, directly elected president. Since there are a large number of relatively strong parties, government is almost always by coalition. Elections have resulted in shifts in coalition membership. Soviet pressure has influenced the maintenance of the current president in office for over twenty years; by treaty foreign policy cannot be anti-Soviet. The provinces have centrally appointed governors. *Subnationalities*: The rural Swedish minority (seven percent) has its own political party and strong cultural ties to Sweden. The Swedish-speaking Åland Islands have local autonomy and other special rights.

**Civil Liberties.** The press is private. Most of the radio service is government controlled, but there is an important commercial television station. Discussion in the media is controlled by a political consensus that criticism of the Soviet Union should be highly circumspect. Those who cross the line are often admonished by the government to practice self-censorship. There is a complete rule of law, and private rights are secured.

**Comparatively:** Finland is as free as Greece, freer than Turkey, less free than Sweden.


# FRANCE

**Economy:** capitalist                  **Political Rights:** 1
**Polity:** centralized multiparty        **Civil Liberties:** 2
**Population:** 53,400,000                **Status of Freedom:** free

An ethnic state with major territorial subnationalities

**Political Rights.** France is a parliamentary democracy. However, the directly elected president is more powerful than the premier and assembly. There is also a constitutional council that oversees elections and passes on the constitutionality of assembly or executive actions on the model of the United States Supreme Court. The multiparty system ensures that governments are generally coalitions. *Subnationalities*: Territorial subnationalities continue to have few rights as ethnic units and have little power under a rigidly centralized provincial administration. However, the recent election of a Paris mayor for the first time in a century and hesitant steps toward regionalization has slightly improved the situation. At present the Alsatian minority seems well satisfied, but there is a demand for greater autonomy among many Bretons, Corsicans, and Basques.

**Civil Liberties.** The French press is free, although often party-related. The news agency is private; radio and television are divided among a variety of theoretically independent companies under indirect government control. In spite of recent changes there is still an authoritarian attitude in government-citizen relations, publications may be banned at the behest of foreign governments, and arrest without explanation still occurs, particularly of members of subnationalities. Information and organization in regard to conscientious objection is restricted. France is, of course, under the rule of law, and rights to occupation, residence, religion, and property are secured. Both through extensive social programs and the creation of state enterprises France is quite far from a pure capitalist form.

**Comparatively:** France is as free as Germany (West), freer than Spain, less free than the United Kingdom.

# GABON

**Economy:** noninclusive capitalist  **Political Rights:** 6
**Polity:** nationalist one-party  **Civil Liberties:** 6
**Population:** 535,000  **Status of Freedom:** not free

A transethnic heterogeneous state

**Political Rights.** Gabon is a moderate dictatorship operating in the guise of a one-party state, with noncompetitive elections characteristic of this form. Candidates must be party approved. Major cities have elected local governments; provinces are administered from the center.

**Civil Liberties.** All media are government controlled, and no legitimate opposition voices are raised. Some critical items appear in local or available foreign media. There is no right of political assembly, and political opponents may be imprisoned. Only one labor union is sanctioned. The authoritarian government generally does not care to interfere in private lives, and respects religious freedom and private property.

**Comparatively:** Gabon is as free as Jordan, freer than Angola, less free than Ghana.

# GAMBIA

**Economy:** noninclusive capitalist  **Political Rights:** 2
**Polity:** centralized multiparty  **Civil Liberties:** 2
**Population:** 600,000  **Status of Freedom:** free

A transethnic heterogeneous state

**Political Rights.** There appears to be a fully functioning parliamentary democracy, although the same party and leader have been in power since independence in 1965. In the last election (1977) the ruling party won twenty-five seats and the opposition parties seven, an increasing but still very small share. Yet there is no evidence of serious irregularities. There is local, mostly traditional, autonomy, but not regional self-rule. (The maintenance of the system may be partly explained by the small size of the government and the lack of an army.)

**Civil Liberties.** The private and public newspapers and radio stations provide generally free media. An independent judiciary maintains the rule of law. Labor unions operate, but within limits. The agricultural economy is largely dependent on peanuts, but remains traditionally organized. The illiteracy rate is very high.

**Comparatively:** Gambia is as free as Papua New Guinea, freer than Senegal, less free than Barbados.

# GERMANY, EAST

**Economy:** socialist
**Polity:** communist one-party
**Population:** 16,700,000

**Political Rights:** 7
**Civil Liberties:** 6
**Status of Freedom:** not free

A relatively homogeneous population

**Political Rights.** East Germany is in practice a one-party communist dictatorship. No electoral competition is allowed that involves policy questions; all citizens are compelled to vote for a government-selected list of candidates. In addition, the presence of Soviet troops and direction from the Communist Party of the Soviet Union significantly reduces the sovereignty (or group freedom) of the East Germans.

**Civil Liberties.** Media are government owned and controlled. Dissidents are repressed by imprisonment and exclusion; the publication of opposing views is forbidden. Among the thousands of political prisoners, the most common offense is trying to leave the country illegally (or in some cases even seeking permission to leave), or propaganda against the state. Political reeducation may be a condition of release. The average person is not allowed freedom of occupation or residence. Once defined as an enemy of the state, a person may be barred from his occupation and his children denied higher education. Particularly revealing has been the use of the "buying out scheme" by which West Germany has been able intermittently to obtain the release of prisoners in the East through cash payments and delivering goods such as bananas and coffee. There is considerable religious freedom, with the Catholic and Protestant hierarchies possessing some independence. Freedom exists within the family, although there is no right to privacy or the inviolability of the home, mail, or telephone.

**Comparatively:** Germany (East) is as free as Rumania, freer than Bulgaria, less free than Poland.

# GERMANY, WEST

**Economy:** capitalist
**Polity:** decentralized multiparty
**Population:** 61,200,000

**Political Rights:** 1
**Civil Liberties:** 2
**Status of Freedom:** free

A relatively homogeneous population

**Political Rights.** West Germany is a parliamentary democracy with an indirectly elected and largely ceremonial president. Both major parties have ruled since the war. The weak Senate is elected by the assemblies of the constituent states and loyally defends states' rights. Successive national governments have been based on changing party balances in the powerful lower house. The states have their own elected assemblies; they control education, internal security, and culture.

**Civil Liberties.** The papers are independent and free, with little governmental interference by European standards. Radio and television are organized in public corporations under direction of the state governments. Generally the rule of law has been carefully observed, and the full spectrum of private freedoms is available. In recent years jobs have been denied to some individuals with radical leftist connections; terrorist activities have led to tighter security regulations, invasions of privacy, and less acceptance of nonconformity. Arrests have been made for handling or producing inflammatory literature, or for calling in question the courts or electoral system. Government participation in the economy is largely regulatory; in addition, complex social programs and worker participation in management have limited certain private freedoms while possibly expanding others.

**Comparatively:** West Germany is as free as France, freer than Italy, less free than the United States of America.

# G H A N A

Economy: capitalist-statist
Polity: centralized multiparty
Population: 11,300,000

**Political Rights:** 4
**Civil Liberties:**   4
**Status of Freedom**: partly free

A transethnic heterogeneous state with subnationalities

**Political Rights.** Since Fall 1979 Ghana is ruled by a parliament and elected president. However, the continuing military tendency to intervene violently was again expressed in 1979. On the local level traditional sources of power are still significant. There are elected district and local councils.

*Subnationalities.* The country is composed of a variety of peoples, with those in the south most self-conscious. The latter are the descendants of a number of traditional kingdoms, of which the Ashanti was the most important. A north-south, Muslim-Christian opposition exists but is weakly developed, because of the economic and numerical weakness and the incomplete hold of Islam in the north. In the south and center of the country a sense of Akan identity is developing among the Ashanti, Fanti, and others; since they include forty-five percent of the people, this amounts to strengthening the ethnic core of the nation. The leaders of the one million Ewe in the southeast (a people divided between Ghana and Togo) have on occasion asked for separation or enhanced self-determination.

**Civil Liberties.** The critical press is both government and private; there is a degree of autonomy to the government-owned radio and television systems. Journalists have continually struggled against censorship or closures. Private opinion is freely expressed on most matters, and freedom of assembly is honored. There are few if any prisoners of conscience, but military intervention led to political executions in 1979. Private businesses and independent organizations such as churches and labor unions thrive. There has been a great deal of government control in some areas—especially in cocoa production, on which the economy depends, and in modern capital-intensive industry. Like Senegal, Ghana has a relatively highly developed industry and its agriculture is dependent on world markets.

**Comparatively:** Ghana is as free as Morocco, freer than Togo, less free than Gambia.

# GREECE

**Economy:** capitalist
**Polity:** centralized multiparty
**Population:** 9,500,000

**Political Rights:** 2
**Civil Liberties:** 2
**Status of Freedom:** free

A relatively homogeneous state

**Political Rights.** Greece is a parliamentary democracy with a theoretically strong, but indirectly elected, president. The stabilization of free institutions is proceeding rapidly: recent elections have been competitive and open to a wide spectrum of parties. Provincial administration is centrally controlled; there is local self-government.

**Civil Liberties.** Newspapers are private and the judiciary is independent. Because of the recent revolutionary situation all views are not freely expressed (a situation similar to that in post-fascist Portugal). One can be imprisoned for insulting the authorities. Private rights are respected.

**Comparatively:** Greece is as free as Portugal, freer than Turkey, less free than France.

# GRENADA

**Economy:** mixed socialist  
**Polity:** centralized dominant-  
    party  
**Population:** 100,000

**Political Rights:** 5  
**Civil Liberties:** 5  
**Status of Freedom:** partly free

A relatively homogeneous population

**Political Rights.** In 1979 a major opposition party came to power by force. The change was initially popular, but the new leaders have increasingly monopolized power and have now postponed elections indefinitely.

**Civil Liberties.** Radio is government controlled and the only private paper was closed by the government in 1979. Opposition assemblies have regularly been broken up. Political detentions are not subject to review. Unions and private business are under government pressure.

**Comparatively:** Grenada is as free as Panama, freer than Haiti, less free than the Dominican Republic.

# GUATEMALA

**Economy:** noninclusive capitalist  
**Polity:** centralized multiparty  
    (military dominated)  
**Population:** 6,800,000

**Political Rights:** 4  
**Civil Liberties:** 5  
**Status of Freedom:** partly free

An ethnic state with a major potential territorial subnationality

**Political Rights.** Guatemala is a constitutional democracy on the American model. In recent elections not all parties were allowed to participate nationally, and there was significant organized abstention. Only the communist party remains illegal. The 1974 presidential election results were apparently altered in favor of the ruling coalition's candidate; in 1978 counting irregularities and resulting challenges were resolved in favor of a candidate less clearly identified with the government, and congressional seats went to a variety of parties. The provinces are centrally administered. Military and other security forces maintain decisive extra-constitutional power. *Subnationalities*: Various groups of Mayan and other Indians make up half the population; they do not yet have a subnationalist sense of unity.

**Civil Liberties.** The press and a large portion of radio and television are privately controlled. The press is generally free, although rural journalists have been harassed by the police. In the cities, at least, opposition political activity is open. However, the continuing operation of death squads on both the right and left inhibits discussion and expression. The struggle against rural guerrillas has led to frequent denial of rights in rural areas by security forces. The judiciary is not entirely free of governmental pressures in political or subversive cases, but some members of rightist death squads have been tried. Official political imprisonment and torture occur. Illegal armed groups, often associated with the government, are responsible for thousands of deaths, including important opposition leaders. Unions are intimidated, but other private rights seem fairly well respected by the government. Largely an agricultural country, fifty percent of those in agriculture own their own farms.

**Comparatively:** Guatemala is as free as El Salvador, freer than Nicaragua, less free than Jamaica.

# GUINEA

**Economy:** preindustrial socialist
**Polity:** socialist one-party
**Population:** 4,900,000

**Political Rights:** 7
**Civil Liberties:** 7
**Status of Freedom:** not free

A transethnic heterogeneous state

**Political Rights.** Guinea is a one-party socialist dictatorship. Elections for president and parliament are uncontested. Provincial and local governments are highly centralized.

**Civil Liberties.** All media are government or party owned and censorship is rigid. Ideological purity is demanded in all areas except religion. There are many prisoners of conscience; torture has been common and execution frequent. Everyone must participate in guided political activity. Few private rights, such as those to organize unions, develop property, or choose one's education are recognized. Private lawyers are not permitted. Movement within the country or over the border seems relatively easy. There is no legal sanctity of the home.

**Comparatively:** Guinea is as free as Ethiopia, less free than Ghana.

# GUINEA-BISSAU

**Economy:** noninclusive socialist
**Polity:** socialist one-party
**Population:** 600,000

**Political Rights:** 6
**Civil Liberties:** 6
**Status of Freedom:** not free

A transethnic heterogeneous state

**Political Rights.** Guinea-Bissau is administered by one party; all other parties are illegal. Constitutionally the secretariat of the party is the highest organ of the state; the party is recognized as the expression of the "sovereign will" of the people. There is apparently limited local freedom to reject candidates; the national assembly is indirectly elected. Local economic control under party guidance is emphasized.

**Civil Liberties.** The media are government controlled, and criticism of the system is forbidden. There are prisoners of conscience. Union activity is government directed. All land has been nationalized; rights of private property are minimal. As the system develops, many other personal rights are likely to be sacrificed, but whether an attempt will be made to adhere strictly to a communist model is unclear.

**Comparatively:** Guinea-Bissau is as free as Tanzania, freer than Guinea, less free than Senegal.

## G U Y A N A

| | |
|---|---|
| **Economy:** mixed socialist | **Political Rights:** 4 |
| **Polity:** centralized multiparty | **Civil Liberties:** 4 |
| **Population:** 820,000 | **Status of Freedom**: partly free |

An ethnically complex state

**Political Rights.** Guyana is a parliamentary democracy. However, in the last three elections the government has been responsibly charged with irregularities that resulted in its victory. The 1978 referendum was criticized for the way it was presented, for campaign restriction, and for the inflation of participation figures. The ruling party has been co-opting the position of the opposition communist party and may be headed toward a one-party state as it moves to the left. Administration is generally centralized but there are some elected local officials.

**Civil Liberties.** The media are both public and private (including party). Several opposition newspapers have been nationalized; the last opposition daily was forced to a weekly schedule in 1979. There is a right of assembly, but harassment occurs. All private schools have recently been nationalized, and the government has interfered with university appointments. It is possible to win against the government in court; there are no prisoners of conscience. Art and music are under considerable government control. Unions are under increasing pressure. Private property (as distinct from personal property) is no longer considered legitimate.

**Comparatively:** Guyana is as free as Morocco, freer than Panama, less free than Mexico.

# HAITI

**Economy:** noninclusive capitalist     **Political Rights:** 7
**Polity:** dominant party               **Civil Liberties:** 6
**Population:** 5,700,000                **Status of Freedom:** not free

A relatively homogeneous population

**Political Rights.** Haiti is a dictatorship with an ephemeral ruling party. Elections in 1979 were the first to allow an opposition candidate to be elected, but this candidacy was a notable exception. Other parties have been organized.

**Civil Liberties.** The media are both private and public. Censorship is legal for all media, including films and theatre; yet considerable courage has been shown by journalists and broadcasters. Rights of assembly and organization are restricted. A government-sponsored militia has suppressed opposition; political murders, imprisonment without trial, exile, and torture have characterized the system in the past, but brutality and short-term arrest are more common now. An acceptable rule of law has been in abeyance during a prolonged "state of siege." Many people attempt to flee the country illegally every year. Union activity is restricted. Corruption seriously infringes rights to political equality.

**Comparatively:** Haiti is as free as Benin, freer than Guinea, less free than Panama.

# HONDURAS

**Economy:** noninclusive capitalist     **Political Rights:** 6
**Polity:** military nonparty            **Civil Liberties:** 3
**Population:** 3,100,000                **Status of Freedom:** partly free

A relatively homogeneous population

**Political Rights.** The government is a military dictatorship, with continued political party activity. The system will change after a 1980 election, although some parties will remain excluded. Advisory councils assist the government. Provincial government is centrally administered.

**Civil Liberties.** The media are largely private and free of prior censorship. In spite of some pressure there is general freedom. Militant peasant organizations and political parties continue to function outside government control. In 1979 partisan political demonstrations were not allowed, but other forms of party activity were. The previous government imprisoned some of the peasants' most violent oppressors. Most private rights are respected—insofar as government power reaches. Labor unions are relatively strong, especially in plantation areas. There is freedom of religion and movement.

**Comparatively:** Honduras is as free as Peru, freer than Cuba, less free than Mexico.

# HUNGARY

Economy: socialist                      **Political Rights:** 6
**Polity:** communist one-party          **Civil Liberties:** 5
**Population:** 10,700,000               **Status of Freedom:** not free

A relatively homogeneous population

**Political Rights.** Hungary is ruled as a one-party communist dictatorship. Although there is an elective national assembly as well as local assemblies, all candidates must be approved by the party, and the decisions of the politburo are decisive. Within this framework recent elections have allowed at least a restricted choice among candidates. The group rights of the Hungarian people are diminished by the government's official acceptance of the right of the Soviet government to interfere in the domestic affairs of Hungary by force.

**Civil Liberties.** Media are under government or party control. Basic criticism of top leaders, communism, human rights performance, or the Soviet presence is inadmissable, but some criticism is allowed, especially through papers, plays, books, and the importation of foreign publications or listening to foreign broadcasts. Prisoners of conscience are detained regularly, though usually for short periods. Control over religious affairs is more relaxed than in most communist states. Although private rights are not guaranteed, in practice there is considerable private property, and permission to travel into and out of the country is easier to obtain than in most of Eastern Europe. (January 1980 the border with Austria became essentially open.) Unions are party directed and have no right to strike.

**Comparatively:** Hungary is as free as Yugoslavia, freer than Czechoslovakia, less free than Egypt.

# ICELAND

Economy: capitalist                     **Political Rights:** 1
**Polity:** centralized multiparty       **Civil Liberties:** 1
**Population:** 223,000                  **Status of Freedom:** free

A relatively homogeneous population

**Political Rights.** Iceland is governed by a parliamentary democracy. Recent years have seen important shifts in voter sentiment, resulting successively in right- and left-wing coalitions. Although a small country

Iceland has pursued a highly independent foreign policy. Provinces are ruled by central government appointees.

**Civil Liberties.** The press is private or party and free of censorship. There are no political prisoners and the judiciary is independent. Private rights are respected; few are poor or illiterate.

**Comparatively:** Iceland is as free as Norway, freer than Portugal.

# INDIA

**Economy:** noninclusive capitalist-statist
**Polity:** decentralized multiparty
**Population:** 661,000,000

**Political Rights:** 2
**Civil Liberties:** 2
**Status of Freedom:** free

A multinational and complex state

**Political Rights.** India is a parliamentary democracy in which the opposition has had an opportunity to rule. The strong powers retained by its component states have been compromised in recent years by the central government's frequent imposition of direct rule. Calling immediate state elections where the opposition continues to rule after a national change of government is a recent practice compromising the federal system.

*Subnationalities.* India contains a diverse collection of mostly territorially distinct peoples united by historical experience and the predominance of Hinduism. India's dominant peoples are those of the north central area who speak as a first language either the official language, Hindi (Hindustani), or a very closely related dialect of Sanskrit origin. The other major subnational peoples of India may be divided into several groups: (1) peoples with separate states that are linguistically and historically only marginally distinct from the dominant Hindi speakers (for example, the Marathi, Gujerati, or Oriya); (2) peoples with separate states that are of Sanskirt background linguistically, but have a relatively strong sense of separate identity (for example, Bengalis or Kashmiris); (3) peoples with separate states that are linguistically and to some extent racially quite distinct (for example, Telegu or Malayalam); and (4) peoples that do not have states of their own and are often survivors of India's pre-Aryan peoples (for example, Santali, Bhuti-Lapcha, or Mizo). With the exception of the last group, the Indian federal system accords a fair amount of democratic rights to all peoples. Several peoples from groups (2), (3), and (4) have shown through legal (especially votes) and illegal means a strong desire by a significant part of the population for independence or greater autonomy (notably Kashmiris, Nagas, and

Mizos). This accounting leaves out many *nonterritorial* religious and caste minorities, although, here again, the system has granted relatively broad rights to such groups to reasonable self-determination.

**Civil Liberties.** The Indian press is strong and independent. The fact that radio and television are not independent in this largely illiterate country is disquieting. Although there have been illegal arrests, questionable killings, and reports of torture, in general the police and judiciary are now thought to be responsive, fair, and independent. The problem of extreme trial delay has recently been addressed. There are few, if any, prisoners of conscience, but there are hundreds imprisoned for political violence, and demonstrations may lead to fatalities and large-scale jailings. Due to the decentralized political structure there is a great deal of regional variation in the operation of security laws. Kashmir has especially repressive security policies in relation to the press and political detention; Sikkim is treated as an Indian colony, and the same might be said for other border areas. Indians enjoy freedom to travel, to worship as they please, and to organize for mutual benefit, especially in unions. Lack of education, extreme poverty, and surviving traditional controls certainly reduce the meaning of such liberties for large numbers of Indians.

**Comparatively:** India is as free as Portugal, freer than Malaysia, less free than Japan.

# INDONESIA

**Economy:** noninclusive capitalist-statist
**Polity:** centralized dominant-party
**Population:** 141,000,000

**Political Rights:** 5
**Civil Liberties:** 5
**Status of Freedom**: partly free

A transethnic heterogeneous state with active and potential sub-nationalities

**Political Rights.** Indonesia is a controlled parliamentary democracy under military direction. Recent parliamentary elections showed the ability of the rather tame opposition parties to gain ground at the expense of the governing party, but the government's majority is still overwhelming. The number and character of opposition parties is carefully controlled, parties must refrain from criticizing one another, candidates of both government and opposition require government approval, and opposition activities in rural areas are restricted. In any event parliament does not have a great deal of power. Provincial governors are indirectly elected from centrally approved lists. Local assemblies are elected.

*Subnationalities.* Indonesia includes a variety of ethnic groups and is divided by crosscutting island identities. Although the island of Java is numerically dominant, the national language is not Javanese, and most groups or islands do not appear to have strong subnational identifications. Both civilian and military elites generally attempt to maintain religious, ethnic, and regional balance. Groups demanding independence exist in Sulawesi, the Moluccas, Timor, West Irian, and northern Sumatra, and continue to mount revolts against the government.

**Civil Liberties.** Most newspapers are private. All are subject to fairly close government supervision; criticism of the system is muted by periodic suppressions. Radio and television are government controlled. Freedom of assembly is restricted, but citizens are not compelled to attend meetings. After years of large-scale imprisonment, there now appear to be very few prisoners of conscience. Thousands of released prisoners remain in a second-class station, especially in regard to residence and employment. In this area the army rather than the civilian judiciary is dominant. Torture appears to be infrequent recently; the army has been responsible for many thousands of unnecessary deaths in its suppression of revolt in, or conquest of, East Timor. Union activity is closely regulated; movement, especially to the cities, is restricted; other private rights are generally respected. The Indonesian bureaucracy has an unenviable reputation for arbitrariness and corruption, practices that reduce the effective expression of human rights.

**Comparatively:** Indonesia is as free as Nicaragua, freer than Burma, less free than Bangladesh.

# I R A N

**Economy:** noninclusive capitalist-statist
**Polity:** quasi-dominant party
**Population:** 36,300,000

**Political Rights:** 5
**Civil Liberties:** 5
**Status of Freedom:** partly free

An ethnic state with major territorial subnationalities

**Political Rights.** The year saw the end of Iran's monarchical system and step by step movement toward a theocratic democracy. Many parties reemerged, but a number were later forcibly disbanded or forced underground. Several elections were held: a simple referendum replacing monarchy with the Islamic republic—overwhelmingly approved but hardly a free and fair vote; the election of a constituent assembly—much lower participation, but at least a restricted choice; and the constitutional referendum—again less enthusiasm and not a free and fair choice.

(1980 saw the further institutionalization of the system and more open elections.) *Subnationalities*: Among the most important non-Persian peoples are the Kurds, the Azerbaijani Turks, the Baluchi, and a variety of other (primarily Turkish) tribes. Many of these have striven for independence in the recent past when the opportunity arose; they were very active in 1979.

**Civil Liberties.** Newspapers are private or party, but were repeatedly suppressed or otherwise controlled during the year. Other media are largely government owned and are official propaganda organs. The right of assembly has been sporadically denied to those who do not approve of the new system. Many prisoners were released early in 1979; subsequently hundreds of political executions and thousands of political imprisonments took place without due process. Anarchy led to vigilante groups competing with the official security system, and many private rights became highly insecure. Thousands fled; other thousands appear to have been denied exit.

**Comparatively:** Iran is as free as Egypt, freer than Iraq, less free than Bangladesh.

# I R A Q

| | |
|---|---|
| **Economy:** noninclusive socialist | **Political Rights:** 7 |
| **Polity:** socialist one-party | **Civil Liberties:** 7 |
| **Population:** 12,900,000 | **Status of Freedom:** not free |

An ethnic state with a major territorial subnationality

**Political Rights.** Iraq is essentially a one-party state under military leadership. Communists and other participants in government prior to 1979 were eliminated during the year. Provinces are governed from the center. *Subnationalities*: The Kurds have been repeatedly denied self-determination, most recently through re-occupation of their lands and an attempt to disperse them about the country.

**Civil Liberties.** Newspapers are largely public or party and are closely controlled by the government; both foreign and domestic books and movies are censored. Radio and television are government monopolies. The strident media are emphasized as governmental means for active indoctrination. Political imprisonment, execution, brutality, and torture are very common. The families of suspects are often imprisoned. Rights are largely de facto or those deriving from traditional religious law. Religious freedom and freedom to organize for any purpose is very limited. Education is intended to serve the party's purposes. Iraq has a dual economy, with a large preindustrial sector. The government has taken over much of the modern petroleum-based economy and, through land reform leading to collectives and state farms, has increasingly limited private economic choice.

**Comparatively:** Iraq is as free as Laos, less free than Syria.


# IRELAND

**Economy:** capitalist
**Polity:** centralized multiparty
**Population:** 3,200,000

**Political Rights:** 1
**Civil Liberties:** 1
**Status of Freedom:** free

A relatively homogeneous population

**Political Rights.** Ireland is a parliamentary democracy which successfully shifts national power among parties. The bicameral legislature has an appointive upper house with powers only of delay. Local government is not powerful, but is elective rather than appointive. The referendum is also used for national decisions.

**Civil Liberties.** The press is free and private, and radio and television are under an autonomous corporation. Strong censorship has always been exercised over both publishers and the press, but since this is of social rather than political content, it lies within that sphere of control permitted a majority in a free democracy. The rule of law is firmly established and private rights are guaranteed.

**Comparatively:** Ireland is as free as Canada, freer than France.


# ISRAEL

**Economy:** mixed capitalist
**Polity:** centralized multiparty
**Population:** 3,800,000

**Political Rights:** 2
**Civil Liberties:** 2
**Status of Freedom:** free

An ethnic state with microterritorial subnationalities

**Political Rights.** Israel is governed under a parliamentary system. Recent elections have resulted in major shifts of power among the many political parties. Provinces are ruled from the center, although there are important local elective offices in the cities. *Subnationalities:* National elections do not involve the Arabs in the occupied territories; Arabs in Israel proper participate in Israeli elections as a minority. Arabs both in Israel and the occupied territories must live in their homeland under the cultural and political domination of twentieth-century immigrants.

**Civil Liberties.** Newspapers are private or party, and free of censorship except for restrictions relating to the always precarious national security. Radio and television are government owned. In general the rule of law is observed, although Arabs in Israel are not accorded the full rights of citizens, and the Orthodox Jewish faith holds a special position in the country's religious, customary, and legal life. Detentions, house arrest, and brutality have been reported against Arabs opposing Israel's Palestine policy. Because of the war, the socialist-cooperative ideology of its founders, and dependence on outside support, the role of private enterprise in the economy has been less than in most of Euro-America. Arabs are, in effect, not allowed to buy land from Jews, and Arab land has been expropriated for Jewish settlement. Freedom House's rating of Israel is based on its judgment of the situation in Israel proper and not that in the occupied territories.

**Comparatively:** Israel is as free as Portugal, freer than Egypt, less free than France.

# I T A L Y

| | |
|---|---|
| **Economy:** capitalist | **Political Rights:** 2 |
| **Polity:** centralized multiparty | **Civil Liberties:** 2 |
| **Population:** 56,900,000 | **Status of Freedom:** free |

A relatively homogeneous population with small territorial sub-nationalities

**Political Rights.** Italy is a bicameral parliamentary democracy. Elections are generally free, but the political process is not free of corruption on both right and left. Since the 1940's governments have been dominated by the Christian Democrats, with coalitions shifting between dependence on minor parties of the left or right. The fascist party is banned. Referendums are used to supplement parliamentary rule. Opposition parties gain local political power, but regional and local power are generally quite limited.

**Civil Liberties.** Italian newspapers are free and cover a broad spectrum. Radio and television are both public and private and provide unusually diverse programming. Laws against defamation of the government and foreign and ecclesiastical officials exert a slight limiting effect on the media. Freedom of speech is inhibited in some areas and for many individuals by the violence of both right- and left-wing extremist groups. Since the bureaucracy does not promptly respond to citizen desires, it represents, as in many countries, an additional impediment to the full expression of the rule of law. Detention may last for years without trial. Since major industries are managed by the government, and the government has undertaken major reallocations of land, Italy is only marginally a capitalist state.

**Comparatively:** Italy is as free as Greece, freer than Morocco, less free than France.

# IVORY COAST

**Economy:** noninclusive capitalist
**Polity:** nationalist one-party
**Population:** 7,700,000

**Political Rights:** 6
**Civil Liberties:** 5
**Status of Freedom:** partly free

A transethnic heterogeneous state

**Political Rights.** Ivory Coast is ruled by a one-party, capitalist dictatorship. Under these constraints presidential and assembly elections have little meaning; in the most recent election there was no choice and the president received ninety-nine percent of the vote. Organized in the 1940's, the ruling party incorporates a variety of interests and forces; there are democratic elements at the local level in the selection of assembly candidates. Provinces are ruled directly from the center. Contested mayoralty elections have occurred recently.

**Civil Liberties.** Although the legal press is mostly party or government controlled, it presents a limited spectrum of opinion. Foreign publications are widely available. While opposition is discouraged, there is no ideological conformity. Radio and television are government controlled. Short-term imprisonment and other pressures are used to control opposition. Travel and religion are generally free. There is a limited right to strike and organize unions. Economically the country depends on small private farms; in the modern sector private enterprise is encouraged.

**Comparatively:** Ivory Coast is as free as Poland, freer than Niger, less free than Kenya.

# JAMAICA

**Economy:** mixed capitalist
**Polity:** centralized multiparty
**Population:** 2,200,000

**Political Rights:** 2
**Civil Liberties:** 3
**Status of Freedom:** free

A relatively homogeneous population

**Political Rights.** Jamaica is a parliamentary democracy in which power changes from one party to another. However, political life has become increasingly violent: the last election was accompanied by murders, a state of siege, bans on political rallies, and government supervision of publicity. Regardless of who is to blame, and both sides may be, this degrades the meaning of political rights. The opposition refused to participate in by-elections in 1978 because of violence and poor electoral procedures. Regional and local administrations do not have independent power.

**Civil Liberties.** The free press is endangered by nationalization, government attacks, and court actions. Government radio and television present a pro-government view and private outlets are denied. Freedom of assembly has been curtailed. The rule of law and respect for rights remain, yet in many districts a climate of fear inhibits their expression. Aside from the media, nationalization of the economy has emphasized so far the takeover of foreign companies.

**Comparatively:** Jamaica is as free as Colombia, freer than Panama, less free than Dominica.

# JAPAN

**Economy:** capitalist
**Polity:** centralized multiparty
**Population:** 115,900,000

**Political Rights:** 2
**Civil Liberties:** 1
**Status of Freedom:** free

A relatively homogeneous population

**Political Rights.** Japan is a bicameral, constitutional monarchy with a relatively weak upper house. The conservative-to-centrist Liberal Democratic Party ruled with solid majorities from independence in the early 1950's until the mid-1970's. Although the Liberal Democrats have lost considerable support in recent elections, through coalitions with independents they have maintained control at the national level, and have recently showed increased strength at the local level. Concentrated business interests have played a strong role in maintaining Liberal Party hegemony through the use of their money, influence, and prestige. In addition, a heavy weighting of representation in favor of rural areas tends to maintain the Liberal Party position. Opposition parties are fragmented. They have local control in some areas, but the power of local and regional assemblies and officials is limited. Since electoral and parliamentary procedures are democratic, we assume that Japan's system would freely allow a transfer of national power to an opposition group should the majority desire it, but as in Italy this is not yet proven by events. Democracy within the Liberal Party is increasing.

**Civil Liberties.** News media are generally private and free, although many radio and television stations are served by a public broadcasting corporation. Television is excellent and quite free. Courts of law are not as important in Japanese society as in Europe and America; both the courts and police appear to be relatively fair. Travel and change of residence are unrestricted. The public expressions and actions of many people are more restricted than in most modern democracies by traditional controls. Japanese style collectivism leads to strong social pressures, especially psychological pressures, in many spheres (unions, corporations, or religious-political groups, such as Soka Gakkai).

**Comparatively:** Japan is as free as West Germany, freer than Italy, less free than the United Kingdom.

# JORDAN

Economy: capitalist
Polity: traditional nonparty
Population: 3,000,000

Political Rights: 6
Civil Liberties: 6
Status of Freedom: not free

A relatively homogeneous population

**Political Rights.** Jordan is an absolute monarchy in the guise of a constitutional monarchy. There are no parties; parliament provides no check on the king's broad powers, since it has not met since 1967. In 1978 an appointive National Consultative Council was established. Provinces are ruled from the center and local governments have very limited autonomy. The king and his ministers are regularly petitioned by citizens.

**Civil Liberties.** Papers are private but self-censored and occasionally suspended. Television and radio are government controlled. Free private conversation and mild public criticism are allowed. Under continuing emergency laws normal legal guarantees for political suspects are suspended, and organized opposition is not permitted. There are prisoners of conscience and instances of torture. Labor has a limited right to organize and strike. Private rights such as those to property, travel, or religion appear to be respected.

**Comparatively:** Jordan is as free as Saudi Arabia, freer than South Yemen, less free than Syria.

# KAMPUCHEA (Cambodia)

Economy: socialist
Polity: communist one-party states
Population: 4–8,000,000

Political Rights: 7
Civil Liberties: 7
Status of Freedom: not free

A relatively homogeneous population

**Political Rights.** Kampuchea in 1979 was divided between the remnants of the Pol Pot tyranny and the only slightly less tyrannical, imposed Vietnamese regime. The people had little part in either regime.

**Civil Liberties.** The media were completely controlled in both areas. Political execution has been a common function of government; enforced starvation remains a tactic employed by both sides. People have been prevented from harvesting their crops or receiving international supplies. There is no rule of law; private freedoms are not guaranteed. Kampucheans continue to be one of the world's most tyrannized peoples.

**Comparatively:** Kampuchea is as free as Ethiopia, less free than Thailand.

# KENYA

**Economy:** noninclusive capitalist
**Polity:** nationalist one-party
**Population:** 15,400,000

**Political Rights:** 5
**Civil Liberties:** 4
**Status of Freedom:** partly free

A formally transethnic heterogeneous state with active and potential subnationalities

**Political Rights.** Kenya is a one-party capitalist state with Kikuyu domination, at least until recently. Only the ruling party competes in elections. Election results often express popular dissatisfaction, but candidates avoid discussion of basic policy or the president. Selection of top party and national leaders is by consensus or acclamation. The administration is centralized, but elements of tribal and communal government continue at the periphery. *Subnationalities*: Comprising twenty percent of the population, the Kikuyu are the largest tribal group. In a very heterogeneous society, the Luo are the second most important subnationality.

**Civil Liberties.** The press is private. It is not censored but under government pressure to avoid criticism. Radio and television are under government control. Rights of assembly, organization, and demonstration are limited. The courts have considerable independence. There are few if any prisoners of conscience. Unions are active but strikes generally illegal; private rights are generally respected. Land is gradually coming under private rather than tribal control.

**Comparatively:** Kenya is as free as Guatemala, freer than Tanzania, less free than Mauritius.

# KIRIBATI

**Economy:** noninclusive capitalist-
statist
**Polity:** decentralized nonparty
**Population:** 56,000

**Political Rights:** 2
**Civil Liberties:** 2
**Status of Freedom:** free

A relatively homogeneous population with a territorial subnationality.

**Political Rights.** Both the legislature and chief minister are elected in a fully competitive system. Local government is significant.

**Civil Liberties.** Public expression appears to be free and the rule of law guaranteed. The modern economy is dominated by government-controlled phosphate mining and investments.

**Comparatively:** Kiribati is as free as Fiji, freer than Western Samoa, less free than Australia.

## K O R E A , N O R T H

Economy: socialist
Polity: communist one-party
Population: 17,500,000

Political Rights: 7
Civil Liberties: 7
Status of Freedom: not free

A relatively homogeneous state

**Political Rights.** North Korea is a hard-line communist dictatorship in which the organs and assemblies of government are merely a facade for party rule. National elections allow no choice. The politburo is under one-man rule; the dictator's son was his expected successor until recently. Military officers are very strong in top positions.

**Civil Liberties.** The media are all government controlled, with glorification of the leader a major responsibility. No individual thoughts are advanced publicly or privately. Individual rights are minimal. Rights to travel internally and externally are perhaps the most restrictive in the world. Social classes are politically defined in a rigidly controlled society. There are large numbers of prisoners of conscience; torture is reportedly common.

**Comparatively:** North Korea is as free as Albania, less free than South Korea.

## K O R E A , S O U T H

Economy: capitalist
Polity: dominant party
Population: 37,600,000

Political Rights: 4
Civil Liberties: 5
Status of Freedom: partly free

A relatively homogeneous state

**Political Rights.** South Korea has had a strong presidential system. The president was indirectly elected by a special elective body, and he appointed one-third of the assembly. 1978 assembly elections gave a plurality to the opposition party; however appointive members and the large number of independents prevented its gaining control. Provinces are headed by national governmental appointees. The president's assassination in October 1979 led to an interim regime based initially on the same forms.

**Civil Liberties.** Most newspapers are private, as are many radio stations and one television station. Because of government pressure, self-censorship is the rule. Special laws against criticizing the constitution, the government, or its policies have resulted in many prisoners of conscience and the use of torture. The resulting climate of fear in activist circles has been sharpened by extralegal harassment of those who were not imprisoned, and the inability of the courts to effectively protect the rights of political suspects or prisoners. Yet demonstrations and expressions of open dissent have continued. Most political prisoners were released in late 1979 and restrictive laws were abrogated or moderated. Outside this arena private rights have been generally respected. Unions were free to organize, but not to strike. Religious freedom (but not religious political activism) and freedom of movement within the country were respected. Rapid, capitalistic economic growth has been combined with a relatively egalitarian income distribution.

**Comparatively:** South Korea is as free as Kenya, freer than China (Mainland), less free than Bangladesh.

# K U W A I T

**Economy:** mixed capitalist-
   statist
**Polity:** traditional nonparty
**Population:** 1,300,000

**Political Rights:** 6
**Civil Liberties:** 4
**Status of Freedom:** partly free

The citizenry is relatively homogeneous

**Political Rights.** Kuwait is a traditional monarchy in retreat from an experiment in constitutional monarchy. (Representative government is promised again in 1980.) The recent monarchical succession was uneventful, and citizens have access to the monarch. More than half the population are immigrants; their political, economic, and social rights are much inferior to those of natives.

**Civil Liberties.** Although the private press presents diverse opinions and ideological viewpoints, papers are subject to suspension for "spreading dissension." Radio and television are government controlled. Freedom of assembly is curtailed. Public critics may be detained, expelled, or have their passports confiscated. Private discussion is open and few, if any, political prisoners are held. Private freedoms are respected, and independent unions operate. There is a wide variety of enabling government activity in fields such as education, housing, and medicine that is not based on reducing choice through taxation.

**Comparatively:** Kuwait is as free as Panama, freer than Saudi Arabia, less free than Lebanon.

# L A O S

**Economy:** noninclusive socialist   **Political Rights:** 7
**Polity:** communist one-party   **Civil Liberties:** 7
**Population:** 3,700,000   **Status of Freedom:** not free

An ethnic state with active or potential subnationalities

**Political Rights.** Laos has established a traditional communist party dictatorship in which the party is superior to the external government at all levels. The government is subservient to the desires of the Vietnamese communist party, upon which the present leaders must depend. There is continued resistance in rural areas, where many groups have been violently suppressed. *Subnationalities*: Pressure on the Hmong (Meo) hill people has caused the majority of them to flee the country.

**Civil Liberties.** The media are all government controlled. There are many political prisoners; large numbers remain in re-education camps. There are few accepted private rights, but there has been some relaxation of opposition to traditional ways recently. Travel within and exit from the country is highly restricted.

**Comparatively:** Laos is as free as Vietnam, less free than China (Mainland).

# L E B A N O N

**Economy:** capitalist   **Political Rights:** 4
**Polity:** decentralized multiparty   **Civil Liberties:** 4
**Population:** 3,000,000   **Status of Freedom:** partly free

A complex, multinational, microterritorial state

**Political Rights.** In theory Lebanon is a parliamentary democracy with a strong but indirectly elected president. In spite of the calamities of the last few years the constitutional system still functions to varying degrees in much of the country. Parliament meets sporadically. Palestinians, local militias, and Syrian forces reduce its sovereignty. *Subnationalities*: Leading administrative and parliamentary officials are allocated among the several religious or communal groups by complicated formulas. These groups have for years pursued semi-autonomous lives within the state, although their territories are often intermixed.

**Civil Liberties.** Renowned for its independence, the press still offers a highly diverse selection to an attentive audience. Most censorship is now self-imposed, reflecting the views of the locally dominant military force. Radio is government owned; television has been in private hands. Widespread killing in recent years has inhibited the nationwide expression of most freedoms and tightened communal controls on individuals.

In many areas the courts cannot function effectively, but within its power the government secures most private rights. Few if any prisoners of conscience are detained by the government.

**Comparatively:** Lebanon is as free as Ghana, freer than Syria, less free than Turkey.

# LESOTHO

**Economy:** noninclusive capitalist
**Polity:** partially centralized
    dominant party
**Population:** 1,300,000

**Political Rights:** 5
**Civil Liberties:** 5
**Status of Freedom:** partly free

A relatively homogeneous population

**Political Rights.** Lesotho is a constitutional monarchy essentially under the one-man rule of the leader of the ruling political party who suspended the constitution to avoid being defeated in 1970. Opposition parties as well as the king have been repressed, and at the end of the year the repression appeared to be growing as the flow of refugees increased. Yet major elements of the traditional system (chiefs) remain, and members of other parties have been introduced into the government. Although there are frequent expressions of national independence, Lesotho remains under considerable South African economic and political pressure. Lesotho is populated almost exclusively by Basotho people, and the land has never been alienated. However, a large percentage of the male citizenry works in South Africa.

**Civil Liberties.** Radio is government and church controlled, as are most papers. There are, however, opposition publications and South African media offer a readily available alternative. Freedom of assembly is restricted. The judiciary seems to preserve considerable independence vis-à-vis the government. Limited union activity is permitted. Internal travel is unrestricted, as are most private rights.

**Comparatively:** Lesotho is as free as Indonesia, freer than South Africa, less free than Botswana.

# LIBERIA

**Economy:** noninclusive capitalist
**Polity:** nationalist dominant party
**Population:** 1,800,000

**Political Rights:** 6
**Civil Liberties:** 5
**Status of Freedom:** partly free

A formally transethnic heterogeneous state

**Political Rights.** Liberian government is formally modeled on that of the United States. However, there is no independent provincial power.

There is only one significant party (an opposition party was legalized in early 1980). Elections are characterized by lack of opposition, a limited electorate, and the easy election of the party's candidates. Although attempts are made to increase the participation of the native population, the country is still ruled by the very small Americo-Liberian community. (April 1980 a military coup replaced the system.)

**Civil Liberties.** The press is private but consists primarily of the organs of the ruling party. Radio and television are partially government controlled. Pressure is brought against those who become too critical either through the media or other channels. The government often acts under special "emergency powers" suspending many constitutional guarantees, yet there are few, if any, long-term political prisoners. Travel and other private rights are generally respected. Only blacks can become citizens. Union organization is partly free.

**Comparatively:** Liberia is as free as Ivory Coast, freer than Gabon, less free than Senegal.

# LIBYA

**Economy:** capitalist-statist
**Polity:** socialist quasi-one-party
        (military dominated)
**Population:** 2,800,000

**Political Rights:** 6
**Civil Liberties:** 6
**Status of Freedom:** not free

A relatively homogeneous state

**Political Rights.** Libya is a military dictatorship apparently effectively under the control of one person. Although officially there is no party, the effort to mobilize and organize the entire population for state purposes follows the socialist one-party model. The place of a legislature is taken by the direct democracy of large congresses. Whatever the form, no opposition is allowed on the larger questions of society. Institutional self-management has been widely introduced in schools, hospitals, and factories. Sometimes the system works well enough to provide a meaningful degree of decentralized self-determination.

**Civil Liberties.** The media are government controlled means for active indoctrination. There are many political prisoners; the use of military and people's courts for political cases suggests little respect for the rule of law. Torture and mistreatment are alleged. Oil and oil-related industry are the major government enterprises. Although ideologically socialist, even some of the press remains in private hands. Socialization tends to be announced at the top and imposed rather anarchically and sporadically at the bottom. Respect for Islam provides some check on arbitrary government.

**Comparatively:** Libya is as free as China (Mainland), freer than Iraq, less free than Egypt.

# LUXEMBOURG

**Economy:** capitalist
**Polity:** centralized multiparty
**Population:** 350,000

**Political Rights:** 1
**Civil Liberties:** 1
**Status of Freedom:** free

A relatively homogeneous state

**Political Rights.** Luxembourg is a constitutional monarchy on the Belgian model, in which the monarchy is somewhat more powerful than in the United Kingdom or Scandinavia. The legislature is bicameral with the appointive upper house having only a delaying function. Recent votes have resulted in important shifts in the nature of the dominant coalition.

**Civil Liberties.** The media are private and free. The rule of law is thoroughly accepted in both public and private realms.

**Comparatively:** Luxembourg is as free as Iceland, freer than France.

# MADAGASCAR

**Economy:** noninclusive mixed
          socialist
**Polity:** nationalist one-party
          (military dominated)
**Population:** 8,500,000

**Political Rights:** 6
**Civil Liberties:** 6
**Status of Freedom:** not free

A transethnic heterogeneous state

**Political Rights.** Madagascar is a military dictatorship with a very weak legislature. In 1977 the parliamentary election was restricted to candidates selected by parties grouped in a "national front," a government sponsored coalition; parliament appears to play a very small part in government. Anarchical conditions also called into question the extent to which the people are willing to grant the regime legitimacy. Emphasis has been put on developing the autonomy of local Malagasy governmental institutions, but the restriction of local elections to approved front candidates belies this emphasis.

**Civil Liberties.** There is a private press, but papers are carefully censored and may be suspended. Broadcasting is government controlled. Movie theatres have been nationalized. The government replaced the national news agency with one which will "disregard information likely to be harmful to the government's socialist development policies." There is no right of assembly; one must be careful of public speech.

There are few political prisoners but short-term political detentions are common. Labor unions and the judiciary are not strong, but religion is free and most private rights respected. Public security is very weak. Overseas travel is restricted. While still encouraging private investment, most businesses and large farms are nationalized.

**Comparatively:** Madagascar is as free as Tanzania, freer than Mozambique, less free than Egypt.

# MALAWI

**Economy:** noninclusive capitalist
**Polity:** nationalist one-party
**Population:** 5,900,000

**Political Rights:** 6
**Civil Liberties:** 7
**Status of Freedom:** not free

A transethnic heterogeneous state

**Political Rights.** Malawi is a one-man dictatorship with party and parliamentary forms. A 1978 election allowed some choice among individuals for the first time. Administration is centralized, although the paramount chiefs retain power locally through control over land.

**Civil Liberties.** The press is private or religious but under strict government control, as is the government-owned radio service. Private criticism of the administration remains dangerous. Foreign publications are carefully screened. The country has been notable for the persecution of Jehovah's Witnesses (including a demand they join the ruling party), treason trials, expulsion of Asian groups, the detention of journalists, torture and brutality (including admitted attempts to kill opponents outside the country). In recent years there have been fewer political prisoners. Asians suffer discrimination. Corruption and economic inequality are characteristic. Traditional courts offer some protection against arbitrary rule, as do the comparatively limited interests of the government. Foreign travel and union activity are closely controlled.

**Comparatively:** Malawi is as free as South Yemen, freer than Somalia, less free than Zambia.

# MALAYSIA

**Economy:** capitalist
**Polity:** decentralized dominant
          party
**Population:** 13,300,000

**Political Rights:** 3
**Civil Liberties:** 4
**Status of Freedom:** partly free

An ethnic state with major nonterritorial subnationalities

**Political Rights.** Malaysia is a parliamentary democracy with a weak, indirectly elected and appointed senate and a powerful lower house. The relatively powerless head of state is an elective monarch, rotating among the traditional monarchs of the constituent states. A multinational front has dominated electoral and parliamentary politics. By such devices as imprisonment or the banning of demonstrations the opposition is not given an equal opportunity to compete in elections. The states of Malaysia have their own rulers, parliaments, and institutions, but it is doubtful if any state has the power to leave the federation. *Subnationalities*: Political, economic, linguistic, and educational policies have favored the Malays (forty-four percent) over the Chinese (thirty-six percent), Indians (ten percent), and others. Traditionally the Chinese had been the wealthier and better educated people. Although there are Chinese in the ruling front, they are not allowed to question the policy of communal preference.

**Civil Liberties.** The press is private and highly varied. However, nothing that might influence communal relations can be printed, and editors are constrained by the need to renew their publishing licenses annually. Foreign journalists are closely controlled. Radio is mostly government owned, television entirely so. Universities have been put under government pressure and foreign professors encouraged to leave. There have been several reports of the development of an atmosphere of fear in both academic and opposition political circles, as well as widespread discrimination against non-Malays. In 1978 an attempt to establish a private university for Chinese language students was blocked. At least 1000 political suspects are detained indefinitely, generally on suspicion of communist activity. Some are clearly prisoners of conscience; several have held responsible political positions. Confessions are often extracted. Nevertheless, significant criticism appears in the media, and in parliament campaigns are mounted against government decisions. Unions are partly free and have the right to strike. Economic activity is free, except for government favoritism to the Malays.

**Comparatively:** Malaysia is as free as Mexico, freer than Indonesia, less free than Sri Lanka.

# MALDIVES

**Economy:** noninclusive capitalist  **Political Rights:** 5
**Polity:** traditional nonparty  **Civil Liberties:** 5
**Population:** 140,000  **Status of Freedom:** partly free

A relatively homogeneous population

**Political Rights.** The Maldives have a parliamentary government in which a president (elected by parliament and confirmed by the people) is the real ruler. Regional leaders are presidentially appointed. Both economic and political power are concentrated in the hands of a very small, wealthy elite. Islam places a check on absolutism.

**Civil Liberties.** Newspapers present some diversity of views but are under pressure to conform; the radio station is owned by the government. Foreign publications are received; political discussion is limited. There are few if any long-term political prisoners. Law is traditional Islamic law; most of the people rely on a traditional subsistence economy; the small elite has developed commercial fishing and tourism.

**Comparatively:** Maldives is as free as Qatar, freer than Seychelles, less free than Mauritius.

# MALI

**Economy:** noninclusive mixed socialist
**Polity:** nationalist one-party (military dominated)
**Population:** 6,500,000

**Political Rights:** 7
**Civil Liberties:** 6
**Status of Freedom:** not free

A transethnic heterogeneous state

**Political Rights.** Mali is a military dictatorship with a recently constructed political party to lend support. The regime appears to function without broad popular consensus. National elections allow no choice, though there is some at the local level. *Subnationalities*: Although the government is ostensibly above ethnic rivalries, repression of the northern peoples has been reported.

**Civil Liberties.** The media are all government controlled. Antigovernment demonstrations are forbidden. Private conversation is relatively free. Political imprisonment and torture occur. Religion is free. Unions are controlled; travelers must submit to frequent police checks. Private economic rights in the modern sector are minimal, but collectivization has recently been deemphasized for subsistence agriculturists, the majority of the people.

**Comparatively:** Mali is as free as Benin, freer than Somalia, less free than Liberia.

# MALTA

**Economy:** mixed capitalist-statist
**Polity:** centralized multiparty
**Population:** 322,000

**Political Rights:** 2
**Civil Liberties:** 3
**Status of Freedom:** free

A relatively homogeneous population

**Political Rights.** Malta is a parliamentary democracy in which power has shifted between the major parties. The most recent election, maintaining the governing party in its position, was marked by violence. The government also altered the composition of a constitutional court in the middle of a case concerning alleged coercion of voters in a particular district.

**Civil Liberties.** The press is free, but foreign and domestic journalists are under government pressure. Broadcasting is under a licensed body; Italian media are also available. Although the rule of law is generally accepted, the government is suspected of fomenting gang violence against its opponents. The government has concentrated a great deal of the economy in its hands, and social equalization programs have been emphasized. The governing party and major union have been amalgamated.

**Comparatively:** Malta is as free as Italy, freer than Turkey, less free than the United Kingdom.

# MAURITANIA

**Economy:** noninclusive capitalist-statist
**Polity:** military nonparty
**Population:** 1,600,000

**Political Rights:** 7
**Civil Liberties:** 6
**Status of Freedom:** not free

An ethnic state with minor territorial subnationalities

**Political Rights.** Mauritania is ruled by a military committee without formal popular or traditional legitimation. *Subnationalities*: There is a subnational movement, concerned particularly with linguistic questions in the non-Arab, southern part of the country.

**Civil Liberties.** The media are government owned and censored, but foreign publications and broadcasts are freely available. There are a few political prisoners. Conversation is free; no ideology is imposed, but assembly is restricted. Travel may be restricted for political reasons. Union activity is government controlled. There is religious freedom. The government controls much of industry and mining, as well as wholesale trade, but the new regime has moved to reduce government involvement.

**Comparatively:** Mauritania is as free as Rumania, freer than Iraq, less free than Morocco.

# MAURITIUS

**Economy:** capitalist
**Polity:** centralized multiparty
**Population:** 900,000

**Political Rights:** 2
**Civil Liberties:** 4
**Status of Freedom:** partly free

An ethnically complex state

**Political Rights.** Mauritius is a parliamentary democracy. The last election showed an important gain for the opposition, but the government managed to retain power through coalition (and amidst controversy). A variety of different racial and religious communities are active in politics, although they are not territorially based. There are a number of semi-autonomous local governing bodies.

**Civil Liberties.** The press is private or party and without censorship. Broadcasting is under a single corporation, presumably private in form. Freedom of assembly is restricted: opposition members of parliament have been imprisoned recently for illegal demonstration. The labor union movement is quite strong, as are a variety of communal organizations. Strikes are frequent. There is religious and economic freedom; taxes can be quite high.

**Comparatively:** Mauritius is as free as Western Samoa, freer than the Comoro Islands, less free than Barbados.


# MEXICO

**Economy:** capitalist-statist
**Polity:** decentralized dominant-
    party
**Population:** 67,700,000

**Political Rights:** 3
**Civil Liberties:** 4
**Status of Freedom:** partly free

An ethnic state with potential subnationalities

**Political Rights.** Mexico is ruled by a governmental system formally modeled on that of the United States; in practice the president is much stronger and the legislative and judicial branches much weaker. The states have independent governors and legislatures. The ruling party has had a near monopoly of power on all levels since the 1920's. In the last presidential election the party candidate received ninety-four percent of the vote. Political competition has been largely confined to factional struggles within the ruling party. However, in 1979 new parties participated, and the new election law gave twenty-five percent of the seats to minor parties by proportional representation; the resulting congress showed unusual independence. Voting and campaign irregularities have been common, particularly on the local level. *Subnationalities*:

There is a large Mayan area in Yucatan that has formerly been restive; there are also other smaller Indian areas.

**Civil Liberties.** The media are mostly private. Although they have operated under a variety of direct and indirect government controls (including take-overs), newspapers are generally free of censorship. Literature and the arts are free. The judicial system is not strong. However, decisions can go against the government; it is possible to win a judicial decision that a law is unconstitutional in a particular application. The clergy are prohibited from political activity, but religion is free. Widespread bribery and lack of control over the behavior of security forces greatly limits operative freedom. Disappearances occur, detention is prolonged, torture and brutality have been common. Private economic rights are respected; government ownership predominates in major industries.

**Comparatively:** Mexico is as free as Malaysia, freer than Nicaragua, less free than Colombia.

# MONGOLIA

**Economy:** socialist
**Polity:** communist one-party
**Population:** 1,600,000

**Political Rights:** 7
**Civil Liberties:** 7
**Status of Freedom:** not free

A relatively homogeneous population

**Political Rights.** A one-party communist dictatorship, for many years Mongolia has been firmly under the control of one man. Power is organized at all levels through the party apparatus. Those who oppose the government cannot run for office. In the 1977 parliamentary elections, 99.9 percent of eligible voters participated; only two persons failed to properly vote for the single list of candidates. Mongolia has a subordinate relation to the Soviet Union, which it depends on for defense against Chinese claims. It must use the USSR as an outlet for nearly all of its trade, and its finances are under close Soviet supervision.

**Civil Liberties.** All media are government controlled, and apparently quite effectively. Religion is greatly restricted, Lamaism having been nearly wiped out. Freedom of travel, residence, and other civil liberties are denied.

**Comparatively:** Mongolia is as free as Bulgaria, less free than the USSR.

# MOROCCO

**Economy:** noninclusive capitalist      **Political Rights:** 4
**Polity:** centralized multiparty        **Civil Liberties:** 4
**Population:** 19,400,000                 **Status of Freedom:** partly free

An ethnic state with active and potential subnationalities

**Political Rights.** Morocco is a constitutional monarchy in which the king has retained major executive powers. Recent elections at both local and national levels were fair and well contested in most localities. Most parties participated (including the communist); independents (largely supporters of the king) were the major winners. Opposition leaders were included in the subsequent government. The autonomy of local and regional elected governments is limited. *Subnationalities*: Although people in the newly acquired land of the Western Sahara participate in the electoral process, it has an important resistance movement. In the rest of the country the large Berber minority is a potential subnationality.

**Civil Liberties.** Newspapers are private or party, and quite diverse. Recently there has been no formal censorship; there are other pressures, including the confiscation of particular issues. Monarchical power must not be criticized. Both public and private broadcasting stations are under government control. In the past the use of torture has been quite common and may continue; the rule of law has also been weakened by the frequent use of prolonged detention without trial. There are many political prisoners; some are probably prisoners of conscience. Private organizational activity is vigorous, including student and party. There are strong independent labor unions; religious and other private rights are respected.

**Comparatively:** Morocco is as free as Guyana, freer than Algeria, less free than Spain.

# MOZAMBIQUE

**Economy:** noninclusive socialist      **Political Rights:** 7
**Polity:** socialist one-party          **Civil Liberties:** 7
**Population:** 10,200,000               **Status of Freedom:** not free

A transethnic heterogeneous state

**Political Rights.** Mozambique is a one-party communist dictatorship in which all power resides in the party leadership. The Liberation Front has now officially been converted into a "vanguard party." All candidates are selected by the ruling party at all levels, but there is electoral competition at local levels. Regional administration is controlled from the center.

**Civil Liberties.** All media are rigidly controlled; no public criticism is allowed. Rights of assembly and foreign travel do not exist. There are no private lawyers. Secret police are powerful; thousands are in reeducation camps. Police brutality is common. Unions are prohibited. Heavy pressure has been put on all religions and especially Jehovah's Witnesses. Villagers are being forced into communes, leading to revolts in some areas. The emigration of citizens is restricted.

**Comparatively:** Mozambique is as free as Angola, less free than Tanzania.

# NAURU

Economy: capitalist-statist
Polity: traditional nonparty
Population: 8,500

Political Rights: 2
Civil Liberties: 2
Status of Freedom: free

An ethnically complex state

**Political Rights.** Nauru is a parliamentary democracy with a recent change of government by elective and parliamentary means. Realignments have led to considerable political instability. The country is under Australian influence.

**Civil Liberties.** The media are free of censorship but little developed. The island's major industry is controlled by the government, but otherwise private economic rights are respected.

**Comparatively:** Nauru is as free as Fiji, freer than the Maldives, less free than New Zealand.

# NEPAL

Economy: noninclusive capitalist
Polity: traditional nonparty
Population: 13,700,000

Political Rights: 5
Civil Liberties: 4
Status of Freedom: partly free

An ethnic state with active and potential subnationalities

**Political Rights.** Nepal is a constitutional monarchy in which the king is dominant. The national parliament is elected indirectly through a series of tiers of government in which the lower levels are directly elected. Parliament has had little power, but 1979 saw some gain. The government's movement generally selects those elected; some members of the opposition have been included in the government. A referendum on continuation of this system is to be held in 1980. *Subnationalities*: There are a variety of different peoples, with only fifty percent of the people speaking Nepali as their first language. Hinduism is a unifying force for the vast majority. The historically powerful ruling castes continue to dominate.

**Civil Liberties.** Newspapers are public and private; criticism is allowed of the government but not the king. Foreign publications may be banned. Radio is government owned. Private contacts are relatively open. In 1979–80 opposition groups campaigned legally for the restoration of multiparty rule. Political arrests, banishment from the capital, and exile have occurred. The judiciary is not independent. Religious proselytizing and conversion is prohibited, and the emigration of those with valuable skills or education is restricted. The population is nearly all engaged in traditional occupations; illiteracy levels are very high.

**Comparatively:** Nepal is as free as Bahrain, freer than Burma, less free than Malaysia.

# NETHERLANDS

**Economy:** mixed capitalist
**Polity:** centralized multiparty
**Population:** 14,000,000

**Political Rights:** 1
**Civil Liberties:** 1
**Status of Freedom:** free

A relatively homogeneous population

**Political Rights.** Netherlands is a constitutional monarchy in which nearly all the power is vested in a directly elected legislature. The results of elections have periodically transferred power to coalitions of the left and right. There is some diffusion of political power below this level, but not a great deal. The monarch retains more power than in the United Kingdom both through the activity of appointing government in frequently stalemated situations, and through the advisory Council of State.

**Civil Liberties.** The media are free and private, with broadcasting more directly supervised by the government. The courts are independent, and the full spectrum of private rights guaranteed. The burden of exceptionally heavy taxes limits economic choice.

**Comparatively:** The Netherlands is as free as Belgium, freer than Portugal.

# NEW ZEALAND

**Economy:** capitalist
**Polity:** centralized multiparty
**Population:** 3,200,000

**Political Rights:** 1
**Civil Liberties:** 1
**Status of Freedom:** free

A relatively homogeneous state with a native subnationality

**Political Rights.** New Zealand is a parliamentary democracy in which power alternates between the two major parties. There is elected local government, but it is not independently powerful. *Subnationalities*: About eight percent of the population are Maori, the original inhabitants.

**Civil Liberties.** The press is private and free. Television and most radio stations are owned by the government. The rule of law and private rights are thoroughly respected. Since taxes (a direct restriction on choice) are not exceptionally high, and industry is not government owned, we label New Zealand capitalist. Others, emphasizing the government's highly developed social programs and penchant for controlling prices, wages, and credit might place New Zealand further toward the socialist end of the economic spectrum.

**Comparatively:** New Zealand is as free as the United States, freer than Japan.

# NICARAGUA

**Economy:** capitalist-socialist
**Polity:** quasi-nonparty
**Population:** 2,500,000

**Political Rights:** 5
**Civil Liberties:** 5
**Status of Freedom:** partly free

A relatively homogeneous population

**Political Rights.** Government is in the hands of the Sandinista political-military movement and a governing junta installed by them. Although not elected, the new government initially had widespread popular backing.

**Civil Liberties.** The journals and radio stations are private and diverse, but television is firmly in government hands. There is pressure on dissident or radical journalists. No organizations representing previous Somoza movements are allowed to exist. Torture, widespread killing, and brutality have occurred, especially in rural areas. The independence of the judiciary is not well developed, but the government does not always win in the courts. Unions are under pressure to join the new government-sponsored federation.

**Comparatively:** Nicaragua is as free as the Philippines, freer than Cuba, less free than Guatemala.

# NIGER

**Economy:** noninclusive capitalist
**Polity:** military nonparty
**Population:** 5,100,000

**Political Rights:** 7
**Civil Liberties:** 6
**Status of Freedom:** not free

A transethnic heterogeneous state

**Political Rights.** Niger is a military dictatorship with no elected assembly or legal parties. All districts are administered from the center.

**Civil Liberties.** Niger's very limited media are government owned and operated. Dissent is seldom tolerated, although ideological conformity is not demanded. A military court has taken the place of a suspended Supreme Court, and political prisoners are held. Labor unions are closely controlled. Foreign travel is relatively open; outside of politics the government does not regulate individual behavior.

**Comparatively:** Niger is as free as Mali, freer than Togo, less free than Liberia.

# NIGERIA

**Economy:** noninclusive capitalist-statist
**Polity:** decentralized multiparty
**Population:** 85,000,000*

A multinational state

**Political Rights:** 2
**Civil Liberties:** 3
**Status of Freedom:** free

**Political Rights.** A multiparty democracy with an elected president and elected provincial governments was reestablished in 1979. Only five strong parties have been authorized, but these seem to include the full spectrum of known leaders.

*Subnationalities.* Nigeria is made up of a number of powerful subnational groupings. Speaking mainly Hausa, the people of the north are Muslim. The highly urbanized southwest is dominated by the Yoruba; and the east by the Ibo. Within each of these areas and along their borders there are other peoples, some of which are conscious of their identity and number more than one million persons. Strong loyalties to traditional political units—lineages or kingdoms—throughout the country further complicate the regional picture. With nineteen states, and independent institutions below this level, the present rulers seem dedicated to taking into account the demands of this complexity in the new federal structure.

**Civil Liberties.** Traditionally, Nigeria's media have been some of the freest in Africa. Television and radio are now wholly federal or state owned, as are all but two of the major papers, in part as the result of a Nigerianization program. However, in spite of occasional suppressions, the media have considerable editorial independence. Political organization, assembly, and publication are now freely per-

---

* Population may be 68,000,000–100,000,000.

mitted. The universities, secondary schools, and the trade unions have been brought under close government control or reorganization in the last few years. Apparently the judiciary remains strong and independent, including, in Muslim areas, *sharia* courts. No prisoners of conscience are held; citizens can win in court against the government. There is freedom of religion and travel, but rights of married women are quite restricted. The country is in the process of moving from a subsistence to industrial economy—largely on the basis of government-controlled oil and oil-related industry. Government intervention elsewhere in agriculture (cooperatives and plantations) and industry has been considerable. Since private business and industry are also encouraged, this is still far from a program of massive redistribution. General corruption in political and economic life has frequently diminished the rule of law. Freedom is respected in most other areas of life.

**Comparatively:** Nigeria is as free as Turkey, freer than Ghana, less free than Spain.

# NORWAY

**Economy:** mixed capitalist  
**Polity:** centralized multiparty  
**Population:** 4,100,000

**Political Rights:** 1  
**Civil Liberties:** 1  
**Status of Freedom:** free

A relatively homogeneous population with a small Lapp minority

**Political Rights.** Norway is a centralized, constitutional monarchy. Labor remains the strongest party, but other parties have formed several governments since the mid-1960's. There is relatively little separation of powers. Regional governments have appointed governors, and cities and towns their own elected officials.

**Civil Liberties.** Newspapers are privately or party owned; radio and television are state monopolies. This is a pluralistic state with independent power in the churches and labor unions. Relatively strong family structures have also been preserved. Norway is capitalistic, yet the extremely high tax burden, perhaps the highest in the noncommunist world, the government's control over the new oil resource, and general reliance on centralized planning reduce the freedom of economic activity.

**Comparatively:** Norway is as free as the United Kingdom, freer than West Germany.

# OMAN

**Economy:** noninclusive capitalist-
        statist
**Polity:** centralized nonparty
**Population:** 600,000

**Political Rights:** 6
**Civil Liberties:** 6
**Status of Freedom:** not free

An ethnic state with a territorial subnationality

**Political Rights.** Oman is an absolute monarchy with no political parties or elected assemblies. Regional rule is by centrally appointed governors, but the remaining tribal structure at the local and regional level gives a measure of local autonomy. The government is under British influence because of their long record of aid and advice. *Subnationalities*: Quite different from other Omani, the people of Dhofar constitute a small subnationality in periodic revolt.

**Civil Liberties.** The media are very limited and government controlled. Foreign publications are censored regularly. Except in private, criticism is not generally allowed. Although the preservation of traditional institutions provides a check on arbitrary action, the right to a fair trial is not guaranteed. Freedom of assembly and freedom of public religious expression are curtailed. There are no independent unions. There is freedom of travel; private property is respected.

**Comparatively:** Oman is as free as Saudi Arabia, freer than South Yemen, less free than the United Arab Emirates.

# PAKISTAN

**Economy:** noninclusive capitalist-
        statist
**Polity:** military nonparty
**Population:** 80,000,000

**Political Rights:** 6
**Civil Liberties:** 5
**Status of Freedom:** not free

A multinational state

**Political Rights.** Pakistan is under centralized military rule. The political parties, religious leaders, provincial leaders, and judiciary (and bar association) continue to be factors in a situation with many elements of consensus. Some party leaders have been brought into the government. The former prime minister was executed in 1979 in a political trial; political parties were officially disbanded and promised elections put off indefinitely. Local elections of limited significance were held. *Subnationalities*: Millions of Pathans, Baluchis, and Sindhis have been represented since the origin of Pakistan as desiring greater regional autonomy or independence. Provincial organization has sporadically offered a measure of self-determination.

**Civil Liberties.** Newspapers are censored; the frequent detention of journalists and closing of papers lead to strict self-censorship. Radio and television are government controlled. For crime punishments are often severe; torture is alleged, and executions have been common. Thousands of members of the opposition have been imprisoned or flogged in the violent political climate. The officially dissolved parties retain considerable de facto organization. There is a human rights society. Rights of assembly are limited, as are those of travel for some political persons. Courts preserve some independence. Unions organize freely, have the right to strike, but are not strong. Emphasis on Islamic conservatism curtails private rights, especially freedom of religion: religious minorities suffer discrimination. Private property is respected, although many basic industries have been nationalized.

**Comparatively:** Pakistan is as free as Yugoslavia, freer than Afghanistan, less free than Bangladesh.

# PANAMA

Economy: capitalist-statist
Polity: quasi-nonparty
    (military dominated)
Population: 1,900,000

Political Rights: 5
Civil Liberties: 5
Status of Freedom: partly free

A relatively homogeneous population

**Political Rights.** Officially Panama is governed by a president elected for a six-year term by the assembly. Assembly members are elected from very unequal districts and assembly powers are very limited. Although elections are nonparty, organized opposition functions at least in major cities and for referendums. The National Guard retains major political power. The provinces are administered by presidential appointees.

**Civil Liberties.** Most newspapers are directly or indirectly government controlled. Censorship and self-censorship still exist in practice. Radio has had periods of considerable freedom. Political parties maintain their opposition role. The judiciary is not independent; the rule of law is very weak in both political and nonpolitical areas. Although common in the past, political arrest has recently been only for brief periods. The government owns major concerns; private property is generally respected; labor unions are under some restrictions. There is general freedom of religion, although foreign priests are not allowed. Travel is generally free.

**Comparatively:** Panama is as free as the Philippines, freer than Haiti, less free than Guatemala.

# PAPUA NEW GUINEA

**Economy:** noninclusive capitalist   **Political Rights:** 2
**Polity:** decentralized multiparty   **Civil Liberties:** 2
**Population:** 3,100,000              **Status of Freedom:** free

A transethnic heterogeneous state with subnationalities

**Political Rights.** Papua New Guinea is an independent parliamentary democracy, although it remains partially dependent on Australia economically, technically, and militarily. Elections appear fair and seats are divided among two major and several minor parties—party allegiances are still fluid. Because of its dispersed and tribal nature, local government is in some ways quite decentralized. Elected provincial governments with extensive powers have been established. *Subnationalities*: Development of provincial government is meant to contain strong secessionist movements in the Solomon Islands, Papua, and elsewhere.

**Civil Liberties.** The press is not highly developed but apparently free. Radio is government controlled but presents critical views; Australian stations are also received. There are no political prisoners. Rights to travel, organize, demonstrate, and practice religion are legally secured. The legal system adapted from Australia is operational, but a large proportion of the population lives in a preindustrial world with traditional controls, including violence, that limit freedom of speech, travel, occupation, and other private rights.

**Comparatively:** Papua New Guinea is as free as Portugal, freer than Malaysia, less free than Australia.

# PARAGUAY

**Economy:** noninclusive capitalist-   **Political Rights:** 5
                      statist           **Civil Liberties:** 5
**Polity:** centralized dominant-party  **Status of Freedom:** partly free
          (military dominated)
**Population:** 3,000,000

A relatively homogeneous state with small Indian groups

**Political Rights.** Paraguay has been ruled as a modified dictatorship since 1954. In addition to an elected president there is a parliament that includes members of opposition parties. Elections are regularly held, but they have limited meaning: the ruling party receives eighty to ninety percent of the vote, a result guaranteed by direct and indirect pressures on the media, massive government pressure on voters, especially in the countryside, and interference with opposition party organization. The most important regional and local officials are appointed by the president. *Subnationalities*: The population represents a mixture of Indian (Guarani) and Spanish peoples; ninety percent continue to speak Guarani as well as Spanish. Several small tribes of primitive forest peoples are under heavy pressure from both the government and the public.

**Civil Liberties.** There is a private press, and a combination of private, government, and church radio and television. In spite of censorship and periodic suppression of publications, dissenting opinion is expressed, especially by the church hierarchy and opposition newspapers. Opposition political organization continues, as do human rights organizations. Torture, imprisonment, and execution of political opponents have been an important part of a sociopolitical situation that includes general corruption and anarchy. There are now few if any long-term prisoners of conscience. Union organization is restricted. Political opponents may be refused passports. Beyond the subsistence sector, private economic rights are restricted by government intervention and control. Perhaps a majority of peasants now own land, partly as a result of government policy.

**Comparatively:** Paraguay is as free as Nicaragua, freer than Cuba, less free than Brazil.

# PERU

**Economy:** noninclusive mixed capitalist

**Polity:** military nonparty

**Population:** 17,300,000

**Political Rights:** 5

**Civil Liberties:** 4

**Status of Freedom:** partly free

An ethnic state with a major potential territorial subnationality

**Political Rights.** Peru is ruled by a military junta of varying composition. The government responds to the pressure of a variety of organized groups, such as unions, peasant organizations, and political parties. In 1978 a constituent assembly with broad party representation was fairly elected. (Illiterates, perhaps twenty percent of the voting age population, could not vote.) At least informally its powers went beyond those of writing a constitution. Parliamentary elections are to be held in 1980. Provincial administration is not independent. *Subnationalities*: Several million people speak Quechua in the highlands, and it has recently become an official language. There are other important Indian groups.

**Civil Liberties.** National dailies, radio, and television are directly under government control. Other journals are frequently suppressed but continue to be highly critical. The existence of a variety of political parties allows diverse positions to be expressed; the parties have limited access to broadcasting services and have a limited right of assembly. Political prisoners are taken, and union leaders are frequently detained, in some cases justifiably because of violence or threats of violence. By the end of the year all prisoners of conscience appeared to be freed. Reports of torture and death during interrogation have been publicized in the recent past, but a successful trial of an accused policeman in 1979 signaled an improvement. Rights to religion, travel, and occupation are generally respected. Land reform, nationalization, and experiments in compulsory worker control of factories or other institutions have characterized recent years, but private property now has regained governmental acceptance.

**Comparatively:** Peru is as free as Kenya, freer than Paraguay, less free than Guyana.

# PHILIPPINES

**Economy:** noninclusive capitalist
**Polity:** dominant party
**Population:** 46,200,000

**Political Rights:** 5
**Civil Liberties:** 5
**Status of Freedom:** partly free

A transethnic heterogeneous state with active and potential subnationalities

**Political Rights.** The Philippines is ruled as a plebiscitory family dictatorship with the aid of a docile assembly. The present ruler was elected in a fair election, but more recent referendums affirming his rule, his constitutional changes, and martial law have not been conducted with open competition, free discussion, or acceptable voting procedures. Previously legitimate political parties exist, but they have no part to play in current political life. Assembly elections in 1978 were held with severely restricted opposition activity and were boycotted by the major parties. The results were subject to questionable tabulations. There is some decentralization of power to local assemblies, but provincial and local officials are centrally appointed. *Subnationalities*: The Philippines includes a variety of different peoples of which the Tagalog speaking are the most important (although a minority). A portion of the Muslim (Moro) subnationality is in active revolt along the front of Christian-Muslim opposition. There are several major potential subnationalities that may request autonomy in the near future on the basis of both territorial and linguistic identity.

**Civil Liberties.** Newspapers and broadcasting are largely private but under indirect government control. Only minor opposition papers exist; diverse foreign publications are widely available. Access to radio and television as well as freedom of assembly for the opposition are restricted. The courts have retained some independence although it has been much reduced. Hundreds of prisoners of conscience are held; torture is used but is sporadically condemned by the top levels of government—torturers have been brought before the courts. Unions have only limited independence, but strikes are permitted. Military actions against insurgents have led to many unnecessary arrests, killings, and destruction. The Church still maintains its independence. The private economy is marginally capitalist, but there has been rapid growth in government intervention, favoritism, and direct ownership of industries.

**Comparatively:** The Philippines is as free as Singapore, freer than Vietnam, less free than Malaysia.

# POLAND

**Economy:** mixed socialist | **Political Rights:** 6
**Polity:** communist one-party | **Civil Liberties:** 5
**Population:** 35,400,000 | **Status of Freedom:** partly free

A relatively homogeneous population

**Political Rights.** Poland is effectively a one-party communist dictatorship, with noncompetitive, one-list elections. However, a few nonparty persons are in the assembly and recent sessions have evidenced more than pro forma debate. There are elected councils at provincial levels. The party apparatus operating from the top down is in any event the locus of power. The Catholic Church, academics, peasants, and workers have countervailing power. The Soviet Union's right of interference and continual pressure diminishes Poland's independence.

**Civil Liberties.** The Polish newspapers are both private and government, and broadcasting is government owned. The independent press occasionally differs cautiously with the government. Censorship is pervasive; yet there are legal anti-Marxist publications with limited circulations. Underground publications are suppressed. There are prisoners of conscience, no right of assembly, nor concept of an independent judiciary. Short imprisonment, beating, and harassment are now the most common means of restricting opposition. Illegal attempts to leave Poland frequently lead to arrest, but travel is now permitted for most citizens. There is no right to organize independently or strike. However, strikes and demonstrations occur, and nongovernmental organizations develop; the Church is an especially important alternative institution. Most agriculture and considerable commerce remain in private hands.

**Comparatively:** Poland is as free as Tunisia, freer that Yugoslavia, less free than Egypt.


# PORTUGAL

**Economy:** mixed capitalist
**Polity:** centralized multiparty
**Population:** 10,000,000

**Political Rights:** 2
**Civil Liberties:** 2
**Status of Freedom:** free

A relatively homogeneous population

**Political Rights.** At present Portugal is a parliamentary democracy with the military command playing a relatively strong role through the presidency and the Council of the Revolution. There is vigorous party competition over most of the spectrum (except the far right), and fair elections. 1979 saw the opposition gain power by election. Provincial government is centrally directed.

**Civil Liberties.** The most important papers and journals are private or party owned, and are now quite free. Radio and television are government owned except for one Catholic station. The government has restored the rule of law. There are probably few prisoners of conscience, yet one can be imprisoned for insult to the government or military. Long periods of detention without trial occur in isolated instances. Imprisonment for "fascist" organization or discussion was promulgated in 1978. The Catholic Church, unions, peasant organizations, and military services remain alternative institutions of power. Although there is a large nationalized sector, capitalism is the accepted form for much of the economy.

**Comparatively:** Portugal is as free as Greece, freer than Turkey, less free than France.


# QATAR

**Economy:** capitalist-statist
**Polity:** traditional nonparty
**Population:** 250,000

**Political Rights:** 5
**Civil Liberties:** 5
**Status of Freedom:** partly free

A relatively homogeneous citizenry

**Political Rights.** Qatar is a traditional monarchy. The majority of the residents are recently arrived foreigners; of the native population perhaps one-fourth are members of the ruling family. The role of consensus is suggested by the fact that extravagance and lack of attention to affairs of state recently led the ruling family to replace the monarch.

**Civil Liberties.** The media are public and private, and passively loyalist. Discussion is fairly open; foreign publications are rarely censored. Political parties are forbidden. This is a traditional state still responsive to Islamic and tribal laws that moderate the absolutism of government. The family government controls the nation's wealth through control over oil, but there are also independently powerful merchant and religious classes. There are no organized unions.

**Comparatively:** Qatar is as free as the United Arab Emirates, freer than Saudi Arabia, less free than Lebanon.

# R H O D E S I A
(See Zimbabwe Rhodesia)

# R U M A N I A

Economy: socialist
Polity: communist one-party
Population: 22,100,000

Political Rights: 7
Civil Liberties: 6
Status of Freedom: not free

An ethnic state with territorial subnationalities

**Political Rights.** Rumania is a now-traditional communist state. Assemblies at national and regional levels are subservient to the party hierarchy. Although the party is very large, all decisions are made by a small elite and especially the dictator. Elections involve only candidates chosen by the party; for some assembly positions the party may propose several candidates. Soviet influence is relatively slight. *Subnationalities*: The Magyar and German minorities are territorially based. If offered self-determination one Magyar area would surely opt for rejoining neighboring Hungary; many of the Germans evidently wish to migrate to Germany, and this movement has been developing. In Rumania the cultural rights of both groups are narrowly limited.

**Civil Liberties.** The media include only government or party organs; self-censorship committees replace centralized censorship. Private discussion may be relatively candid. Dissenters are frequently imprisoned. Forced confessions, false charges, and psychiatric incarceration are characteristic. Treatment may be brutal; physical threats are common. Many arrests have been made for attempting to leave the country or importing foreign literature (especially Bibles and material in minority languages). Contacts with foreigners must be reported if not given prior approval. Religious and other personal freedoms are quite restricted. Outside travel and emigration are not considered rights, and are very difficult. Private museums have been closed. Independent labor and management rights are essentially nonexistent. Attempts to form a trade union in 1979 were crushed.

**Comparatively:** Rumania is as free as East Germany, freer than Bulgaria, less free than Hungary.

# RWANDA

**Economy:** noninclusive mixed
**Polity:** nationalist one-party
    (military dominated)
**Population:** 4,900,000

**Political Rights:** 6
**Civil Liberties:** 6
**Status of Freedom:** not free

An ethnic state with a minority nonterritorial subnationality

**Political Rights.** Rwanda is a military dictatorship with an auxiliary party organization. Elections are not free and candidates are pre-selected. There is no legislature and districts are administered by the central government. There are elected local councils. *Subnationalities*: The former ruling people, the Tutsi, have been persecuted and heavily discriminated against, but the situation has improved.

**Civil Liberties.** The weak press is private or governmental; radio is government owned. Public criticism is very constrained. Political prisoners are held, and beating of prisoners and suspects may be common. Considerable religious freedom exists. Travel is restricted both within the country and across its borders. Labor unions are very weak. There are no great extremes of wealth. The government is socialist in intent, but missionary cooperatives dominate trade, and private business is active in the small nonsubsistence sector. Traditional ways of life rather than government orders regulate the lives of most.

**Comparatively:** Rwanda is as free as Gabon, freer than Burundi, less free than Zambia.

# ST. LUCIA

**Economy:** mixed capitalist
**Polity:** centralized multiparty
**Population:** 115,000

**Political Rights:** 2
**Civil Liberties:** 3
**Status of freedom:** free

A relatively homogeneous state

**Political Rights.** This is a functioning parliamentary democracy in which the incumbent party was replaced through election in 1979. However, the resulting government was partially paralyzed by factional struggles.

**Civil Liberties.** The media are largely private and uncensored. Organization and assembly are free, but harassment and violence accompany their expression. Personal rights are secured.

**Comparatively:** St. Lucia is as free as Colombia, freer than Guyana, less free than Venezuela.

# ST. VINCENT AND
# THE GRENADINES

**Economy:** mixed capitalist
**Polity:** centralized multiparty
**Population:** 110,000

**Political Rights:** 2
**Civil Liberties:** 2
**Status of Freedom:** free

A relatively homogeneous state

**Political Rights.** St. Vincent is an operating multiparty state. In a 1979 election the ruling party was returned to office, winning 11 of 13 seats with fifty-three percent of the vote.

**Civil Liberties.** The election period suggested access by all groups to the public through assemblies, demonstrations, and the media. Radio was accused of progovernment policies. There is a rule of law.

**Comparatively:** St. Vincent is as free as Gambia, freer than Guyana, less free than Barbados.

# SAO TOME AND PRINCIPE

**Economy:** inclusive socialist
**Polity:** socialist one-party
**Population:** 85,000

**Political Rights:** 6
**Civil Liberties:** 6
**Status of Freedom:** not free

A relatively homogeneous population

**Political Rights.** Sao Tome and Principe are governed under strongman leadership by the revolutionary party that led the country to independence. The degree of implementation of the post-independence constitutional system remains unclear. Popular dissatisfaction and factional struggles appear serious. Angolan troops have been used to maintain the regime.

**Civil Liberties.** The media are government controlled; opposition voices are not heard; there is no effective right of political assembly. The largely plantation agriculture has been socialized, as has most of the economy. Labor unions are not independent. On the other hand, there seems to be an operating legal system, freedom of religion, and little evidence of brutality, torture, or political imprisonment.

**Comparatively:** Sao Tome and Principe appears to be as free as Guinea-Bissau, freer than Guinea, less free than Senegal.

# SAUDI ARABIA

**Economy:** capitalist-statist
**Polity:** traditional nonparty
**Population:** 8,100,000

**Political Rights:** 6
**Civil Liberties:** 6
**Status of Freedom:** not free

A relatively homogeneous population

**Political Rights.** Saudi Arabia is a traditional family monarchy ruling without assemblies. Political parties are prohibited. The right of petition is guaranteed. Regional government is by appointive officers; there are some local elective assemblies.

**Civil Liberties.** The press is both private and governmental; strict self-censorship is expected. Radio and television are mostly government owned, although ARAMCO also has stations. Private conversation is relatively free; there is no right of political assembly or political organization. Islamic law limits arbitrary government, but the rule of law is not fully institutionalized. There are political prisoners and torture is reported; there may be prisoners of conscience. Citizens have no freedom of religion—all must be Muslims. Unions are forbidden. Private rights in areas such as occupation or residence are generally respected, but marriage to a non-Muslim or non-Saudi is closely controlled. Women may not marry non-Muslims, and suffer other special disabilities, particularly in the right to travel. The economy is overwhelmingly dominated by petroleum or petroleum-related industry that is directly or indirectly under government control.

**Comparatively:** Saudi Arabia is as free as Algeria, freer than Iraq, less free than Syria.

# SENEGAL

**Economy:** mixed capitalist
**Polity:** centralized dominant-party
**Population:** 5,500,000

**Political Rights:** 4
**Civil Liberties:** 4
**Status of Freedom:** partly free

A transethnic heterogeneous state

**Political Rights.** After several years under a relatively benevolent one-party system, limited multiparty activity is allowed; the number and nature of political parties remains under arbitrary control. In parliamentary elections eighteen of one hundred seats were obtained by an opposition party. Decentralization is restricted to the local level where contested elections occur.

*Subnationalities.* Ethnically eighty percent are Muslims; the Wolof people represent thirty-six percent of the population, including most of the elite, the urban population, and the more prosperous farmers.

However, regional loyalties, both within and outside of this linguistic grouping, seem to be at least as important as communal groupings in defining potential subnationalities. In addition, rapid assimilation of rural migrants in the cities to Wolof culture has reduced the tendency toward ethnic cleavage. The fact that the ruler since independence is a member of the second largest ethnic group (Serer) and minority religion (Catholic) also retards the development of competing subnationalisms.

**Civil Liberties.** The press is predominantly public, and government regulations restrict the independence of private publications. Opposition papers and journals appear. Nineteen seventy-nine saw trials for nonviolent political organization. Unions have gained increasing independence. Religion, travel, occupation, and other private rights are respected. Although much of the land remains tribally owned, government-organized cooperatives, a strong internal private market, and dependence on external markets have transformed the preindustrial society.

**Comparatively:** Senegal is as free as Ghana, freer than Ivory Coast, less free than Gambia.

## SEYCHELLES

**Economy:** mixed capitalist
**Polity:** socialist one-party
**Population:** 65,000

**Political Rights:** 6
**Civil Liberties:** 6
**Status of Freedom:** not free

A relatively homogeneous population

**Political Rights.** Seychelles is a one-party state allowing personal competition for parliament but not president. The former ruling party is said to have "simply disappeared." Tanzanian troops continue to help maintain the government in power. There is no local government.

**Civil Liberties.** There is no independent opinion press, and radio is largely governmental. No opposition in publication or even conversation is legal. Individuals have little judicial protection. There is no right of political assembly and the security services have broad powers of arrest. Opposition party activities are banned; people have frequently been arrested on political charges. Labor and government are interconnected. Private rights, including private property, are generally respected, despite the extensive government services of a largely urban, if improverished, welfare state.

**Comparatively:** Seychelles is as free as Tanzania, freer than Somalia, less free than Maldives.

# SIERRA LEONE

**Economy:** noninclusive capitalist
**Polity:** socialist one-party
**Population:** 3,700,000

**Political Rights:** 5
**Civil Liberties:** 5
**Status of Freedom:** partly free

A formally transethnic heterogeneous state

**Political Rights.** After progressively excluding opposition candidates from power by violence, arrest, parliamentary exclusion, or electoral malpractice, in 1978 Sierra Leone's rulers used a possibly fraudulent referendum to establish a one-party state. The new cabinet included, however, members of the former opposition. There is little independent local government.

**Civil Liberties.** The press is private and governmental. Radio is government controlled. Both are now closely controlled, but there is considerable freedom of private speech. The courts do not appear to be very powerful or independent. Special emergency powers have given the government untrammeled powers of detention, censorship, restriction of assembly, and search for the last two years. There may now be no prisoners of conscience. Identity cards have recently been required of all citizens. Labor unions are relatively independent and travel is freely permitted. The largely subsistence economy has an essentially capitalist modern sector. Corruption is pervasive.

**Comparatively:** Sierra Leone is as free as Nicaragua, freer than Gabon, less free than Senegal.

# SINGAPORE

**Economy:** mixed capitalist-
statist
**Polity:** centralized dominant-party
**Population:** 2,400,000

**Political Rights:** 5
**Civil Liberties:** 5
**Status of Freedom:** partly free

An ethnically complex state

**Political Rights.** Singapore is a parliamentary democracy in which the ruling party has won all of the legislative seats in recent elections. Reasonable grounds exist for believing that economic and other pressures against all opposition groups (exerted in part through control of the media) make elections very unfair. After the last election three opposition leaders were sentenced to jail terms for such crimes as defaming the prime minister during the campaign. The opposition still obtains thirty percent of the votes. There is no local government.

**Civil Liberties.** The press is nominally private, but owners of shares with policy-making power must be officially approved; in some cases the government owns the shares. Broadcasting is largely a government monopoly. By closing papers and imprisoning editors and reporters, the press is kept under close control. University faculties are also under considerable pressure to conform. Most opposition is treated as a communist threat and, therefore, treasonable. Prisoners of conscience are held; in internal security cases the protection of the law is weak—the prosecution's main task appears to be obtaining forced confessions of communist activity. Torture is used. Trade union freedom is inhibited by the close association of government and union. Private rights of religion, occupation, or property are generally observed, although a large and increasing percentage of manufacturing and service companies are government owned.

**Comparatively:** Singapore is as free as Sierra Leone, freer than Vietnam, less free than Malaysia.

## SOLOMON ISLANDS

**Economy:** preindustrial capitalist    **Political Rights:** 2
**Polity:** primarily nonparty    **Civil Liberties:** 2
**Population:** 200,000    **Status of Freedom:** free

A relatively homogeneous state with subnational strains

**Political Rights.** The Solomon Islands are a parliamentary democracy under the British monarch. Parties exist, but government and parliament are largely nonparty. There is some decentralization of power at the local level; further decentralization at the provincial level is planned.

**Civil Liberties.** Media are little developed. The rule of law is maintained in the British manner, alongside traditional ideas of justice. Published incitement to inter-island conflict has led to banishment for several persons.

**Comparatively:** The Solomon Islands are as free as Tuvalu, freer than Mauritius, less free than New Zealand.

## SOMALIA

**Economy:** noninclusive mixed    **Political Rights:** 7
     socialist    **Civil Liberties:** 7
**Polity:** socialist one-party    **Status of Freedom:** not free
     (military dominated)
**Population:** 3,500,000

A relatively homogeneous state

**Political Rights.** The Somali Republic is under one-man military rule combining glorification of the ruler with one-party socialist legitimization.

1979 elections with 99 percent approval allowed no choice. Ethnically the state is homogeneous, although until the military coup in 1969 the six main clan groupings and their subdivisions were the major means of organizing loyalty and power. While politics is still understood in lineage terms, in its centralizing drive the government has tried to eliminate both tribal and religious power.

**Civil Liberties.** The media are under strict government control, private conversation is controlled, and those who do not follow the government are considered to be against it. There are many political prisoners, including prisoners of conscience. There have been jailings for strikes and executions of rebels. Travel is restricted. Beyond the dominant subsistence economy, some individual freedoms have been curtailed by establishing state farms, state industries, and welfare programs. However, a definite private sector of the economy has also been defined.

**Comparatively:** Somalia is as free as Ethiopia, less free than Kenya.

# SOUTH AFRICA

**Economy:** capitalist-statist     **Political Rights:** 5
**Polity:** centralized multiparty     **Civil Liberties:** 6
**Population:** 25,000,000     **Status of Freedom:** partly free

An ethnic state with major territorial and nonterritorial subnationalities

**Political Rights.** South Africa is a parliamentary democracy in which over eighty percent of the people are excluded from participation in the national political process because of race. For the white population elections appear fair and open. There is, in addition, a limited scope for the nonwhites to influence affairs within their own communities. *Subnationalities*: In the several Bantustans that have not yet separated from the country, black leaders have some power and support from their people. Most black political parties are banned, but operating political parties among Indians and people of mixed blood work for the interests of their respective peoples. Regionally, government within the white community includes both central government officials and elected councils.

**Civil Liberties.** The white South African press is private and quite outspoken, although pressures have been increasing, especially on reporters. Freedom for the nonwhite press is restricted. Broadcasting is under government control. The courts are independent, but do not effectively control security forces. There are political prisoners and torture—especially for black activists, who live in an atmosphere of terror. Private rights are generally respected for whites. Rights to labor organization greatly improved for blacks in 1979. Legal separation of the races remains, but has relaxed in some respects recently. Rights to choice of residence and occupation remain very restricted for nonwhites.

**Comparatively:** South Africa is as free as Syria, freer than Tanzania, less free than Morocco.

# S P A I N

**Economy:** capitalist
**Polity:** centralized multiparty
**Population:** 37,600,000

**Political Rights:** 2
**Civil Liberties:** 2
**Status of Freedom:** free

An ethnic state with major subnationalities

**Political Rights.** Spain has recently established a constitutional monarchy in the European manner. The current parliament has been fairly elected from a wide range of parties. Municipalities are often controlled by the opposition. Regional and local government is changing the previous centralized character of the state. *Subnationalities*: The Basque and Catalan territorial subnationalities have had their rights greatly expanded in the last two years, and regional power is being extended to the other parts of the country.

**Civil Liberties.** The press is private and is now free. The television network and some radio stations are government owned. Radio is no longer a state monopoly and television is controlled by an all-party committee. By the end of 1979 there were no prisoners of conscience; imprisonment still threatens those who insult the security services. Although police brutality and use of torture are still reported, generally the rule of law has been reestablished and private freedoms are respected. Continued terrorism and reaction to terrorism affect some areas. Union organization is quite free and independent.

**Comparatively:** Spain is as free as Greece, freer than Egypt, less free than France.

# S R I   L A N K A

**Economy:** capitalist-statist
**Polity:** centralized multiparty
**Population:** 14,500,000

**Political Rights:** 2
**Civil Liberties:** 3
**Status of Freedom:** free

An ethnic state with a major subnationality

**Political Rights.** Sri Lanka is a parliamentary democracy in which power has alternated between the major parties. The constitution was changed in 1977–78 to a presidential system along French lines. Regional government is centrally controlled, but local government is by elected councils. A number of individuals have been barred from government for breach of trust. *Subnationalities*: Receiving a large vote in the most recent election, the Tamil minority constitutes an important secessionist tendency. Repression or private violence against the Tamils occurs; the present government is inclined to meet Tamil demands up to but not including that for independence or equal linguistic standing.

**Civil Liberties.** The press has been strong, both private and party. However, under the previous regime some of the largest papers were nationalized; the new government has maintained ownership; editorial policy of these papers appears to be influenced by the government in power. Broadcasting is under government control, but differing views are presented. Limited censorship has been applied to prevent violence at particular places and times. Th rule of law has been threatened by communal violence. Courts remain independent of the government. A few prisoners of conscience have been arrested, at least for advocating Tamil independence; and torture or brutality is alleged. There is freedom of assembly but not demonstration. Private rights to movement, residence, religion, and occupation are respected. Strikes in public services are restricted, but unions are well developed. There has been extensive land reform; the State has nationalized a number of enterprises in this largely plantation economy. The system has done an excellent job in providing for basic nutrition, health, and educational standards within a democratic framework.

**Comparatively:** Sri Lanka is as free as Turkey, freer than Malaysia, less free than the United Kingdom.

# SUDAN

**Economy:** noninclusive mixed
**Polity:** nationalist one-party
    (military dominated)
**Population:** 17,900,000

**Political Rights:** 5
**Civil Liberties:** 5
**Status of Freedom:** partly free

An ethnic state with a major but highly diverse subnationality

**Political Rights.** Sudan is a military dictatorship with a supportive single party and legislature. There has been a general reconciliation of the government and its noncommunist opposition. 1978 legislative elections allowed the participation and frequent victory of individuals from de facto opposition groups. Several cabinet and party central committee members were subsequently selected from these groups. There is considerable power "in the streets" and devolution of power to the regions. *Subnationalities*: The Southern (Negro) region has been given a separate assembly; its former guerrillas form a part of the Southern army. A former guerrilla leader is now head of a regional government based on an assembly controlled by independents.

**Civil Liberties.** The press is weak and nationalized. Radio and television are government controlled. The media have been used for active indoctrination, but the messages in the last few years have necessarily been mixed. Limited criticism is allowed, especially in private. The university campus maintains a tradition of independence, but the courts are not strong. There are political prisoners, reports of torture, and detention without trial. Religion is relatively free. Unions are government organized but nevertheless lead illegal strikes. Sudan is socialist theoretically, but in business and agriculture the private sector has recently been supported by denationalizations.

**Comparatively:** Sudan is as free as Egypt, freer than Ethiopia, less free than Kenya.

# S U R I N A M

Economy: capitalist                    **Political Rights:** 2
**Polity:** centralized multiparty     **Civil Liberties:** 2
**Population:** 470,000                **Status of Freedom:** free

An ethnically complex state

**Political Rights.** In 1979 Surinam remained a parliamentary democracy with authentic elections. Its two main parties represented separate ethnic groups. Although they were not as territorially distinct, negotiation between them resulted in a division of communal rights analogous to that in Belgium or Canada. There were no autonomous regional governments. (A military coup in early 1980 established an appointed, nonparty government.)

**Civil Liberties.** The press and radio were free and varied. Political prisoners and torture did not exist. There was a rule of law and private rights were respected.

**Comparatively:** Surinam was as free as India, freer than Guyana, less free than Barbados.

# S W A Z I L A N D

Economy: noninclusive capitalist      **Political Rights:** 5
**Polity:** traditional nonparty      **Civil Liberties:** 5
**Population:** 500,000               **Status of Freedom:** partly free

A relatively homogeneous population

**Political Rights.** Swaziland is ruled directly by the king with the aid of his royal advisors. The majority of the people probably support the king who is both a religious and political figure and has been king since 1900. An indirect election for an advisory legislature was held in 1978 and local councils invite popular participation. South African political and economic influence is extensive.

**Civil Liberties.** Private media exist alongside governmental; there is little criticism; South African and other foreign media present available alternatives. Opposition leaders have been repeatedly detained, and partisan activity is forbidden. Parliamentary and council criticism occurs, but public assemblies are restricted, unions limited, emigration difficult. Religious, economic, and other private rights are maintained. The traditional way of life is continued, especially on the local level. Several thousand whites in the country and in neighboring Transvaal own the most productive land and business.

**Comparatively:** Swaziland is as free as Lesotho, freer than South Africa, less free than Botswana.

# S W E D E N

**Economy:** mixed capitalist
**Polity:** centralized multiparty
**Population:** 8,300,000

**Political Rights:** 1
**Civil Liberties:** 1
**Status of Freedom:** free

A relatively homogeneous population

**Political Rights.** Sweden is a parliamentary democracy in which no party monopolizes power. Referendums are held. Although there are some representative institutions at regional and local levels, the system is relatively centralized. The tendency of modern bureaucracies to regard issues as technical rather than political has progressed further in Sweden than elsewhere.

**Civil Liberties.** The press is private or party; broadcasting is by state-licensed monopolies. Although free of censorship, the media are accused of presenting a rather narrow range of views. There is the rule of law. The defense of those accused by the government may not be as spirited as elsewhere, but, on the other hand, the ombudsman office gives special means of redress against administrative arbitrariness. Most private rights are respected; but state interference in family life is unusually strong. The national church has a special position. In many areas, such as housing, individual choice is restricted more than in other capitalist states—as it is of course by the very high tax load.

**Comparatively:** Sweden is as free as Denmark, freer than West Germany.

# SWITZERLAND

**Economy:** capitalist
**Polity:** decentralized multiparty
**Population:** 6,300,000

**Political Rights:** 1
**Civil Liberties:** 1
**Status of Freedom:** free

A trinational state

**Political Rights.** Switzerland is a parliamentary democracy in which all major parties are given a role in government determined by the size of the vote for each party. Parties that increase their vote above a certain level are invited to join the government, although such changes in party strength rarely occur. The lack of a decisive shift in power from one party to another in the last fifty years is the major limitation on the democratic effectiveness of the Swiss system. However, its dependence on the grand coalition style of government is a partial substitute, and the Swiss grant political rights in other ways that compensate for the lack of a transfer of power. Many issues are decided by the citizenry through national referendums or popular initiatives. After referendums, in keeping with the Swiss attitude, even the losing side is given part of what it wants if its vote is sufficiently large. *Subnationalities*: The three major linguistic groups have separate areas under their partial control. Their regional and local elected governments have autonomous rights and determine directly much of the country's business. National governments try to balance the representatives of the primary linguistic and religious groups; this is accomplished in another way by the upper house that directly represents the cantons (regions) on an equal basis.

**Civil Rights.** The high quality press is private and independent. Broadcasting is government operated, although with the considerable independence of comparable West European systems. The rule of law is strongly upheld; as in Germany it is against the law to question the intentions of judges. Private rights are thoroughly respected.

**Comparatively:** Switzerland is as free as the United States, freer than Italy.

# SYRIA

**Economy:** mixed socialist
**Polity:** centralized dominant-party
      (military dominated)
**Population:** 8,400,000

**Political Rights:** 5
**Civil Liberties:** 6
**Status of Freedom:** partly free

A relatively homogeneous population

**Political Rights.** Syria is a military dictatorship assisted by an elected parliament. The election of the military president is largely pro forma, but in recent assembly elections a few opposition candidates defeated candidates of the National Front, organized under the leadership of the governing party. The ruling Front includes several ideologically distinct parties, and cabinets have included representatives of a variety of such parties. Some authenticity to the election procedure is suggested by the fact that due to apathy and a boycott by dissident party factions in 1977 elections, the government had such great difficulty achieving the constitutionally required voter participation that it was forced to extend the voting period. Because of its position in the army the Alawite minority (ten percent) has a very unequal share of national power. Provinces have little separate power, but local elections are contested.

**Civil Liberties.** The media are in the hands of government or party. Broadcasting services are government owned. Although the media are used as governmental means for active indoctrination, a limited number of legalized political parties articulate a narrow range of viewpoints, and individuals feel free to discuss politics. Lawyers show considerable independence. The courts are neither strongly independent nor effective in political cases where long-term detention with trial occurs. Political prisoners are often arrested following violence, but there are prisoners of conscience. Torture has frequently been employed in interrogation. Private rights, such as those of religion, occupation, or residence are generally respected; foreign travel and emigration are closely controlled for certain groups. Syria's economy is a mixture of governmental and private enterprise; labor is not independent of the party.

**Comparatively:** Syria is as free as Tunisia, freer than Iraq, less free than Lebanon.

# TANZANIA

**Economy:** noninclusive socialist          **Political Rights:** 6
**Polity:** socialist one-party              **Civil Liberties:** 6
**Population:** 17,000,000                    **Status of Freedom:** not free

A transethnic heterogeneous nation in union with Zanzibar

**Political Rights.** Tanzania is a union of the paternalistic socialist mainland with the radical socialist Zanzibar. Although the governments are still not unified except in name, the single parties of each state have joined to form one all-Tanzanian party. Elections offer choice between individuals, but no issues are to be discussed in campaigns; all decisions come down from above, including the choice of candidates. *Subnationalities*: Ethnically, the country is divided into a large number of peoples (none larger than thirteen percent); most are not yet at the subnational level. The use of English and Swahili as national languages enhances national unity. Since the two subnations (Zanzibar and Tanganyika) are in a voluntary union at present, there is no question of dominance of one over the other.

**Civil Liberties.** Civil liberties are essentially subordinated to the goals of the socialist leadership. No contradiction of official policy is allowed to appear in the government-owned media, or in educational institutions. The people learn only of those events the government wishes them to know. There is no right of assembly or organization. Millions of people have been forced into communal villages; people from the cities have been abruptly transported to the countryside. Thousands have been detained for political crimes, and torture has occurred. There are now few prisoners of conscience. Lack of respect for the independence of the judiciary and individual rights is especially apparent in Zanzibar. Union activity is government controlled. Neither labor nor capital have legally recognized rights—strikes are illegal. Most business and trade and much of agriculture are nationalized. Religion is free, at least on the mainland; overseas travel is restricted.

**Comparatively:** Tanzania is as free as Algeria, freer than Malawi, less free than Zambia.

# THAILAND

**Economy:** noninclusive capitalist　　**Political Rights:** 4
**Polity:** centralized multiparty　　　**Civil Liberties:** 4
　　　(military dominated)　　　　　**Status of Freedom:** partly free
**Population:** 46,200,000

An ethnic state with a major territorial subnationality

**Political Rights.** Under the controlled parliamentary system introduced this year, fair elections won by the opposition were partly nullified by the appointed senate's role in reappointing the prime minister. Repeated military interventions in recent years limit the freedom of civilian politicians. Government is highly centralized. *Subnationalities*: There is a Muslim Malay community in the far south, and small ethnic enclaves in the north.

**Civil Liberties.** The press is private, but periodic suppressions and warnings lead to self-censorship. Broadcasting is government or military controlled. There are few if any long-term prisoners of conscience, but in rural areas arrest may be on vague charges and treatment brutal. "Reeducation centers" have been established for former guerrillas. Human rights organizations are active. Labor activity is relatively free, but strikes are illegal. Private rights to property, choice of religion, travel, or residence are secure. However, corruption limits the expression of all rights. Government enterprise is quite important in the basically capitalist modern economy.

**Comparatively:** Thailand is as free as Ghana, freer than Indonesia, less free than Bangladesh.

# TOGO

**Economy:** noninclusive mixed
**Polity:** nationalist one-party
**Population:** 2,400,000

**Political Rights:** 7
**Civil Liberties:** 7
**Status of Freedom:** not free

A transethnic heterogeneous state

**Political Rights.** Togo is a military dictatorship ruled in the name of a one-party state. In this spirit there is a deliberate denial of the rights of separate branches of government, including a separate judiciary, or even of private groups. National elections allow little or no choice. Below the national level only the cities have a semblance of self-government. *Subnationalities*: The southern Ewe are culturally dominant and the largest group (twenty percent), but militant northerners now rule.

**Civil Liberties.** No criticism of the government is allowed in the media, and foreign publications may be confiscated. There is little guarantee of a rule of law: people have been imprisoned and beaten on many occasions for offenses such as the distribution of leaflets or failure to wear a party badge. There are, however, few if any long-term prisoners of conscience. Religious freedom is limited. There is occasional restriction of foreign travel. Union organization is closely regulated. In this largely subsistence economy the government is heavily involved in trade, production, and the provision of services. All wage earners must contribute heavily to the ruling party.

**Comparatively:** Togo is as free as Burundi, less free than Niger.

# TONGA

**Economy:** noninclusive capitalist
**Polity:** traditional nonparty
**Population:** 115,000

**Political Rights:** 5
**Civil Liberties:** 3
**Status of Freedom:** partly free

A relatively homogeneous population

**Political Rights.** Tonga is a constitutional monarchy in which the king and nobles retain power. Only a minority of the members of the legislative assembly are elected directly by the people; in any event the assembly has little more than veto power. Regional administration is centralized.

**Civil Liberties.** The main paper is a government weekly and radio is under government control. There is a rule of law, but the king's decision is still a very important part of the system. Private rights within the traditional Tonga context seem guaranteed.

**Comparatively:** Tonga is as free as Morocco, freer than Seychelles, less free than Western Samoa.

# TRANSKEI

**Economy:** noninclusive capitalist    **Political Rights:** 5
**Polity:** centralized dominant-party    **Civil Liberties:** 6
**Population:** 2,400,000    **Status of Freedom:** partly free

A relatively homogeneous population

**Political Rights.** In form Transkei is a multiparty parliamentary democracy; in fact it is under the strong-man rule of a paramount chief supported by his party's majority. The meaning of recent elections was largely nullified by governmental interference, including the jailing of opposition leaders. Chiefs remain very important in the system, but beyond that there is little decentralization of power. South Africa has a great deal of de facto power over the state, particularly because of the large number of nationals that work in South Africa. However, Transkei is more independent than the Soviet satellites; in 1978 it severed relations with South Africa.

**Civil Liberties.** The press is private, but under strong government pressure. Broadcasting is government controlled. Many members of the opposition have been imprisoned; new retroactive laws render it illegal to criticize Transkei or its rulers. Freedom of organization is very limited, although an opposition party still exists. Private rights are respected within the limits of South African and Transkei custom. Capitalist and traditional economic rights are diminished by the necessity of a large portion of the labor force to work in South Africa.

**Comparatively:** Transkei is as free as Syria, freer than Mozambique, less free than Swaziland.

# TRINIDAD AND TOBAGO

**Economy:** capitalist    **Political Rights:** 2
**Polity:** centralized multiparty    **Civil Liberties:** 2
**Population:** 1,100,000    **Status of Freedom:** free

An ethnically complex state

**Political Rights.** Trinidad and Tobago is a parliamentary democracy in which one party has managed to retain power since the 1950's.

Elections have been boycotted in the past but now appear reasonably fair. A new opposition party has recently gained almost thirty percent of the assembly seats. There is local government. An independence movement has developed in Tobago.

**Civil Liberties.** The private or party press is generally free of restriction; broadcasting is under both government and private control. Opposition is regularly voiced. There is the full spectrum of private rights, although violence and communal feeling reduce the effectiveness of such rights for many.

**Comparatively:** Trinidad and Tobago is as free as Dominica, freer than Grenada, less free than Bahamas.

# TUNISIA

| | |
|---|---|
| **Economy:** mixed capitalist | **Political Rights:** 6 |
| **Polity:** socialist one-party | **Civil Liberties:** 5 |
| **Population:** 6,400,000 | **Status of Freedom:** partly free |

A relatively homogeneous population

**Political Rights.** Tunisia is a one-party dictatorship that preserves alongside one-man leadership the trappings of parliamentary democracy. Elections to the assembly are contested within the one-party framework. In 1979 elections the opposition publicly called for abstention. Regional and local government are dependent on central direction.

**Civil Liberties.** The private, party, or government media are controlled. Although frequently banned or fined two major opposition papers have been publishing since 1978. Private conversation is relatively free, but there is no right of assembly. The courts demonstrate only a limited independence, but it is possible to win against the government. Unions have been relatively independent; however, a general strike called in early 1978 led to riots and subsequent large-scale imprisonment, and closer government controls followed. There are prisoners of conscience and torture. The unemployed young are drafted for government work. Overseas travel is occasionally blocked. Most private rights seem to be respected, including economic rights since doctrinaire socialism was abandoned.

**Comparatively:** Tunisia is as free as Poland, freer than Algeria, less free than Egypt.

# TURKEY

**Economy:** capitalist-statist          **Political Rights:** 2
**Polity:** centralized multiparty       **Civil Liberties:** 3
**Population:** 44,300,000               **Status of Freedom:** free

An ethnic state with a major territorial subnationality

**Political Rights.** Turkey is a parliamentary democracy in which power has often shifted between the major parties or their coalitions. A marxist party has recently been legalized, but the communist party is still prohibited. The democratic system has been strongly supported by the military that has intervened against threats to the system from both the right and left. This leaves the miliary in a more powerful political position than is traditionally acceptable in a democracy, a position symbolized by the fact that the largely ceremonial (except in crises) position of the president has come to be occupied by a military leader. Although there are elected councils at lower levels, power is effectively centralized. *Subnationalities*: Several million Kurds are denied self-determination: it is even illegal to teach or publish in Kurdish.

**Civil Liberties.** The press is private and free; the government controls the broadcasting system directly or indirectly, but allows dissident views. Although public expression and assembly cover a wide spectrum, there are laws against extremist publications, assembly, and organization that are regarded as threats to the democratic order. Together with antigovernment violence this has led to frequent political imprisonment (often followed by accusations of torture). Government generally observes the law, but nongovernmental extremists have been responsible for many deaths. Martial law was imposed in some areas after extensive political violence in late 1978. Private rights are generally respected in other areas such as religion. Nearly fifty percent of the people are subsistence agriculturists. State enterprises make up more than one-half of Turkey's industry.

**Comparatively:** Turkey is as free as Colombia, freer than Morocco, less free than Portugal.

# TUVALU

**Economy:** noninclusive capitalist   **Political Rights:** 2
**Polity:** traditional nonparty        **Civil Liberties:** 2
**Population:** 9,000                    **Status of Freedom:** free

A relatively homogeneous state

**Political Rights.** Tuvalu is a parliamentary democracy under the

British monarch. Each island is represented; seats are contested individually. An opposition bloc has been formed in the assembly.

**Civil Liberties.** Media are little developed. The rule of law is maintained in the British manner, alongside traditional ideals of justice.

**Comparatively:** Tuvalu is as free as Malta, freer than Tonga, less free than New Zealand.


# UGANDA

**Economy:** noninclusive, mixed
    capitalist
**Polity:** quasi-one-party
**Population:** 13,000,000

**Political Rights:** 6
**Civil Liberties:** 6
**Status of Freedom:** not free

A transethnic heterogeneous state with major subnationalities

**Political Rights.** Uganda is ruled by a transitional government established in 1979 with the aid of exile groups and the Tanzanian army. The "Front" and an appointed parliament in the names of which the government rules contain a variety of factions. Political parties cannot operate outside this framework. Tanzanian influence remained decisive at least through the end of 1979. *Subnationalities*: The population is divided among a wide variety of peoples, some of which are subnationalities based on kingdoms that preceded the present state. The most important of these is Buganda, a kingdom with special rights within the state, that was suppressed in 1967. Sixteen percent of the people are Ganda.

**Civil Liberties.** The government and private media have limited freedom under the new regime. Assembly and travel are similarly restricted within the country. Arbitrary arrests were frequent at times during the year; politicians were arbitarily killed by the government or murdered by unknown assailants. Torture occurred as Tanzanian troops roamed the country. Religious freedom was reestablished.

**Comparatively:** Uganda was as free as Tanzania, freer than Mozambique, less free than Kenya.


# UNION OF
# SOVIET SOCIALIST REPUBLICS

**Economy:** socialist
**Polity:** communist one-party
**Population:** 262,400,000

**Political Rights:** 6
**Civil Liberties:** 6
**Status of Freedom:** not free

A complex ethnic state with major territorial subnationalities

**Political Rights.** The Soviet Union is ruled by parallel party and governmental systems: the party system is dominant. Elections are held for both systems, but in neither is it possible for the rank and file to determine policy. Candidacy and voting are closely controlled and the resulting assemblies do not seriously question the policies developed by party leaders (varying by time or issue from one individual to twenty-five). The Soviet Union is in theory elaborately divided into subnational units, but in fact the all-embracing party structure renders local power minimal.

*Subnationalities.* Russians account for half of the Soviet population. The rest belong to a variety of subnational groupings ranging down in size from the forty million Ukrainians. Most groups are territorial, with a developed sense of subnational identity. The political rights of all of these to self-determination, either within the USSR or through secession, is effectively denied. In many cases Russians or other non-native peoples have been settled in a subnational territory in such numbers as to make the native people a minority in their own land (for example, Kazakhstan). Expression of opinion in favor of increased self-determination is repressed at least as much as anticommunist opinion. Most of these peoples have had independence movements or movements for enhanced self-determination in the years since the founding of the USSR. Several movements have been quite strong since World War II (for example, in the Ukraine or Lithuania); the blockage of communication by the Soviet government makes it very difficult to estimate either the overt or latent support such movements might have. In 1978 popular movements in Georgia and Armenia led to the retention of the official status of local languages in the Republics of the Caucasus.

**Civil Liberties.** The media are totally owned by the government or party and are, in addition, regularly censored. Elite publications occasionally present variations from the official line, but significant deviations are generally found only in underground publications. Crimes against the state, including insanity (demonstrated by perverse willingness to oppose the state), are broadly defined; as a result political prisoners are present in large numbers both in jails and insane asylums. Nearly all imprisonment and mistreatment of prisoners in the Soviet Union are now carried out in accordance with Soviet security laws—even though these laws conflict with other Soviet laws written to accord with international standards. Since the Bolshevik Revolution there has never been an acquittal in a political trial. Insofar as private rights, such as those to religion, education, or choice of occupation, exist, they are de facto rights that may be denied at any time. Travel within and outside of the USSR is highly controlled; many areas of the country are still off-limits to foreigners—especially those used as areal prisons for dissidents. Nearly all private entrepreneurial activity is outside the law; there are rights to nonproductive personal property. Other rights such as those to organize an independent labor union are strictly denied. Literacy is high, few starve, and private oppression is no more.

**Comparatively:** The USSR is as free as Cuba, freer than East Germany, less free than Hungary.

# UNITED ARAB EMIRATES

**Economy:** capitalist-statist
**Polity:** decentralized nonparty
**Population:** 800,000

**Political Rights:** 5
**Civil Liberties:** 5
**Status of Freedom:** partly free

A relatively homogeneous citizenry

**Political Rights.** The UAE is a confederation of seven shaikhdoms in which the larger are given the greater power both in the assembly and the administrative hierarchy. There is a great deal of consultation in the traditional pattern. Below the confederation level there are no electoral procedures or parties. Each shaikhdom is relatively autonomous in its internal affairs. The majority of the people are recent immigrants and noncitizens.

**Civil Liberties.** The press is private or governmental. There is self-censorship, but some opposition is expressed. Broadcasting is under UAE control. There are no political assemblies or labor unions, but there are also few, if any, prisoners of conscience. The courts dispense a combination of British, tribal, and Islamic law. Private rights are generally respected; there is freedom of travel and some religious freedom. Many persons may still accept the feudal privileges and restraints of their tribal position. The rights of the alien majority are less secure: "troublemakers" are deported. Private economic activity exists alongside the dominance of government petroleum and petroleum-related activities.

**Comparatively:** United Arab Emirates are as free as Kuwait, freer than North Yemen, less free than Tonga.

# UNITED KINGDOM

**Economy:** mixed capitalist
**Polity:** centralized multiparty
**Population:** 55,800,000

**Political Rights:** 1
**Civil Liberties:** 1
**Status of Freedom:** free

An ethnic state with major subnationalities

**Political Rights.** The United Kingdom is a parliamentary democracy with a symbolic monarch. Fair elections are open to all parties, including those advocating secession. There are elected local and regional governments, but to date these are primarily concerned with administering national laws. The devolution of more substantial powers is currently under discussion and development. *Subnationalities*: Scots, Welsh, Ulster Scots, and Ulster Irish are significant and highly self-conscious territorial minorities. In 1978 parliament approved home rule for Scotland and Wales, but the Welsh and (more ambiguously) the Scots voters rejected this opportunity in 1979. Northern Ireland's home rule is in abeyance because of an ethnic impasse. Ulster Scots and Irish live in intermixed territories in Northern Ireland. Both want more self-determination—the majority Ulster Scots as an autonomous part of the United Kingdom, the minority Ulster Irish as an area within Ireland.

**Civil Liberties.** The press is private and powerful; broadcasting has statutory independence although it is indirectly under government control. British media are comparatively restrained because of strict libel and national security laws, and a tradition of accepting government suggestions for the handling of sensitive news. In Northern Ireland a severe security situation has led to the curtailment of private rights, to imprisonment, and on occasion to torture and brutality. However, these conditions have been relatively limited, have been thoroughly investigated by the government, and improved as a result. Elsewhere the rule of law is entrenched, and private rights generally respected. In certain areas, such as medicine, housing, inheritance, and general disposability of income, socialist government policies have limited choice for some while expanding the access of others.

**Comparatively:** The United Kingdom is as free as the United States, freer than West Germany.


# UNITED STATES OF AMERICA

**Economy:** capitalist      **Political Rights:** 1
**Polity:** decentralized multiparty      **Civil Liberties:** 1
**Population:** 220,000,000      **Status of Freedom:** free

An ethnically complex state with minor territorial subnationalities

**Political Rights.** The United States is a constitutional democracy with three strong but separate centers of power: president, congress, and judiciary. Elections are fair and competitive. Parties are remarkably weak: in some areas they are little more than temporary means of organizing primary elections. States, and to a lesser extent cities, have powers in their own rights; they often successfully oppose the desires of national administrations. Each state has equal representation in the upper house, which in the USA is the more powerful half of parliament.

*Subnationalities.* There are many significant ethnic groups, but the only clearly territorial subnationalities are the native peoples. The largest Indian tribes, the Navaho and Sioux, number 100,000 or more each. About 150,000 Hawaiians still reside on their native islands, intermingled with a much larger white and oriental population. Spanish-speaking Americans number in the millions; except for a few thousand residing in an area of northern New Mexico, they are mostly twentieth-century immigrants living among English-speaking Americans, particularly in the large cities. Black Americans make up over one-tenth of the U.S. population; residing primarily in large cities they have no major territorial base. Black and Spanish-speaking Americans are of special concern because of their relative poverty; their ethnic status is quite comparable to that of many other groups in America, including Chinese, Japanese, Filipinos, Italians, or Jews.

**Civil Liberties.** The press is private and free; both private and public radio and television are government regulated. There are virtually no government controls on the content of the printed media (except in nonpolitical areas such as pornography) and few on broadcasting. There are no prisoners of conscience or sanctioned uses of torture; some regional miscarriages of justice and police brutality have political and social overtones. Widespread use of surveillance techniques and clandestine interference with radical groups or groups thought to be radical has occurred; as a reduction of liberties the threat has remained largely potential; in recent years these security excesses have been greatly attenuated if not eliminated. Wherever and whenever publicity penetrates, the rule of law is generally secure, even against the most powerful. The government often loses in the courts. Private rights in most spheres are respected. Although a relatively capitalistic country, the combination of tax loads with the decisive government role in agriculture, energy, defense, and other industries restricts individual choice as it increases majority power.

**Comparatively:** The United States is as free as Australia, freer than Italy.

# UPPER VOLTA

**Economy:** noninclusive capitalist
**Polity:** centralized multiparty
**Population:** 6,700,000

**Political Rights:** 2
**Civil Liberties:** 3
**Status of Freedom:** free

A transethnic heterogeneous state

**Political Rights.** Upper Volta has a president and parliament on the French model. Presidential and parliamentary elections held in 1978 maintained the previous ruler in power. The election result appeared reasonably fair: successful M.P.'s represented a number of parties, the presidential election was only decided after a run-off, and the resulting government included all major parties. In 1979 the rule banning all but the three largest parties was enforced. There is little official decentralization of power.

**Civil Liberties.** Media are both government and private; criticism appears regularly in both, but not of named officials. There are no political prisoners. The rule of law seems fairly well established and within traditional limits private rights are respected. Trade unions are important. Travel is unrestricted. Essentially the economy remains dependent on subsistence agriculture, with the government playing the role of regulator and promoter of development.

**Comparatively:** Upper Volta is as free as Turkey, freer than Ghana, less free than Gambia.

# U R U G U A Y

Economy: mixed capitalist
Polity: military nonparty
Population: 2,900,000

Political Rights: 6
Civil Liberties: 6
Status of Freedom: not free

A relatively homogeneous population

**Political Rights.** Uruguay is a military dictatorship supplemented by an appointed civilian head of state and appointed advisory council. The leading parties are inactive but still exist legally. The state is highly centralized.

**Civil Liberties.** The press is private, and broadcasting private and public. Both are under heavy censorship and threats of confiscation or closure, as are book and journal outlets. (Special permission is required to see old newspapers.) The right of assembly is very restricted. The independence of the judiciary and the civil service has been drastically curtailed. There are about 1,500 political prisoners, many of which are prisoners of conscience. Torture has been routinely used until recently; convictions have been generally based on written confessions. Many parties have been banned, but there is still considerable room for political discussion of alternatives beyond the limits of the present system. All organizations, including unions, are under close government supervision. Private rights are generally respected. The tax load of an overbuilt bureaucracy and emphasis on private and government monopolies have also restricted choice in this now improverished welfare state.

**Comparatively:** Uruguay is as free as Tanzania, freer than Ethiopia, less free than Chile.

# VENEZUELA

**Economy:** capitalist-statist
**Polity:** centralized multiparty
**Population:** 13,500,000

**Political Rights:** 1
**Civil Liberties:** 2
**Status of Freedom:** free

A relatively homogeneous population

**Political Rights.** Venezuela is a parliamentary democracy in which power has alternated between major parties in recent years. Campaigns and voting appear fair. The opposition presidential victory in 1978 provided a good example of the power of the average voter. Regional and local assemblies are relatively powerful, but governors are centrally appointed. Each state has equal representation in the upper house.

**Civil Liberties.** The press is private and free; most broadcasting is also in private hands. Censorship occurs only in emergencies. The rule of law is generally secured, but in the face of guerrilla actions the security services have on occasion arbitrarily imprisoned persons, used torture, and threatened to prosecute for antimilitary statements. A paper may be confiscated for slandering the president. Many persons have been detained for long periods without trial; on rare occasions members of parliament have been arrested. However, there is little evidence that those detained have been prisoners of conscience, and the government has taken steps to prevent torture. The court can rule against the government. Most private rights are respected; government involvement in the petroleum industry has given it a predominant economic role.

**Comparatively:** Venezuela is as free as France, freer than Italy, less free than Costa Rica.

# VIETNAM

**Economy:** socialist
**Polity:** communist one-party
**Population:** 50,000,000

**Political Rights:** 7
**Civil Liberties:** 7
**Status of Freedom:** not free

An ethnic state with subnationalities

**Political Rights.** Vietnam is a traditional communist dictatorship with the forms of parliamentary democracy. Actual power is in the hands of the communist party; this is in turn dominated by a small group at the top. Officially there is a ruling national front as in several other communist states, but the noncommunist parties are essentially meaningless. Administration is highly centralized, with provincial boundaries arbitrarily determined by the central government. The flow of refugees and other evidence suggest that the present regime is very unpopular, especially in the South which is treated as an occupied country. *Subnationalities*: Continued fighting has been reported in the Montagnard areas in the South. Combined with new resettlement schemes non-Vietnamese peoples are under pressure in both North and South Vietnam. Many Chinese appeared to be driven out of the country in 1978.

**Civil Liberties.** The media are under direct government, party, or army control; only the approved line is presented. While the people do not suffer the fears and illegalities of anarchy, they have essentially no rights against the interests of the state. Severe repression of the Buddhist opposition has led to many immolations—pressure on the Hoa Hao and Catholics is comparable. In spite of superficial appearances religious freedom is generally denied. Perhaps one-half million persons have been put through reeducation camps, hundreds of thousands have been forced to move into new areas, or to change occupations; hundreds of thousands remain political prisoners or in internal exile. By placing a trusted, usually Northern, leader over each group of ten families in the South, at least half of the country has been turned into a prison camp. There are no independent labor union rights, rights to travel, choice of education, and so forth.

**Comparatively:** Vietnam is as free as Korea (North), less free than China (Mainland).

# WESTERN SAMOA

**Economy:** noninclusive capitalist  **Political Rights:** 4
**Polity:** traditional nonparty  **Civil Liberties:** 2
**Population:** 171,000  **Status of Freedom:** partly free
A relatively homogeneous population

**Political Rights.** Western Samoa is a constitutional monarchy in which the assembly is elected by 9,500 "family heads." There have been important shifts of power within the assembly as the result of elections, although there are no political parties. Village government has preserved traditional forms and considerable autonomy; it is also based on rule by "family heads."

**Civil Liberties.** The press is private and government; radio is government owned; television is received only from outside. There is general freedom of expression, organization, and assembly. The rule of law and private rights are respected within the limits set by the traditional system.

**Comparatively:** Western Samoa is as free as Mauritius, freer than Malaysia, less free than Nauru.


# YEMEN, NORTH

**Economy:** noninclusive capitalist      **Political Rights:** 6
**Polity:** military nonparty             **Civil Liberties:** 5
**Population:** 5,800,000                  **Status of Freedom:** not free

A complex but relatively homogeneous population

**Political Rights.** North Yemen is a collective military dictatorship supplemented by an appointive People's Assembly. Leaders are frequently assassinated. The tribal and religious structures still retain considerable authority, and the government must rely on a wide variety of different groups in an essentially nonideological consensual regime. Some local elective institutions have recently been developed. Political parties are forbidden. The country is divided between city and country, a variety of tribes, and two major religious groupings.

**Civil Liberties.** The weak media are largely government owned; there is limited freedom of expression. Proponents of both royalist and far left persuasions are openly accepted in a society with few known prisoners of conscience. Politically active opponents may be encouraged to go into exile. The traditional Islamic courts give some protection; private rights such as those to religion and property are respected. There is no right to strike or to engage in religious proselytizing. Economically the government has concentrated on improving the infrastructure of Yemen's still overwhelmingly traditional economy.

**Comparatively:** North Yemen is as free as Argentina, free than South Yemen, less free than Syria.


# YEMEN, SOUTH

**Economy:** noninclusive socialist       **Political Rights:** 6
**Polity:** socialist one-party           **Civil Liberties:** 7
**Population:** 1,900,000                  **Status of Freedom:** not free

A relatively homogeneous population

**Political Rights.** South Yemen considers itself a communist country governed according to the communist one-party model. It is doubtful that the party retains the tight party discipline of its exemplars; it is government by coup and violence. Parliamentary elections in 1978 followed the one-party model; they allowed some choice among individuals. Soviet influence in internal and external affairs is powerful.

**Civil Liberties.** The media are government owned and controlled, and employed actively as a means of indoctrination. Even conversation with foreigners is highly restricted. In the political and security areas the rule of law hardly applies. Thousands of political prisoners, torture, and hundreds of "disappearances" have instilled a pervasive fear in those who would speak up. Death sentences against protesting farmers have been handed down by people's courts. Independent private rights are few, although some traditional law and institutions remain. Industry and commerce have been nationalized.

**Comparatively:** South Yemen is as free as Malawi, freer than Somalia, less free than Oman.

# YUGOSLAVIA

**Economy:** mixed socialist
**Polity:** communist one-party
**Population:** 22,200,000

**Political Rights:** 6
**Civil Liberties:** 5
**Status of Freedom:** not free

A multinational state

**Political Rights.** Yugoslavia is governed on the model of the USSR, but with the addition of unique elements. These include: the greater role given the governments of the constituent republics; and the greater power given the assemblies of the self-managed communities and industrial enterprises. The Federal Assembly is elected indirectly by those successful in lower level elections. In any event, the country is directed by a small elite of the communist party; evidence suggests that in spite of some earlier liberalizing tendencies to allow the more democratic formal structure to work, Yugoslavia is now no more democratic than Hungary. No opposition member is elected to state or national position, nor is there public opposition in the assemblies to government policy on the national or regional level.

*Subnationalities.* The several peoples of Yugoslavia live largely in their historical homelands. The population consists of forty percent Serbs, twenty-two percent Croats, eight percent Slovenes, eight percent Bosnian Muslims, six percent Macedonians, six percent Albanians, two percent Montenegrins, and many others. The Croats have an especially active independence movement.

**Civil Liberties.** The media in Yugoslavia are controlled directly or indirectly by the government, although there is ostensible worker control. There is no right of assembly. Hundreds have been imprisoned for ideas expressed verbally or in print that deviated from the official line (primarily through subnationalist enthusiasm, anticommunism, or communist deviationism). Psychiatric hospitals are also used to confine prisoners of conscience. As long as the issue is not political, however, the courts have some independence; there is a realm of de facto individual freedom that includes the right to seek employment outside the country. Travel outside Yugoslavia is often denied to dissidents, and religious proselytizing is forbidden. Labor is not independent but has rights through the working of the "self-management" system. Although the economy is socialist or communalist in most respects, agriculture in this most agricultural of European countries remains overwhelmingly private.

**Comparatively:** Yugoslavia is as free as Hungary, freer than Rumania, less free than Morocco.

# ZAIRE

**Economy:** noninclusive capitalist-statist
**Polity:** nationalist one-party
**Population:** 28,000,000

**Political Rights:** 6
**Civil Liberties:** 6
**Status of Freedom:** not free

A transethnic heterogeneous state with subnationalities

**Political Rights.** Zaire is under one-man military rule, with the ruling party essentially an extension of the ruler's personality. Elections in 1977 at both local and parliamentary levels were restricted to one party, but allowed for extensive choice among individuals. The majority of the party's ruling council was also elected in this manner. A subsequent presidential election offered no choice. The broadcasting of live parliamentary debates has revealed sharp questioning of ministers. Regions are deliberately organized to avoid ethnic identity: regional officers all are appointed from the center, generally from outside of the area, as are officers of the ruling party.

*Subnationalities.* There are such a variety of tribes or linguistic groups in Zaire that no one group has as much as twenty percent of the population. The fact that French remains the dominant language reflects the degree of this dispersion. Until recently most of the Zaire people have seen themselves only in local terms without broader ethnic identification. The revolts and wars of the early 1960's saw continually shifting patterns of affiliation, with the European provincial but not ethnic realities of Katanga and South Kasai being most important. The most self-conscious ethnic groups are the Kongo people living in the west (and Congo and Angola) and the Luba in the center of the country. In both cases ethnicity goes back to important ancient kingdoms. There is continuing disaffection among the Lunda and other ethnic groups.

**Civil Liberties.** Private newspaper ownership remains. There is some freedom to criticize, but censorship is pervasive. There is no right of assembly, and union organization is controlled. Government has been arbitrary and capricious. The judiciary is not independent; political arrest is common, as are execution and torture. Individual names as well as clothing style have had to be changed by government decree. All ethnic organizations are forbidden. Arrested conspirators have been forbidden their own lawyers. Major churches retain some autonomy, but independent churches have been proscribed. When founded on government power, the extravagance and business dealings of those in high places reduces economic freedom. Nationalization of land has often been a prelude to private development by powerful bureaucrats. Pervasive corruption and anarchy reduce human rights. There is also considerable government enterprise.

**Comparatively:** Zaire is as free as Gabon, freer than Benin, less free than Zambia.

# ZAMBIA

**Economy:** preindustrial mixed
**Polity:** socialist one-party
**Population:** 5,600,000

**Political Rights:** 5
**Civil Liberties:** 5
**Status of Freedom:** partly free

A transethnic heterogeneous state

**Political Rights.** Zambia is ruled as a one-party dictatorship, although there have been elements of freedom within that party. Party organs are constitutionally more important than governmental. Although elections have had some competitive meaning within this framework, recently the government has repressed opposition movements within the party. Expression of dissent is possible through abstention. A 1978 presidential election allowed no choice and little opposition campaigning; it allowed negative votes.

**Civil Liberties.** All media are government controlled. A considerable variety of opinion is expressed, but it is a crime to criticize the president, the parliament, or the ideology. Foreign publications are censored. There is a rule of law and the courts have some independence: cases have been won against the government. Hundreds of political opponents have been detained, and occasionally tortured, yet most people talk without fear. There were few political prisoners in 1979. Traditional life continues. The government does not fully accept private rights in property or religion; important parts of the economy, especially copper mining, have been nationalized.

**Comparatively:** Zambia is as free as Indonesia, freer than Angola, less free than Morocco.

# ZIMBABWE RHODESIA

**Economy:** noninclusive capitalist-
              statist
**Polity:** centralized multiparty
**Population:** 7,200,000

**Political Rights:** 4
**Civil Liberties:** 4
**Status of Freedom:** partly free

An ethnically complex state with a territorial subnationality

**Political Rights.** Zimbabwe is a parliamentary democracy in which the overwhelming power has been in the hands of the white minority (four percent). Elections under a new constitution in 1979 ostensibly transferred power to the black majority. However, the constitution provided for a gradual transfer of effective military and administrative power. The continued white role and the self-exclusion of the major external parties (because of their opposition to the constitution) led to a series of conferences and the transfer of power to a British caretaker regime at the end of the year in preparation for more inclusive elections. (1980 began with advances in all freedoms, but the relatively free election brought a party to power with antidemocratic credentials.)*

*Subnationalities.* The formerly dominant white, Indian, and colored populations (five percent) are largely urban. The emerging dominant people are the majority Shona-speaking groups (seventy-four percent). The Ndebele (eighteen percent) are territorially distinct and politically self-conscious.

**Civil Liberties.** The press is private. It is under pressure to conform, but offers a spectrum of opinion within the white community. (Opposition publications appeared in January 1980.) Broadcasting is government controlled. For whites there was a generally fair application of the rule of law, with freedom of residence and occupation (except for conscription). Black parties had general freedom of speech, assembly, and organization, as long as they did not support the guerrilla movements based outside the country. Racial discrimination was officially outlawed, especially in residence, occupation, and conscription. Much of the country was under martial law during the year. The forced movement of large numbers of blacks into fortified villages because of the security situation was resented by many. The war and security situation has led to widespread political imprisonments, executions, and reported torture. Both agricultural and nonagricultural economic development has moved Rhodesia most of the way toward a capitalist society, while government restrictions on the movement and employment of black

---

* For the conclusions of the Freedom House missions to observe the elections in Zimbabwe Rhodesia see Part III (above).

citizens in the recent past and the many government corporations have created a form of corporate state economy.

**Comparatively:** In 1979 Zimbabwe Rhodesia was as free as Ghana, freer than Zambia, less free than Botswana.

# Index

For countries, peoples, and related territories, *see also* the Tables.